P9-CET-821

Smoothie heaven

Smoothie heaven

Hundreds of divine recipes to take you to smoothie paradise

WENDY SWEETSER

METRO BOOKS
New York

METRO BOOKS
New York

An imprint of Sterling Publishing
387 Park Avenue South
New York, NY 10016

METRO BOOKS and the distinctive Metro Books logo are trademarks of Sterling Publishing Co., Inc.

This 2010 edition published by Metro Books by arrangement with Quintet Publishing.

This book was conceived, designed, and produced by
Quintet Publishing Limited
6 Blundell Street
London N7 9BH
United Kingdom
QTT.SMHE

Project Editor: Martha Burley
Editorial Assistant: Carly Beckerman-Boys
Designers: Susi Martin, Chris Taylor
Food Stylist: Liz Martin
Photographer: Michael Dannenberg
Art Editors: Zoë White, Jane Laurie
Art Director: Michael Charles
Managing Editor: Donna Gregory
Publisher: Mark Searle

ISBN: 978-1-4351-2251-2

For information about custom editions, special sales, and premium and corporate purchases, please contact Sterling Special Sales at 800-805-5489 or specialsales@sterlingpublishing.com.

Manufactured in China

4 6 8 10 9 7 5 3

www.sterlingpublishing.com

Contents

Introduction

There can be few more satisfying ways to start your day than with a glass of deliciously thick homemade smoothie. Just saying the word smoothie makes you feel good and if you've made it yourself, you'll know it will do you good too, as you'll have chosen what's gone into it.

But, as this book shows, smoothies aren't just for breakfast, they're an all-day treat that the whole family can enjoy and a great way to ensure your children get plenty of nutrients without E-numbers and additives. Try a smoothie as a mid-morning reviver when you're having a hard day or have been burning calories in the gym, include one as part of your children's packed lunch to keep their energy levels up and, come evening, relax with friends by whizzing up a decadent smoothie cocktail of chocolate, ice cream, strawberries, and a dash of spirit for a long, cool wind-down.

Smoothies originated in the United States, where cafés devoted entirely to these divinely creamy treats enticed customers through their doors. Europe and the rest of the world followed and the drink's popularity rose steeply as more and more reluctant fruit and vegetable eaters discovered that a smoothie was an easy and extremely pleasant way to boost their "5 a day."

What is a smoothie?

Unlike fresh juices, where just the juice is extracted from fruit or vegetables leaving the pulp behind, smoothies are made by processing the whole fruit or vegetable with added juice, milk, or yogurt. A glass of juice can count as only one of our "5 a day" regardless of how many different kinds of fruit and vegetables have been used to make it. A smoothie, on the other hand, contains much higher levels of fiber, carbohydrate, fruit sugars, and vitamin C, so one glass is much more nutritionally satisfying.

Making the perfect smoothie

How should I prepare ingredients?

When making smoothies, fruit and vegetables need to be peeled and any pips, cores, seeds, and stalks removed before being blended with fruit juice, vegetable juice, milk, or yogurt. Exceptions are strawberries and raspberries where it's impossible to remove their tiny seeds; figs and kiwi fruit where the seeds can be left in; and any fruits that are too small to peel such as grapes, cherries, or blueberries.

How thick should a smoothie be?

Smoothies are thicker than plain juices and a very pulpy smoothie, especially one with added starch such as lentils or bulghur wheat, will thicken up on standing. If a smoothie becomes too thick for your liking, dilute it with water, milk, extra fruit, or vegetable juice. Alternatively, add a few chunks of watermelon or cucumber (both of which contain a lot of liquid) and process again to reach the desired consistency. How thick a drink should be is also down to personal preference so if your perfect smoothie is one you eat with a spoon—enjoy!

Does a smoothie need sweetening?

Most smoothies will be sweet enough already due to the natural sugars contained in the fruit and vegetables but if you find a drink too sharp, sweeten it with a little clear honey or maple syrup rather than refined sugar, as both contain added health benefits. If a smoothie is too sweet for your taste, sharpen it by adding a squeeze of fresh lemon or lime juice. When sweetening or sharpening the flavor of a smoothie, do this just before drinking as its flavor, including its natural sweetness, will become more pronounced the longer it is left to stand.

How long will a smoothie keep?

Ideally smoothies are best drunk as soon as they are made as the longer they're kept the more their vitamin count goes down. Once exposed to the air, fruit starts to oxidize and drinks containing apples or bananas can discolor and turn brown, while citrus flavors become more pronounced and begin to dominate more delicate fruits.

Why has my blueberry and yogurt smoothie curdled?
If a smoothie is made by blending citrus fruits, berries (particularly blueberries), or pineapple with dairy products such as milk, yogurt, or ice cream, it needs to be drunk immediately as the longer it is left to stand the more it will thicken and take on an unappetizing, curdled appearance. This is caused by the reaction of a protein found in cow's milk called casein with the fruit. All is not lost, however, as you can rescue the smoothie by pushing it through a sieve or returning it to the blender and processing again. The result will be nearer a mousse than a drink, but still irresistible!

If you do need to prepare a smoothie in advance, blitz fruit or vegetables and juice together without adding any dairy ingredients. Store it in a covered container in the fridge and either whisk or blend in the milk or yogurt before serving.

To avoid the problem of curdling, you can replace dairy products with soy milk, soy yogurt, soy "ice cream," or silken tofu, as they do not contain casein.

How can I remove too much froth from a smoothie?
Some fruits, notably apples and pears, produce a thicker head of froth than others and the easiest way to remove or reduce this is by

skimming off the froth with a spoon. The alternative is to serve the smoothie with a straw so the juice can be drunk from the bottom of the glass and the froth left behind.

I made my kids a raspberry smoothie but they wouldn't drink it because of the "bits."

It's not called a "smoothie" for nothing and your kids are right—what's in their glass should be as smooth as silk. While most adults will put up with raspberry and fig pips and specks of pulverized blueberry or cherry skin in their drinks, children are more picky so it's best to strain the pips and any other bits out to keep them smiling.

If I create my own smoothie recipes, can I use any combination of fruit and vegetables?

In theory, yes, but a smoothie needs to look fresh and luscious so when selecting your ingredients try to picture what the final color of the drink will be. A glass of something resembling pond water is unlikely to tempt your taste buds!

It's best to avoid combining too many strong flavors as they'll battle for domination in the finished drink. Fruit and vegetables that have dense flesh like mango, banana, and avocado should also be balanced with juicier ones like melon, cucumber, and orange.

Equipment

If you want to treat yourself by all means invest in a special smoothie maker but all the recipes in this book can be made using a blender. For soft fruits and vegetables a stick blender is fine but for coarser ingredients a jug blender, where the jug is narrower at the bottom than the top, gives the best results. If you add ice cubes to your smoothies, a jug blender with a motor strong enough to break up the ice is essential. If you're unsure whether yours can cope, crush the ice first by putting the cubes in a plastic bag and bashing them with a rolling pin before adding to the blender.

If you own a juice extractor you can also make the orange, pineapple, grapefruit, carrot, apple, and other juices used in the recipes, rather than buying these ready-made. Citrus juices can be made using a traditional lemon squeezer or manual press.

Food processors are less successful for making smoothies as they tend to chop ingredients rather than purée them finely.

Choosing ingredients

Fruit and vegetables that are ripe but still feel firm to the touch and smell fragrant and sweet have the greatest concentration of antioxidants and make the most satisfying smoothies. Unripe fruit is likely to contain more fiber but could make a smoothie taste bitter and sharp unless balanced with riper, sweeter ingredients. Avoid using any produce that's past its best or damaged with bruises or blemishes as nutrient levels diminish with age.

Looking good

Smoothies can be served in any style of glass, although tall, slender tumblers look the most attractive and also give you scope to add final flourishes such as fresh fruit skewers, strawberry fans, or twists of citrus peel. For a whole chapter of garnish and decoration ideas, see page 226. Vary the size of a glass according to the richness and thickness of the drink and use smaller glasses when making smoothies for children.

About this book

The chapters in this book will provide you with recipes for sublime smoothies for every occasion from simple, perennially popular fruit and vegetable combinations and tasty, nutritious specials just right for kids, to low-fat, between-meal snacks and heavenly, oh-so-irresistible smoothie desserts.

Quantities and servings given on individual recipes should be used as a guide as they will vary according to the size of the fruit and vegetables used and how much juice and pulp they produce. Similarly the thickness of a smoothie will also depend on fruit and vegetable size, how much pulp they make and, if you are adding yogurt, how thick that is.

Eternal Smoothies

Eternal smoothies are simple and inexpensive combinations. Instead of paying the marked-up price, you can make these smoothies at home for a better-value, fresher, and tastier trip to smoothie heaven.

Eternal Smoothies

Smoothies are, generally, simple, delicious, and cheap. Yet we spend a small fortune on them in shops and cafés. This chapter is on a crusade to get you to put down your purse and start blending yourself.

Moving from the simplest of simple shakes, Classic Banana, and taking you through to flavor combinations that you may never have considered, like Blueberry, Strawberry & Orange or Cherry & Coconut, this will take you from beginner blender to specialized smoothie-maker before you know it.

Key ingredients in this chapter are milk, yogurt, ice cream, and sorbet, although there are plenty which have juice as the base for a healthier alternative. Stock up your storecupboard with these basics and you will find that it becomes habit to start trying different ingredients together. Use these recipes as flavor inspiration, and your tastebuds will guide you from there.

Classic Banana

The oldest shake in the book, this classic banana smoothie is thick, creamy, and just what you'd expect!

1 small, ripe banana, peeled and chopped, with extra to decorate
1 cup whole milk
2 scoops vanilla ice cream
1 tsp. sugar (optional)
1 tsp. lemon juice (optional)
grated nutmeg to decorate

Place the banana, milk, ice cream, sugar, and lemon juice in a blender and process until smooth. Pour into glasses and decorate with grated nutmeg and banana slices.

Serves 2

Plain Vanilla

Serve this shake in its basic form or use with a variety of different toppings, stirred into the ice cream for flavor and interest.

1 cup whole milk
2 scoops vanilla ice cream
2 tbsp. whipped cream
grated good-quality chocolate or nutmeg, to decorate

Place the milk and vanilla ice cream in a blender and process until smooth and frothy. Serve in a tall glass over ice. Decorate with whipped cream and grated chocolate or nutmeg.

Serves 1

TIP

Make your ice cubes from milk to reduce the diluting effect of water.

Magnificent Mango

A basic recipe that can be adapted to suit most fruits.

½ ripe mango, peeled, pitted, and chopped, extra pulp reserved to decorate
2 scoops mango sorbet
¾ cup whole milk
1 tsp. lime juice
lime wedge, to decorate

Place the mango in a blender and process until smooth. Add the sorbet, milk, and lime juice and process for 30 seconds. Pour into the glass and garnish with the passion fruit pulp. Alternatively, stir the pulp into the mixture for a textured shake.

Serves 1

TIP

Omit the mango and lime juice and add 1 ripe peach, pitted and chopped, to make a Peachy Shake. You could also try ½ cup of hulled strawberries, raspberries, or blueberries. For a smoother shake, press the berries through a non-metallic strainer.

Fruit Combo

Choose complementary flavors and good-quality ripe fruit to make a perfect shake every time. For a really smooth shake, process the fruit in a blender, then press through a non-metallic strainer.

TIP

The addition of lemon or lime juice often brings out the flavor of the fruit. Adjust to suit your own taste.

2 scoops vanilla ice cream
½ cup whole milk
½ cup diced ripe cantaloupe
¼ cup raspberries
sugar syrup (optional)
4 to 5 raspberries, mint leaves, and melon slices, to decorate

Place the ice cream, milk, cantaloupe, and raspberries in a blender and process until smooth. Taste and sweeten, if desired. Pour into the glass and decorate with a few additional raspberries, mint leaves, and melon slices.

Serves 1

Strawberry Frappé

This drink is a great hit in all the restaurants around Hollywood.

6 strawberries, hulled
1½–2 tbsp. strawberry syrup
½ tsp. lime juice
3–4 ice cubes
1 scoop strawberry or vanilla ice cream
club soda
strawberry slices, orange slices, and mint leaves, to decorate

Place the strawberries, strawberry syrup, lime juice, ice cubes, and ice cream in a blender and process until the mixture becomes a creamy froth. Pour into a chilled glass and top off with club soda. Stir and then decorate with a flourish of fruit slices and mint leaves.

Serves 1

TIP

You could try using strawberry sorbet in place of the ice cream.

Easy Frozen Yogurt

This simple frozen yogurt is best made with Greek-style yogurt, which imparts a creamy richness. Mandarin makes a good choice of flavor for a basic yogurt because it blends well with most other fruits and can be substituted in the recipes given over the next few pages.

2 tsp. cornstarch
15 fl. oz can mandarin oranges in their natural juices
2 tbsp. honey
1½ cups yogurt

Blend the cornstarch to a paste with a little of the liquid from the mandarins and pour in a blender along with the remaining contents of the can. Pour over the honey and process until smooth. Add the yogurt and process just long enough to combine. Transfer to the ice-cream machine and churn until firm. Put in a frozen glass before serving. Use immediately or freeze until required. Transfer to the refrigerator for about 15–20 minutes before using to allow for easier serving.

Serves 1

TIP

Substitute fresh or canned strawberries, apricots, pineapple, or pitted cherries. Bananas work well too. If using fresh fruit, add ½ cup fruit juice. For a smooth texture, strain the fruit through a non-metallic strainer before combining with the yogurt.

Frozen Mint Lassi

These drinks are popular in India where there are many variations based on fruits, spices, and flower waters. The following is an iced lassi. Vanilla frozen yogurt may be used but, for an authentic taste, make your own frozen yogurt omitting all flavorings.

8 fresh mint leaves
½ cup low-fat milk
2 scoops plain or vanilla frozen yogurt
sugar, to taste
ice, to serve
mint leaves and whole raspberries, to decorate

Place the mint leaves and the milk together in a blender and process until the leaves are finely chopped. Add the frozen yogurt and sugar to taste. (The quantity of sugar will vary depending on the sweetness of the frozen yogurt.) Pour in a glass and top off with extra milk, as necessary. Serve over ice and decorate with fresh mint leaves.

Serves 1

TIP

To make a rose water lassi, you could omit the mint and use 1–2 teaspoons of rose water.

Kiwi Fruit & Raspberry Slush

The indefinable sweet-tart flavor of kiwi fruit and the sharp tangy kick of raspberry combine wonderfully to make this a drink to wake up all the senses.

2 scoops kiwi fruit sorbet
1 scoop raspberry sorbet
½ cup chilled water
kiwi fruit slices, to decorate

Place the sorbets and water in a blender and process on a low speed until combined. Serve in a tall glass and decorate with slices of kiwi fruit.

Serves 1

TIP

Slushes always look good in sugar-rimmed glasses. Dip the rim of the glass in lemon juice, sugar syrup, or cane syrup and then dip in granulated sugar.

Pineapple & Coconut Smoothie

Cool, creamy, and refreshing, serve this virgin cousin of the Piña Colada in a tall glass with plenty of ice.

½ banana, peeled and chopped
7 fl. oz pineapple juice
3 fl. oz coconut milk
ice

Place the banana, pineapple juice, and coconut milk in a blender and process until smooth. Pour into a tall glass half-filled with ice and serve with a straw.

Serves 1

TIP

Add a dash of Grenadine to the drink and stir before drinking, for a Sunrise Moclada Smoothie.

Clementine Crush

Tantalize your tastebuds with this delicious, tangy treat. Clementines are a natural source of vitamins and antioxidants, perfect for any time of day.

lime wedge
superfine sugar
1 tbsp. freshly squeezed lime juice
½ tsp. sugar syrup, or to taste
1 peeled clementine
2 fl. oz apple juice

Rub the rim of a cocktail glass with the lime wedge, and dip in the superfine sugar to coat in an even layer. Place the lime juice, sugar syrup, clementine, and apple juice in a blender and process until smooth, then strain the mixture into the glass.

Serves 1

TIP

Replace 1 peeled clementine with 2 pitted apricots, for an apricot crush. Add a little more apple juice if the drink is too thick.

Woodland Smoothie

These classic woodland flavors make this the perfect fall smoothie.

1 cup blackberries
½ cup black currants
½ cup plain low-fat yogurt
¼ cup apple juice

Place the blackberries, black currants, yogurt, and the apple juice in a blender and process for 1 minute or until smooth. Pour into a glass to serve.

Serves 1

TIP

Replace the apple juice with the same amount of orange juice for a citrus flavor.

Plum Smoothie

This combination makes a deliciously creamy smoothie with a wonderful color.

TIP

You could try adding ¼ cup stewed rhubarb to the mixture before processing.

3 red or purple plums, halved and pitted, with extra slices to decorate
½ cup plain low-fat yogurt
¼ cup milk

Place the plums, yogurt, and milk in a blender and process for 1 minute or until smooth. Pour into a glass to serve, decorated with plum slices on a cocktail stick.

Serves 1

Blueberry, Strawberry & Orange Smoothie

Take advantage of the fresh wild blueberries available in late summer if you can.

½ cup blueberries
1 cup strawberries, hulled
½ cup plain low-fat yogurt
¼ cup orange juice

Place the blueberries, strawberries, yogurt, and orange juice in a blender and process for 1 minute or until smooth. Pour into a glass to serve.

Serves 1

TIP

Replace the orange juice with the same quantity of milk for a creamier smoothie.

Papaya & Lime Smoothie

A thick and sustaining smoothie, but delicately fragrant with the scents of tropical fruits.

1 cup papaya, peeled, pitted, and chopped
juice of 1 lime
½ cup plain low-fat yogurt
¼ cup milk
melon slices and mint leaves, to decorate

Place the papaya, lime juice, yogurt, and milk in a blender and process for 1 minute or until smooth. Pour into a glass to serve, decorated with the melon slices and mint.

TIP

If the lime is too tart for your taste, try omitting the lime juice and adding a teaspoon of honey.

Serves 1

Tomato & Parsley Sling

This veggie delight is an ideal pick-me-up. Enjoy the strong flavors and healthy hit of vitamin C.

2½ cups tomato (or mixed vegetable) juice
1 small bunch parsley
ice, to serve
Worcestershire (or soy) sauce to taste

Place the tomato juice and parsley in a blender and process until combined. Pour over ice, and season with Worcestershire or soy sauce to taste.

Serves 4

TIP

You could add 1 measure of vodka for an alcoholic kick.

Apple Shake

Sweet and scrumptious, this smoothie combines tart apple flavor with smooth banana, and just a hint of something spicy.

1 cup of apple juice
½ tsp. powdered cinnamon
2 tsp. grated fresh gingerroot
2 bananas, peeled and chopped
cucumber, julienned, to decorate

Put the apple juice, cinnamon, and fresh gingerroot in a blender and process gently until combined. Next add the sliced bananas and process again until smooth. Pour the smoothie mixture into two glasses, and decorate with the cucumber slices.

Serves 2

Peach & Raspberry Smoothie

This classic combination relies on the sweetness of a ripe peach to work well—but be sure the peach is not overripe, or it will have an unpleasant taste.

TIP

Try adding a couple of mint leaves to the blend, as well as decorating with them.

1 peach, pitted and chopped
½ cup raspberries plus extra to decorate
½ cup plain low-fat yogurt
¼ cup milk
mint leaves, to decorate

Place the peach, raspberries, yogurt, and milk in a blender and process for 1 minute or until smooth. Pour into a glass and serve, decorated with extra raspberries and mint leaves.

Serves 1

Watermelon Smoothie

Mouthwatering melon makes wonderful smoothies. Sweet and smooth, this one has a raspberry kick.

2½ cups watermelon flesh, plus slices to decorate
⅔ cup galia melon flesh
1–2 tsp. raspberry jelly
1 tbsp. yogurt
crushed ice
fresh mint leaves, to decorate

Remove any seeds from the watermelon flesh and process finely with the galia melon, yogurt, and raspberry jelly. Pour the blend into two glasses and fill up with plenty of crushed ice. Add a teaspoon of raspberry jelly to each and serve decorated with fresh mint leaves.

Serves 2

Cranberry Smoothie

There's no need to save cranberries for the holiday season. This tart and creamy smoothie is delicious all year round.

2 cups frozen cranberries
1 tbsp. confectioners' sugar
8½ fl. oz full-cream yogurt

Place the frozen cranberries into a blender, add the yogurt and confectioners' sugar and process. Transfer to chilled glasses, or put the creamy mixture into a piping bag and pipe into chilled glasses. Serve at once.

Serves 2

TIP

If no frozen cranberries are available, freeze fresh cranberries yourself. This smoothie can also be made in exactly the same way with whipping or heavy cream. Just make sure that the cranberries are frozen.

Grape & Kiwi Smoothie

This celestial smoothie is bursting with fruity flavors. Enjoy the mild grape, tangy kiwi, and addictive honey combination.

1 ripe kiwifruit, peeled and chopped, plus slices, to decorate
1 cup white grapes, skinned and pitted, plus two grapes with skin, to decorate
2 tsp. freshly squeezed lemon juice
2 tbsp. acacia honey
2 tbsp. full-cream yogurt

Put the kiwifruit and grapes into a blender with the lemon juice, acacia honey, and yogurt, and process. Chill for about 30 minutes, then pour into glasses at once and serve cold decorated with grapes and kiwifruit slices on cocktail sticks.

Serves 2

TIP

Keep pitted grapes in the freezer, and add to recipe as normal. You won't need to chill this scrumptious smoothie at all.

Cherry & Coconut Smoothie

The ultimate sweet smoothie, this tropical combo always goes down well with friends and family.

2 untreated limes
2 cups cherries, stoned
10 fl. oz cherry juice
4 tbsp. coconut syrup
2 tbsp. flaked coconut
1 banana, peeled and chopped
6 ice cubes

TIP

If you can't find coconut syrup, substitute vanilla syrup and 1 teaspoon coconut flavoring from the baking aisle.

Wash the limes, remove a few strips of zest for the garnish and squeeze the limes.

Put the cherries, cherry juice, lime juice, coconut syrup, flaked coconut, banana, and ice cubes into a blender and process for several minutes, until very finely puréed.

Pour the smoothie into two large glasses and decorate with lime zest.

Serves 2

Smoothies for Cherubs

These days you have to be so careful about what your kids are eating, looking for additives, E-numbers, and high salt and sugar contents, but you know exactly what's in a smoothie. Kids love the taste, and you can make sure they're getting the nutrients they need.

Smoothies for Cherubs

It is hard to get kids excited about fruit and vegetables. However, present them as something different and give them a new name, and sure enough they will see them in a new light. The bright, colorful, and neatly presented smoothie recipes in this chapter are separated into different categories—"Healthy eyes," "Healthy minds," "Healthy bones & teeth," "Healthy bodies," and perfect for birthday parties, "Special treats."

Children will go crazy for the bright colors of smoothies such as Kiwi Fruit & Lemon and Peach Melba, and you can be satisfied knowing that they are getting a great source of vitamin C. Some of the recipes include raw eggs for a protein extra, however, there are always suggestions for egg-free alternatives if you are concerned about safety.

Most of these recipes require the use of a blender—however, it is also worth consideration to invest in a juice extractor for recipes like Monster Juice or Orange & Carrot Juice, which are perfect for kids who prefer a thinner texture to their drink. There are a many different types of extractors which vary in price and quality—helping you to get those important vitamins and nutrients into your kids' diet.

Black Currant & Pomegranate Smoothie

Healthy Eyes

Your cherubs will love the tasty flavors of this smoothie, while you can rest assured that they are getting all the necessary healthy ingredients for well-being.

1 large, ripe pomegranate
½ cup fresh blueberries
½ cup fresh black currants
5 fl. oz natural yogurt
confectioners' sugar
about 9 fl. oz milk

Roll the pomegranate over a work surface with the flat of your hand, applying light pressure. Then cut off top and bottom, cut into sections lengthwise, and turn inside out to release the seeds. Reserve a couple of pieces for decoration. Finely process the rest of the fruit and push through a sieve.

Place the pomegranate juice into a blender with the washed blueberries, black currants, and yogurt and process. Sweeten to taste with a little confectioners' sugar.

Add enough milk to produce the desired consistency and process again. Decorate with pomegranate seeds.

Serves 3–4

Apricot & Mandarin Smoothie

Healthy Eyes

The rich flavor of apricots is delicious, however, this basic recipe can be adapted easily by changing the fruit.

10 apricots, canned or fresh
1 cup apple juice
2 scoops mandarin or orange frozen yogurt
2–3 tsp. honey
ice, to serve
fresh mint, to decorate

Place the apricots in a blender with the juice and process until smooth. For a smooth smoothie, pass the fresh fruit purée through a non-metallic strainer and return to the blender. Add the frozen yogurt and honey to taste, and process until smooth. Serve over ice, and decorate with fresh mint.

Serves 1

TIP

You could try removing the skin and stone from a very ripe nectarine and substituting it for the apricots for a nectarine and mandarin combination.

Carrot & Orange Juice

Healthy Eyes

Carrots are high in beta-carotene (a pro-vitamin), which converts into Vitamin A. In terms of eyesight, Vitamin A plays an important role in maintaining healthy vision.

2 apples, peeled, cored, and chopped
3 carrots, trimmed
2 oranges, peeled

Put the apples, carrots, and oranges through a juice extractor. Pour into a glass to serve.

Serves 1

Passion Fruit & Nut Smoothie

Healthy Minds

Nuts are a great source of protein, fiber, healthy monounsaturated fats, vitamins, nutrients, and antioxidants.

- pulp and juice of 1 passion fruit (sift if preferred)
- 1½ mangoes, peeled, pitted, and chopped
- 1 cup pineapple juice
- 1 banana, peeled and chopped
- 2 Brazil nuts
- 4 walnut halves
- 3 blanched almonds
- pineapple, to decorate

Place the passion fruit pulp and juice, the mangoes, pineapple juice, banana, and nuts in a blender and process for 1 minute or until smooth. Pour into a glass to serve. Decorate with a piece of fresh pineapple.

Serves 1

Banana, Prune & Flax Oil Smoothie

Healthy Minds

This smoothie aids digestion and brain power. Flax oil is known to be a great source of Omega-3.

1 banana, peeled and chopped
5 prunes, pitted, plus 1 extra to decorate
¼ cup orange juice
1 cup plain low-fat yogurt
1 tbsp. flax oil

Place the banana, prunes, juice, yogurt, and flax oil in a blender and process for 1 minute or until smooth. Pour into a glass or mug to serve.

Serves 1

TIP

If you can't find flax oil, try linseed oil. This is available in most drug stores and some supermarkets.

Bittersweet Choconana Smoothie

Healthy Minds

The high antioxidant levels and healthy potassium in this smoothie make it perfect for growing healthy minds.

¼ cup bittersweet chocolate, 70% cocoa, plus extra for decoration
14 fl. oz milk
2 ripe bananas, peeled and chopped
2 tsp. confectioners' sugar

Melt the chocolate over a warm bain-marie or in the microwave. Warm the milk to room temperature, then process the banana and confectioners' sugar with the milk. Pour into glasses and add 2–3 teaspoons of the melted chocolate to create swirls of chocolate in the smoothie. Serve at once, decorated with a few pieces of chocolate.

Serves 2

TIP

Bananas that are a rich yellow with small brown streaks or spots will have the right level of ripeness and the best flavor for this smoothie.

Blueberry & Yogurt Drink

Healthy Minds

Kids love blueberries, and they just adore this tasty blue smoothie. Eggs give them protein, yogurt cultures contribute to a strong immune system, and berries help to build brain cells. Your cherubs won't even realize this treat is healthy!

TIP

If you're worried about raw eggs, substitute with pasteurized egg beaters. Use the amount recommended on the carton.

2 eggs
2 cups plain yogurt
¼ cup blueberry preserves
1 cup milk
1 tsp. bitters
crushed ice

Place the eggs, yogurt, preserves, milk, and bitters in a blender. Process for about 30 seconds or until smooth. Serve over crushed ice.

Serves 4

Soy Banana Smoothie

Healthy Bones & Teeth

A thick and filling smoothie, with soy milk which is a great alternative for kids with an intolerance or allergy to dairy produce.

1½ bananas, peeled and chopped
1 tbsp. smooth peanut butter
1 cup soy milk

Place the bananas, peanut butter, and soy milk in a blender and process for 1 minute or until smooth. Pour into a glass to serve.

Serves 1

Kid's Eggnog

Healthy Bones & Teeth

This is high in calcium—perfect for your kids' bones and teeth.

1 large egg, separated
1½ tsp. superfine sugar
few drops of vanilla extract
5 fl. oz low-fat milk
2 fl. oz heavy cream
freshly grated nutmeg, to dust

Place the egg yolk, sugar, and vanilla in a bowl and whisk together until pale and creamy. Gradually whisk in the milk. In a separate bowl, whisk the egg white until it stands in soft peaks. Fold the egg yolk mixture into the whisked white. Whip the cream until it just holds its shape and then fold it in as well. Spoon into a glass and serve dusted with a little freshly grated nutmeg.

Serves 1

TIP

If you're worried about raw eggs, substitute with pasteurized egg beaters. Use the amount recommended on the carton.

Mango & Coconut Refresher

Healthy Bodies

Coconut milk is a great alternative to dairy; it's a good source of calcium and low in saturated fat.

¼ ripe mango, peeled, pitted, and chopped
2 fl. oz thick coconut milk
ice cubes
about 4 fl. oz seltzer

Place the mango and coconut milk in a blender, and process until smooth. Pour into a glass half filled with ice cubes and top off with seltzer. Decorate with a fun cocktail stick.

Serves 1

Orange Tang

Healthy Bodies

The fruity flavor of the orange juice blends well with the buttermilk and you can hardly tell that there is any buttermilk there. This drink makes a nice nutritious treat for a child who is not feeling well and aids digestion.

half 6-oz can frozen orange juice concentrate, slightly defrosted
1 cup chilled buttermilk
1 tsp. honey
2 tsp. wheat germ (optional)
2 scoops orange, or pineapple–lemon sherbet
ice, to serve
orange slices, to decorate

Place the orange juice, buttermilk, honey, wheatgerm (if using), and sherbet in a blender and process until smooth and frothy. Pour into an ice-filled glass. Decorate with orange slices.

Serves 1

Monster Juice

Healthy Bodies

The spooky green makes this healthy smoothie fun to drink—especially for Halloween.

1 kiwi fruit, peeled
1 cup seedless white grapes
1 cup honeydew melon, peeled and chopped
3 green apples, peeled, cored, and chopped
3 tbsp. milk

Place the kiwi fruit, grapes, melon, apples, and milk in a blender and process until smooth and frothy. Pour into a glass, and serve.

Serves 1

Kiwi Fruit & Lemon Smoothie

Healthy Bodies

Bright and fun, these healthy smoothies are perfect for getting your kids into fruity and healthy flavors. A good Halloween idea too!

2 kiwi fruit, peeled and chopped
1 lemon
1–2 tbsp. honey
7–9 fl. oz pineapple juice
2 tbsp. crushed ice

Finely purée the chopped kiwi fruit. Squeeze the lemon, strain the juice through a sieve, and mix with the honey. Place the fruit, lemon and honey mixture, juice, and ice in a blender and process until smooth. Pour into glasses and decorate with cocktail sticks.

Serves 2

Peach Melba Smoothie

Healthy Bodies

A swirly, colorful delight, this is fun to make with kids too.

for the coulis
½ cup raspberries
squeeze of lemon juice
1 tsp. honey

for the smoothie
2 peaches, pitted and chopped
½ cup plain low-fat yogurt
¼ cup milk

For the coulis, place the berries, juice, and honey in a blender and process until smooth. Pour out and set aside. If you do not want any seeds, pour the coulis through a mesh strainer. Don't worry about washing the blender, because it will give the peach smoothie a lovely pink color.

For the smoothie, place the peaches, yogurt, and milk in the blender and process the mixture for 1 minute or until smooth. Pour into a large bowl, swirl in the raspberry coulis, then pour into a glass to serve.

Serves 1

Peanut Punch

Healthy Bodies

A healthy peanut delight.

⅓ cup smooth peanut butter
 or 1 cup roasted peanuts,
 finely ground
14-oz can evaporated milk
14-oz can condensed milk
1 cup water
1 tbsp. sugar (optional)
1 egg
zest of 1 lime or lemon
1 tsp. vanilla extract
1 cup milk (optional)
1 scoop ice cream, to serve

Mix the peanut butter or ground peanuts with the evaporated milk. Add the condensed milk and water and mix together well. Taste and, if it is not sweet enough, add the sugar. Beat the egg, zest, vanilla, and milk into the peanut and milk mixture. Serve with ice cream.

Serves 4

PBJ Shake

Special Treats

The classic combination of peanut butter and jelly for the all-American kid.

3 tbsp. grape jelly
1 cup whole milk
3 scoops ice cream
2 tbsp. crunchy peanut butter

Place the grape jelly, milk, and ice cream in a blender and process for 30 seconds. Add the peanut butter and process until evenly mixed. Do not over-process or the crunch may be lost. Serve in paper cups.

Serves 2

TIP

Preserves can be used to produce sweet shakes that are similar to those made with syrups; however, they have more texture. Look out for preserves that are sweetened with natural fruit sugars and those with a reduced sugar content.

Momma's Strawberry Shake

Special Treats

This is a strawberry shake of childhood memories.

½ can strawberries
¾ cup whole milk
¼ cup half and half
2 scoops vanilla or strawberry ice cream
ice cubes, to serve

Drain the strawberries and place in a blender. Process until puréed. Add the milk, half and half, and ice cream and process until smooth. Pour over ice cubes.

Serves 1

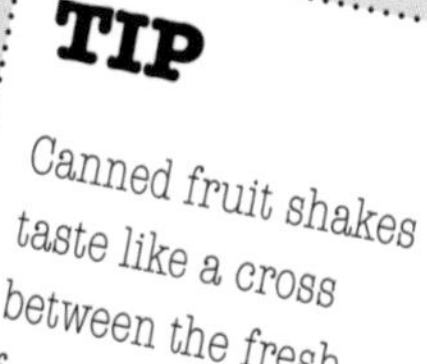

TIP

Canned fruit shakes taste like a cross between the fresh fruit and the preserve shakes. Use fruits in natural juices where possible as these are less sweet.

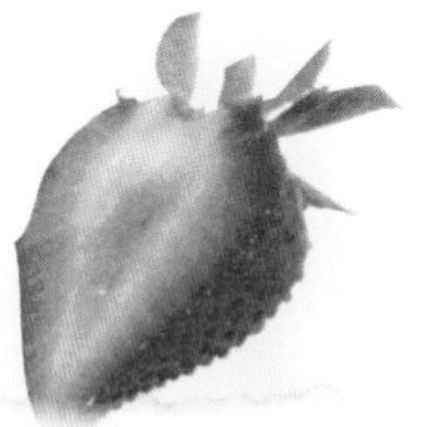

Banana & Toffee Smoothie

Special Treats

This irresistibly rich smoothie is made sweet by the dulce de leche and satiny smooth by the yogurt.

1½ bananas, peeled and chopped
1 tbsp. dulce de leche
½ cup plain low-fat yogurt
¼ cup milk
1 ginger cookie

Place the bananas, dulce de leche, yogurt, and milk in a blender. Process for 1 minute or until smooth. Pour into glasses and crumble the cookie on top.

Serves 2

Marshmallow Foam

Special Treats

This shake will remind you of summer camp—especially if you serve it with a toasted marshmallow.

1 cup whole milk
¼ cup mini marshmallows
2 scoops raspberry ice cream
mini marshmallows or one large toasted marshmallow, to decorate
mint leaves, to decorate

Heat the milk and the marshmallows together until the marshmallows are beginning to melt. Let chill in the refrigerator. Place in a blender with the raspberry ice cream and process until smooth and very foamy.
Pour into a glass, and decorate with a few mini marshmallows or 1 large toasted marshmallow on a toothpick, and mint leaves.

Serves 1

TIP

For a delicious alternative, substitute chocolate ice cream for raspberry, and sprinkle crushed graham crackers over the top to decorate.

Breakfast Smoothies

Although it's the most important meal of the day, breakfast is often forgotten or neglected. Our busy lifestyles mean it's easier to skip the meal, go hungry, and possibly risk our health. Instead, try a delicious breakfast smoothie. You can make them the night before to store in the fridge, and start the day in smoothie bliss.

Breakfast Smoothies

Breakfast is often cited as the most important meal of the day, and what better way to start your morning than a healthy and nutritious smoothie. Kick-starting your metabolism into action, this chapter brings the best breakfast recipes together so you will never get bored of porridge again.

These filling smoothies will easily keep hunger at bay, with ingredients like wheat germ, granola, and oatmeal. There are favorite staple flavors such as coffee, maple and banana, and orange and date, as well as some unexpected choices—the Wake-up Call smoothie has to be tried to be believed.

All the recipes have fruit at their base, meaning you'll get started on your five-a-day in delicious style. The great thing about smoothies is although they do taste at their best when the fruit is freshest, they can be a delicious way of using up fruit which is a little soft to eat alone—our tips often provide different fruit variations so you can tailor the recipe to the fruit that needs to be blended first.

Breakfast Orange

This recipe makes a great start to the day. Add honey to break the taste buds in more gently, but remember that the frozen yogurt is usually pretty sweet.

1 cup chilled orange juice (fresh if possible)
2 scoops vanilla or orange frozen yogurt or ice cream
1 egg
2 tsp. wheat germ
1 tbsp. honey (optional)
orange slice, to decorate

Place the orange juice, yogurt, egg, wheat germ, and honey, in a blender and process until smooth. Pour into a chilled glass, decorate with an orange slice, and serve.

Serves 1

TIP

This smoothie is delicious served with a wholewheat raisin muffin.

Blue Banana Breakfast

This eye-opening smoothie is an ideal breakfast. Filling and delicious, it even has more healthy fiber than your average breakfast cereal.

- 1 cup fresh or frozen blueberries, plus extra to decorate
- 1 banana, peeled and chopped
- 1 tbsp. wheat germ
- ¼ tsp. lemon juice
- 2 scoops vanilla frozen yogurt
- 1 tbsp. maple syrup

Place the blueberries, banana, wheat germ, lemon juice, yogurt, and maple syrup in a blender and process until smooth. Pour into a glass, and decorate with some whole blueberries.

Serves 1

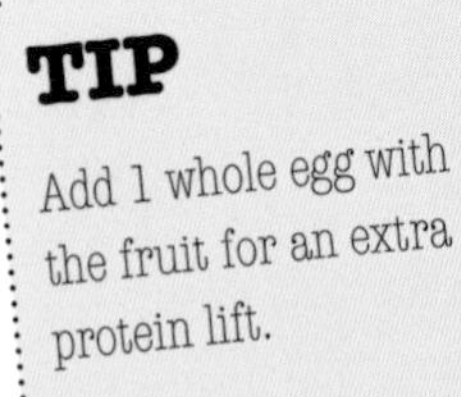

TIP

Add 1 whole egg with the fruit for an extra protein lift.

Banana Strawberry Surprise

The surprise comes from all the goodies slipped into the blender; the creaminess of the banana and strawberries, the tang of lemon frozen yogurt, and the nutty flavor of wheat germ that adds nutrition to the shake.

1 very small banana, peeled and chopped
6 large strawberries, hulled
½ cup whole milk
2 tbsp. skim milk powder
1 tbsp. malt powder
2 tsp. wheat germ
2 tsp. unrefined sugar
2 scoops lemon frozen yogurt
powdered cinnamon

Place the banana, strawberries, whole milk, milk powder, malt powder, wheat germ, and sugar in a blender and process until the banana and strawberry is puréed and the sugar dissolved. Add the frozen yogurt and a good shake of cinnamon. Process until smooth. Serve in a chilled glass.

Serves 2

Maple Banana Smoothie

Feeling a craving for home-cooked banana pancakes in the morning? Try this oh-so-good smoothie for a faster option.

TIP

The riper the banana, the sweeter the flavor.

- 1 small ripe banana, peeled and chopped, plus extra to decorate
- 1 cup whole milk
- 2 scoops maple-syrup-flavored ice cream
- 1 tsp. sugar (optional)
- 1 tsp. lemon juice (optional)
- a drizzle of maple syrup, to decorate

2 scoops plain yogurt
2 "scoops" maple syrup

Place the banana, milk, ice cream, sugar, and lemon juice in a blender and process for 30 seconds until smooth. Pour into glasses and decorate with a drizzle of maple syrup, and banana slices.

Serves 1

Banana & Maple Soy Shake

Start the day the healthy way with this creamy soy smoothie, perfect for watching your weight or your cholesterol.

1 banana, peeled and chopped
1 cup cold soy milk
2 tsp. lemon juice
1 tbsp. maple syrup, plus extra to decorate
2 tsp. wheat germ

Place the banana, soy milk, lemon juice, syrup, and wheat germ in a blender and process until smooth and frothy. Refrigerate until well chilled. Pour into a glass and drizzle with maple syrup.

Serves 1

TIP

For a low-carb or sugar-free version, try substituting sugar-free maple syrup and unsweetened soy milk.

Honest Coffee Shake

Forget the high-price coffee smoothie you buy on the way to work. Make your own version that's just as delicious and easier on the wallet!

for the smoothie
1 cup strong coffee (instant or ground), chilled
½ cup whole milk or half and half
1 scoop coffee ice cream
ice
½–2 tsp. coffee syrup (see page 238)
whipped cream, to decorate

TIP

For a lighter smoothie, try using sugar-free syrup, non-fat milk, and cool whip for the topping.

Place the coffee, milk or half and half, and ice cream in a blender along with ice, if your blender can take it. Process until smooth. Pour into a glass with a little more ice and sweeten to taste with the coffee syrup. Top with whipped cream, if desired.

Serves 1

Spiced Country Breakfast Smoothie

Using stewed fruit is a novel approach to smoothie-making, but this fruit adds a mellow flavor that you don't get from fresh fruits.

1 apple, peeled, cored, and chopped
1 pear, peeled, cored, and chopped
1 cup chopped rhubarb
¼ cup blackberries
squeeze of lemon juice
1 tsp. honey
½ cup plain low-fat yogurt
1 tsp. pumpkin pie spice
honey, to decorate

TIP

Stewed rhubarb is also delicious in a smoothie, and stewing makes it a lot easier to process the fruit together.

Place all of the fruits into a pan with 2 tablespoons water, the lemon juice, and the honey. Bring to a boil, then turn down to a simmer. Poach the fruit for 10 minutes or until it is tender. Remove from the heat and let cool. Place the stewed fruit in a blender with the yogurt and add 1 teaspoon pumpkin pie spice to the stewed fruit before blending. Process for 1 minute or until smooth. Pour into a glass to serve. Drizzle a little extra honey over the smoothie if desired.

Serves 1

Apricot Breakfast Smoothie

The wheat germ in this breakfast smoothie provides a slow release of energy through the morning, helping you to keep satisfied until lunch. It also adds a creamy texture to the smoothie.

- 3 apricots, halved and pitted, with 1 slice reserved to decorate
- ¾ cup apple juice
- ¾ cup plain low-fat yogurt
- 1 tsp. honey
- 1 tbsp. wheat germ

Put the apricots, juice, yogurt, honey, and wheat germ in a blender and process for 1 minute. Pour into a glass to serve.

Serves 1

TIP

You could try replacing the apricot with 1 cup of blueberries for another morning delight.

Orange & Date Smoothie

Dates give this smoothie a slight toffee taste and yogurt keeps you full for longer, a perfect substitute for the sugary morning Danish.

zest and juice of 2 oranges
5 dried dates, pitted
1 cup plain low-fat yogurt

Place the zest, juice, dates, and yogurt in a blender and process until smooth. Pour into a glass to serve.

Serves 1

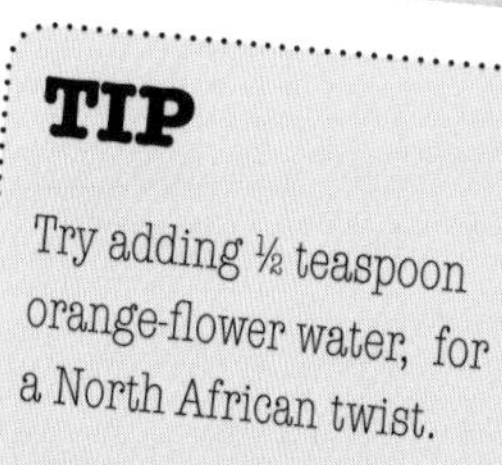

TIP

Try adding ½ teaspoon orange-flower water, for a North African twist.

Wake-up Call

If you have an important appointment the morning after a heavy night, this will probably get you up in time to do business better than the most insistent alarm! Warning: Do not attempt to drive after drinking one of these!

- 1 fl. oz gold rum
- 1 fl. oz Amaretto Disaronno
- 2 tbsp. whipping cream
- 1 fl. oz cold, strong black coffee or a shot of espresso
- ice cubes
- grated bittersweet chocolate, to decorate

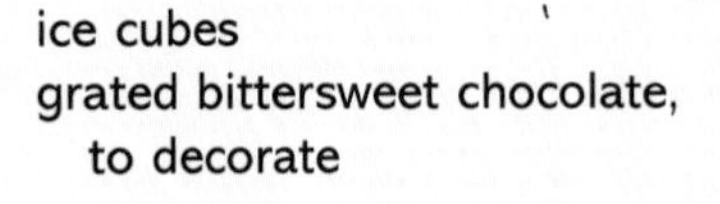

Place the rum, Amareto Disaronno, cream, and coffee into a cocktail shaker with plenty of ice cubes. Shake vigorously. Strain into a cocktail glass and grate a little bittersweet chocolate on top.

Serves 1

TIP

For a real espresso wake-up call, replace the gold rum with dark rum and double the amount of coffee.

Peach & Oatmeal Drink

Everyone loves morning oatmeal, and combining the wholesome goodness of oats with tasty peach makes a fun and fruity breakfast.

TIP

Try 3 tablespoons of fruit muesli in place of the rolled oats for a more flavorful breakfast drink.

- 2½ cups water
- 3 tbsp. rolled oats
- 1 very ripe peach, pitted and chopped
- 2 tbsp. peach preserves
- ¼ cup orange juice

Place the water and oats in a small pan. Bring to a boil; then reduce the heat and simmer for 3 minutes. Remove from the heat and let cool. Place the oat mixture in a blender and process until very smooth. Add the peach, preserves, and orange juice. Process until smooth.

Serves 2

Breakfast Yogurt Eggnog

Keep the holiday spirit all year round with this rich and creamy smoothie. There's no alcohol, so it's great for a sweet treat in the early morning.

TIP

If you need a little fruit in the morning, this recipe tastes great with an added banana.

- 2 eggs, separated
- 1½ tbsp. sugar
- 1 cup milk
- 1 cup plain yogurt
- ½ tsp. pure vanilla extract
- freshly grated nutmeg, to decorate

Place the egg yolks and sugar in a bowl and beat until thick and lemon-colored. Add milk, yogurt, and vanilla and stir well. In another bowl, using clean, dry beaters, beat egg whites until stiff. Fold into yogurt mixture. Sprinkle with nutmeg.

Serves 4

Grapefruit & Carrot Cocktail

For all your vitamin-C needs, this smoothie combines tart grapefruit with smooth carrot flavor for a breakfast pick-me-up that helps guard against colds and flu.

TIP

Replace the grapefruit juice with the same quantity of milk for a creamier smoothie.

3 carrots, peeled and coarsely chopped
3 cups water
4 cups unsweetened grapefruit juice
1½ tbsp. honey
⅛ tsp. powdered ginger

Place the carrots in a small pan and add ½ cup water. Cover and cook over a low heat for 10 minutes or until carrots are tender. Drain well, reserving ¼ cup cooking liquid. Purée carrots and reserved ¼ cup cooking liquid in a blender. Add grapefruit juice, honey, ginger, and the remaining water. Process until frothy. Pour into glasses to serve.

Serves 4

Date & Almond Drink

Toffee notes and smooth almond flavor make this smoothie a scrumptious alternative to pastries for breakfast or brunch.

1 cup milk
1 cup plain yogurt
4 ice cubes
12 dates, pitted and coarsely chopped
4 unsalted almonds

Place the milk, yogurt, ice cubes, dates, and almonds in a blender and process for about 2 minutes or until smooth. Pour into glasses to serve.

Serves 2

TIP

For an indulgent date drink, add 2 tablespoons of chocolate chips to the mix.

Strawberry & Almond Smoothie

A healthy strawberry and almond delight, this will keep hunger at bay until lunchtime.

1 ⅓ cups ripe strawberries, hulled, plus extra to decorate
1 tbsp. clear honey
2 tbsp. ground almonds
10 fl. oz chilled yogurt
1 tbsp. almond syrup
1 tbsp. strawberry syrup, for color, plus extra if necessary
flaked almonds, to decorate

Put the strawberries into a shallow dish and transfer to the freezer for about 30 minutes. Then put in a blender with the honey, ground almonds, and yogurt and process. Add the almond syrup and strawberry syrup and process again briefly. Push through a sieve if necessary and pour into 2 glasses. Decorate with flaked almonds and strawberry slices.

Serves 2

Egg, Wheat Germ & Honey Smoothie

Sugar and spice, and all things nice—tease your tastebuds and get a hit of morning protein with this fragrant smoothie.

2 eggs
2 tbsp. acacia honey
14 fl. oz whole milk
2 tbsp. wheat germ
freshly grated nutmeg
powdered cinnamon

Separate the eggs. Beat the egg yolks and honey with an electric whisk until pale and foamy. Heat the milk until bubbles form at the edge of the pan. Do not let it boil. Whisk the egg whites until stiff. Add the warm milk and the wheat germ to the egg yolk mixture and process with a hand blender until homogenized. Add nutmeg and cinnamon to taste, then carefully stir in the beaten egg whites. Pour into glasses and serve at once, with fresh fruit on the side.

Serves 2

TIP

The fresher the eggs, the easier they will be to separate and the best they will be for this smoothie.

Minty Orange Coffee

This shake has a fragrant, refreshing taste and is a good "pick-me-up" brunch shake. Prepare the coffee the day before, cover, and leave in the refrigerator overnight.

TIP

If you can't find orange-flavored coffee, use regular coffee and 1 teaspoon orange flavoring from the baking aisle.

- 1 cup orange-flavored coffee
- 1 sprig of fresh mint, plus extra, to decorate
- 1 thin strips of orange zest, plus extra to decorate
- 1 scoop coffee ice cream

Pour the coffee over the mint and orange peel. Leave until cold. Cover and refrigerate until chilled. Place the coffee and the ice cream in a blender and process until smooth. Float a couple of strips of orange peel on the top of the coffee, and decorate with mint leaves.

Serves 1

Smoothie Snacks

During the day, it's easy to feel those little twinges of hunger between meals and reach for the chips or the cookie jar, but choosing a smoothie for a snack is healthier and often more satisfying. These recipes are like mini-meals, mostly healthy and vegetable-based to help you beat those devilish mid-afternoon hunger pangs.

Smoothie Snacks

Sweet smoothies are more popular than they have ever been, but waiting in the wings are the savory smoothies. A perfect alternative to soup, these vegetable-based smoothies are great for a quick snack or a healthy meal.

Often combining fruit with spices and herbs like chili, parsley, cinnamon, or pesto, these are unique recipes to try when you grow tired of your favorite mango smoothie.

They are often more time-consuming, but far more rewarding—both for taste and nutritional value. For instance, the Zucchini Refresher (right), contains four different types of vegetables.

For the savory smoothie beginner, it may be worth starting with the Tomato & Parmesan Smoothie—combining one of the greatest Italian flavor combinations, it is a simple and delicious smoothie which is presented so well it is worthy of a dinner-party appetizer.

Zucchini Refresher

This fiery, refreshing smoothie makes a deliciously unusual appetizer or snack. It takes only minutes to prepare and is perfect for entertaining.

2 tbsp. olive oil
1 small onion, thinly sliced
2 cups zucchini, chopped
1 medium potato, peeled and chopped
2 small carrots, peeled and thinly sliced
1 tsp. dried leaf tarragon, plus extra to garnish
1 tbsp. chopped fresh dill weed or 1 tsp. dried dill weed
2 cups chicken broth
1 cup milk

Heat oil in a large pan. Add the onion, zucchini, potato, and carrots. Cook, stirring, until vegetables start to soften. Add the tarragon, dill weed, and broth and bring to a boil. Reduce heat, cover, and simmer until vegetables are tender. Remove from heat; cool, pour in a blender and process until smooth. Pour into a pitcher and refrigerate until well chilled. Stir in 1 cup milk just before serving; add more milk if desired. Serve garnished with tarragon.

Serves 6

TIP

Add a tablespoon of chili powder to give a kick to your filling smoothie.

Emerald Blend

A filling smoothie with a tasty Asian feel, this recipe is full of vitamins and minerals for a perfect low-fat snack.

⅓ cup chopped fresh parsley
6 cups unsweetened pineapple juice
10 lettuce leaves, chopped
⅓ cup chopped celery leaves
⅓ cup alfalfa sprouts, plus extra to garnish
parsley sprigs, to garnish

Place the chopped parsley, pineapple juice, lettuce, celery leaves, and alfalfa sprouts in a blender. Process until smooth. Refrigerate until well chilled. Garnish with parsley sprigs and alfalfa sprouts.

Serves 6

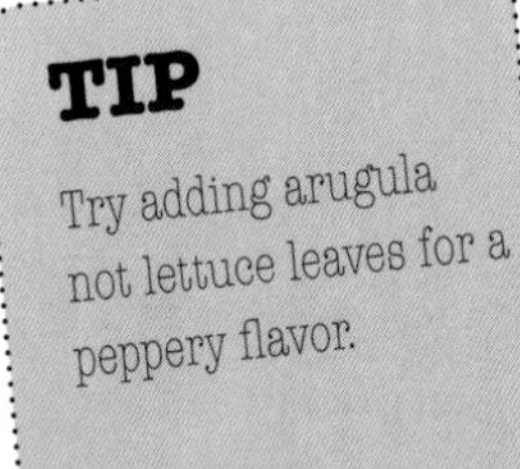

TIP

Try adding arugula not lettuce leaves for a peppery flavor.

Cucumber Frappé

Cooling and calming cucumber makes a stress-relieving smoothie snack, easy to make in advance and take to work.

3 large cucumbers, peeled, seeded, and chopped
3 cups plain yogurt
¼ cup chopped fresh parsley
¼ cup chopped fresh mint
9 ice cubes

Reserve the peel of one cucumber and set aside. Place the yogurt, parsley, and mint in a blender. Process until smooth. Add the chopped cucumber, a third at a time, and process until smooth. Add the ice cubes and process until crushed. Garnish with reserved cucumber peel—curl the cucumber around a toothpick to get this striking serving suggestion.

Serves 6

TIP

Parsley could also make an interesting, effortless garnish.

Strawberry & Chili Smoothie

This fiery, refreshing smoothie makes a deliciously unusual appetizer or snack. It takes only minutes to prepare and is perfect for entertaining.

2 cups ripe strawberries, hulled
juice of 3 oranges
1½ fresh red chilies, seeded and chopped
pinch of salt
ice cubes, to serve (optional)
fresh mint leaves, to garnish

Place the strawberries, orange juice, and chilies in a food processor or blender and process until smooth. Add a pinch of salt and pulse to mix it in.

Pour the soup into small bowls, add a couple of ice cubes to each portion, if desired, and serve garnished with mint.

Serves 4

TIP

You could try replacing the orange juice with 1 cup of fruity red wine.

Mexicali

Snacking south of the border means aromatic herbs and spicy chili. Enjoy this hot and healthy Mexican smoothie for a mid-afternoon jolt to the system.

1 cup tomato juice
½ small green hot chili pepper, seeded
1 fresh cilantro sprig
⅛ teaspoon dried leaf oregano
2 avocado slices

Place the tomato juice, chili, herbs, and avocado in a blender and process for 30 seconds. Pour into a glass to serve.

Serves 1

TIP

You could try roasting the chili pepper over an open flame before you add it to the dish, giving an additional smoky flavor to the drink.

Celery & Apple Berry Delight

An excellent hydrating juice to get you back to peak performance to face the day ahead.

1 apple, peeled and cored
1 carrot, peeled and trimmed
2 celery stalks, trimmed
¾-inch piece of peeled gingerroot
1½ cups mixed dried berries and currants

Place the apple, carrot, celery, gingerroot, and berries through a juice extractor. Pour into a glass to serve.

Serves 1

TIP

You could try omitting the berries and adding 2 small beets, trimmed, into the juice extractor.

Melon & Pesto Soup Smoothie

A chilled melon smoothie that is perfect for summer entertaining because it actually benefits from being made up to a day in advance. It's a marvelous way of using up the shells of melons that you have balled for other dishes.

2 lb galia melon purée
1 mild green chili, seeded and finely chopped
18 fl. oz water
3 tbsp. best-quality pesto
salt and white pepper, to season
lime juice, to taste
crushed ice, to serve

Place the melon purée, chili, water, and pesto in a blender, and process until smooth. Add enough lime juice to lift the flavor of the soup. Season to taste, and chill the soup for at least 2 hours. Serve over a little crushed ice.

Serves 4

TIP

It is essential to use the very best pesto sauce—it should be sweet and made just with basil, garlic, Parmesan, olive oil, and pine nuts.

Kiwi Fruit, Coconut & Lime Smoothie

Fruity smoothie snacks are always popular. Try this tropical mix for something sweet and satisfying between meals.

1 ripe kiwi fruit, peeled and sliced
2 tbsp. cream of coconut
2 tbsp. lime juice
¾ cup cold seltzer

Reserve 1 kiwifruit slice. Place the remaining kiwi fruit, cream of coconut, and lime juice in a blender. Process about 10 seconds or until smooth. Pour into a glass to serve. Add seltzer; stir. Decorate with reserved kiwi fruit slice.

Serves 1

TIP

For an authentic Caribbean taste, substitute the flesh of ½ a ripe mango for the kiwi fruit.

Grape Feast Smoothie

This smoothie is guaranteed to fill you up. Packed with fruit and protein, this really is the perfect snack.

2½ cups red grape juice
½ cup plain yogurt
½ cup milk
2 egg yolks
1 banana, peeled and chopped
1 cup melon cubes

Place the juice, yogurt, milk, yolks, banana, and melon in a blender and process until smooth. Pour into glasses to serve.

Serves 4

Spinach Yogurt Smoothie

Mom always told you to eat your spinach, so here's an unexpectedly delicious way to get the green vegetable into your daily diet.

3 cups fresh baby spinach
1 tsp. sunflower oil
14 fl. oz yogurt (10% fat)
salt
½ tsp. chili powder
lemon juice (optional)
sprig of thyme, to garnish

Wash the spinach and spin dry. Heat the oil in a pan and heat the spinach over a medium heat until it wilts. Let the spinach cool, then process finely with the yogurt. Season with salt and chili powder. Add a dash of lemon juice if you wish. Chill in the refrigerator for 20 minutes. Pour into glasses and serve well chilled, with a thyme garnish.

Serves 2

TIP

If fresh spinach is not available, frozen spinach can be used, but it should be heated and left to cool before using.

Beet Smoothie

Beets are an excellent source of iodine, sulphur, copper, vitamin B1, and vitamin B2, so try this smoothie for a very healthy snack.

1 small beet, cooked, peeled, and chopped
5 fl. oz freshly squeezed orange juice
1½ cups full-cream yogurt
2 tsp. gingerroot, freshly grated
2 tbsp. agave syrup
orange slices, to decorate

Put the beet in a blender with the orange juice, yogurt, gingerroot. and agave syrup and process finely. Pour into glasses, garnish with orange slices, and serve at once.

Serves 2

TIP

You can use acacia honey instead of the agave syrup, if you wish, but only use 1 tablespoon.

Tomato & Parmesan Smoothie

The Italian flavors in this scrumptious smoothie make it perfect for a light lunch on the go.

4–5 ripe tomatoes, skinned, seeded, and chopped
1 tbsp. Parmesan, grated
6 basil leaves
1 clove garlic, peeled
2 tbsp. cold-pressed olive oil
salt and freshly ground pepper
wedges of Parmesan, to garnish
1 tbsp. arugula leaves, to garnish

Place the tomatoes, grated Parmesan, basil, garlic, and olive oil in a blender and process until smooth. Season well with salt and pepper. Chill for 30 minutes, then pour into glasses and serve garnished with a wedge of Parmesan and the arugula leaves.

Serves 2

Pear & Cinnamon Yogurt Shake

Sweet and spicy, this smoothie gives you a mouthwatering combination you won't find at the average café or juice bar.

TIP

The pears should be ripe and soft, but not mushy. The yogurt and cream should be well chilled.

2 medium-sized, ripe pears, peeled, cored and chopped
10½ fl. oz full-cream yogurt
3½ fl. oz whipping cream
1 tbsp. acacia honey
1 tsp. powdered cinnamon
pinch of nutmeg
pinch of cinnamon sugar, to decorate

Put the chopped pears in a blender with the yogurt, cream, honey, cinnamon, and nutmeg and blend. Pour into glasses, sprinkle with a little cinnamon sugar, and serve at once.

Serves 2

Spicy Papaya & Chili Smoothie

Papaya is often paired with chili in Thai-style salads or relishes. This smoothie combines them both for a drink that is not too sweet, and packs a real punch!

1 large papaya, peeled, pitted, and chopped
8 fl. oz pineapple juice
juice of 1 fresh lime
4 fl. oz low-fat milk
1 cup banana, peeled and chopped
4 ice cubes
1 red poblano chili, seeded and finely chopped
1 tbsp. honey
mint leaves, to decorate

Place the papaya, juices, milk, banana, ice, chili, and honey in a blender and process until smooth. Pour into tall glasses to serve. Decorate with mint leaves.

Serves 2

TIP

Wedges of lime work well as decoration, bringing out the zesty bitter flavor.

Parsley, Chive & Basil Smoothie

Aromatic, utterly delicious, and bursting with antioxidants, this amazing smoothie will have you addicted in no time.

14 fl. oz full-cream yogurt
2 tbsp. parsley, chopped
1 tbsp. chives, chopped
1 tbsp. basil, chopped
2 tbsp. cold-pressed olive oil
1 tbsp. freshly squeezed lemon juice
salt
pinch salt and pepper
freshly grated nutmeg
parsley, to garnish

Place the yogurt, the herbs, oil and lemon juice in a blender, and process until smooth. Season with salt and pepper and add nutmeg to taste. Pour into tall glasses and serve cold, garnished with a little parsley.

Serves 2

Dessert Smoothies

Need something sweet after your evening meal? Smoothies can be fantastic desserts, and whether you fancy something light and sweet or rich and decadent, *Smoothie heaven* answers your prayers with the ideal ooey-gooey dessert.

Dessert Smoothies

Smoothies have a healthy image—and so they should when most have low-fat yogurt and fruit at their base. However, they can become luxurious desserts with the right recipe. Here are a selection of the most devilish smoothies allowed in smoothie heaven—drinks positively drowning in chocolate, toffee, marshmellow, and cream.

Favorite desserts such as apple or cherry pies, peaches and cream, tiramisu, cheesecake, and good old-fashioned strawberry trifle are transformed and updated into delicious smoothies and shakes.

Many of the recipes—for ease—are shown in quantities for one person, but no doubt these are recipes you will want to share. Simply double the quantities, and don't be afraid with your toppings. For more ideas about presentation, see Garnishes & Decorations on page 226.

Double Fudge Treat Smoothie

Taking the dessert category by storm, this fudge ice cream and topping is almost too good to be true.

1 cup whole milk
3 scoops fudge chunk or toffee swirl ice cream
¼ cup fudge sauce
1 tbsp. chopped roasted almonds

Place the milk and 2 scoops of ice cream in a blender and process until just smooth. Avoid over-blending, particularly if you are using the textured fudge chunk ice cream, otherwise the chunks will be blended into the shake. Pour the shake into a chilled glass and top with the additional scoop of ice cream. Drizzle over the fudge sauce and sprinkle with nuts.

Serves 2

TIP

Avoid hot fudge sauce because it warms up the shake too quickly and can make it sickly.

Key Lime Smoothie

This shake is refreshing and has a pleasant tartness, which offsets the sweetness of the ice cream and chocolate. This shake fits into a regular tumbler-sized glass.

½ lemon
½ lime, plus extra to decorate
1½–2 tbsp. sugar
1 cup whole milk
2 scoops vanilla ice cream
3 tbsp. semisweet chocolate chips or sprinkles
whipped cream (optional)
semisweet chocolate chips or sprinkles and citrus peel curls, to decorate

Wash the lemon and lime well and cut into pieces. Place in a blender with the sugar and milk and process until only tiny flecks of skin are visible. Sift through a non-metallic strainer, pressing out all the liquid.

Return to the blender and add the ice cream. Process until smooth. Pour into a glass and stir in the chocolate chips or sprinkles. Top with whipped cream, if using, and decorate with chocolate chips or sprinkles, slice of lime, and citrus peel curls.

Serves 1

TIP

Make your ice cubes from milk to reduce the diluting effect of water.

Apple Pie Smoothie

Apple pie with ice cream is an iconic all-American dessert, and here the pie and ice cream are blended into one angelic smoothie.

1 cup stewed apples, with extra peel and slices to decorate
¼ tsp. cinnamon
1 cup vanilla ice cream
3 tbsp. heavy whipping cream

Put all the ingredients except the crumbled cookie into a blender and process for 1 minute. Pour into a glass and with the peel and slices of apple. Serve immediately.

Serves 1

TIP

Prepare the basic recipe, adding ¼ cup stewed rhubarb to the other ingredients before processing.

Caramel Candy Bar Smoothie

Candy bar ice creams are very popular. The ones that are prepared in an ice cream parlor can be used in shakes but those that are individually wrapped and sold in the market do not make successful shakes. Try this homemade version. It does not contain a candy bar, but it has all their indulgent ingredients.

½ cup whole milk
1 scoop rich chocolate ice cream
2 scoops vanilla ice cream
1 tbsp. butterscotch sauce, plus extra to decorate
2 tbsp. semisweet chocolate chips
chopped, toasted unsalted peanuts or almonds, to decorate

TIP

You could go a step further and decorate the glass with a caramel star.

Place the milk, chocolate and 1 scoop of vanilla ice cream, and butterscotch sauce in a blender and process until smooth. Pour into a glass, then stir in the chocolate chips.

Top with the remaining vanilla ice cream and drizzle over plenty of butterscotch sauce. Sprinkle with the chopped nuts.

Serves 1

Chocolate Truffle Smoothie

The chocolate complements the coffee flavor very well in this delicious smoothie.

1 cup strong chocolate truffle coffee, chilled
½ cup whole milk
1 scoop vanilla ice cream
ice
½–2 tsp. coffee syrup or sugar
whipped cream, to decorate
grated chocolate, to decorate

Place the coffee, milk, and ice cream in a blender and process until smooth. Pour into a glass with a little ice and sweeten to taste with the coffee syrup. Top with a swirl of the whipped cream and decorate with the grated chocolate.

Serves 1

Peaches & Cream Smoothie

The addition of a peach liqueur gives a little kick to this delightfully refreshing shake.

½ can peach halves, with juice
½ cup whole milk
¼ cup half and half
1½ scoops vanilla ice cream
3 tbsp. peach liqueur
1 scoop peach ice cream
and peach slices

Place the peach halves with about ¼ cup juice in a blender and process until smooth. Pour about one-quarter of the purée into a jug and set aside. Add the milk, half and half, ice cream, and the peach liqueur to the blender. Process until smooth.

Pour into the glass and top with the remaining scoop of ice cream. Drizzle the reserved peach purée over the ice cream and decorate the glass with peach slices.

Serves 1

TIP

When using canned fruits in smoothies choose fruits in natural juices where possible as these are less sweet.

Cherry Pie Smoothie

The almond extract brings out the flavor of the cherries in this smoothie while adding an interesting hint of almonds.

15 pitted black cherries, either very ripe or canned
¾ cup cranberry juice
2 scoops vanilla frozen yogurt
¼ tsp. almond extract
fresh cherries, to decorate

Place the cherries, juice, frozen yogurt, and almond extract in a blender and process until smooth. Sift through a non-metallic strainer into an ice-filled glass. Decorate with fresh cherries.

Serves 1

TIP

Place a few berries or small pieces of chopped fruit in the base of the glass. Serve the smoothie with a long-handled spoon so that the goodies at the bottom can all be scooped out.

Banorange Cream Smoothie

Topped with whipping cream, this smoothie makes a wonderful end-of-meal treat.

1 cup chilled orange juice
1 very small or ½ medium banana, peeled and chopped
½ cup half and half
orange slices, to decorate
1–2 tbsp. whipped cream, to decorate

Place orange juice, banana, and half and half in a blender and process until smooth. Pour into chilled glasses and decorate with the orange slices.

Serves 2

TIP

If you can't use half and half in this one, use whole milk and a dash of cream.

Raspberry Cheesecake Smoothie

The addition of cottage cheese increases the nutritional value of this shake and adds a slight sharpness to the flavor.

1 cup whole milk
2 tbsp. cottage cheese
1–2 tbsp. raspberry syrup
few drops lime juice, plus extra if needed
frozen raspberries, to decorate

TIP

Try this smoothie with other sweet syrups too, such as strawberry, cherry, or blueberry.

Place the milk, cheese, raspberry syrup, and juice in a blender and process until smooth. Taste and add more lime juice, if required. Serve in a chilled glass and decorate with a few frozen raspberries.

Serves 1

Banoffee Smoothie

A traditional dessert in a not-so-traditional form, this banana and toffee delight is best served with a spoon!

1 small ripe banana, peeled and chopped
1 cup whole milk
2 scoops toffee ice cream
1 tsp. sugar (optional)
1 tsp. lemon juice (optional)
grated chocolate and whipping cream, to decorate

Place the banana, milk, ice cream, sugar, and lemon juice in a blender and process for 30 seconds until smooth. Pour into glasses and decorate with grated chocolate and the whipping cream.

Serves 2

Strawberry Trifle Smoothie

This once-maligned British dessert has been revalued and reworked in many kitchens recently. It's especially delicious as a smoothie.

1 cup strawberries, hulled
1 cup vanilla ice cream
½ cup ready-made custard
1 ladyfinger, crumbled
sugar sprinkles, to decorate

Place the strawberries, ice cream, and custard in a blender and process for 1 minute. Pour into a glass and stir the crumbled ladyfinger through the mixture. Serve with the sugar sprinkles scattered on top.

Serves 1

TIP

Add 2 tablespoons sherry to the other ingredients before blending.

Baileys Tiramisu Smoothie

The sensational Italian dessert converts easily into a luxurious drink that would make a stylish conclusion to a party meal.

1 cup vanilla ice cream
½ cup mascarpone
1 tbsp. heavy whipping cream
1 tsp. instant coffee dissolved in
1 tbsp. boiling water
2 tbsp. Baileys liqueur
1 ladyfinger
cocoa powder, for dusting

Place the ice cream, mascarpone, and cream in a blender and process for 1 minute. Pour into a glass. Mix together the dissolved coffee and Bailey's liqueur and crumble the ladyfinger into the mixture. Stir the mixture into the glass. Dust the top of the mixture with the cocoa powder.

Serves 1

TIP

You could try replacing the Baileys for 2 tablespoons Amaretto liqueur.

Apple Crumble Smoothie

Apple crumble topped with vanilla ice cream is a very popular dessert, especially in the fall. Here the crumble and ice cream are blended into one rich smoothie.

1 cup stewed apples
¼ tsp. cinnamon
1 cup vanilla ice cream
3 tbsp. heavy whipping cream
1 oatmeal cookie, crumbled

Place the apples, cinnamon, ice cream, and heavy whipping cream in a blender and process for 1 minute. Pour into a glass and top with the crumbled cookie.

Serves 1

Ginger & Pear Dessert Smoothie

Ginger brings a spicy warmth to this fruity smoothie.

1 ripe pear, peeled, cored, and chopped
1¼ cups ginger ice cream
3 tbsp. heavy whipping cream
2 ginger cookies, crumbled

Place the pear, ice cream, and heavy whipping cream in a blender and process for 1 minute. Pour into a glass and top with the crumbled cookies.

Serves 1

Chocolate Shake

Simple, rich, delicious, this is the basic but ultimate chocolate shake.

1 cup whole milk
1 scoop chocolate ice cream
sliced strawberries, to decorate

Place the milk and the ice cream in a blender and process until smooth. Pour into a glass.

Serves 1

TIP

You can select the chocolate ice cream of your choice: Belgian chocolate, rich chocolate, malt chocolate, etc.
You could also stir 2 tablespoons semisweet chocolate chunks or chips in.

Coconut Hula Scream

The delicious flavor of coconut is satisfying and refreshing.

1 cup whole milk
2 scoops coconut ice cream
ice, to serve
pineapple wedges, to decorate

Place the milk and ice cream in a blender and process until smooth and frothy. Serve over ice, and decorate with fresh pineapple wedges.

Serves 2

TIP

Add 2 tablespoons semisweet chocolate chips after blending and top with chocolate shavings.

Maple Leaf Frappé

This drink is very refreshing and works well with soda or milk.

2 tbsp. maple syrup
3–4 ice cubes
1 scoop vanilla ice cream
club soda or whole milk

Place the maple syrup, ice cubes, and ice cream in a blender and process until the ice cubes are incorporated and the mixture is smooth and frothy. Pour into a cold glass and top off with club soda or milk. Stir and serve.

Serves 1

TIP

Serve frappés in tall, thin glasses that have been chilled in the freezer.

Rocky Road Chocolate Shake

Rocky Road is made from white chunks of soft and spongy marshmallow together with crunchy peanuts, all enrobed in a silk-smooth dark chocolate. It works so well in a shake!

1 cup whole milk
1 scoop chocolate ice cream
2 tbsp. mini marshmallows
2 tbsp. mixed chopped nuts
1 tbsp. mini marshmallows, to decorate

Place the milk, ice cream, the mini marshmallows, and chopped nuts in a blender and process until smooth. Pour into a glass and top with marshmellows.

Serves 1

Neapolitan Shake

Relive your summer vacation with this fabulously colorful Italian shake.

1 cup whole milk
1 scoop chocolate ice cream
¼ cup strawberries, hulled, plus 1 extra, to decorate

Place the milk, ice cream, and strawberries in a blender and process until smooth. Pour into a glass and top with strawberry sauce and toasted coconut.

Serves 1

TIP

You could decorate with strawberry sauce and toasted coconut for a real Italian feel.

Workout Smoothies

If you're working out, your muscles need protein to rebuild themselves, but after a hard run or hour at the gym, it's difficult to stomach a heavy, meaty meal. Smoothies provide the perfect substitute; using whey or soy protein as well as naturally protein-rich ingredients, you can ensure your workouts retain their glory.

Workout Smoothies

Protein shakes have never tasted so good!

This chapter has recipes bursting with natural protein (found in eggs, nuts, lentils, bulgur wheat, and split peas) alongside workout classics (whey powder, protein powder, and Guarana powder), so you are able to choose the flavor and approach which works best for you.

Although they are healthy and energy-boosting, these smoothies should not be seen to help with weight-loss. The nuts, avocado, and other ingredients prevalent in the recipes have high levels of fat (although it is heart-healthy mono-unsaturated fat). You should consume the smoothies as part of a healthy diet, plus plenty of exercise, to really get the benefits.

These recipes will have you running on the treadmill, stacking up those weights, and breaking records before you know it.

Berry Protein Smoothie

Whey protein powder is a common source of workout energy, and this berry-flavored health smoothie disguises the unappealing taste.

½ cup strawberries, hulled
1 tbsp. clear honey
1 tbsp. lemon juice
1 tbsp. protein powder
1¾ fl. oz low-fat milk
2½ fl. oz kefir

Put the strawberries, honey, and lemon juice in a blender and process until smooth. Add the protein powder and milk and blend thoroughly, then fill up with the kefir. Stir and pour into a glass. Serve at once.

Serves 1

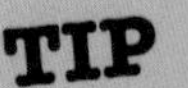

The same quantity of raspberries also works well in this recipe.

Fat-burner Smoothie with Ginger

Strictly speaking, this smoothie doesn't burn fat. Guarana, however, is said to speed up our metabolism.

TIP

Green tea can also work as a good substitution for the apple juice.

¼ cup strawberries, hulled
¼ cup raspberries
¼ cup blueberries
¼ cup cranberries
¼ cup apple juice
1 tsp. Guarana powder
1 tbsp. Aloe vera juice
1 tsp. gingerroot, grated

Place the berries, apple juice, powder, aloe vera juice, and ginger in a blender and process for 1 minute or until smooth. Pour into a glass to serve.

Serves 1

Guarana Drink

Guarana is a great energy booster as it contains almost twice the amount of caffeine as coffee beans. Guarana powder is very bitter and rather unpleasant if drunk with water—here is a delicious way to drink it.

1 tsp. Guarana powder
generous cup unsweetened yogurt
1 banana or papaya, peeled and chopped
1 tbsp. clear honey
milk or soy milk

Place the Guarana powder, yogurt, banana or papaya, and honey in a blender and process until smooth. Add milk or soy milk according to the consistency you like.

Serves 2

Yogurt & Wheat Germ Smoothie

This simple smoothie is best made with Greek-style yogurt, which imparts a creamy richness. Blackstrap molasses is a healthy sweetener that contains significant amounts of a variety of minerals that can promote your health.

TIP

This is a very basic recipe which can be embellished with fruit yogurt, or ½ cup of soft fruit.

1 cup yogurt
1 tbsp. blackstrap molasses
1 tsp. wheat germ

Place the yogurt, molasses, and wheat germ in a blender and process for about 10 seconds or until smooth. Pour into a glass to serve.

Serves 1

Orange & Cashew Nut Cooler

Cashew nuts have a high energy density and high amount of dietary fiber, both of which have been said to have a beneficial effect on weight management, but only when eaten in moderation.

½ cup coarsely chopped unsalted cashew nuts
4 cups water
¼ cup honey
4 cups orange juice

Put the nuts, water, honey, and orange juice in a blender and process until smooth. Strain into a pitcher and refrigerate until well chilled.

Serves 4

Orange Almond Milk

The ultimate energy boost.

1½ cups unsalted roasted almonds
1⅔ cups confectioners' sugar
4 cups water
⅓ cup orange flower water
12 cups milk

Drop the almonds into a pan filled with boiling water and blanch for 30 seconds. Drain the almonds well, then rub in a towel to remove the skins. Place the almonds and half the sugar in a blender and process until the nuts are very finely ground. Combine the almond mixture and the water in a large bowl, cover, and let stand overnight. Stir in the orange flower water.

Place the milk in a large jug and add the remaining sugar. Strain the almond mixture through cheesecloth into milk. Stir and refrigerate until well chilled.

Serves 8

Power Smoothie

Spirulina is a true super food. Packed full of antioxidants and crammed with vitamins, it has real health benefits. Because it is not to everyone's taste, it is added to a delicious smoothie to make it more drinkable.

½ cup mixed berries
1 cup plain low-fat yogurt, plus 1 tsp. to garnish
¼ cup orange juice
1 tbsp. Spirulina powder

Place the berries, yogurt, orange juice and powder in a blender and process for 1 minute or until smooth. Pour into a glass to serve. Swirl in an extra teaspoonful of yogurt in the glass to garnish.

Serves 1

TIP

You could try omitting the Spirulina powder and replacing it with 2 teaspoons honey.

Cucumber & Wasabi Drink

Wasabi has surprising health benefits—and tastes great too. This low-calorie smoothie is a perfect snack after exercising to keep energy levels high.

⅔ cup cucumber, peeled and chopped omitting a strip (1 in. x 2 in.) for the garnish
½ tsp. fresh dill
dash salt
1 tsp. wasabi paste
white pepper
1¾–2½ fl. oz milk

Slice the 1 in. x 2 in. strip cucumber thinly lengthwise for about two thirds of its length and thread on a wooden cocktail stick. Fan out the slices and reserve for the garnish. Place the cucumber in a blender with the dill and salt. Then drain the cucumber through a sieve lined with a cloth.

Process the cucumber juice with the wasabi, pepper, and milk and season to taste with salt. Pour into a glass and serve with the cucumber garnish.

Serves 1

Hazelnut Shake

Hazelnuts contain high levels of energy, and with the additional protein powder this shake will help you well on the way to Muscle Beach.

2 tbsp. hazelnut butter
1 tbsp. protein powder
5 fl. oz low-fat milk
½ tsp. powdered cinnamon
1–2 tsp. sugar
powdered cinnamon, to decorate

Place the butter, protein powder, and low-fat milk in a blender and process thoroughly. Pour into a glass and served dusted with cinnamon.

Serves 1

Avocado & Peanut Shake

With avocado, peanuts, and kefir, this filling shake is bursting with natural energy!

1 small avocado
2–3 tbsp. lime juice
4 tbsp. roasted, salted peanuts
4½ fl. oz kefir
dash cayenne pepper
1 tbsp. fresh cilantro
2½ fl. oz low-fat milk
salt
1 tsp. cilantro and paprika, to garnish

TIP

Replace the cilantro leaves with parsley for a different flavor.

Halve the avocado, remove the stone and spoon out the flesh. Put in a blender with the lime juice, peanuts, kefir, cayenne pepper, and half of the cilantro, and process finely. Fill up with milk and season to taste with salt. Pour into two glasses and sprinkle with paprika. Serve garnished with the cilantro leaves.

Serves 2

Australian Smoothie

Completely natural fruit sugars combine to create this Oz-influenced power drink.

pulp and juice of 1 passion fruit
1½ mangoes, peeled, pitted, and chopped
1 cup pineapple juice
1 banana, peeled and chopped
5 macadamia nuts
slice of pineapple, to decorate

Place the passion fruit, mangoes, pineapple juice, banana, and nuts in a blender and process for 1 minute. Pour into a glass to serve. Garnish with a piece of fresh pineapple if desired.

Serves 1

TIP

You could try walnut halves and blanched almonds instead of the macadamia nuts.

Banana & Lentil Smoothie

Lentils come in a variety of colors, and all can be found in health food stores, larger supermarkets, and Asian food stores. As with other types of pulses, lentils are high in fiber and help to lower bad cholesterol, plus they also keep blood sugar levels from rising too quickly after a meal. Split red lentils, that are more orange than red in color, are used to make this satisfying smoothie.

TIP

Unlike dried peas and beans, red lentils need no pre-soaking before being cooked.

2 oz split red lentils
1 banana, peeled and chopped
10 fl. oz freshly squeezed orange juice
5 fl. oz milk
finely grated orange zest, to garnish

Place the lentils in a saucepan, cover with plenty of cold water, and bring to the boil. Lower the heat and simmer for 30–35 minutes until the lentils are soft. Drain and set aside to cool. Place the banana in a blender. Add the lentils and orange juice and process until smooth. Pour in the milk and process again until combined. Pour into glasses and serve with a little finely grated orange zest on top.

Serves 2

Split Pea & Blueberry Smoothie

Packed with soluble fiber that helps lower cholesterol and keep your heart healthy, split peas come in two varieties—green and yellow. Either can be used to make this smoothie, although the yellow will result in a fresher-looking, more appealing drink.

2 oz split peas
4 oz blueberries
10 fl. oz pineapple juice
5 fl. oz soy milk
pineapple wedges, to garnish

Soak the split peas in a bowl of cold water overnight. Drain the peas, place in a saucepan, and cover with plenty of fresh cold water. Bring to a boil, lower the heat, and simmer for about 40 minutes or until the peas are soft. Drain and set aside to cool. Place the split peas, blueberries, and pineapple juice in a blender and process until smooth. Add the soy milk and blend again until combined. Pour into glasses and serve with a wedge of pineapple over the side of each glass.

Serves 2

TIP

When cooking the split peas, don't add salt to the water or the peas will not soften. As split peas are quite time-consuming to cook and only a small quantity is used, it's worth making the smoothie when you're cooking a larger quantity for another recipe.

Apple–broccoli Smoothie

Despite all the good news about broccoli's super-healthy image, the tufted green florets are never going to be top of everyone's list of favorite vegetables. But try blending broccoli with sweeter fruit and vegetables and you'll transform it into a refreshing and colorful drink the whole family will love.

4 oz small raw broccoli florets, chopped
1 stalk of celery, chopped
1 apple, peeled, cored, and chopped
10 fl. oz carrot juice
apple wedges, to garnish

Place the broccoli, celery, apple, and carrot juice into a blender and process until smooth. Pour into glasses and garnish each glass with apple wedges.

Serves 2

TIP

Carrot juice gives the smoothie a gorgeous golden glow but substitute apple juice if you prefer. You could also use 8 spears of raw tenderstem broccoli instead of the florets.

Bulgur Wheat & Apricot Smoothie

The main ingredient of the popular Middle Eastern salad, tabbouleh, bulgur wheat adds a pleasantly nutty flavour to a smoothie. Made by parboiling, drying, and then grinding whole grains of wheat, it is high in protein and fiber, low in fat—and therefore calories—plus it has useful amounts of B and E vitamins and iron.

TIP

Bulgur wheat doesn't need pre-cooking, simply soak it in boiling water for a few minutes until it swells.

2 peaches
2 tbsp. bulgur wheat
1 cup milk
½ cup lemon yogurt
2 tbsp. finely chopped pecans, to garnish

Put the peaches in a heatproof bowl and pour over boiling water to cover. Let stand for 1 minute. Put the bulgur wheat in a cup, pour over boiling water so the wheat is just covered, and let stand until it has absorbed the water. Drain the peaches and, when cool enough to handle, cut into quarters, remove the stones, and peel off the skins. Place the peaches in a blender, add the bulgur wheat and milk and process until smooth. Add the lemon yogurt and blend again until combined. Pour into glasses and sprinkle the chopped pecans on top.

Serves 2

Healing Smoothies

Whether you're fighting off the common cold or suffering after a wild night out, your body sometimes needs a little T.L.C. These smoothie recipes have the right amount of vitamins and minerals, rehydrating elements, and great tastes to help you rebuild your temple in no time.

Healing Smoothies

You have started to feel under-the-weather and the concept of a week in bed is looming—what do you do? Brimming with rejuvenating goji berry, echinacea, ginger, ginseng, and nutmeg, fight off your cold with the recipes in this chapter.

These are healthy, natural recipes which are packed full of vitamins to get anyone back on their feet after a hard week. There are also simple, soothing recipes to reassure and comfort those who are ill—such as Mango Buttermilk and Pear & Pomegranate Yogurt Smoothie.

The recipes will also help when preparing or starting a detox. Once you start making them, you may find they become easy additions to your daily routine, and a quick effortless way to avoid those colds and headaches.

Vitamin Bomb

Beetroot is valued by health professionals for its tonic and revitalizing qualities. This vitamin-C delight is a perfect detox choice.

2 oranges, with extra slices, to decorate
4 tbsp. crushed ice
4½ fl. oz unsweetened beet juice
1–2 tbsp. natural honey
mineral water

Thread two slices of orange on each bamboo skewer. Squeeze the oranges and strain the juice through a sieve. Divide the crushed ice between 2 glasses. Place the orange juice, beet juice, and honey in a blender and process. Pour over the crushed ice. Fill up with mineral water and serve garnished with the orange skewers.

Serves 2

Goji Berry Ice Bite

Goji berries have been used for 6,000 years by herbalists in China, Tibet, and India to protect the liver, help eyesight, improve sexual function and fertility, strengthen the legs, boost immune function, improve circulation, and promote longevity.

2 fl. oz goji berry juice
4 fl. oz cranberry juice
juice of ½ lime, plus extra slices to decorate
crushed ice
glacé cherry, to decorate

Put the goji berry juice, cranberry juice, and lime juice into a cocktail shaker. Shake well. Fill a tall glass with crushed ice and pour in the drink. Decorate with a glacé cherry and slices of lime.

Serves 1

TIP

Be careful when purchasing your goji berry juice, as many companies claim to be producing "pure" goji juice which is usually mixed in order to preserve the freshness. Juice squeezed from berries should have an orange color, while reconstituted juices normally have a coffee color and a prunelike flavor.

Lemon Tea Coolie

Iced tea is a popular summertime drink. This version is even cooler. With a tea basis which serves as a natural antioxidant, this high-energy citrus drink is perfect for a hot day.

2 cups boiling water
1 tsp. loose tea or 1 tea bag
2 strips lemon zest
2 tsp. sugar, plus extra to taste
2 tbsp. lemon juice
4 scoops lemon sorbet
ice
lemon zest curls, to decorate

Make the tea by pouring boiling water over the loose tea or tea bag. Add the lemon zest and the sugar, and allow to steep for 15 minutes. Strain or discard bag, cool, and chill. Mix in the lemon juice and place 1 cup of tea in a blender with the lemon sorbet. Process and adjust sweetness to taste. Pour over ice and top off with additional tea. Stir and decorate with lemon zest curls.

Serves 1

TIP

Look for mint sorbet which could replace the lemon.

Grapeberry Smoothie

This smoothie is a wonderful color. An easy way to get a lot of natural energy is to start drinking grape juice. Give it a try and see if you don't feel refreshed and energized.

TIP

For an extra lemon balm flavor, you could process ¼ cup leaves in with the ingredients.

⅔ cup fresh raspberries, with 3 or 4 extra to decorate
1 cup red grape juice
2 scoops raspberry frozen yogurt
2 tsp. honey
few drops vanilla extract
sliced grapes, to decorate

Place the berries, grape juice, yogurt, honey, and vanilla in a blender and process until smooth. Sift through a non-metallic strainer into an ice-filled glass. Decorate with fresh raspberries and grape slices.

Serves 1

Twist in the Tail

Ginger has a remarkable amount of benefits. It is known to tackle nausea, digestive problems, aid circulation, and the effects of arthritis. Try this deliciously spicy drink to settle your stomach.

2 large bananas, peeled and chopped
2 limes, juice and grated zest of 2 limes
sugar
1 cup ginger ale
1 tsp. grated gingerroot
crushed ice

Place the banana, the lime juice and zest, sugar, half of the ginger ale, and grated gingerroot in a blender. Process until smooth. Pour over ice in a tall glass then top off with the rest of the ginger ale to taste.

Serves 2

TIP

Ginger can be added to most smoothies—try stirring in 1 teaspoon grated gingerroot before blending.

Cucumber & Avocado Blend

Avocado, as well as being a delicious addition to a smoothie, is known to protect against cholesterol-related heart diseases. Avocado includes necessary minerals like potassium, calcium, vitamins C and K, folic acid, copper, sodium, and dietary fibers. It is also a good antioxidant.

TIP

Avocado goes brown quickly—to avoid this, keep the avocado stone in the bowl with the chopped avocado until processing.

- 1 medium avocado, peeled, pitted, and chopped
- 1 large cucumber, peeled, seeded, chopped, and peel reserved
- ½ cup chopped fresh parsley
- 3 tbsp. lemon juice
- 1 tbsp. olive oil
- 2 cups crushed ice

Place the avocado, chopped cucumber, parsley, lemon juice, and oil in a blender and process until smooth. Add crushed ice and process until smooth. Strain into glasses. Garnish with the reserved cucumber peel.

Serves 4

Mango Buttermilk

Buttermilk is lower in fat than regular milk, because the fat has been removed to make butter. It is also high in potassium, vitamin B12, calcium, and riboflavin as well as a good source of phosphorus. Those with digestive problems are often advised to drink buttermilk rather than milk, because it is more quickly digested.

TIP

Make sure you check the labels when purchasing buttermilk, because some brands are higher in fat than others.

1 cup mango, peeled, pitted, and chopped
½ cup buttermilk
1 tsp. honey
½ tsp. lemon juice
¼ tsp. grated lemon peel
⅓ cup crushed ice
strawberries, to decorate

Place the mango, buttermilk, honey, lemon juice, lemon peel, and crushed ice in a blender and process until smooth. Decorate with strawberries.

Serves 2

Mango & Passion Fruit Smoothie

The astringent flavor of passion fruit cuts through the rich sweetness of mango, lightening the effect of this aromatic smoothie. When ingested orally, rose water is known to ease a heavy or troubled digestion process.

TIP

Sprinkle a few passion fruit seeds over the top of the smoothie if desired.

1 medium mango, peeled, pitted, and chopped
pulp of 2 passion fruit
½ cup plain low-fat yogurt
½ cup milk
½ tsp. rose water

Place the mango, passion fruit, yogurt, milk, and rose water in a blender and process for 1 minute or until smooth. Pour into a glass to serve.

Serves 1

Prune Smoothie with Flax Oil

This fiber-rich smoothie will aid your digestion system and, aside from its health benefits, it tastes wonderful. Flax oil is a great source of Omega 3.

1 banana, peeled and chopped
5 prunes, pitted
¼ cup orange juice
1 cup plain low-fat yogurt
1 tbsp. pure flax oil

Place the banana, prunes, juice, yogurt, and oil in a blender and process for 1 minute or until smooth. Pour into a glass or mug to serve.

Serves 1

TIP

You could try mixing 1 tablespoon ground flax seeds instead of the flax oil into the mixture. The seeds actually have even more nutritional value than the oil—they contain more protein, fiber, vitamins, and lignins.

Herb Kefir with Bean Sprouts

Kefir is a fermented milk drink and has many reputed health benefits. It has antibiotic and antifungal properties. Tryptophan, one of the essential amino acids abundant in kefir, is well known for its relaxing effect on the nervous system.

2 tbsp. bean sprouts
3–4 tbsp. mixed herbs, chopped
9 fl. oz kefir
2 tbsp. lemon juice
½ tsp. honey
salt
white pepper

Wash the sprouts and drain in a sieve. Put the herbs in a blender with the kefir, lemon juice, honey, and a little salt and process finely. Season to taste with salt and pepper. Pour into two glasses, garnish with the sprouts and serve at once.

Serves 2

TIP

Alfalfa sprouts could replace the bean sprouts for a slightly more peppery flavor.

Persimmon Smoothie with Grapefruit

Persimmon is an Asian fruit growing in popularity. It is not only high in fiber but is also a wonderful source of vitamin A. A contrast to the bitter grapefruit, this fruit is sweet and tangy.

1 persimmon, peeled and chopped
sugar, to taste
1–2 tbsp. lemon juice
3–4 tbsp. apple juice
3–4 grapefruit segments, to decorate

Put the persimmon in a blender with a little sugar, lemon juice, and apple juice and process finely. Push through a sieve. Add more sugar if necessary. Pour into a glass and serve decorated with grapefruit segments.

Serves 1

TIP

You must always eat persimmons after the fruit is soft and fully ripe—unripe fruit tastes astringent and bitter.

Pear & Pomegranate Yogurt Smoothie

Pomegranate is said to be rich in antioxidants. Its subtle flavor works well with the mellow pear flavor for a truly healing, relaxing smoothie.

1 small pomegranate
1¾ fl. oz pear juice
5 fl. oz yogurt
sugar, to taste
lemon balm leaves, to decorate

Squeeze the pulp of a pomegranate, place in a blender with the pear juice and yogurt and process thoroughly. Push through a sieve. Sweeten to taste with sugar to taste. Pour into two glasses and decorate with lemon balm leaves.

Serves 2

White Tea & Ginseng Smoothie

Although all tea is good for us, white tea is the best, as it is the least processed and so retains the highest levels of antioxidants that fight free radicals in the body. The buds and small early leaves are picked from the tea bushes and then steamed, dried and slightly oxidized to produce a more subtly flavored tea than green or black, where the leaves are rolled and left to oxidize for longer. As with green tea, white tea is best brewed using very hot but not boiling water, which damages and scalds the delicate leaves.

TIP

It's best not to add milk to white tea as this reduces its levels of antioxidants.

1 tsp. white tea leaves or 1 white tea bag
1 tsp. sliced ginseng root or ginseng powder
8 fl. oz water, very hot not boiling
1 small wedge of honeydew melon, peeled, seeded, and chopped
2 pineapple rings, chopped
5 fl. oz freshly squeezed orange juice

Put the tea leaves or tea bag in a heatproof jug, add the ginseng and pour over the water. Leave to stand for 2–3 minutes, then strain if using tea leaves and ginseng root, or remove the tea bag. Let cool, a process that can be speeded up by adding 2–3 ice cubes to the jug. Place the melon and pineapple in a blender with the orange juice. Pour in the tea and process until smooth. Pour into two glasses and serve immediately.

Serves 2

Passion Fruit & Sage Smoothie

Its wrinkled purple-brown skin might not win passion fruit any prizes for its appearance but this egg-shaped tropical fruit is packed with good things. The vivid orange pulp is a valuable source of dietary fiber, potassium, and vitamins A and C, plus it contains plant sterols that help lower cholesterol. Passion fruit also helps the body to relax so drunk before bedtime this smoothie should guarantee a peaceful night's sleep. The seeds can be added to the blender with the pulp or removed, as preferred.

TIP

Whole, low-fat, skim cow's milk, or soy milk can all be used to make this smoothie.

- 2 passion fruit
- 1 small mango, pitted, peeled, and chopped
- 1 small banana, peeled and chopped
- 2 cups milk
- 4 fresh sage leaves, roughly chopped

Cut the passion fruit in half and scrape the pulp and seeds into a liquidizer. If you prefer to remove the seeds, heat gently until the seeds separate from the pulp and then push through a sieve. Place the mango and banana in a blender with the milk, and sage leaves. Process until smooth, pour into glasses, and serve.

Serves 2

Apple & Nutmeg Smoothie

"An apple a day keeps the doctor away" as our grandmothers used to tell us and, despite a rather unpromising start in the Garden of Eden, the apple has emerged as one of nature's superfoods. The malic and tartaric acids found in apples break down fat in the body, aiding digestion and helping to lower cholesterol. When liquidized or juiced for a smoothie, apples produce quite a large head of froth, which can either be skimmed off or left on and the smoothie drunk from the bottom of the glass through a straw.

TIP

Instead of nutmeg, try adding the same quantity of powdered cinnamon or cardamom.

- 1 apple, peeled, cored, and chopped
- 7 fl. oz coconut milk
- 7 fl. oz apple juice
- ¼ tsp. freshly grated nutmeg, plus a little extra for sprinkling

Place the apple in a blender with the coconut milk, apple juice, and nutmeg. Process until smooth and pour into glasses. Serve with a little extra nutmeg grated over the top.

Serves 2

Echinacea Tea Smoothie

A herbaceous plant with large colorful flowers that have long, thin petals and spiny centers, echinacea is native to east and central North America where it grows on prairies and open woodland. Also known as purple cornflower, echinacea acts as a natural antibiotic, boosting the immune system and helping the body fight off infection, particularly winter colds.

TIP

Gingerroot gives this smoothie a sweet, spicy warmth but omit it if you prefer.

1 tsp. dried echinacea root
1 tsp. finely chopped gingerroot
1 green tea bag
10 fl. oz very hot but not boiling water
1 tsp. clear honey
1 nectarine or peach
1 pear, peeled, cored, and quartered

Put the echinacea root, ginger, and green tea bag in a heatproof jug and pour over the water. Leave to stand for 15 minutes, removing the tea bag after 5 minutes. Strain the tea and stir in the honey. Let cool completely—this process can be speeded up by adding a few ice cubes to the jug. Meanwhile, put the nectarine or peach in a heatproof bowl and pour over boiling water to cover. Let stand for 1 minute, then drain and, when cool enough to handle, cut the nectarine or peach into quarters, remove the stone, and strip off the skin. Place the nectarine or peach and pear in a blender and add the tea. Process until smooth, pour into glasses, and serve.

Serves 2

Citrus Smoothie

Oranges have always been recognized as an excellent source of vitamin C but what is less well documented is that kiwi fruit contain twice as much of the valuable vitamin. Blitzed with potassium-rich banana and the sharp tang of grapefruit, the resulting smoothie not only tastes divine but is packed with health-giving nutrients too.

TIP

Use pink grapefruit juice if available as it will give the smoothie a delicate pastel pink hue. Use fruits in natural juices where possible as these are less sweet.

1 banana, peeled and chopped
1 large orange, peeled and pithed
1 kiwi fruit, peeled and chopped
5 fl. oz freshly-squeezed orange juice
5 fl. oz grapefruit juice
2 lime wedges, to serve

Place the banana, orange slices and kiwifruit in a blender, add the orange and grapefruit juices, and process until smooth. Pour into glasses and serve with a wedge of lime to squeeze into the smoothie before drinking.

Serves 2

Summer Smoothies

Summer days aren't complete without delicious smoothies. Whether you're lazing in the garden or at a BBQ with friends, the right smoothie can feel like divine intervention on a hot day. These light and fun recipes will take you to your very own smoothie heaven anytime in the summer months.

Summer Smoothies

The sun is shining and you want to be out in that garden soaking up the rays. Before you reach for those ice creams, try something new with these seasonal smoothies and shakes.

Often with sorbet, ice cream, or frozen yogurt at the base, these recipes can refresh, invigorate, and keep you hydrated.

For a nice alternative to ice, you could add further flavor by pouring cranberry, orange, or apple juice into icetrays and forming fruity ice cubes. When they melt, they can also add extra zest to the smoothie.

Frosted Summer Fruits

Frozen fruit works really well when combined with milk. It tastes like a smoothie, with all the thickness and richness you would expect. Simple flavors work well too—for instance, strawberries on their own are delicious.

TIP

You could replace the milk with 2 scoops berry icecream for an indulgent alternative.

½ cup mixed frozen summer fruits
1 cup whole milk
1–1½ tbsp. sugar syrup, sugar, or honey, plus extra to taste
fresh lemon balm or mint leaves, to decorate

Place the fruits straight from the freezer in a blender. Add the milk and sugar syrup, sugar, or honey and process until smooth. Taste and add a little more sugar, if required. Sift into a chilled glass through a non-metallic strainer. Decorate with fresh lemon balm or mint leaves.

Serves 1

Strawberry & Pineapple Crush

Lay back in the sunshine with this refreshingly tangy crush.

7 large strawberries, hulled
pineapple slice
juice of ½ orange
juice of ½ lemon
2 dashes of fraise (strawberry syrup)
sugar
½ cup crushed ice

Place 6 large strawberries with the pineapple slice, juice, strawberry syrup, sugar, and crushed ice in a blender and process until frothy. Pour into a glass, with the remaining strawberry to decorate.

Serves 1

TIP

You can crown this with fraise-soaked sugar frosting around the rim of a highball glass, and decorate with a strawberry.

Frozen Apples & Pears

Apples work better with yogurt than with ice cream. If you make frozen yogurt at home, try using an apple and pear-flavored yogurt as the base. Alternatively, use the Easy Frozen Yogurt recipe given on page 24, omitting the mandarins and substituting 2 ripe pears, peeled and cored, and half a cup apple concentrate.

½ cup apple juice
1 large, very ripe pear, peeled, cored, and chopped
2 scoops vanilla or apple and pear frozen yogurt
¼ tsp. apple pie spices
apple pie spices, to decorate

Place the apple juice and pear in a blender and process until smooth. Add the frozen yogurt and spices, and process until blended and frothy. Decorate with a light dusting of apple pie spices.

Serves 1

Winter Summer Berry Smoothie

This store-cupboard smoothie can remind you of summer all year round.

3 tbsp. strawberry ice cream
1 cup summer fruits juice
½ cup frozen mixed summer fruits, plus extra to decorate
2 scoops strawberry frozen yogurt
few drops natural vanilla extract

Place the ice cream, summer fruit juice, frozen summer fruits, strawberry frozen yogurt, and vanilla extract in a blender and process until smooth. Sift into an ice-filled glass through a non-metallic strainer. Decorate with frozen berries. (Use a small bunch of frozen berries, if available.)

Serves 1

TIP

For a milkier taste use only 2 tablespoons of strawberry topping and reduce the mixed summer fruits juice to ½ cup. Add ½ cup whole milk.

Simple Home-made Sherbet

This is a basic recipe that can be adapted by simply using other flavored juices. Great sherbets can be made from orange, mango, summer fruits, and tropical juices as well as peach and apricot nectar.

½ cup unsweetened pineapple juice
1 tsp. grated lemon peel
⅓ cup lemon juice
½ cup sugar
pinch of salt
2 cups cold whole milk

Place the pineapple juice, lemon peel, lemon juice, sugar, salt, and milk in a bowl and mix together. The milk may curdle slightly but this is usual and will not be noticeable in the final sherbet. Place in an ice-cream machine and churn for 20–25 minutes until stiff. Transfer to a freezer box. Place in the refrigerator for 15–20 minutes before using.

Serves 2

TIP

Buttermilk can be substituted for the milk, if desired, in which case reduce the lemon juice to 1 tablespoon.

Pinemelon Sherbet Shake

A very basic sherbet that can be adapted to include your favorite fruits and sherbets.

1 cup pineapple juice
½ cup chopped chanterelle or cantaloupe melon, plus extra to decorate
2 scoops pineapple–lemon sherbet
crushed ice
sliced pineapple, to decorate
maraschino cherry, to decorate

Place the pineapple juice, melon, and sherbet in a blender and process until smooth. Pour over crushed ice and serve with a maraschino cherry, melon, and pineapple.

Serves 1

Waterkey Cooler

This subtle cooler is for summertime and needs no additional fruit juice other than that from the watermelon.

2 kiwi fruit, peeled, plus ½ to decorate
2 cups chopped watermelon
2 scoops lemon sorbet
sugar syrup or honey (optional)

Place the kiwi fruit, watermelon, and sorbet in a blender and process until smooth. Pass through a non-metallic strainer to remove stray seeds. Taste and add sugar syrup or honey, as required. Pour over ice and decorate with kiwi fruit—chopped in half with peel on.

Serves 1

TIP

Make ice cubes from frozen orange or other fruit juice. They won't dilute your drink as they melt.

Cranberry–orange Cooler

A basic, but fantastic cooler—just admire that color!

1 cup cranberry juice
2 scoops orange sorbet
2–4 tsp. sugar syrup or honey
crushed ice
orange slices, to decorate

Place the cranberry juice, orange sorbet, and 2 teaspoons sugar syrup or honey in a blender and process until smooth. Taste for sweetness and add more sugar syrup or honey, if desired. Pour over crushed ice into a glass and decorate with orange slices.

Serves 1

TIP

Try using melonberry juice in place of cranberry. Add ½ cup chopped melon too.

Berry Cooler

Everyone loves sumptuous summer berries and here their sparkling taste is captured perfectly.

- ½ cup raspberries
- ½ cup strawberries, hulled
- ½ cup blueberries
- ½ cup summer berry juice
- 2 scoops raspberry sorbet
- 2–4 tsp. sugar syrup or honey
- fresh berries, to decorate

Place the berries, juice, sorbet, and 2 teaspoons sugar syrup or honey in a blender and process until smooth. Taste and add extra sugar syrup or honey, as required. Sift into ice-filled glasses through a non-metallic strainer. Decorate with fresh berries.

Serves 2

TIP

Any sorbet that has gone icy in the freezer can be used up by making coolers.

Dried Apricot Smoothie

Dried apricots have a more intense flavor than their fresh counterparts and make excellent flavorsome drinks.

10 dried apricots
2 tbsp. sugar syrup
2 scoops orange sorbet
1 cup orange, peach, and apricot (or similar) juice
½ fresh peach, chopped, to decorate

Cook the apricots in a little water and cool. Place in a blender with the sugar syrup and 3 tablespoons of the cooking liquor. Add the sorbet and fruit juice, and process until smooth. Strain before serving. Decorate with fresh peach slices.

Serves 1

Pear Smoothie

Share a smoothie out by the poolside for a delicious fruity recipe.

1½ cup diced pears
½ cup peach yogurt
½ cup pear nectar
1 tsp. lemon juice
¼ tsp. grated fresh gingerroot
3–5 ice cubes

Place the pears, yogurt, nectar, lemon juice, and gingerroot. Process until smooth. Add the ice cubes, and process until the ice is small enough to fit through a straw, but large enough to crunch on. Pour into glasses.

Serves 2

Tropical Cooler

A real treat on a scorching day that is ready in a flash.

½ cup tropical fruit juice
2 scoops citrus sorbet
tropical soda
pineapple wedge, to decorate

Place the fruit juice and one scoop of sorbet in a blender and process until smooth. Pour into a tall glass and add sufficient tropical soda to three-quarters fill the glass. Add the second scoop of sorbet and top off with more drink. Decorate with a pineapple wedge.

Serves 1

Apricot Nectale

This recipe is made with apricot nectar but any other dense fruit juice could be used.

½ cup apricot nectar
2 scoops vanilla ice cream
ginger ale

Place the apricot nectar and one scoop of vanilla ice cream in the bottom of a tall glass and stir. Add sufficient ginger ale to three-quarters fill the glass. Add the second scoop of ice cream, then top off the glass with more ginger ale.

Serves 1

TIP

If ginger ale is not to your taste, then use a lemon-lime soda.

Ginger Scream

This soda is based on ginger ale, with a hint of spice that goes well with orange.

1 tbsp. heavy cream
1 scoop vanilla ice cream
ginger ale
1 scoop orange sherbet or sorbet
orange slices, to decorate

Place the cream and vanilla ice cream in the bottom of a tall glass with a little ginger ale. Stir and add sufficient ginger ale to three-quarters fill the glass. Add the scoop of orange sherbet or sorbet, then top off the glass with more ginger ale. Decorate with orange slices.

Serves 1

Peach & Apricot Cream Slush

This upmarket slush combines the rich luxuriant flavor of apricots with juicy, refreshing peach, to give a velvety, creamy taste.

TIP

To ensure that you get your slush to the right consistency, make sure that the water and milk are ice cold and that the ingredients are processed well.

1 scoop apricot sorbet
½ cup chilled water
½ cup chilled whole milk or half and half
peach slices, to decorate
raspberries, to decorate

Place all the ingredients in a blender and process on a low speed until smooth. Serve in a tall glass, and decorate with peach slices, and raspberries.

Serves 4

Dragon Fruit Cocktail

Dragon fruit is also known as pitaya, and is a beautiful fruit inside and out. Simple flavors speak for themselves in this exotic fruit mix.

TIP

The skin of a dragon fruit is also known to be edible, providing it is clean and fresh. Try processing a small amount of the skin with the flesh for a slightly stronger flavor.

1 dragon fruit
1 banana
1 cup orange juice

Cut the dragonfruit in half and spoon out the flesh. Place with the banana and orange juice in a blender and process on a low speed for 15 seconds. Serve in a glass immediately.

Serves 1

Frozen Berry and Pineapple Smoothie

Fresh and seasonal, this refreshing frozen drink will be a great hit at a party.

1 cup frozen blueberries
1 cup frozen strawberries
1 cup pineapple and orange juice blend
1 cup fat-free plain vanilla yogurt
2 tsp sugar
6 ice cubes
mint leaves, to decorate

Place the blueberries, strawberries, juice, yogurt and sugar into the container of a blender. Process until smooth. Add the ice cubes, and process until the ice is small enough to fit through a straw, but large enough to crunch on. Pour into glasses, and decorate with the mint leaves.

Serves 2–4

TIP

Try adding a couple of mint leaves to the blend.

Blueberry & Vanilla Shake

The sparkling taste of blueberries contrasts with the smoothness of the vanilla.

3 tbsp. blueberry preserve
1½ tbsp. lime juice
1 cup whole milk
3 scoops vanilla ice cream
4 blueberries to decorate
lime slice, and peel, to decorate

Place the preserve, lime juice, whole milk, and ice cream in a blender and process until smooth. Serve in a tall, clear glass decorated with blueberries threaded onto a toothpick, lime slice, and zest.

Serves 1

Frozen Coffee Smoothie

Get yourself ready to face the day with this caffeine boost for when the sun is shining.

14 fl. oz strong coffee
2 tbsp. brown sugar
½ vanilla bean
2 bananas
2 tsp. maple syrup
2 tbsp. blanched almonds
6 ice cubes
banana slices with skin, mint leaves, to decorate

Add the sugar to the freshly made hot coffee and stir until the sugar has dissolved. Scrape the seeds out of half of a vanilla bean and put into the hot coffee with the bean. Leave to infuse.

Then remove the vanilla bean and let the coffee cool. Chill in the refrigerator for at least 30 minutes. Cut a few slices from one of the bananas before peeling it and brush with maple syrup to stop them going brown. Peel the rest of the bananas and process in a blender with the coffee and almonds. Add the ice cubes and blend again until the ice cubes are roughly crushed. Pour into two glasses, decorate with the prepared banana slices and a little mint and serve at once.

Serves 2

Rejoicing Smoothies

When it's time to celebrate, nothing beats a party cocktail smoothie. Whether you're throwing a party or celebrating at home, these recipes are fast to prepare and easy to make in larger batches. Offer all your friends smooth and creamy smoothie salvation, but make sure you have enough tumblers!

Rejoicing Smoothies

Dance the night away with these boozy beauties. Your favorite cocktails are given a unique smoothie heaven twist. Become a blasting bartender with the best martini, pina colada, daiquiri, and tequila sunrise recipes around.

It will be a good idea to purchase a cocktail shaker for these naughty recipes. Many of the recipes give the option to simply blend, but for a more authentic feel you need to get shaking!

In cooler climates fruit is often less sweet and fragrant than in the tropics, so if you find the cocktail you've made isn't as you'd like, sugar syrup is the easy way to sweeten a drink. Sugar doesn't dissolve easily in alcohol so using syrup means that there are no gritty granules left at the bottom of the glass. Nonalcoholic, ready-made syrups are available at gourmet or liquor stores, or on the internet.

These cocktails are sophisticated, sexy, and fun, but however innocent they taste, they pack a highly intoxicating punch. Drink wisely and don't overindulge—as tempting as it may be!

Frozen Strawberry Daiquiri

This delicious, refreshing drink is perfect to serve at a cocktail party because it is simple to make but looks and tastes stunning. Make the drink with a cocktail shaker for added effect and imagine yourself in Acapulco as you sip this ice-cool daiquiri.

4–6 tbsp. white rum
½ tsp. lime juice
1 tsp. orange juice
3 fresh strawberries, hulled, plus 1 extra, sliced, to decorate
2 scoops strawberry sorbet
ice
strawberry slices to decorate

Place the rum, lime juice, orange juice, strawberries, and the strawberry sorbet in a blender and slowly process until smooth. Alternatively, shake together thoroughly in a cocktail shaker. Pour over ice and serve, and decorate with strawberry slices.

Serves 1

Tom Coolie

This soda is a frozen Tom Collins, a cocktail said to be named after its creator.

6 tbsp. gin
1 tsp. lemon juice
2 scoops lemon sorbet
ice
club soda
lemon slice and a maraschino cherry, to decorate

Place the gin, lemon juice, and sorbet in a blender and process slowly until smooth. Alternatively, shake together thoroughly in a cocktail shaker. Pour over ice in a tumbler, top off with club soda, and decorate with a lemon slice and a cherry.

Serves 1

Pina Colada Smoothie

This makes a delicious shake with or without the rum.

¾ cup crushed pineapple, plus extra to decorate
1 cup whole milk
2 scoops ice cream
2 tbsp. coconut milk powder
6 tbsp. white rum
ice
maraschino cherry, to decorate

Place the crushed pineapple, milk, ice cream, and coconut milk powder in a blender and process until smooth. Add the rum and process to mix. Pour over ice and decorate with pineapple and a cherry.

Serves 1

TIP

For a bit of fun, you can serve this drink in a small, hollowed-out coconut shell.

Singapore Slush

This delicious slush is based on the classic cocktail, the only problem with this slush is that you can't keep going back for more!

3 tbsp. gin
6 tbsp. cherry brandy
ice
2 scoops lemon sorbet
1 cup club soda
orange slices and a maraschino cherry, to decorate

Place the gin and cherry brandy with two ice cubes in a cocktail shaker and shake well. Pour into a glass. Then place the sorbet and a little soda in a blender and process slowly until smooth. Pour into the glass and stir. Top off with additional soda and decorate with orange slices and a cherry.

Serves 1

TIP

Ice does melt in the presence of alcohol, so do not use too much or the frozen edge to the drink will be lost.

Tequila Sunrise

In general, orange-based cocktails work as well as frozen drinks. Tequila Sunrise is particularly good, but try the variations or follow the same method for your own personal favorite.

2 scoops orange sorbet
2 tbsp. fresh orange juice
6 tbsp. tequila
ice cubes
2 tsp. grenadine
mini scoops of orange or pomegranate sorbet
orange slices, to decorate

Combine the orange sorbet and juice with the tequila in a blender and slowly process until smooth. Alternatively, shake together thoroughly in a cocktail shaker. Place 3 or 4 ice cubes in a tall glass and pour over the sorbet mixture. Slowly pour the grenadine into the glass and allow to settle. Stir once and decorate with mini scoops of sorbet, and orange slices.

Serves 1

Replace the tequila for 3 tablespoons of Malibu and 2 tablespoons of rum and stir well after adding the grenadine.

White Prussian

A vanilla ice cream-based variation on the classic Russian. Both Tia Maria and crème de caçao are sometimes used to make this drink. Choose your favorite.

1 scoop vanilla ice cream
3 tbsp. vodka
3 tbsp. Tia Maria or crème de caçao
ice
grated nutmeg, to decorate

Place the vanilla ice cream, vodka, and Tia Maria or crème de caçao in a blender and process slowly until smooth. Alternatively, shake together thoroughly in a cocktail shaker. Pour into a glass over ice cubes and sprinkle with grated nutmeg.

Serves 1

Buttered Rum

The basis for this recipe is the butterscotch ice cream and this can be refrozen for a month or kept in the refrigerator for up to a week. Make it in larger quantities if it proves popular.

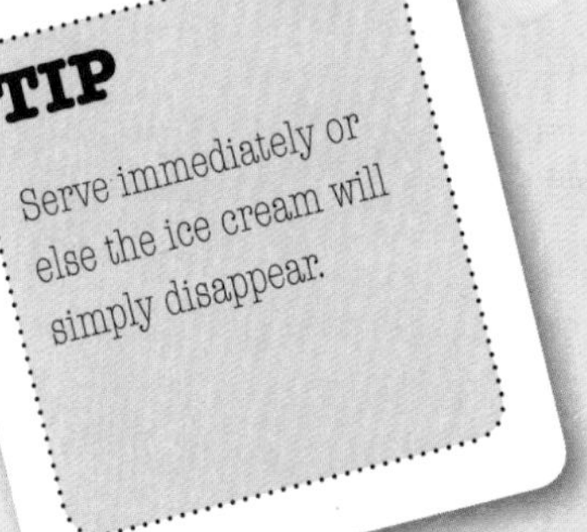

1 cup brown sugar
½ cup butter
1 cup vanilla ice cream, slightly softened
3 tbsp. of rum per serving
boiling water
nutmeg or powdered cinnamon, to decorate

Place the brown sugar and the butter in a pan and cook over a low heat until the butter and sugar has melted. Combine the sugar mixture with the ice cream in a mixer or blender and process until smooth. Place in a refrigerator until cooled, or freeze.

Place 1 scoop of frozen mixture or ¼ cup chilled mixture in a cup with 3 tablespoons of rum. Fill with boiling water, stir, and sprinkle with grated nutmeg or cinnamon.

Serves 8

Prickly Pear Martini

This Mexican-inspired cocktail looks fantastic and is perfect for an exotic cocktail party recipe.

1 prickly pear, peeled, cored, and chopped
6 tbsp. tequila
juice of ½ lemon, plus a twist to serve
ice cubes

Blend the prickly pear to a purée. Put 1 teaspoon of the purée in a cocktail shaker with the tequila and lemon juice. Add plenty of ice and shake thoroughly. Strain into a glass to serve.

Serves 1

TIP

Try replacing the prickly pear with 1–2 guavas for a different flavored martini.

Amaretto & Apricot Smoothie

The Italian combination of apricot and almond makes for a stylish adult-friendly smoothie—especially when the almond flavor comes from an Amaretto liqueur.

4 very ripe apricots, pitted
¼ cup Disaronno amaretto liqueur
¼ cup orange juice
½ cup plain low-fat yogurt
2 amaretto cookies, crumbled, to serve

Place the apricots, amaretto liqueur, orange juice, and yogurt in a blender and process for 1 minute or until smooth. Pour into a glass and serve with crumbled cookies on top.

Serves 1

Papaya & Orange Bourbon Slush

The soft, sweet flesh of a papaya is the perfect foil for the acidic hit of orange juice, and the ice cubes make this drink particularly good in the summer months.

TIP

Try replacing the bourbon with the same amount of rum.

1 papaya, peeled, pitted, and chopped
¼ cup orange juice
juice of 1 lime, plus an extra slice, to decorate
1 tsp. brown sugar
1 tbsp. bourbon
1 cup ice cubes

Place the papaya, orange juice, lime juice, brown sugar, bourbon, and ice cubes in a blender and process for 1 minute or until smooth. Pour into a glass to serve, and decorate with a slice of lime.

Serves 1

Saint Christopher

The barman who created this chocolate extravaganza is called Christopher. The "Saint" was added ironically because you can barely taste any alcohol.

1 fl. oz chocolate liqueur
1 fl. oz Bacardi
⅛ of fresh melon, peeled and seeded
1 tsp. chocolate powder
1 tsp. sugar syrup (to taste)
2 fl. oz milk
six ice cubes
fresh mint leaves and 1 chocolate flake, to decorate

Place the chocolate liqueur, Barcadi, melon, chocolate powder, sugar syrup, milk, and ice cubes in a blender and process until smooth. Pour into a tall glass and decorate with mint leaves and a chocolate flake.

Serves 1

Zabaglione Shake

This shake is almost like a frozen dessert. It is very Italian and very good.

6 tbsp. marsala
4 tbsp. whole milk
2 scoops eggnog ice cream or vanilla ice cream
2 egg yolks (optional)
chocolate curls, to decorate

Place the marsala, whole milk, ice cream, and egg yolks (if desired) in a blender and process until smooth. Pour into a glass and decorate with the chocolate curls.

Serves 1

Classic Eggnog

Everyone needs to know how to make this classic drink, so full of seasonal cheer.

6 tbsp. sugar
6 eggs, separated
½ cup brandy
1 pint whipping cream
6 cups milk
freshly grated nutmeg, to decorate

Put 4 tablespoons of sugar in a large bowl. Beat in the egg yolks, 1 at a time, until mixture is thick and lemon-colored. Beat in the brandy. To make the meringue, place the egg whites and remaining 2 tablespoons of sugar in another bowl. Using clean, dry beaters, beat until stiff. Set aside. Gradually and gently beat cream into the egg-yolk mixture; then slowly beat in milk. Pour into glasses and top with meringue. Sprinkle with nutmeg.

Serves 1

TIP

Dried egg white powder made up according to the manufacturer's instructions can be used as a risk-free substitute for fresh egg white.

Orange Velvet

This simple, flavorsome drink is an old favorite—bring it up to date with some orange segment decorations.

¾ cup orange juice
¼ cup lime juice
1 cup sweet sherry
2 teaspoons sugar
1 egg white
6 ice cubes

Place the orange juice, lime juice, sherry, sugar, egg white, and ice cubes in a blender and process for about 20 seconds or until smooth and frothy.

Serves 2

Abbot's Cocktail

This is another classic alcoholic smoothie, for a true Frangelico fan.

3 tbsp. Frangelico liqueur
¼ banana, peeled and chopped
¼ cup unsweetened pineapple juice
6 tbsp. crushed ice
2 dashes bitters
2 hazelnuts, crushed, to decorate

Place the Frangelico, banana, pineapple juice, crushed ice, and bitters in a blender and process for about 20 seconds or until smooth. Decorate with hazelnuts.

Serves 1

Mango Chardonnay Frappé

Many Chardonnays are described as having fruity undertones, and this cocktail goes one step farther by combining the two together for a perfect aperitif.

1 large ripe mango, peeled, pitted, and sliced
5 ice cubes, crushed
2 tsp. sugar
2½ cups sparkling Chardonnay
3 maraschino cherries, to decorate

Reserve 3–4 slices of the mango for the decoration, then place the remaining flesh in a blender with the crushed ice and sugar and process until smooth. Strain into a serving pitcher, pour in the Chardonnay, stir and pour into glasses. Decorate with the reserved mango slices, and maraschino cherries.

Serves 3–4

Espresso Brandy Smoothie

An afterdinner treat, this is great for retiring into a winter's evening.

2 fl. oz cream
1–2 tbsp. sugar, to taste
a good pinch of powdered cinnamon, plus extra to decorate
a good pinch of grated nutmeg, plus extra to decorate
1¾ fl. oz brandy
1¾ fl. oz strong espresso

Whip the cream lightly with the sugar and spices. Stir in the brandy and espresso and divide between two brandy glasses. Sprinkle with a little cinnamon and nutmeg and serve.

Serves 2

TIP

The cream, brandy, and espresso should all be well chilled.

Pomegranate Margarita

A smoothie favorite, the combination of tequila with pomegranate makes an ultra special cocktail.

9 fl. oz pomegranate juice
¾ fl. oz (4 tsp.) lime juice
1 ¾ fl. oz white tequila
1 fl. oz grenadine syrup
crushed ice cubes

Put the pomegranate juice, lime juice, tequila, and grenadine into a cocktail shaker and mix well. Fill 2 cocktail glasses with ice and divide the margarita between the two glasses. Serve ice cold.

Serves 2

Mocha Milk with Orange Liqueur

Milky with a pistachio twist, this combination works as both a treat and a healing winter warmer.

10½ fl. oz milk
2 small cups freshly made espresso
¾ fl. oz (4 tsp.) Grand Marnier
2 tsp. chopped pistachios
2 orange slices

Heat and froth the milk and pour into glasses. Set the froth aside for the time being. Add one espresso and 2 teaspoons Grand Marnier to each glass. Then put 2 tablespoons of the milk froth on top of each. Sprinkle with chopped pistachios, decorate with a piece of orange on the rim of each glass and serve at once.

Serves 2

Global Smoothies

Although smoothies became popular in America first, the rest of the world has been concocting their own unique recipes and variations. Using regional ingredients, these smoothies have an international flair, a variety of flavors, and will take you on a delicious journey to smoothie Nirvana.

Global Smoothies

The unusual flavors and ingredients in these recipes stem from their diverse origins. Even if you are unable to visit the exotic places mentioned, these smoothies will take your tastebuds there. It is quite remarkable how different many smoothie textured drinks have found themselves as part of cuisine cultures.

You may need to go to specialty stores for some of the ingredients—for instance okra, Antonovka apples, and rambutans—however, each recipe contains replacement ingredient ideas which are more readily available.

It is easy to experiment with recipes which have ice cream or yogurt at the base. Play around with some of the amazing flavors you can get, such as ginger and white chocolate, to make some really exciting drinks. Soy ice cream and soy yogurt are readily available, meaning that those who avoid dairy products can still enjoy a thick and creamy smoothie with international influences.

North African Apple Milkshake (Sarbat)

A rich, cool drink made from milk and fruit or nut milk, sarbat is an ideal "pick me up" for serving in the late afternoon on hot days when dinner will be late and something is needed to sustain guests through the early evening.

2 dessert apples, peeled, cored, and chopped
2 cups cold milk
2 tbsp. superfine sugar
about 1½ tsp. rose water or orange-flower water
shaved ice, to serve, if desired

Place the apples, milk, and sugar in a blender and process until smooth. Add rose water or orange-flower water to taste. Serve over shaved ice, if desired, in chilled glasses.

Serves 2–4

Caribbean Sherbet

A tropical treat—if you don't have the coconut milk, just omit it and decorate with toasted coconut instead. The recipe calls for pineapple–lemon sherbet, but orange, lemon, or even mango could be substituted. Add a few chunks of pineapple with the mango to enhance the mixed tropical taste.

TIP

Top the Caribbean Sherbet with another scoop of sherbet and decorate with passion fruit pulp.

½ fresh mango, peeled, pitted and chopped, or 3 canned mango slices
1 tsp. coconut milk powder
¾ cup orange and passion fruit juice
2 scoops of pineapple–lemon sherbet
toasted coconut, slice of pineapple, and passionfruit, to decorate

Put the mango, coconut milk powder, fruit juice, and sherbet in a blender and process until smooth. Serve over ice, and decorate with toasted coconut or tropical fruit slices.

Serves 1

Indian Melon & Ginger Lassi

Lassi is a popular and traditional yogurt-based drink which originated in the Punjab region of the Indian subcontinent. Traditionally, yogurt is mixed with spices and salt, but this is an updated version with a sweeter taste.

2 oz natural yogurt
3 oz melon flesh
½ tsp. powdered ginger
1–2 tbsp. powdered sweetener
15 fl. oz water
1 cup ice cubes
slice of fresh mango, to decorate

Put the yogurt, melon, ginger, sugar, water, and ice in a blender and process until frothy. Pour into a tall glass and drop in some more ice, if required.

Serves 1

Indian Mango & Okra Smoothie

Native to West Africa, small green okra pods are a popular vegetable in Indian, Cajun, and English-speaking Caribbean island cuisines. In the Deep South and West Indies okra is known as "gumbo," whilst in India the pods become "bindi" or the more romantically dubbed "ladies' fingers". The sticky sap within the pods isn't to everyone's taste but in a smoothie okra works well when pulsed with a sweet, fragrant fruit like mango.

TIP

Depending on the size of the mango used, you may find the smoothie too thick, in which case dilute it to the desired consistency with extra milk or still mineral water.

- 2 oz raw okra, trimmed and coarsely chopped
- 1 medium mango, pitted, peeled, and chopped, plus extra slices with peel to decorate
- juice of 1 lime
- ½ cup natural yoghurt
- 10 fl. oz milk

Place the okra and mango in a blender and add the lime juice, yogurt, and milk. Process until smooth, pour into glasses, and serve, decorated with mango.

Serves 2

Refresco Rosado

Refrescos are blended fruit drinks, popular in Mexico.

4 medium-size carrots, peeled and roughly chopped
3 thick pineapple slices, peeled and chopped, plus extra, to decorate
4 cups water
4 cups crushed ice, to serve
1 tbsp. finely chopped walnuts, to decorate

Place the carrots and pineapple in a blender and process until smooth. Dilute with the water, and serve over crushed ice. Decorate with the chopped walnuts and pineapple slices.

Serves 4

Jalapeño & Tomato Smoothie

Jalapeño chilies are widely used in Mexican cooking where they add a warm heat to dishes rather than the eye-watering fire of tiny birds' eye chilies or Caribbean Scotch bonnets. Cone-shaped and around 2 inches long, jalapeños vary in color from emerald to dark green, turning red when ripe. As with all chilies their heat is fiercest in the seeds and membranes so cut these away before using, taking care not to rub your eyes as you do so.

TIP

The seeds and skins of the tomatoes are removed as they can impart a bitter taste to the smoothie if blitzed with the other ingredients.

6 medium tomatoes
1 jalapeño chili, green or red
1 celery stalks, chopped into 1-in. lengths
2-in. piece of cucumber, peeled, seeded, and chopped
4 fresh basil leaves, chopped
2 cups carrot juice
juice of 1 lime
strips of orange zest, to decorate

Put the tomatoes in a heatproof bowl, pour over boiling water to cover them, and set aside for 30 seconds. Drain, cool the tomatoes under cold water, then cut each one into quarters and remove the skins and seeds. Chop the tomato quarters into small pieces, spread out on a tray and freeze for 20–30 minutes until firm.

Remove the stalk from the chili, cut in half lengthwise, and scrape out the seeds and membranes. Coarsely chop the chili.

Put the frozen tomatoes into a blender, add the chili, celery, cucumber, basil leaves, and carrot juice and process until smooth. Add half the lime juice, blend again, and then taste, adding the rest of the lime juice according to taste. Pour into glasses and decorate with orange zest.

Serves 2

Cactus Detox Smoothie

Mexico's nopal cactus, also known as the prickly pear or paddle cactus, is one of nature's most valuable foods. The spiky green pads contain not just a rich concentration of antioxidants but also dietary fiber, iron, and vitamins A, B, and C that help cleanse the liver and detox the digestive system. A glass of nopal cactus juice is a favorite breakfast drink south of the border and if the pads are puréed with orange, yogurt, and banana the resulting smoothie is a healthy and sustaining way to kick-start to anyone's day.

1 medium nopal cactus pad, spines removed and chopped, or 2 tsp. nopal cactus powder
1 banana, peeled and chopped, plus extra to decorate
½ cup natural yogurt
10 fl oz freshly squeezed orange juice
2 slices of orange, to decorate

Put the cactus pad or cactus powder into a blender, add the banana and yogurt and process to a purée. Pour in the orange juice and process again until smooth and evenly mixed. Pour into glasses and serve, decorated with the orange slices and extra banana slices.

Serves 2

TIP

If using a fresh cactus pad, it's important that all the spines have been removed and that the pad is as young and fresh as possible. Cactus pads are available from supermarkets mainly in Texas and California, but if you can't find them, nopal cactus powder from health food shops makes a good substitute.

Turkish Yogurt Drink (Ayran)

This is a very simple and refreshing drink, generally served very cold with doner kebab, sandwiches, or burgers. It can be purchased ready mixed in bottles or cartons all over Turkey, and locals will flavor the drink by adding fresh fruit of their choice.

2 cups thick plain yogurt
2 cups cold water
pinch of salt

Put the yogurt, water, and salt in a blender and process until frothy. Divide the froth among four glasses, followed by the remainder of the drink.

Serves 4

Turkish Raki Grape–Fig Smoothie

Raki is a potent brandy distilled from grapes and raisins and flavored with aniseed, like the French aperitif, Pernod. The Turkish drink it two ways—neat, alternating mouthfuls of raki with mouthfuls of water, or in a tall glass diluted with water, which turns the raki cloudy and gives it its nickname of "lion's milk."

4 large or 6 small figs, quartered
6 oz seedless green grapes, stalks removed, plus 2 small bunches of seedless green grapes, to decorate
6 fl. oz plain yogurt
6 fl. oz freshly squeezed orange juice
2 tbsp raki

Put the figs, grapes, and yogurt into a blender and process until smooth. Add the orange juice and raki and process again until evenly mixed. Pour into glasses and decorate the side of each with a small bunch or grapes.

Serves 2

TIP

If the aniseed in raki is not to your taste, try making the smoothie with another type of fruit liqueur such as orange-flavored Curacao or Grand Marnier, lemon-flavored limoncello, or cherry-flavored Kirsch.

American Malt Vanilla Shake

A simple, yet satisfying shake—reminiscent of afternoons at the local diner.

1 cup whole milk
1 tbsp. malt powder
2 scoops vanilla ice cream
sugar or honey (optional)
chocolate powder or powdered cinnamon, to decorate

Place the milk, malt powder, and vanilla ice cream in a blender and process until smooth. Taste and add sugar or honey to sweeten as desired. Pour over ice and decorate with a sprinkle of chocolate powder or powdered cinnamon.

Serves 1

American Blueberry Pie Smoothie

Your favorite fruit pie in a glass! Loaded with antioxidants that boost the immune system and fight disease, the humble blueberry might look innocuous but with a list of superfood credentials ranging from keeping our blood flowing smoothly to boosting collagen levels so our skin stays younger-looking, it's a small fruit that packs a giant punch.

1 cup blueberries, stalks removed
1 cup buttermilk
½ cup semi-skimmed milk
2 tsp. maple syrup
½ tsp powdered cinnamon
2 graham crackers, crushed
1 tbsp. demerara sugar

Place the blueberries in a blender. Add the buttermilk, milk, maple syrup, and cinnamon and process until smooth and creamy. Pour into glasses and sprinkle the crushed crackers and demerara sugar on top.

Serves 2

TIP

Ring the changes by using strawberries or raspberries instead of blueberries or a selection of different berries. If using frozen blueberries, don't bother to defrost them first, simply process them with the other ingredients for a chill-out drink.

Hungarian Cherry Soup Smoothie

This sweet and sour cherry soup smoothie is rich and creamy, and traditionally served in small portions as an elegant appetizer. Instead of bowls, try serving the soup in stylish cups on saucers.

2 lb. Morello (sour) cherries, pitted
⅔ cup superfine sugar
2 cinnamon sticks
1¾ cup red wine
1¾ cups water
½ cup light cream
lemon juice, to taste
crème fraiche, to serve

Place the cherries in a large pan and sprinkle with the sugar. Tuck in the cinnamon sticks and pour in the wine and water. Bring to a boil, then reduce the heat, cover, and simmer for about 20 minutes.

Remove the cinnamon sticks. Stir in the light cream, then check the flavor, adding a squeeze of lemon juice to taste. Ladle the smoothie into cups and serve topped with crème fraiche.

Serves 4

TIP

Try using 1½ cup red wine and ½ cup port instead of all red wine for an even heartier flavor.

Japanese Ginger & Melon Smoothie

Mioga ginger from Japan is a relative of the common ginger we're more familiar with in the West but it is more highly prized for its buds and stems, that are used to garnish and season dishes, than for its root. Common ginger is fine for this smoothie and you can either make your own ginger juice by squeezing the peeled, chopped gingerroot through a garlic press or buy a bottle of ready-prepared juice from a health food store.

2 lb wedge of watermelon, peeled, seeded, and chopped
½ tsp. ginger juice
5 fl. oz red grape juice
1 tbsp. lemon juice

Place the watermelon in a blender with the ginger, grape, and lemon juices and process until smooth. Pour into glasses and serve.

Serves 2

TIP

The smoothie can be made ahead but the longer it is left to stand the more the flavor of the ginger will develop and strengthen.

Russian Antonovka Apple Smoothie

Russia's notoriously cold winters can make apple growing a hit and miss affair, the exception being the sour Antonovka variety. Harvested in late fall or early winter when they are at their best, Antonovka apples can survive extreme temperatures and store well, the fruit becoming more aromatic and sharper-tasting the longer it is left on the tree.

2 Antonovka apples, peeled, cored, and quartered, plus extra apple slices to decorate
1 small banana, peeled and chopped
1 cup cranberry juice
5 fl. oz apple juice
1 tsp. honey, or to taste
1 tbsp. cranberries, to decorate

Put the apples and banana in a blender, add the cranberry and apple juices, and process until smooth. Add the honey, process again, and then taste for sweetness, adding more honey and processing again, as necessary. Pour into glasses and serve, decorated with apples and cranberries.

Serves 2

TIP

If Antonovkas are not available, substitute another tart apple such as Granny Smith, adjusting the amount you sweeten the smoothie accordingly.

Australian Guada Bean Smoothie

Trailing guada bean plants that cling to huge trellises are a familiar sight in subtropical regions of Australia and South Africa where they are cultivated instead of zucchini, the latter being difficult to grow as they develop mould and spoil in a hot, damp climate. When picked young, guada beans can replace zucchini in any recipe and, similarly, if you live in a cool place where the beans are not available, use zucchini for this smoothie.

- 2 guada beans, trimmed and chopped
- 2 oz fresh spinach leaves, roughly chopped
- 1 pear, peeled, cored, and chopped
- 2 tbsp. roughly chopped fresh parsley
- 2 cups white grape juice
- cucumber sticks, to garnish

Put the guada beans, spinach, pear, and parsley in a blender, add the grape juice and process until smooth. Pour into glasses and serve with a couple of sticks of cucumber tucked into each glass.

Serves 2

The grape juice and pear should sweeten this smoothie sufficiently but process in a little honey or maple syrup at the end if necessary.

French Chocolate & Pear Smoothie

Rich, creamy and darkly decadent, this is a real "spoil yourself" smoothie. Pears and chocolate are a match made in heaven and appear together in many popular French desserts. Here they combine to make a truly delicious drink.

½ lemon
¼ cup (1 oz) bittersweet chocolate, grated
1 large or 2 small pears, peeled, cored, and chopped
3 scoops rich bittersweet chocolate ice cream
¾ cup low-fat milk

Rub the rims of two glasses with the cut side of the lemon. Spread out the grated chocolate on a plate and dip the glasses into it so the rims are evenly coated.

Place the pears in a blender, add the ice cream, milk, and any grated chocolate left on the plate. Squeeze in the juice from the lemon half, process until smooth and pour into the chocolate-rimmed glasses. Serve with long spoons to scoop out the last of the smoothie mixture from the bottom of the glasses.

Serves 2

TIP

The stronger the flavor of the chocolate ice cream, the better the smoothie will taste, so look for one with a high proportion of cocoa solids.

Greek Frappé

Found in every café in Greece, this refreshing drink is the perfect way to take your coffee on a hot day. It is important to use instant coffee rather than fresh-ground coffee in order to get a long-lasting foamy top. Greek frappés are served with a straw, which is used to mix the coffee and sugar as it settles on the bottom of the glass.

2 tsp. instant coffee
¾ cup of cold water
1 tsp. sugar, optional
2 ice cubes
1 tbsp. evaporated milk (optional)

Put the coffee, sugar, and a little water (4–5 tablespoons) in a shaker. Shake hard until the mix is thick and foamy (around 2 minutes). Pour into a tall glass over the ice cubes, and add the remaining water and milk, if adding.

Serves 1

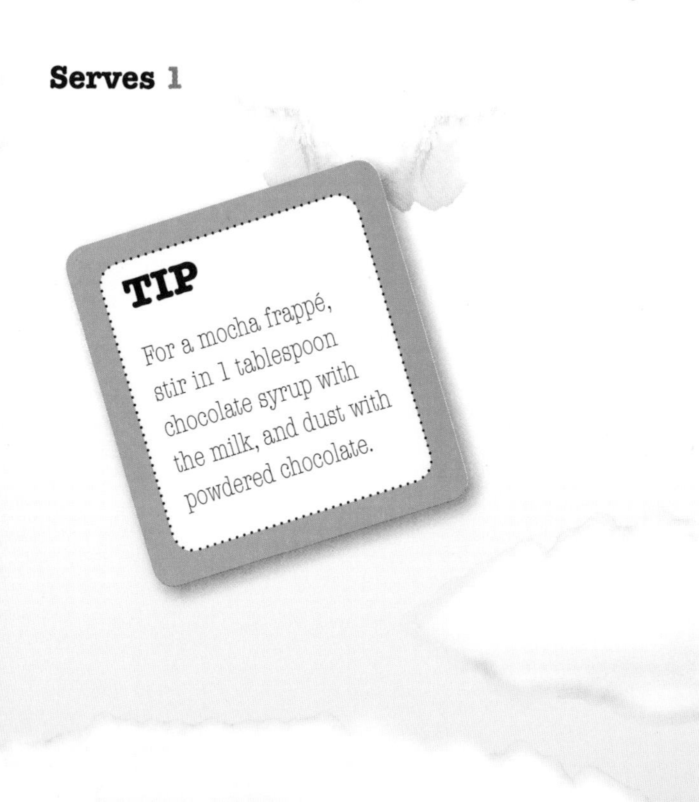

Vietnamese Avocado Shake

This may seem like an odd combination of flavors, but it really works! Avocado shakes are available on every street corner in Vietnam, and variations abound throughout South-east Asia. Delicious as it is, this smoothie is very calorific, so if you're keeping an eye on your waistline, perhaps save this for an occasional treat.

1 ripe medium avocado
1 cup ice
⅓ cup condensed milk
½ cup milk

Scoop the avocado flesh into a blender, and add the ice, condensed milk, and milk. Process until completely smooth. Chill for 15 minutes before serving into small glasses.

Serves 3–4

TIP

The Indonesian version of this shake, es apokat, adds a couple of tablespoons of either strong coffee or chocolate syrup to the blend. Both really bring out the grassy, buttery flavors of the avocado.

Malaysian Rambutan Smoothie

One look at a rambutan's coat of spiky red and yellow tendrils and you'll be in no doubt how it got its name from the Malay word "rambut," meaning hair. Under the "hair" the brittle orange rind is peeled away to reveal firm, white, translucent flesh. Sweet, juicy and delicately flavored, rambutans combine well with two other prolific Malaysian fruits, papaya and pineapple, in this smoothie.

TIP

Substitute fresh or canned lychees for rambutans if you find them difficult to get hold of.

8 rambutans, peeled and seeded
½ medium papaya, weighing about 6 oz, peeled, seeded, and chopped
10 fl. oz pineapple juice
crushed ice
small papaya wedges, to decorate

Place the rambutans and papaya in a blender and add the pineapple juice. Process until smooth, pour into glasses over crushed ice and decorate each glass with a small wedge of papaya.

Serves 2

Smoothies can be a snack on the run or an elegant beverage. If you'd like to give your smoothies a little something extra, why not try a garnish or decoration? These fun and fruity ideas range from simple to more advanced, and will make your smoothies look truly angelic.

Simple Toppings

When you are making smoothies, the easiest topping ideas are those of the fruits or vegetables within the smoothie itself. You could twist, cut, or style your ingredient as described in the following pages. However, you could top your smoothie or shake with any of the following ingredient ideas alone or in combination.

Whipped cream or ice cream
Whipped cream can instantly add a more luxurious feel to a drink. You could also add an extra scoop of ice cream—try vanilla, white chocolate, or egg-nog for extra creaminess; raspberry for a Neapolitan-style shake; macadamia, pecan, or almond for a nutty crunch; or chocolate chip for a chocolate crunch.

Sauces
Chocolate, strawberry, fudge, or butterscotch sauce—these are really good over an extra scoop of ice cream. A sprinkling of chocolate powder also works well.

Liqueurs
Liqueurs are good over extra ice cream—choose a simple, untextured chocolate or vanilla ice cream.

Chocolate chips and candies
Especially when preparing for kids, chocolate chips and candies can instantly make a healthy smoothie seem more of a treat. M&Ms, sprinkles, jelly beans, and marshmellows are popular choices.

Syrups
Syrups are best poured over extra ice cream. Try some of the more unusual ones such as toasted marshmallow or an alcoholic flavoring (without the alcohol) such as rum or Irish Cream.

Spices

Powdered cinnamon, nutmeg, or apple pie spices are used throughout this book to add both color and flavor to a smoothie. For a more adventurous idea, try a dash of chili powder or saffron.

Nuts

Nuts can add protein to a smoothie but also a change in texture and flavor. Popular nuts for smoothies are toasted pecans, almonds, macadamia nuts, or hazelnuts.

Fruit Slices

Slices of fruit make the simplest of garnishes and decorations for both savory and sweet dishes. With a sharp knife, cut thin, even slices. Use them whole or halved. Citrus fruit, apples with bright peel, Chinese gooseberries, star fruit, mango, and peach are a few examples of fruit that makes an attractive garnish.

Citrus Twists

Cut thin slices, then make a slit into the center of each. Move the slit in the fruit in opposite directions to stand the slice up and form the twist.

Sliced Fruit Fans

Prepare and thinly slice the fruit into neat, even pieces. As you work, try to keep the slices in the original form of the fruit. Lift the slices together onto the plate to ease the pieces neatly into position. Pears, lime halves, star fruit, mango halves, and peaches are a few examples of fruit to fan. Strawberries make excellent fans—leave their stems on and the slice attached together at the stem end.

Citrus Zest

Citrus zest is often used as a garnish because the oils in the peel add a subtle aroma to drinks. You can cut strips of citrus zest with a vegetable peeler or a sharp knife, but the best tool for the job is an inexpensive gadget called a zester. This little device makes it extra-easy to remove strips of zest with no white pith attached.

Citrus Vandyke-Cut Melon

Use a fine-bladed, sharp knife. Make a cut halfway down the length of the fruit in as far as the center and at a slight angle. Remove the knife and make another cut in the same way but at the opposite angle to create a "V" shape. Continue cutting all around the middle of the fruit, linking all the "V" cuts to halve the fruit. Gently pull the halves apart.

Frosted Fruit

Brush a small whole fruit or pieces of fruit with a little lightly whisked egg white, then coat with superfine sugar. Strawberries, bunches of currants, kumquats, and mandarin segments are all suitable.

Fruit Sticks

Thread small chunks or slices of the fruits that have been used to make the smoothie onto cocktail sticks and rest two "kabobs" across the top of each glass. Tuck a sprig of fresh mint or a small bunch of red currants between the sticks for added effect.

Chocolate Decorations

Chocolate can complement the flavors of a milky smoothie or shake and can contrast very effectively with fruity flavors. These ideas can really vamp up delicious smoothies, if you are serving as a dessert or a special treat.

Chocolate shapes

Pour melted chocolate onto a sheet of parchment paper and use a palette knife to spread it out to 1½-inch thickness. Let cool until the chocolate becomes cloudy but has not set. Dip a cookie cutter in hot water and use to stamp out chocolate shapes. Let the shapes set on a separate sheet of parchment paper.

Chocolate ribbons

Chocolate ribbons can only be made from unsweetened chocolate as it contains no cocoa butter and is very flexible and easy to work with. Spread the melted chocolate onto a nonstick cookie sheet and let set. Working away from you, push a spatula, or preferably a clean wallpaper scraper shallowly into the sheet of chocolate. Let the end curl over and hold this up gently with your other hand. Continue pushing the scraper or spatula down the sheet of chocolate to form a long, wide ribbon. Use immediately.

Chocolate curls

Hold a block of room-temperature white or unsweetened chocolate and run a vegetable peeler up and down one side to make curls. The cheaper the chocolate the better it tends to curl.

Coffee syrup

The amount of sugar added to a coffee shake is a matter of individual taste. Even people who take their hot coffee without sugar will find that the flavor of a shake is improved with a little sugar, or better still, coffee syrup.

TIP

The sugar needs to be added to the blender and the syrup can be added afterward, drop by drop, until it is just right.

6 scoops of coffee
1 cup of boiling water
¾ cup light brown sugar

Make a coffee syrup by adding the coffee to the boiling water. Infuse for 10 minutes, then strain. This will make about ¾ cup coffee. Add the sugar and heat gently until dissolved. This syrup is too sweet to form the basis for a coffee shake but is the best sweetener. Place in a sterilized bottle and it will keep for one month in the refrigerator.

Stir It Up

Some smoothies separate on standing and need a good stir before drinking. Instead of using a swizzle stick or long spoon to do this, cut long, thin sticks of fruit or vegetables such as melon, mango, carrot, celery, or pepper, tie three or four different ones together with a length of fresh chive stem, and pop in the drink.

Curly Wurly

To garnish vegetable smoothies, cut long, very thin, julienne strips of celery, carrot, white radish, green beans, or snow peas, and leave in a bowl of cold water in the fridge for several hours until they curl—this process can be speeded up by adding a few ice cubes to the water. When ready to serve the smoothie, drain the vegetable curls and pile on top of the drink, tucking a few small leaves of parsley, dill, chervil, watercress, or basil between the curls.

Sun Umbrella

Rather than decorate a smoothie made from exotic fruits with a paper cocktail umbrella, why not make your own parasol? Cut a slice from an unpeeled orange, mango, apple, pear, or other fruit that will give the round, slightly domed shape of a parasol. Push a wooden satay skewer through the slice, followed by a fruit of a contrasting color such as a whole strawberry, grape or raspberry, or a slice of star fruit or fig. Finally add a Cape gooseberry on top of the "parasol," opening out the fruit's papery covering, or an exotic bloom such as an orchid flower.

Melon Balls

Use a melon baller for this. These gadgets are available in two sizes. When scooping perfect melon balls, be prepared to leave about a quarter of the flesh on the skin—this can of course be eaten separately. For the majority of salads, the best compromise is to scoop out as many perfect melon balls as possible, then to scoop out those with a small amount of flesh on the skin. The discarded shapes can usually be mixed into a fruit salad and making individual cocktails it is best only to use perfect balls as the appearance is marred by untidy pieces.

Index of Recipes

A

B

C

D

E

F

G

H

I

J

K

L

M

watermelon smoothie 36
white prussian 190
white tea & ginseng smoothie 155
winter summer berry smoothie 166
woodland smoothie 29

Y

yogurt & wheat germ smoothie 128

Z

zabaglione shake 196
zucchini refresher 85

Index of Ingredients

D

E

F

G

H

I

K

L

M

N

O

P

R

S

T

V

W

Y

Z

Picture Credits

A = above, B = below, L=left, R=right

iStock 4; 24; 34; 46; 62 L, R; 64 L; 68; 75; 84 R; 87; 121; 149; 200; 212; 214; 223;
Fotolia 17; 18; 20; 28; 33 A, B; 47; 69; 92; 110; 173; 209; 228; 240 B;
Shutterstock 9 B-R; 11; 12 A, B; 13 L, R; 15; 16 L, R; 21; 32; 38; 39; 40 L; 42 L; 44; 48; 49; 57; 59; 63; 66; 67; 98; 100 L; 100 R; 102 R; 106; 109; 127; 140 L; 159; 161; 171; 174; 178; 179; 181; 182 R; 184 R; 184 R; 187; 189; 197; 207; 224; 229 L, R; 230 L, T, R; 231 A; 231 B; 232 A; 233; 234 A; 234 B; 234 B; 235 A; 236 R; 236 B; 243; 247 L, R; 256 L, R.
StockFood 1 © Eriksson, Ingvar; 3 © Eriksson, Ingvar; 36 © Coelho; 37 © Giblin, Sheri; 43 © Arras, K.; 55 © Cazals, Jean; 79 © Giblin, Sheri; 80 © Lister, Louise; 94 © Arras, K.; 95 © Arras, K.; 96 © Arras, K.; 97 © Sporrer/Skowronek; 99 © Schieren, Bodo A.; 105 © Westermann, Jan-Peter; 120 © Garlick, Ian; 125 © Boyny, Michael; 132 © Sklar, Evan; 133 © Carlott, Caspar; 134 © Bender, Uwe; 143 © Bischof, Harry; 152 © Bender, Uwe; 153 © Arras, K.; 154 © Urban, Martina; 201 © King, Dave; 202 © Grablewski, Alexandra; 203 © Mewes, K.

 While every effort has been made to credit contributors, Quintet Publishing would like to apologize should there have been any omissions or errors—and would be pleased to make the appropriate correction for future editions of the book.

"There are very few processes described in this book that I have not performed myself – albeit, perhaps, some of them ineptly.

madness. It is time to cut out what we do not need so we can live more simply and happily. Good home- and locally-produced food, comfortable clothes, serviceable housing, and true culture—these matter. The only way this can happen is by ordinary people, us, boycotting the huge multinational corporations that are destroying our Earth, and by creating a new Age—an Age of Healing to replace the Age of Plunder.

I would like to acknowledge my fellow self-supporters, Will Sutherland and Angela Ashe, for their unfailing help. They have shared the trials and labors as well as the joys of this way of life, and have come into partnership with me to start a school of self-sufficiency in Ireland, to which all honest men, women, and children are most welcome, provided they can find the fees!

Of course, I have learned a lot since I wrote the first edition (when you cease learning things they take you away in a box), and I always tried to live a pretty self-sufficient life. There are very few processes described in this book that I have not performed myself—albeit, perhaps, some of them ineptly. I have embarked on many an enterprise without the faintest idea of how to do it—but I have always ended up with the thing done and with a great deal more knowledge than I had when I started.

Would I advise other people to follow this lifestyle? I wouldn't advise anybody to do anything. The purpose of this book is not to shape other people's lives but simply to help people to do things if they decide to. It's a way of life that has suited me: it kept me fighting fit and at least partly sane into my 88th year, and it prevented me from doing too much harm to our poor planet.

I would perhaps pass on this sage advice: do not try to do everything at once. This is an organic way of life and organic processes tend to be slow and steady. I would also like to offer this motto: "I am only one. I can only do what one can do. But what one can do, I will do!" Happy grub-grubbing! (Better than money-grubbing any day!)

John Seymour

Introduction

In the lives we lead today, we take much for granted, and few of us indeed remember why so many so-called advanced civilizations of the past simply disappeared. When I left college I went to Africa and roamed for six years. I rode the veld in the Karroo, in South Africa, looking after sheep; I managed a sheep farm in Namibia on the verge of the Namib Desert; I hunted buck and shot lions. I spent a year deep sea fishing and six months working in a copper mine in what is now Zambia. And then I traveled all over central Africa for two years inoculating native cattle.

One of the best friends I made during my time in Africa was a man of the Old Stone Age. White people, unable to get their tongues around his real name, which was a conglomeration of clicks, called him Joseph. He was a bushman of the Namib desert but he had been caught by a white farmer and made to work so he knew Afrikaans. I knew some of this Cape Dutch language and so could communicate with him.

I used to go hunting with Joseph. First he would hand over the flock of sheep to his wife, and then we would walk out into the bush in search of gemsbok or oryx. Joseph had what seemed to be an amazing knack for knowing where they were. When he knew me better he asked me to leave my rifle behind, and he used to put his arm into a thorn bush and pull out the head of a spear. It was quite illegal for a "native" to own a spear. He would cut a shaft from a bush and fit the spearhead, and using three dogs we would bring a buck to bay and Joseph would kill it with the spear. Later Joseph took me on an expedition to meet his people. They lived in the most desolate and inhospitable part of Africa, but they still lived well. They hunted food by lying in wait near waterholes and shooting game with small poisoned arrows. They found water by cutting open the stomach of the gemsbok and drinking the contents—as I learned to do myself. Or they would find an insignificant looking creeper, dig down under it and bring up a soggy mass of vegetation as big as a football. They sucked the liquid from this, and very nasty it tasted too, but very welcome when it could keep you alive.

These people did not work as you and I might understand it. They could walk 40 miles (65 kilometers) in a night and had endless patience whilst waiting for game. Life was hard in this fierce climate, but they spent most nights dancing and singing and telling stories in the light of their fires. They were completely at home in the natural world around them and they knew every living being in it. They never felt for one moment that they were in any way special or apart from the rest of nature.

I tell all this because I want to point out the enormous change in lifestyle which took place when humans began to practice agriculture. Suddenly, only 10,000 to 12,000 years ago, people discovered they could plant crops and, just as important, domesticate animals. But there were only a few places where natural conditions were such as to allow this to be possible year after year (mostly fertile river valleys) and thus permit development of cities. As history shows, very few civilizations developed cultures sufficiently wise and robust to last for more than a thousand years: they simply exhausted their soils or were conquered by more aggressive neighbors.

Now we have had the Agricultural, Industrial, Technological, Information, and Internet Revolutions, all of which have brought great changes. However, those who benefit materially are the relative few who have their hands on or adjacent to the levers of power. Elsewhere most men and women live in appalling conditions.

For most of the global population it is a forced trek to work in slum cities for starvation wages and sing to the tunes of the big multinationals. Farmers and farm workers today are either starving or being forced to adopt methods which they know are damaging the land. All over the earth the soil is going, eroded by tractor cultivation and slowly poisoned by chemicals from agribusinesses. And so we have created lifestyles which are simply not sustainable nor pleasant. But there are many simple changes which individuals can make to their lifestyles which could change all this. And, if we are wise, we will not wait for the apocalypse before making some adjustments. I do not ask you to blindly follow my suggestions, but merely consider them as you think about the future.

ENERGY

One day I was invited to attend a public symposium on energy, and a public relations officer for the nuclear power industry was there. He showed us all a frightening graph showing the world's energy consumption from 1800 to the present day. The graph started at virtually zero and went up at increasing speed until it was almost vertical. What he had not noticed was that the line pointed straight at the "EXIT" sign above! Now surely a moment's reflection is enough to tell us that everyone in the world simply cannot live at the energy levels favored by the 21st-century Western ideal.

Of course, for thousands of years muscle energy and the heat from fires were all that humans had to depend on. When I was born in 1914, things began to change radically with the discovery of how to exploit oil, and today we have released so much carbon back into the atmosphere that no one can predict the consequences. But what difference will it make (you may ask) if I walk up the stairs instead of using the elevator, or turn down the heating a couple of notches, or use my bike instead of the car? I get no substantial cash benefits because no-one can really pay me for benefitting the commons, the common land and seas we share. This is called the tragedy of the commons—no one pays us to keep the oceans or the air clean.

But if it's true that the only person over whom I have control of actions is myself, then it does matter what I do. It may not matter a jot to the world at large, but it matters to me. And there is by good fortune one important factor that can help us make progress in saving energy. For not only does using our muscles help the planet, but it also keeps us fit and healthy.

Of course there are many other sources of benign energy. Solar energy, wind energy, and water power are three obvious alternatives which are increasingly easy to harness with modern technology. I count planned tree planting and coppicing as one of the best solar energy collecting devices. And let us never forget that energy saved is as good as energy bought. It is often much cheaper to buy energy-saving equipment than to pay for the energy used by less effective arrangements.

TRANSPORTATION

Unless we come from a race of traveling peoples, we are all pretty much "locals." We live somewhere, and what goes on in the locality of where we live is much more important than what goes on in Paris, London, Tokyo or Washington, DC. If we could once again run our world on a local scale, with decisions made on a local community basis, then many of our problems would be stopped in their tracks. Let me explain my definition of local by comparing two villages: these happen to be in Crete but they could be anywhere.

One village is high up in the mountains, just to the south of the cave where Zeus was born. It can only be reached by an unpaved road full of potholes and quite unsuitable for buses. The only contact with the outside world that I could see with this mountain community was a man with a very tough truck braving the potholes once each week to bring a load of fish from the small fishing port down on the coast. Sheep were exported from the village to bring in the cash for this exchange.

Apart from this exchange, the community on this mountain was self-supporting. There were enough tiny terraced fields to grow wheat, wine, and olives. There was an oil mill for pressing the olives. There were plenty of nut trees as well as lemon groves, fig trees, and many other kinds of fruits. There were beehives, and the sheep provided meat in abundance. The mountain village houses were beautiful, simple, and comfortable in that climate. Clothes were made by the women. There was a loom maker in a neighboring village, a boot-maker in another, and a knife-maker in yet another. Was there culture, you might ask? Well, there was singing and dancing and music in plenty. There were few books, but if the villagers had wanted them, they could have been available. The villagers paid no taxes and had just one policeman. They knew their own laws and kept to them.

Now the other Cretan village I wish to describe was lower down the mountain and had a "good" road. This gave access to the city but also gave the city access to the countryside. City money came in and bought much of the land, uprooting the old trees and vineyards and planting quick-growing olive trees, so providing an olive crop for cash sale. Now the villagers had to pay for their olive oil and were dragged quickly into the money economy. All sorts of traders had access to the village and a small supermarket opened. Suddenly the villagers found they "needed" all sorts of things they had never needed before. Television arrived and brought with it aspiring visions. Young people in the village no longer sang or danced; they wanted Western pop music and Coca-Cola. Even though their fine road looked like a road to freedom, it was actually a road to sadness, wage slavery, and discontent, and one from which the youngsters could not return.

WORK

I once knew an old lady who lived by herself in the Golden Valley of Herefordshire, England. She was one of the happiest old women I have met. She described to me all the work she and her mother used to do when she was a child: washing on Monday, butter-making on Tuesday, market on Wednesday, and so on. "It all sounds like a lot of hard work," I said to her. "Yes, but nobody ever told us then," she said in her Herefordshire accent. "Told you what?" "Told us there was anything wrong with work!" Today work has become a dirty

> This book is about changing the way we live, and I am well aware that the subject is fraught with difficulties.

word, and most people would do anything to get out of work. To say that an invention is labor-saving is the highest praise, but it never seems to occur to anyone that the work might have been enjoyable. I have plowed all day behind a good set of horses and been sad when the day came to an end!

This book is about changing the way we live, and I am well aware that the subject is fraught with difficulties. The young couple who have mortgaged themselves to buy a house, have to pay huge monthly sums for their season ticket to get to work, have a bank overdraft and debts with the credit card sharks, are in no position to be very choosy about what work they do. But why should we get into such a situation?

Why should we all labor to enrich the banks? (For that is what we are doing.) There is not necessarily anything wrong with doing things that are profitable. It is when "profit" becomes the dominant motive that the cycle of disaster begins. In my work with self-sufficiency I have met hundreds of people in many countries across the world who have withdrawn themselves from conventional work in big cities and moved out into the countryside. Almost all of them have found good, honest, and useful ways of making a living. Some are fairly well off in regard to money; others are poor in that regard but they are all rich in things that really matter. They are the people of the future. If they are not in debt they are happy men and women.

HOME

A true home should be the container for reviving real hospitality, true culture and conviviality, real fun, solid comfort, and above all, real civilization. And the most creative thing that anybody can do in this world is to make a real home. Indeed, the homemaker is as important as the house, and the "housewife" is the most creative, most important job on Earth. One of the essential characteristics of a good home is craftsmanship. It seems to me that all human artifacts give off a sort of cultural radiation, depending on how much love and art has gone into their production. A mass-produced article of furniture comes from a high-speed, high-tech factory, using plastics and often working with wood that has been destroyed by chipping and glueing. The noise and

smell of these places is quite terrifying. And this factory-made rubbish, although it may look fine for a few years, is fit only for the landfill site (you cannot burn it, for it gives off dioxins).

Furniture made by a craftsman, on the other hand, is full of care and made with sympathy for the wood. It will last for generations and be a constant beacon of beauty in the home. Of course I am not suggesting that everyone should or can build their own home or make their own furniture. After all, if houses were well built and the population was stable, everyone should inherit a good house. What I am saying is that if you can build your own furniture, or indeed house, either with your own hands or with the help of a builder, it is a marvelous thing to do.

FOOD

It is true that our friends in the supermarkets have made many advances in the complexity of sourcing our food as well as in the sophistication of creating ready meals. But the sad fact is that our food now travels thousands—yes thousands—of miles between the place it is produced and our mouths. Most people never get an opportunity to taste real local-grown fresh food; they do not know what they are missing. This book is about quality of life, and I submit that if there is no quality in the food we eat, then we must just hope to get through life as quickly as possible. Because the sources of our food are getting further away from our tables and the food goes through more and more processing, the only quality now deemed important is long shelf life. Such food is dead food: all the life has been taken out of it. The best food of all comes from our own garden and therefore not surprisingly you will find a big chunk of this self-sufficiency guide showing you how to sow, plant, nurture, pick, harvest, and preserve this wonderful produce. But there is still good locally-produced organic food you can source from a local farm, or farmers' markets, and local shop. If we take the trouble to seek out good, "flavour-full," real food we will be benefitting ourselves and, just as important, giving support to those who take the trouble to produce such food.

CHAPTER ONE

THE MEANING OF SELF-SUFFICIENCY

"We had never had any real conscious drive to self-sufficiency. We had thought, like a lot of other people, that it would be nice to grow our own vegetables. But living here has altered our sense of values. We find that every time we buy some factory-made article we wonder if they enjoyed making it or if it was just a bore? I know that the modern factory worker is supposed to lead an easier life than, say, the peasant. But I wonder whether easier is better? Simpler? Healthier? More spiritually satisfying? Or not? So far as we can, we import our needs from small and honest craftsmen and tradesmen. We subscribe as little as we can to the tycoons, and the Ad-men, and the boys with their expense accounts."

John Seymour *The Fat of the Land*, 1976

The Way to Self-Sufficiency

Self-sufficiency does not mean "going back" to the acceptance of a lower standard of living. On the contrary, it is the striving for a higher standard of living, for food that is fresh and organically grown and good, for the good life in pleasant surroundings, for the health of body and peace of mind which come with hard, varied work in the open air, and for the satisfaction that comes from doing difficult and intricate jobs well and successfully.

In a modern world almost everything we use is dependent on the whim of some international corporation or the operation of a very complex supply chain. So it brings peace of mind and satisfaction to be able to do more and produce more yourself. The old maxim that "you only get out of something what you put into it" could not be more apposite here. And for those who feel their careers and consumer lifestyles are not bringing the satisfaction they need, then what better than to try something new, and re-learn the old skills that made country living so magical in days gone by.

Everyone who owns a piece of land should husband that land as wisely, knowledgeably, and intensively as possible. The so-called "self supporter" sitting among a riot of docks and thistles talking philosophy ought to go back to town. He is not doing any good at all, and is occupying land which should be occupied by somebody who can really make good sustainable use it.

> "You do not need five acres and a degree in horticulture to become self-sufficient.

Size doesn't matter with self-sufficiency

You do not need five acres and a degree in horticulture to become self-sufficient, nor should you feel disappointed if you cannot produce all you need. Self-sufficiency is about taking control and becoming an effective producer of whatever your resources allow. This might be home-made bread, jam, or beer. It might be home produced vegetables or meat. It might be baskets or blockwork. We were not meant to be a one-job animal. We do not thrive as parts of a machine. We are intended by nature to be diverse, to do diverse things, to have many skills. The city person who buys a sack of wheat from a farmer on a countryside visit and grinds his own flour to make his own bread, cuts out the middlemen and furthermore gets better bread. He gets good exercise turning the handle of the grinding machine too. And any suburban gardener can dig up some of that useless lawn and put some of those dreary hardy perennials on the compost heap and grow their own cabbages. An urban garden, an allotment, these are both a sound base for a would-be self supporter (*see pp. 28–35*), and a good-sized suburban garden can practically keep a family. I knew a woman who grew the finest outdoor tomatoes I ever saw in a window box 12 storeys up in a tower-block. They were too high up to get the blight.

The first principles of self-sufficiency

Although this concise edition concentrates on what can be done by the city, town, or village dweller, it is worth considering for a moment some of the basic principles of husbandry on a larger holding. Who knows – some of you may be thinking of taking your ideas on to the next stage

“There should be no need for a dustman on the self-sufficient holding.

and this will give you some pointers. We are talking here about how we combine all the strands of activity on a larger holding including livestock, fields and orchard, as well as a vegetable garden. But my core belief – that nothing should be wasted – applies to the 15-m (50-ft) garden just the same.

In planning the layout of the smallholding the homesteader will take careful account of natural shelter, considering especially the effects of the prevailing wind. Depending on the size of your holding, trees may be planted to create a barrier on the north and east (in the northern hemisphere). If you are lucky enough to own a large holding you'll want permanent thorn hedges established to divide the holding into sensible stockproof fields. Existing water and streams will be carefully assessed for possible use in irrigation, water power, or suitable ponds for ducks and geese. Care will be taken to make good advantage of all natural features of the site. Walls will be constructed to create a south-facing shelter suitable for excellent fruit trees. The buildings will be sited where they are most convenient both to each other and to the productive areas of the smallholding.

Now husbanding homesteaders – those with livestock to consider – will not keep the same species of animal on a piece of land too long, just as they will not grow the same crop year after year in the same place. They will follow their young calves with their older cattle, their cattle with sheep, their sheep with horses, while geese and other poultry either run free or are progressively moved over their grassland and arable land (by arable I mean land that gets ploughed and planted with crops as opposed to land that is grass all the time).

All animals suffer from parasites, and if you keep one domesticated species on one piece of land for too long, there will be a build-up of parasites and disease organisms. As a rule, the parasites of one animal do not affect another and therefore following one species with another over the land will eliminate parasites.

Also, husbanding homesteaders will find that every enterprise on their holding, if it is correctly planned, will interact beneficially with every other. If they keep cows, their dung will manure the land, this will provide food, not only for the cows but for the humans and pigs also. The by-products of the milk of the cows (skimmed milk from butter-making and whey from cheese-making) are a marvellous whole food for pigs and poultry. The dung from the pigs and poultry helps grow the food for the cows. Chickens will scratch about in the dung of other animals and salvage any undigested grain.

All crop residues help to feed the appropriate animals – and such residues as not even the pigs can eat, they will tread into the ground, and activate with their manure, and turn into the finest *in situ* compost without the husbandman or women lifting a spade. All residues from slaughtered birds or animals go either to feed the pigs or the sheepdogs, or to activate the compost heap. Nothing is wasted. This is the basic principle I alluded to before. Nothing is an expensive embarrassment to be taken away to pollute the environment. There should be no need for a dustman on the self-sufficient holding.

Even old newspapers can make litter for pigs, or be composted. Anything that has to be burnt makes good potash for the land. Nothing is wasted – there is no "rubbish". But before the potential self-supporter embarks on the pursuit of true husbandry, he or she should acquaint themselves with some of the basic laws of nature, so that they can better understand why certain things will happen on their holding and why other things will not.

The food chain

Life on this planet has been likened to a pyramid: a pyramid with an unbelievably wide base and a small apex. All life needs nitrogen, for it is one of the most essential constituents of living matter, but most creatures cannot use the free, uncombined nitrogen which makes up a great part of our atmosphere. The base of our biotic pyramid, therefore, is made up of the bacteria that live in the soil, sometimes in symbiosis with higher plants, and these bacteria have the power of fixing nitrogen from the air. The number of these organisms in the soil is unimaginably great: suffice it to say that there are millions in a speck of soil the size of a pin-head.

On these, the basic and most essential of all forms of life, lives a vast host of microscopic animals. As we work up the pyramid, or the food chain, whichever way we like to consider it, we find that each superimposed layer is far less in number than the layer it preys upon. On the higher plants graze the herbivores (plant-eating animals). Every antelope, for example, must have millions of grass plants to support it. On the herbivores "graze" the carnivores (the meat-eaters). And every lion must have hundreds of antelopes to support it. The true carnivores are right at the apex of the biotic pyramid. Humans are somewhere near the top, but not at the top, because they are not true carnivores: they are omnivores. They are one of those lucky animals that can subsist on a wide range of food: vegetable and animal.

Inter-relationships not interference

Up and down the chain, or up and down between the layers of the pyramid, there is a vast complexity of inter-relationships. There are, for example, purely carnivorous micro-organisms. There are all kinds of parasitic and saprophitic organisms: the former live on their hosts and sap their strength, the latter live in symbiosis, or in friendly cooperation, with other organisms, animal, or vegetable. We have said that the carnivores are at the apex of the food chain. Where in it stands a flea on a lion's back? Or a parasite in a lion's gut? And what about the bacterium that is specialized (and you can bet there is one) to live inside the body of the lion flea? A system of such gargantuan complexity can best, perhaps, be understood by the utter simplification of the famous verse:

Little bugs have lesser bugs upon their backs to bite 'em,
And lesser bugs have lesser bugs and so on ad infinitum!

This refers to parasitism alone, of course, but it is noteworthy that all up and down the pyramid everything is consumed, eventually, by something else. And that includes us, unless we break the chain of life by the purely destructive process of cremation. Now humans, the thinking monkeys, have to interfere with this system (of which we should never forget that we are a part), but we do so at our peril. If we eliminate many carnivores among the larger mammals, the herbivores on which these carnivores preyed become overcrowded, overgraze, and create deserts. If, on the other hand, we eliminate too many herbivores, the herbage grows rank and out of control and good pasture goes back to scrub and cannot, unless it is cleared, support many herbivores. If we eliminate every species of herbivore except one, the grazing is less efficiently grazed.

Thus sheep graze very close to the ground (they bite the grass off with their front teeth), while cows like long grass (they rip grass up by wrapping their tongues around it). The hills produce more and better sheep if cattle graze on them too. It is up to us as husbandmen and women to consider very carefully, and act very wisely, before we use our powers to interfere with the rest of the biotic pyramid.

Plants, as well as animals, exist in great variety in a whole host of different natural environments – and for very good reasons. Different plants take different things out of the soil, and put different things back in. Members of the pea-bean-and-clover family, for example, have nitrogen-fixing bacteria in nodules on their roots. With the help of these friendly bacteria they can fix their own nitrogen. But you can wipe the clovers out of a pasture by applying artificial nitrogen. It is not that the clovers do not get on with the artificial nitrogen, but that you have removed the "unfair advantage" that they had previously over the grasses (which are not nitrogen-fixing) by supplying the latter with plenty of free nitrogen and, being naturally more vigorous than the clovers, these grasses smother the clovers out.

It is obvious from observing nature that monoculture is not in the natural order of things. We can only sustain a one-crop-only system by adding the elements that the crop needs from the fertilizer bag and destroying all the crop's rivals and enemies with chemicals. If we wish to farm more in accordance with the laws of nature, we must diversify as much as we can, both with plants and animals.

"... the soil feeds the plants, the plants feed the animals, the animals manure the land, the manure feeds the soil, the soil feeds the plants.

Being part of the natural cycle

Ultimately, it all comes back to the first rule in becoming self-sufficient: that is, to understand the natural cycle: namely, the soil feeds the plants, the plants feed the animals, the animals manure the land, the manure feeds the soil, the soil feeds the plants. True husbanding homesteaders will wish to maintain this natural cycle, but they have to become part of the cycle themselves; as plant-eaters and carnivores they are liable to break the chain unless they observe at all times the "Law of Return".

The Law of Return means that all residues (animal, vegetable, and human) should be returned to the soil, either by way of the compost heap, or the guts of an animal, or the plough, or by being trodden into the ground by livestock. Whatever cannot be usefully returned to the soil, or usefully used in some other way, should be burned; this will make potash for the land. Nothing should be wasted on the self-sufficient holding and I believe this applies as much to a modest allotment as it does to a holding of several acres.

The soil

Huge quantities of usable nitrogen are present in human, animal, and plant wastes. It is much easier for the soil to recycle these than for soil bacteria to "fix" nitrogen from scratch. This is why all effective husbandry places such emphasis on the importance of composting and maintaining a healthy soil.

Because soil derives from many kinds of rock, there are many varieties of soil. As we cannot always get exactly the kind of soil that we require, the husbandman or women must learn to make the best of the soil available. Depending on the size of their particles, soils are classified as light or heavy, with an infinite range of gradations in between. Light means composed of large particles. Heavy means composed of small particles. Gravel can hardly be called soil but sand can, and pure sand is the lightest soil you can get. The kind of clay which is made of the very smallest particles is the heaviest. The terms "light" and "heavy" in this context have nothing to do with weight but with the ease of working of the soil. You can dig sand, or otherwise work with it, no matter how wet it is, and do it no harm. Heavy clay is very hard to dig or plough, gets very "puddingy" and sticky, and is easily damaged by working it when it is wet.

What we call soil generally has a thickness to be measured in inches rather than feet. It merges pretty quickly below with the subsoil, which is generally fairly humus-free (that is without compost, muck or farmyard manure, leaf-mould, green manuring, basically any vegetable or animal residue) but may be rich in mineral foods needed by plants. Deep-rooting plants such as some trees, lucerne or alfalfa, comfrey, and many herbs, send their roots right down into the subsoil, and extract these nutriments (nourishing food) from it.

> The nature of the subsoil is very important because of its influence on drainage. If it is heavy clay, then the drainage will be bad.

The nature of the subsoil is very important because of its influence on drainage. If it is heavy clay, for example, then the drainage will be bad and the land will be wet. If it is sand, gravel, decayed chalk or limestone, then the land will probably be dry. Below the subsoil lies rock, and rock makes up the Earth's crust (surface layer) down to the centre of the Earth. The rock, too, can affect drainage: chalk, limestone, sandstone and other pervious rocks make for good drainage: clay (geologists consider this a rock, too), slate, mudstone, some shales, granite, and other igneous rocks generally make for poor drainage. Badly drained soils can always be drained – provided enough expenditure of labour and capital is put into doing it.

Types of soil

Heavy clay This, if it can be drained and worked with great care and knowledge, can be very fertile soil, at least for many crops. Wheat, oak trees, field beans, potatoes, and other crops do superbly on well-farmed clay. Farmers often refer to it as strong land. But great experience is needed to farm it effectively. This is because clay tends to flocculate (the microscopic particles which make up clay gather together in larger particles). When this happens, the clay is more easily worked, drains better, allows air to get down into it, and allows the roots of plants to penetrate it more easily. In other words, it becomes good soil. When it does, the opposite of flocculate happens, it "puddles" (that is, forms a sticky mass much like the potter uses to make his or her pots on the wheel), becomes virtually impossible to cultivate, and gets as hard as brick when it dries out. The land forms big cracks and is useless.

Factors which cause clay to flocculate are alkalinity rather than acidity, exposure to air and frost, incorporation of humus, and good drainage. Acidity causes it to puddle; so does working it while wet. Heavy machines tend to puddle it. Clay must be ploughed or dug when in exactly the right condition of humidity, and left strictly alone when wet.

Clay can always be improved by the addition of humus, by drainage, by ploughing it up at the right time and letting the air and frost get to it (frost separates the particles by forcing them apart), by liming if acid, even, if you have to, by mixing in sand. Clay soil is "late" soil (i.e. it will not produce crops early in the year). It is difficult soil. It is not hungry soil, that is, if you put humus in it the humus will last a long time. It tends to be rich in potash and is often naturally alkaline, in which case it does not need liming.

Loam This is intermediate between clay and sand, and has many gradations of heaviness or lightness. A medium loam is perhaps the perfect soil for most kinds of farming. Most loam is a mixture of clay and sand, although some loams probably have particles all of the same size. If loam (or any other soil) lies on a limestone or chalk rock, it will probably be alkaline and will not need liming, although this is not always the case: there are limestone soils which, surprisingly, do need liming.

Sand At the lighter end of the heavy–light soil spectrum, sand is generally well-drained, often acid (in which case it will need liming), and often deficient in potash and phosphates. It is "early" soil; that is, it warms up very quickly after the winter and produces crops early in the year. It is also hungry soil (when you add humus, it does not last long). In fact, to make sandy soil productive you must put large quantities of organic manure into it, and inorganic manure gets quickly washed away from it.

Sandy soils are favoured for market gardening, being "early" and easy to work and very responsive to heavy dressings of manure. They are good soils for such techniques as folding sheep or pigs on the land. They are good for wintering cattle on because they do not poach (turn into a quagmire when trodden) like heavy soils do. They recover quickly from treading when under grass. But they won't grow as heavy crops of grass or other crops as heavier land. They dry out very quickly and suffer from drought more than clay soils.

Peat In a class of their own, peat soils are sadly fairly rare. Peat is formed of vegetable matter which has been compressed in anaerobic conditions (underwater) and has not rotted away. Sour wet peatland is not much good for farming, although such soil, if drained, will grow potatoes, oats, celery, and certain other crops. But naturally drained peatlands are, quite simply, the best soils in the world. They will grow anything, and grow it better than any other soil. They don't need manure, they *are* manure! Happy is the self supporter who can get hold of such land for his crops are most unlikely to fail.

Humans and their Environment

If it ever comes to pass that we have used up all, or most of, the oil on this planet, we will have to reconsider our attitude to our only real and abiding asset – the land itself. We will one day have to derive our sustenance from what the land, unaided by oil-derived chemicals, can produce. We may not wish in the future to maintain a standard of living that depends entirely on elaborate and expensive equipment and machinery, but we will always want to maintain a high standard of living in the things that really matter – good food, clothing, shelter, health, happiness, and fun with other people. The land can support us, and it can do it without huge applications of artificial chemicals and manures and the use of expensive machinery. Therefore true homesteaders will seek to husband their land, not exploit it. They will wish to improve and maintain the heart of this land, its fertility.

The art of good husbandry

Other forms of life, too, besides our own, should merit our consideration. Man should be a husbandman to nature, not an exploiter. This planet is not exclusively for our own use. To destroy every form of life except such forms as are obviously directly of use to us is immoral, and ultimately, quite possibly, will contribute to our own destruction. The kind of varied, carefully thought-out husbandry of the self-supporting holding fosters a great variety of life forms, and every self-supporter will wish to leave some areas of true wilderness on his holding, where wild forms of life can continue to flourish undisturbed and in peace. So he or she will learn by observing nature that growing one crop only, or keeping one species of animal only, on the same piece of land is not in the natural order of things. Where they cultivate, they will always keep in mind the needs of the soil, considering each animal and each plant for what beneficial effect it might have on the land.

And then there is the question of our relations with other people. Many people move from the cities back to the land precisely because they find city life, surrounded by people, too lonely. A self-supporter, living alone surrounded by giant commercial farms, may be lonely, too; but if he has other self-supporters near him he will be forced into cooperation with them and find himself, very quickly, part of a living and warm community. There will be shared work in the fields, animal feeding duties when other people go on holiday, the sharing of child-minding duties, as well as bartering of produce for expertise or other produce.

Good relations with the old indigenous population of the countryside are important, too. In my area, the old country people are very sympathetic to the new "drop-ins". They are genuinely pleased to see us reviving and preserving the old skills they practised in their youth, and they take pleasure in imparting them to us. They wax eloquent when they see the hams and flitches of bacon hung up in my chimney. "That's real bacon!" they say, "better than the stuff we get in the shops." "My mother used to make that when I was a boy, we grew all our own food then," they might add. "Why don't you grow it now?" I ask. "Ah! times have changed." Well, they are changing again.

The Urban Garden

It is amazing what can be packed into an urban garden. Even the smallest space can be made productive and what could be more attractive than the sight of well-tended succulent fruit and vegetables right outside your back door. If you have space then think about a small greenhouse which will extend your growing season and offer a chance for more exotic produce. And don't forget that a beehive will send the little foragers out to gather nectar perfectly legally from all your neighbours' flowers.

I remember meeting a fascinating man when I was in California who made his living creating "easy-run" urban vegetable gardens for the old and infirm. These were all on raised beds made of either brick or treated wood constructions. These beds raised the soil level to a comfortable height for weeding and picking while, at the same time, giving the plants more light and providing the garden with a pleasing 3-D effect. These raised container gardens were of the "deep-bed" type, created by using old sleepers, brick or block constructions, and then filled with extremely good quality topsoil to a depth of at least 45 cm (18 in) deep. This allows for very dense planting, high output, and vigorous, drought-resistant rooting. The smaller your plot, the more intensively you can cultivate.

At the other extreme from the raised-bed, easy-run urban garden we have the traditional allotment (*see p.32*). We have all seen these along the side of railways with their little wooden potting sheds, staked runner beans, and well-guarded winter brassicas. Most communities have allotments for hire – check your local shop or library.

Planning your urban garden

The first essential is to think about the orientation of the site: where is the sun and where is the shade? You will not want to have tall plants on the south side of your garden (in the northern hemisphere at any rate); equally, you will want to use any south-facing fence or wall for sun-loving plants – for example, espaliered fruit trees. Ideally, you will want to break up the cultivated area into smaller blocks by using perennials, such as the soft fruit bushes or artichokes.

Some plants, for example, marrows or blackberries, are very large and aggressive and just not suitable for a small urban garden. Equally, potatoes take up too much space for very little gain, and you can source first-rate spuds easily.

As a compromise you might want to plant just a few earlies. The green salad crops are good to grow because they taste so much better pulled up fresh from the garden or allotment. Mange tout or sugar snap peas are also delicious when fresh, while runner beans are a real 3-D plant that produces a mass of food from a very small space. A few soft fruit bushes and raspberries will give good returns on labour and space, as will espaliered fruit trees. Rhubarb is a good early fruit crop choice, but asparagus is a real space guzzler, as is sweet corn. Carrots are ideal for growing, and taste absolutely delicious when pulled fresh from the soil. Tomatoes can also be a brilliantly productive plant in a tight space. Strawberries grow well in specially designed pots; but make sure the pot you buy is frost-proof because many of the cheaper ones are not and will crack, causing you to lose your lovely crop. You can also grow strawberries in little crevices made in stone walls. In the urban garden I think this is the best place for them.

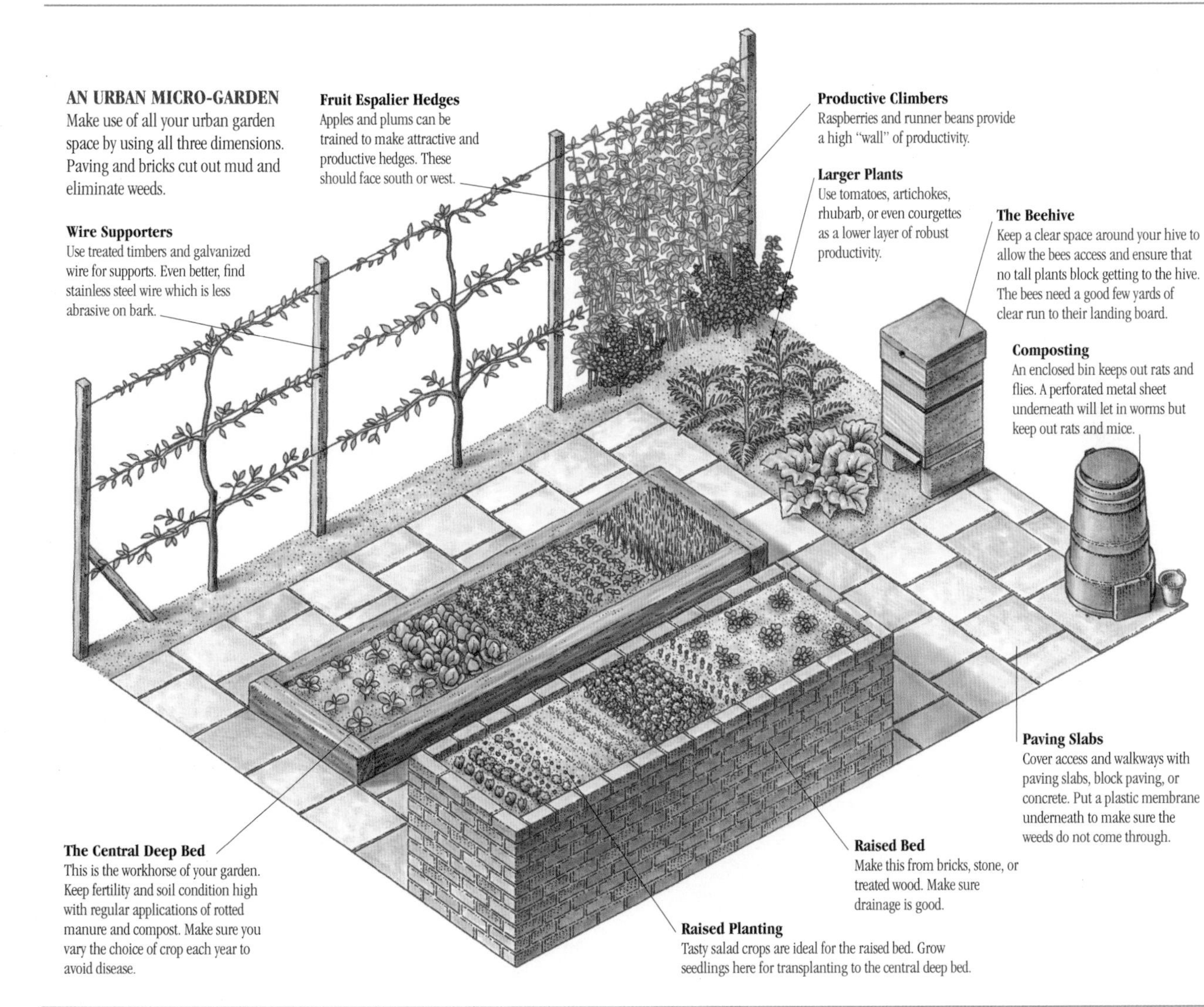
AN URBAN MICRO-GARDEN
Make use of all your urban garden space by using all three dimensions. Paving and bricks cut out mud and eliminate weeds.
Fruit Espalier Hedges
Apples and plums can be trained to make attractive and productive hedges. These should face south or west.
Productive Climbers
Raspberries and runner beans provide a high "wall" of productivity.
Larger Plants
Use tomatoes, artichokes, rhubarb, or even courgettes as a lower layer of robust productivity.
The Beehive
Keep a clear space around your hive to allow the bees access and ensure that no tall plants block getting to the hive. The bees need a good few yards of clear run to their landing board.
Wire Supporters
Use treated timbers and galvanized wire for supports. Even better, find stainless steel wire which is less abrasive on bark.
Composting
An enclosed bin keeps out rats and flies. A perforated metal sheet underneath will let in worms but keep out rats and mice.
Paving Slabs
Cover access and walkways with paving slabs, block paving, or concrete. Put a plastic membrane underneath to make sure the weeds do not come through.
The Central Deep Bed
This is the workhorse of your garden. Keep fertility and soil condition high with regular applications of rotted manure and compost. Make sure you vary the choice of crop each year to avoid disease.
Raised Bed
Make this from bricks, stone, or treated wood. Make sure drainage is good.
Raised Planting
Tasty salad crops are ideal for the raised bed. Grow seedlings here for transplanting to the central deep bed.

Plants and walls

Take some trouble to construct effective paths and walls for your garden. Choose materials that are sympathetic to the rest of your urban environment, but remember that paths must not be a constant source of weeds. Gravel or woodchip paths will become a nightmare of invasive weeds before mid summer – properly laid slabs or brickwork would be much better. Walls too must be maintenance free: you will not want to start re-building when your beautiful espaliered fruit tree is just a few years old! Make sure your walls have a good foundation and waterproof tops. If you decide you have space for an open composting bin (or double bin system) then make sure that you use materials that will not break or rot – old softwood pallets may be cheap but they are certainly not the best solution.

Seedtrays and pricking out

There are many advantages to using indoor seedtrays for the urban garden. If you are relying on seeding direct into the garden itself, then it's quite likely that the local birds and cats could play havoc with the germination. The seedtray process may seem to involve more work but in the long run you will be more successful if you can start off your salad crops and brassicas indoors. Other crops too, like butternut squashes, courgettes and sunflowers should also be more successful started this way. By planting out your own seedlings you avoid the potential problems of buying in diseased seedlings from a nursery. You can start plants off earlier in the year and also save on buying the extra seed packets which you would use if sowing direct into the garden and then thinning out.

We have taken to using one of the heated propagating trays which have a clear plastic cover and are easily available from garden centres. You can get two or three seed trays into one of these (depending on size) and the gentle warmth will produce amazingly fast results. Sometimes it seems to be only a matter of hours before the tiny green shoots appear after you have scattered your seeds onto a moist compost seedbed. If you have a conservatory or large window then these could be ideal places to start off your seeds in early spring. Once the seedlings have a couple of good leaves you can "prick" them out. Do this by selecting them one at a time using a kitchen knife or flat screwdriver as a spade, and popping them into small pots or a large seedtray, so they can reach a more substantial size before taking their chance in the garden.

Soil condition

If you have soil which is in poor condition, you will never have a satisfactory organic garden. In a small urban garden it is particularly important to invest time and care in the improvement of your soil. If we garden without using poisons, then we depend on strong and healthy crops that will resist pests and disease. A good kitchen garden may have been dug, weeded and composted for 20 years or more but we will probably want to get our soil into good condition in much less time than this.

We cover the pros and cons of different soil types elsewhere in this book but the vital ingredient is always what we call "humus". Good soil is a veritable soup of living material all of which depends on the nutrients produced by sweetly rotting vegetation. You can smell the healthy aroma produced by bacteria and fungi as they work on decaying vegetation. The top soil on a typical grass lawn may be only a couple of inches deep but we want the top soil in our vegetable garden to be much deeper than this – 15–30 cm (6–12 in) if we can manage it. This can only be done by regular digging and adding of fresh well rotted compost. Many an urban garden is also contaminated with builder's rubble that may be lying just below the surface – this must most definitely come out.

It is no secret that rotting cow manure is the very best source of the "humus" which will make your garden give a bumper disease-free harvest. The cow is nature's superb storehouse of beneficial bacteria which magically transform grass into protein. However, if you can't get your hands on a few trailer loads of rotted cow manure there are now many other sources of good compost – indeed your local authority may even be enlightened enough to be composting domestic waste. Alternatively, you can buy in compost direct from your local garden centre; but check the packaging to see whether it contains chemical additives.

My choice for the urban garden

Salad crops come top of my list for the urban garden. There are many interesting varieties of lettuce as well as rocket and greek cress which can spice up your salad greenery. If warm and well watered, your salad crops will grow quickly and you can keep planting more to renew your supply over the season. Your main problem is likely to come from the local slug population who will have to be trapped with regular midnight patrols.

Carrots come next on my list although they really do best on sandy light soil. You cannot transplant carrot seedlings, so you will have to sow them *in situ* and guard against cats who love to dig and roll in a dusty carrot seedbed. I find a low chicken wire net fence staked up with bamboo poles is enough to deter most of them. Carrots are slow in germination so be patient; and I must admit that weeding and thinning young carrots is not the most comfortable job for those with back problems. Handle the seedlings with care: thin only when the soil is damp, and dump all damaged carrot leaves straight into the compost and you will avoid damage from the carrot fly.

One or two pumpkins, butternut squashes or courgettes will add some jungle vigour to your garden, and give the kids some excitement as they watch these magical plants grow bigger by the day. But these are definitely plants with attitude so beware or they will take over.

French beans, runner beans, peas, and beetroot would be my other favourites for the urban vegetable garden. These are all easy to grow and pretty well free of pest and disease problems. Plant some blackcurrants and raspberries if you have room, gooseberries too if you can manage it. Just three or four bushes of each will give enough surplus fruit to freeze for the winter. And remember it is a notable feature of the natural world that pests such as aphids or rabbits breed extremely fast. Once they get going, their numbers increase exponentially and your vegetable plot is fast consumed. So there is vital value in having predators ready and waiting right at the start of the breeding season. One or two bushy perennials will provide shelter for these predators over the winter – hence the added benefit of planting blackcurrants or raspberries.

The Allotment

Your allotment will, I do hope, become part of a long-term relationship between your family and the soil. Give some thought as to how you might like it to develop over a number of years. Plants like soft fruit bushes and espaliered fruit trees will grow more than you can imagine – at least that has been my experience, as I always seem to end up having to thin out my bushes after five or six years. The layout of paths, hedges, and perennial plantings needs to be mulled over carefully. Think of leaving enough space to take a rotovator into the heart of the garden – you will certainly need to leave enough room in your allotment for turning at the end of rows.

To start clearing an allotment, first remove all the surface vegetation and set up a composting area. You will need a space about 4.5 sq m (5 sq ft) for this. A scythe is the perfect tool for cutting the weeds as close to the earth as your skill allows.

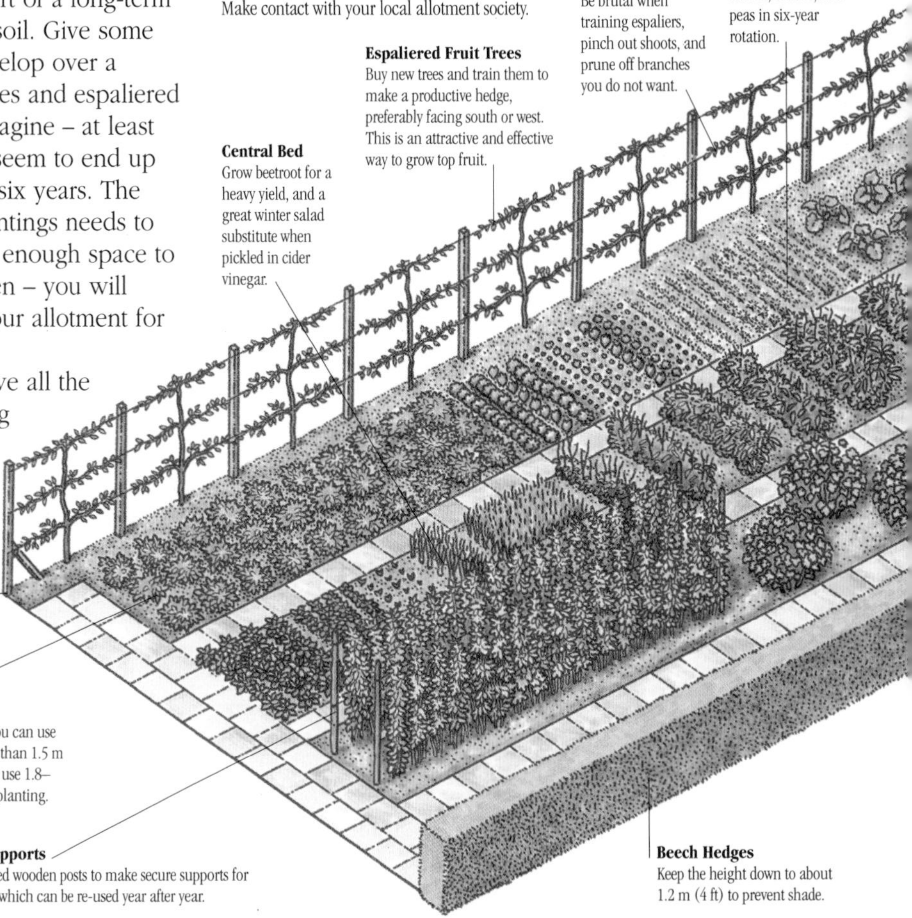

THE URBAN ALLOTMENT
Check with your local library, post office or local council to find out about getting an allotment. Make contact with your local allotment society.

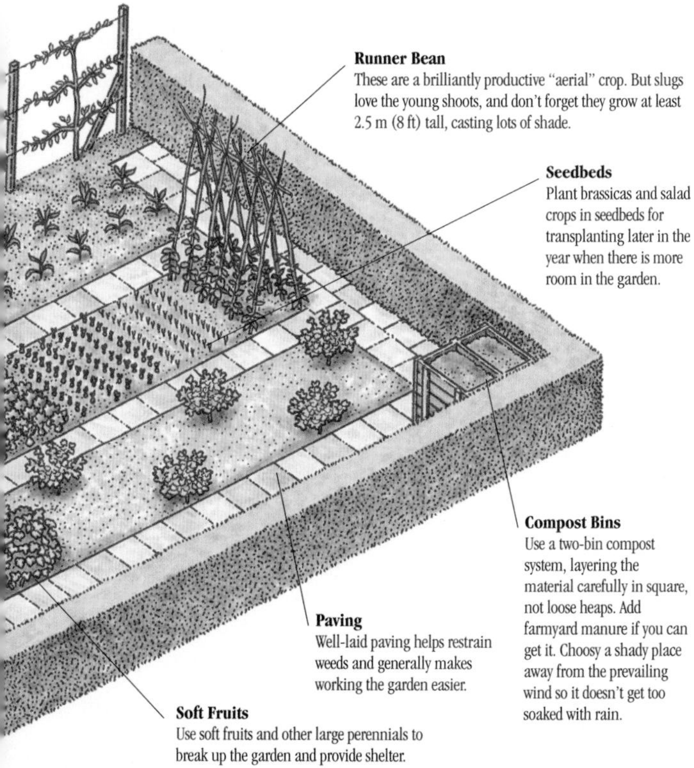

Runner Bean
These are a brilliantly productive "aerial" crop. But slugs love the young shoots, and don't forget they grow at least 2.5 m (8 ft) tall, casting lots of shade.

Seedbeds
Plant brassicas and salad crops in seedbeds for transplanting later in the year when there is more room in the garden.

Compost Bins
Use a two-bin compost system, layering the material carefully in square, not loose heaps. Add farmyard manure if you can get it. Choosy a shady place away from the prevailing wind so it doesn't get too soaked with rain.

Paving
Well-laid paving helps restrain weeds and generally makes working the garden easier.

Soft Fruits
Use soft fruits and other large perennials to break up the garden and provide shelter.

Rake off the cut vegetation with a garden fork. Press the fork down firmly as you pull it towards you to get the surface weeds pulled out. When the surface clearing is complete, get to work with your fork again. By using a fork you will avoid cutting up the deep roots of perennial weeds such as docks or the dreaded spear grass. You will not be able to dig if it is too wet – or too dry. A nice, cool breezy day in winter is best of all, especially if the sun is shining to keep your spirits high. Fork the land over in large lumps, pulling out deep roots and couch strands by hand. Don't worry too much about surface-rooting annual weeds, as you are going to give them a hard time anyway in the weeks to come. Just turn over the biggest square sods that you can with the green side down. Keep your wheelbarrow close by and take the weeds and roots straight to your compost heap which should be in a shady patch. Spread them out in layers to make a stack and not a loose heap.

When you are digging, pace yourself and develop a sort of meditational rhythm. Let your mind wander as your body steadily does the work. It may take several hours or even days to dig the plot, but that's fine. We can't hurry nature. When the job is finished you will have a brown and very lumpy plot spread out. Now you must leave things as they are for at least three or four weeks. This will allow the weather, the wind, and the sun to work on your soil.

Powered digging with a rotovator

Find yourself a good rotovator. This should not go down too deep – 23 cm (9 in) is about right. It's quite a tricky beast for the uninitiated to master and can feel harder at first than manual digging! Take a quick walk over the plot before you start to rotovate and pull out any remaining deep-rooted perennials. Now make at least two passes over the plot with your rotovator. On the last pass try not to leave any footmarks. You want the soil to be left as fluffed up as possible so that weed roots will dry out and die. Let the plot lie again for a couple of weeks, though you could put in some of the larger plantings, for example, rhubarb, soft fruits, artichokes, and espaliered fruit.

Double digging

Once your ground has been properly cleared you must develop a routine of annual cultivation. Most of this will take place in the autumn, winter and spring. It should include constant clearing of stones, the working in of compost and at least some double digging (*see pp.43-45 The Deep Bed for details*).

In our garden we tidy up, removing old plants and the deep-rooted perennial weeds in September. The smaller annual weeds like chickweed and fathen we can simply rotovate in or dig over. Then the whole garden is either dug or rotovated – having said that, we are not touching the winter brassicas, leeks, or strawberry beds, which stay in place all winter.

The whole garden is left to stay this way through the winter winds, frosts, and sun. A lot of small annual weeds will cover the surface, but this is fine as they help to keep the soil in place and stop erosion. Such greenery will easily be turned in by the rotovator when we come to prepare for the spring next March.

Winter is the season when we have time to do some double digging. Each year we try to turnover a small area of the garden in this way. I say a small area because double digging is hard, slow work, and once you have treated an area in this way you will not need to do it again for five or six years, or even longer. But as time goes by, your whole garden will be steadily and significantly improved by extending the topsoil and removing stones in this way. Each year you can move on to work on a different piece of the garden and you will be amazed at the boost this gives to your production.

Fencing, walls and gates

Never underestimate the importance of fencing and walls around your garden. It was not for nothing that the traditional kitchen garden was surrounded by a 2.5 m (8 ft) garden wall. Ideally your barrier should keep out dogs, cats, rabbits, deer, cattle, pigs, sheep as well as the occasional wild child or local scrumper. And make no mistake these are the larger varieties of garden pest that can do huge amounts of damage. We started by using hedging combined with wire rabbit fencing, but we have now moved on to building a complete block wall around the garden. Not only does this really keep out the local rabbit population but it also keeps out dogs and, in our locality, the absolutely disastrous rampaging of the occasional loose bullock. Remember that a wall need not be built in a few days – in fact you can complete your fortifications over a number of years. If you do you will be glad of it!

Rotation

There are whole books and agricultural courses on the science of proper crop rotation. So we won't cover the topic in a couple of paragraphs. Some crops like the salads, beans and peas will not really mind being sown in the same ground for a few years in succession. Others like the brassicas and potatoes will give you a lot of trouble if you do not rotate them around. Potatoes get attacked by wireworm and blight, while brassicas can get clubroot and other nasties so they need to be moved around too.

The simplest way to approach rotation is just to keep a brief garden diary or plan for each year. Then next year try and move everything around to different places.

In our garden we do not grow potatoes in the same ground for five years – so we limit ourselves to a few earlies. As with almost everything in the natural world, variety brings resilience and health, whilst routine and monocropping leads to pest and disease.

Companion planting

Again there are volumes of work you can find on the subtle science of companion planting. The idea is simply to find plants that help each other when planted close together. So if your carrots are sending out lovely carrot smells to the wandering hordes of carrot fly, try planting equally smelly plants like onions next to them. I generally mix rows of rocket or greek cress with my salad crops as their pungent taste seems to deter the local slugs. Again it is the same old story about variety being a benefit in nature, so do not plant large blocks of the same vegetable: if you want a lot of something then spread your planting in smaller blocks around the garden.

Tool shed

Never underestimate the importance of looking after your tools. After use, always clean them and put them back in the tool shed. Never break this habit or sure enough you will find tools missing or broken when you need to use them.

Water

At some stage, global warming or no, you will need water in your garden. It is not a major task to lay in some plastic underground piping and set up a couple of taps (at least) in convenient places. Simply drive in treated fence posts and screw on your taps. You will then have water available for irrigation or puddling in seedlings. If you can lay on your water before you start planting then so much the better, but this will not always be possible. Best of all, set up a holding tank high up somewhere so you can store rainwater from roof run-off, and then use it when everyone else is drying out with a hosepipe ban!

Animals for a smaller plot

Although many of you may live in urban situations where keeping larger animals is more or less impossible, there are often opportunities for keeping rabbits – or even pigs – and possibly poultry in a contained area within your garden. Rabbits are small and need only a relatively small hutch (*see p.139*), whilst pigs can (and traditionally often were) kept in a closed pigsty (*see p.126*). Now if you can keep animals for meat, the benefits will be great not only in having healthy meat which you can trust (and which tastes excellent) but also in using up spoiled or sub-standard produce from your garden which would otherwise simply go onto the compost heap.

Poultry are a very attractive source of eggs and meat but they will need a fair bit of space to be successful (*see p.130*). This means you should include the possibility of keeping poultry when you are planning the layout of your garden. If you are lucky enough to have sufficient garden to include an orchard then this could be a perfect place to keep chickens or ducks. We always have four or five chickens and they provide plenty of eggs without taking up too much space – the more space chickens have, the healthier they will be, and the less mess they will make.

CHAPTER TWO

FOOD FROM THE GARDEN

"We don't bother to do a lot of things in our garden. We let things take their chance, and every year some crops are good and others are bad; but at least there is always enough to eat and we always get a taste of everything. If we did all the spraying and sprinkling and dusting and fumigating that one is told to do in the books, we would spend a fortune on chemicals and have no time left over for anything else. In fact, growing a big variety of crops and never the same crop two years on the same ground, and heavily manuring with the dung of a variety of animals seems to give our crops the strength to resist most pests and diseases. Only sometimes do we come a cropper.

The failure to use artificials is not crankiness. It is simply this: our aim is to grow our food for next to nothing. If we spend money on buying artificial manures we are not doing this. Also we realize now that food tastes a lot nicer if it has been grown with natural and not artificial manures."

John Seymour *The Fat of the Land*, 1976

The Food-Producing Garden

The country garden of my childhood was a mixture of vegetables, flowers, soft fruit, tree fruit (oh, those greengages!) and very often tame rabbits, almost certainly a hen run, often pigeons, and often ferrets. It was a very beautiful place indeed. Now, alas, it has disappeared under a useless velvety lawn and a lot of silly bedding plants and hardy perennials, but of course the owner feels compelled to keep up with the people next door.

However limited the space available, you only need the determination to abandon your space-wasting lawn and flowerbeds in exchange for a program of planned crop rotation for every inch of your garden to become a productive unit. You will save money, your end products will be fresh, and your garden will be a fine example of a dying breed: the cottage garden of yesteryear. But how can we best reproduce the old cottage garden, which was one of the most productive places on Earth? Well, divide the garden area into six parts: seven if you want a small lawn-and-flower area for the sublime fragrance of flowers.

The clever thing to do is to use perennial food plants as hedges to divide up the garden into plots. These are plants that go on from year to year – thus providing valuable overwintering homes for beneficial insects, as well as shelter from the wind and weather. Plants for this purpose are those such as asparagus, globe artichoke, horseradish, rhubarb, and many of the soft fruits, including raspberries. You want to avoid large open areas that encourage spread of disease. At the same time you do not want a garden so claustrophobic that you cannot maneuver the rototiller effectively for the spring cultivations. Larger trees like fruit trees are best kept separate in the orchard, as they really do shade and sterilize a large area of soil. Instead you might consider planting neat espaliered fruit trees as they make excellent and very productive hedges dividing up your beds.

> Each yearly crop is called a break.

Our six parts can then be used in a six-part rotation which will keep potatoes and brassicas from being grown too frequently in the same position. Each yearly crop is called a break. The six yearly crops I use are spuds (which means potatoes and is a very good word!); pea and bean family (legumes); brassicas (cabbages, broccoli, turnips, and so on); reedy plants like corn, pumpkins and cucumbers; salad and catch crops, onions, shallots; and roots (carrots, parsnips, beets, celery, and so on).

Liming

If your land is acid it will need lime. You can test for this with a very simple device bought from any garden shop – or by asking a neighbor. You should lime before the pea and bean break. The peas and beans like the lime and the cabbage tribe that follows them likes what is left of it. Lime has more time to combat the dreaded clubroot disease, which is carried by brassica, if it is in the soil for a few months before the brassica are planted.

Mucking and mulching

If you have muck – farmyard manure – and I hope you have, or if you have compost, concentrate this on your potato break. The potatoes benefit enormously by it. In fact, you won't grow very many without it. It is better not to put it on the root break because some roots, carrots and turnips in particular, are apt to "fork" if they have too much fresh muck. It is better not to put muck on the pea and bean break, because you lime that, and lime and muck don't go very well together in the same year.

It is quite advantageous to put a mulch, a covering of some dead greenstuff, on the surface of the soil between the cabbage-tribe plants, but only after you have hoed them two or three times to suppress the weeds. If you mulch on top of weeds, the weeds will simply grow through the mulch and the mulch will then impede the hoe.

Organic gardening

The aim of the organic gardener should be to get as much humus into his land as possible. By humus I mean soil in which things once living have died and are decaying: muck, compost, seaweed, leaf mold, spoiled hay, nettles, roadside cuttings, anything of vegetable or animal origin: compost it and put it on the land, or just put it on the land. If you dig it in well, you dig it in. If you just leave it on top, the worms will dig it in for you. (I have covered the art of composting as a separate exercise on pp.200-202.)

Unless you keep animals on your garden, you will have to bring in organic matter, or inorganic matter if you are not organically minded, from outside if you want a really productive garden.

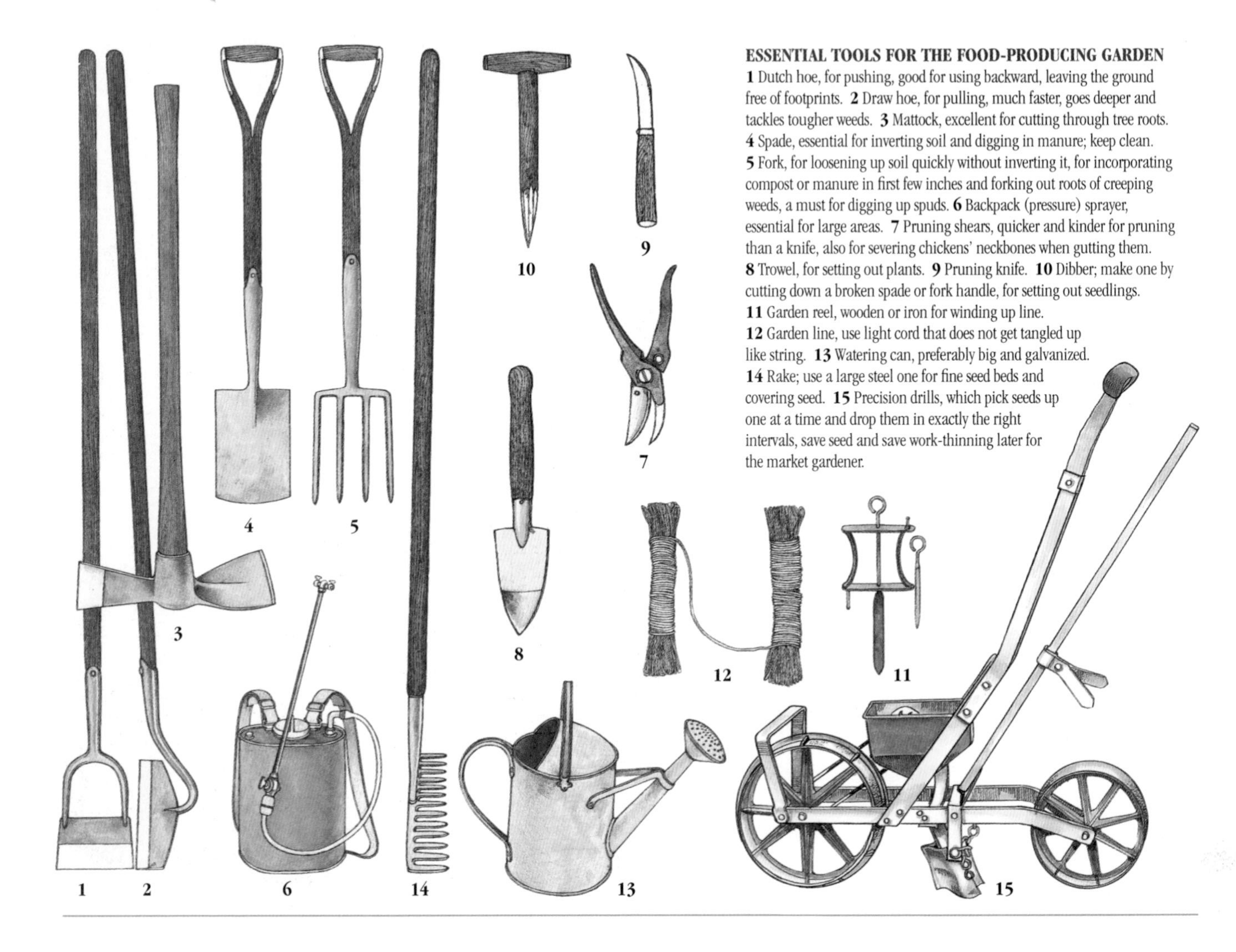

ESSENTIAL TOOLS FOR THE FOOD-PRODUCING GARDEN
1 Dutch hoe, for pushing, good for using backward, leaving the ground free of footprints. **2** Draw hoe, for pulling, much faster, goes deeper and tackles tougher weeds. **3** Mattock, excellent for cutting through tree roots. **4** Spade, essential for inverting soil and digging in manure; keep clean. **5** Fork, for loosening up soil quickly without inverting it, for incorporating compost or manure in first few inches and forking out roots of creeping weeds, a must for digging up spuds. **6** Backpack (pressure) sprayer, essential for large areas. **7** Pruning shears, quicker and kinder for pruning than a knife, also for severing chickens' neckbones when gutting them. **8** Trowel, for setting out plants. **9** Pruning knife. **10** Dibber; make one by cutting down a broken spade or fork handle, for setting out seedlings. **11** Garden reel, wooden or iron for winding up line. **12** Garden line, use light cord that does not get tangled up like string. **13** Watering can, preferably big and galvanized. **14** Rake; use a large steel one for fine seed beds and covering seed. **15** Precision drills, which pick seeds up one at a time and drop them in exactly the right intervals, save seed and save work-thinning later for the market gardener.

PERCENTAGE VALUES OF ORGANIC FERTILIZERS

	Nitrogen	Phosphorus	Potash	Calcium
Average farmyard manure	0.64	0.23	0.32	nil
Pure pig dung	0.48	0.58	0.36	nil
Pure cow dung	0.44	0.12	0.04	nil
Compost	0.50	0.27	0.81	nil*
Deep litter on peat	4.40	1.90	1.90	2.20
Deep litter on straw	0.80	0.55	0.48	nil
Fresh poultry dung	1.66	0.91	0.48	nil
Pigeon dung	5.84	2.10	1.77	nil

**Unless lime has been added*

I subsidize my garden with manure made by animals that eat grass, hay, and crops grown on the rest of the farm. There is much wild talk by would-be organic gardeners who think a garden will produce enough compost material to provide for itself. Well, let them try it. Let them take a rood of land, grow the bulkiest compost-making crop they can on it, compost it, and then see how far the compost it has made goes. It will not go very far. True, deep-rooting plants, such as comfrey and alfalfa, can do great work in bringing up minerals, and phosphates and potash as well, from the subsoil to add to your soil. Trees do an even better job. But the land that is devoted to growing the alfalfa or the trees is out of use for growing food crops.

Of course if your own sewage goes back, in one form or another, into the soil of your garden, one big leakage of plant nutriments is stemmed. The old cottage gardens of the past had all their sewage returned, because the sewage system was a bucket and the contents of that were buried in the garden. Provided the ground in which they were buried was left undisturbed for a time, any pathogens in the sewage would die a natural death. These country gardens owed their phenomenal fertility to the fact that the inhabitants were importing food from outside all the time, as well as eating their garden's own produce, and lots of matter from both sources ended up in the soil. But if you annually extract large amounts of produce from a piece of soil, and either export it or eat it and export the resulting sewage, and don't import any manure or fertilizer, the laws of nature are such that you will ultimately exhaust that soil.

It is vital that your garden be well drained, and it is an advantage if the land beneath it is not too heavy. A well-drained medium loam is most desirable, but sandy soil, provided you muck it well, is very good, too. Heavy clay is difficult to manage, but will grow good brassica crops. Whatever your soil is, you can scarcely give it too much muck, or other humus or humus-forming material.

Green manuring

Green manuring is the process of growing a crop and then digging or plowing it back into the soil, or else just cutting or pulling the crop, and throwing it down on top of the soil. This latter form of green manuring is called mulching. Ultimately, the green matter will rot and the earthworms will drag it down into the soil in their indefatigable manner. If you dig in green manure crops you should do it at least three weeks before you sow the next crop on top of them. The only way round this is to add plenty of available nitrogen to help the green manure to rot down without robbing the soil.

Green manuring improves the quality of the soil for growing because the vegetable matter rots down into humus. The amount of humus added by an apparently heavy crop of green manure is smaller than you might think, but the great value of such crops is that they take up the free nitrogen in the soil. Bare soil would lose this nitrogen to the air, whereas the green crop retains nitrogen and only releases it when it has rotted, by which time the subsequent crop should be ready to use it.

Using weeds

Even weeds can be a green manure crop. Many annual weeds will pop out of nowhere after your crops have been harvested. Tolerate these with good heart for they make an excellent addition to the compost heap when scythed off tight to the ground before they seed. Their roots will help bind the ground against winter rains. But whatever you do, don't let them seed. For one thing, "one year's seeding is seven years' weeding," and for another, all green manure crops should be cut or pulled at the flowering stage, or earlier, when their growth is young, succulent, and high in protein. They then have enough nitrogen in them to provide for their own rotting down.

So look upon annual weeds as friends, provided you can keep them under control. Perennial weeds (those that go on from year to year) should not be tolerated at any cost. They will do you nothing but harm, except perhaps nettles and bracken. If you grow these two crops on otherwise waste land you can cut them and add them to the compost heap. They will do great good, as they are both deep rooting and thus full of material they bring up from below.

Planting green manure

Green manure crops can be divided into winter and summer crops, and legumes and non-legumes. People with small gardens will find winter crops more useful than summer ones, for the simple reason that they will need every inch of space in summer for growing food crops. Legumes make better green manure than non-legumes, because they have bacteria at their roots that take nitrogen from the air, and this is added to the soil when they rot.

Grazing rye

Of winter green manuring crops, grazing rye is probably the best. It can be broadcast at a rate of 2 oz per sq yd (70 g of seed per sq m) after the early potatoes have been lifted. Rake the seed in, leave it to grow all winter, and then dig it in during spring. You can plant grazing rye as late as October, although you won't get such a heavy crop.

Comfrey and *Tagetes minuta*

Comfrey is a perennial to grow for either good green manure or compost. Plant root cuttings from existing plants 2 ft (0.6 m) apart in really weed-clear land in spring and just let it grow. The roots will go down into the soil as far as there is soil for them to penetrate, and they will live for a decade giving heavy yields of highly nitrogenous material, rich in potash, phosphate, and other minerals, too.

Tagetes minuta is a kind of giant marigold growing 10 ft (3 m) high that can kill eelworm and wipes out ground elder (a.k.a. Goutweed or Bishop's weed) and bindweed. It can even suppress quack grass, but is too tough to be dug in as green manure and should be composted.

The Deep Bed

A deep bed is a highly intensive and effective method of producing vegetables in a small space – especially if you are looking for drought resistance and vigorous growth. It is also an excellent way to bring old grassland into vegetable production. The idea seems to have taken root in California, at least that is where I first saw it. The technique is ideal for those with limited space. First we need to understand how to create the bed. Then we have to learn to get the best out of it.

The principles of the deep-bed system follow these three simple steps: first create a highly fertile, deep, and well-drained block of topsoil, working in plenty of good compost so it will give you vigorous root growth as well as drought resistance. Then work your plot from the edges, without the need for walking on the soil. A deep bed should not be any more than 5 ft (1.5 m) wide – and it might need to be narrower for those who have short arms! This way you can do your planting and weeding from the sides. Finally, plant your vegetables in a close pattern that will reduce the need for weeding (much of which you will have to do by hand).

Marking out

Begin by marking out the area you have chosen for your bed. This may well be in established grassland turf, or it may be an area of already cultivated soil convenient for the purpose (perhaps a specifically created area within an urban garden). Size-wise an ideal might be 5 ft (1.5 m) wide by 20 ft (6 m) long. The turf should be turned over well below two "spits" of earth – a "spit" being the countryman's term for the depth of one good spadeful of earth, that is about 9 in (22 cm) – where it will rot. If the bed can follow my recommended size, you will begin by marking off, say, six widths using a garden line or straight batten to guide you. Before you start it is useful to find a large piece of old plastic or even some old pieces of plywood. This will provide a convenient place to dump the diggings from the first row. After cutting the turf, dig out the first row. The process can be tough work, especially if you are working with land that has not been cultivated before.

Now go back to where you started and dig out the next spit of soil. Do not worry if the second spit contains some subsoil. By bringing it to the top you make it available to mix with compost. And as your deep bed matures over the years you will be regularly turning over the top 18 in (45 cm) or so of soil, creating a massively expanded layer of fertile topsoil for your plants. After finishing your first trench you can fork in a 2– to 3–in (5– to 8–cm) layer of good manure into the bottom before turning over the next sod. If you don't have manure, don't worry; your bed will work well anyway – but the manure forms a superb reservoir of moisture for plants in a dry period.

Give the turves a few chops with your spade if they are too lumpy and uneven to fit the trench. Continue the process until you have dug the final trench. At this point you take in the turf and then the soil from the very first trench (from your plastic of plywood sheet). In our Irish garden we have many stones – huge and well hidden underground mostly. Be prepared for this kind of thing with a wheelbarrow, pickaxe, and a strong iron bar. Be prepared,

DIGGING A DEEP BED

1 First mark out the boundaries of your bed. Use all your weight on a sharp spade to cut the turf in two parallel lines right down the length of the first row of the plot before you start to dig.

2 The cut lines should be about 12 in (30 cm) apart, allowing you now to dig out square lumps of turf 6 in (15 cm) thick. Pull out deep rooted weeds like docks or thistles.

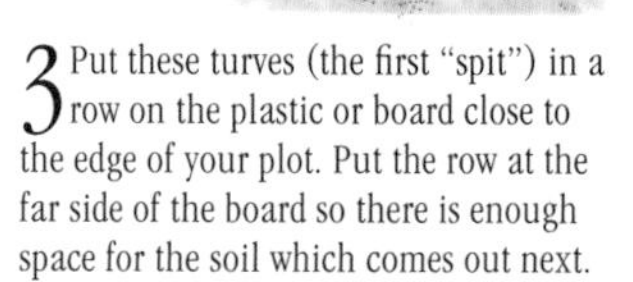

3 Put these turves (the first "spit") in a row on the plastic or board close to the edge of your plot. Put the row at the far side of the board so there is enough space for the soil which comes out next.

4 When you have taken out the whole of the top layer of turf (the top spit), continue to dig the trench by taking out the next spit of soil. Put this on to the board next to the turf.

too, to find tree roots many yards away from large trees. When dealing with roots or a stone, always hold the spade with your two hands grasping the shaft. This way you can use the momentum of the spade's own weight to cut roots or loosen stones without hurting your hands. It is a useful tip, believe me.

Don't be surprised when you find that your deep bed is now raised 9 in (22 cm) above the surrounding garden! This is quite normal; indeed, the heaped effect is beneficial for the use of the bed. But, of course, this is what happens to all soil when disturbed and there will be considerable subsidence with weather and rain.

Making the edges

One feature that makes a deep bed more effective is to add substantial edging of some kind once the bed has been created. I like to use large paving slabs, but you can try aesthetically more pleasing and natural old railroad ties or rot-proof wood or anything similar. Put the slabs onto sheets of building plastic (you can get these from a good local home improvement store) and this will stop weeds from growing through the cracks. Not only does the solid edging allow you to cultivate and harvest the bed more comfortably, it also lets you rest heavy equipment on it without disturbing the bed. Other benefits are that rainfall

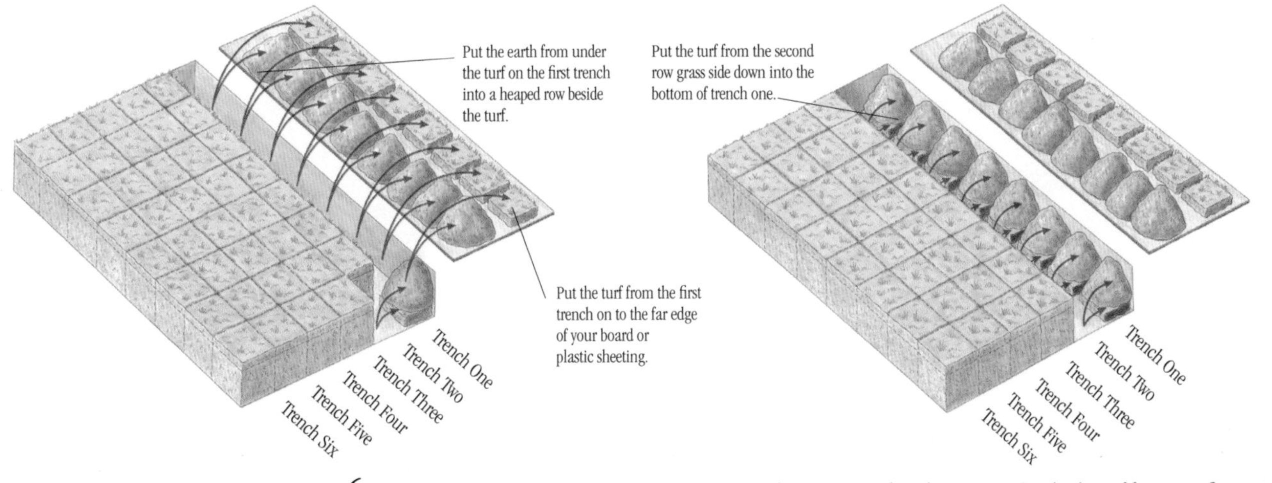

5 After digging out all the soil from the first row, begin the second trench by cutting squares of turf as for the first row; but these go (grass face-down) into the trench you have already dug.

6 The second trench is now completed by digging out the next "spit" of soil and turning it on top of the upturned turf in the first row. Dig out any large stones (you may need a pickaxe).

7 Continue the sequence with each row going upside down into the trench. Add rotted manure under each turf for the ideal result.

8 Take the turf from your first trench and put it face down into the last trench. When you cover this with the soil from the first trench, the bed is complete.

from both sides of the deep bed is gathered from the edges, almost doubling the effective summer rainfall into the cultivated area. The edging also prevents the constant spread of creeping weeds from the edges, while the warm concrete acts as a major deterrent for ever-wandering slugs (especially if you sprinkle on a little salt or ash from time to time). Surprisingly, the sheer capacity of slabs to soak up heat during the day helps to keep off frost and maintain a better temperature through the period of darkness. I have used this feature very effectively to keep frost away from tender young trees like walnuts – try a couple of big 9-in (22-cm) concrete blocks, either side of each young tree.

Let your new bed settle for at least a week before you get it ready for seeding (depending, of course, on the time of year). Fork over the top layer and smooth it around with your fork or a strong rake. Ideally, you will want to work some good compost into the top layer if it contains a high proportion of subsoil. If you don't do this your germination may be poor. You can avoid this risk if you transplant seedlings from elsewhere and this, in my view, is the best approach. You will find that crops such as onions, lettuce, corn, cucumbers, squash, and strawberries simply race away, as will the brassicas. However, plants like carrots and beets must obviously start from seed.

Sowing and Planting

What does a seed want? Moisture, warmth, and soil friable enough for its shoots to grow upward and its roots downward. This soil should be in close contact with the seed, and there really shouldn't be too much soil between the seed and the light, because the plant's growth depends on the energy collected from the sun by photosynthesis in its green leaves. This energy takes over from the energy stored in the seed when that is exhausted, and helps to protect the plant from its enemies. Very broadly speaking, there are two ways to establish vegetables. One is by sowing the seed directly into the ground where it is going to stay. The other is by sowing it somewhere else, and then transplanting later. And there are even occasions when we transplant the plants from where we sowed the seed into another bed, leave them there to grow for a while, and then transplant them again into their final bed.

SOWING

1 Fork over the ground. Mark out the rows, and stretch a garden line along each one. Drive a drill with a draw hoe at a suitable depth.

2 Sprinkle tiny seeds thinly. Large seeds (peas and beans) should be planted at regular intervals, usually recommended by the supplier. Water them gently.

3 When sowing is finished, rake the bed all over, so the entire surface becomes a fine tilth. This top layer of crumbly soil is the most important feature.

4 After you have raked the soil, step it down firmly with your feet or with the base of the rake. This ensures that the seeds are in close contact with the earth.

Why transplant? It seems such a laborious and time-consuming procedure. Well first, by crowding the seed in a seed bed, we release the land that the plants will ultimately take up, and can use it for another, earlier crop. So nearly all our brassicas (cabbage tribe), leeks, and those other plants that will grow through the fall and possibly into winter occupy very little ground for the first half of the summer. Then we put them in ground vacated by earlier crops, such as early spuds or peas, so we get two crops off the land in one year. Secondly, transplanting gives seeds a good start when done in a seed bed under glass, plastic, or other covering. This way, those of us who live in the more temperate climates can start seeds earlier and give them an initial boost, so that they will come to harvest during our short summer.

PLANTING

1 Crowd the seeds into a seed box, so that the land where they will eventually grow will be able to bear another early crop in the meantime.

2 Or you can plant your seeds in pots. As the seedlings grow, thin them out to allow the strongest seedlings more room for their roots to develop.

Soil for seed boxes

The sort of soil you put in your flats, or seed boxes, or pots is very important. If you just put in ordinary topsoil, it will tend to crack, and dry out, and it will have insects and disease organisms in it that may flourish in the hot air of the greenhouse. If you can get and afford prepared potting composts, then get them. The expense is justified by results. These composts are carefully blended and well sterilized. If you can't or don't want to buy them, you will have to manufacture potting composts of your own. The fundamental ingredients of the prepared composts are loam, peat, and sand.

You can make the loam by digging top quality meadow turves and stacking them, grass side down, with a sprinkling of good compost or manure in between each layer of turves. Stack them in 6–ft (1.8–m) layers, and leave them for 6–12 months. The loam should be sterilized. This is best done by passing steam through it: put the loam in any container with holes in the bottom and place it over a vessel of boiling water. Peat can be bought in bales or dug from a peat bog and sterilized by simply in water. There are certain crops which respond better to being grown in peat pots before they are transplanted, rather than in flats or seed boxes – corn, melons, squashes to name a few.

These and other semi-hardy plants don't like having their roots interfered with. When you plant the peat pot direct in the ground, the roots will simply drive their way through the wet peat and the plant won't suffer.

Compost composition

Seed compost, for putting in flats or seed boxes is by volume: 2 parts sterilized loam; 1 part sterilized peat; 1 part coarse sand. To each bushel (25.5 kg) of the above add 1½ oz (40 g) of superphosphate of lime and ¾ oz (20 g) of ground chalk or ground limestone.

Potting compost is by volume: 7 parts sterilized loam; 3 parts sterilized peat; 2 parts coarse sand. To each bushel kg (25.5) add ¼ lb (115 g) of base fertilizer and ¾ oz (20 g) ground chalk or limestone.

Base fertilizer is by weight: 2 parts hoof and horn meal; 2 parts superphosphate of lime; 1 part sulfate of potash.

3 When the seedlings of your first seed box look overcrowded, prick them out. This means thinning and removing to a box or bed for room to grow.

4 Give your seeds a good start by putting them in pots or seed boxes under glass. They will grow and thrive earlier than they would if left in the open air.

Transplanting

Consider what a trauma transplantation must be for a plant, which is a life form evolved for growing all its life in one place. It is wrenched out of the ground, and most of the friendly earth is shaken from its tender roots which themselves are probably severely damaged. Then it is shoved roughly into some alien soil, possibly with much of its root system not in contact with the soil at all and the rest jammed together into a matted ball.

So dig plants out gently and be sure that as much soil adheres to their roots as possible. Transplant them gently into friable soil with their roots spread naturally as they were before. Make sure the soil is well firmed, but not roughly trampled so as to break off tender roots. Then "puddle" (completely saturate) them. It is drying out that kills most transplants. Plant when it is raining, or rain is forecast. Put large plants in with a trowel and smaller ones with a dibber (basically a pointed stick). If a moderate tug on the plant doesn't pull it out, it will be all right. With larger or delicate plants, e.g. tomatoes or corn, keep a ball of soil on the roots and place very carefully in a hole dug with a trowel. Then firm the soil around them.

Growing under Cover

You can get a greenhouse with all the bells and whistles: thermostats, propagators, electric fumigators, and hell knows what. But if you buy this sort of equipment you are spending the money that would buy you out-of-season vegetables for many decades. Consider: is it really worthwhile going to great trouble and expense in order to have some vegetable or fruit ready a couple of weeks earlier than you would otherwise? Unless the self-supporter intends to make greenhouse production a main item of bartering or money earning, only the simplest of greenhouses is justified (see pp.90–91) with maybe some cold frames, hot frames, and a few cloches.

Cold frames

If you make four low walls and put a pane of glass on them, sloping to face the sun, you have a frame. The walls can be made of wood, bricks, concrete blocks, rammed earth, what you will. The glass must be set in wooden frames so that it can be raised or lowered. Frames are fine for forcing on early lettuces and cabbages, for growing cucumbers later in the summer, or for melons and all sorts of other things. Most of them are too low for tomatoes.

Hot frames

These are much used by skillful French market gardeners, and are a fine, economical way to force on early plants, but they do need skill. Start with a hot bed, that is a pile of partly rotted farmyard manure or compost. The best is stable manure: horse manure mixed with straw, mixed with an equal part of leaves or other composting material so it won't be too hot. Turn this a couple of times until the first intense heat of fermenting has gone off and the strong smell of ammonia, then lay it down in your frame with a shallower layer of earth on top. You should manure 2½ ft (75 cm) deep with 12 in (30 cm) of soil over it. The seed should be put in when the temperature falls to about 80 F° (27°C). You can transplant plants into the bed. You need to do this in the late winter or early spring, so that as the hot bed cools, the spring advances, and the heat of the sun replaces the heat of the manure. You will then have lovely, well-rotted horse manure. A well-made compost heap with some activator will work, too. Growing in a hot frame is not as easy as it sounds, get the procedure right and it is highly effective.

> "If I just look at a glass cloche it falls to pieces.

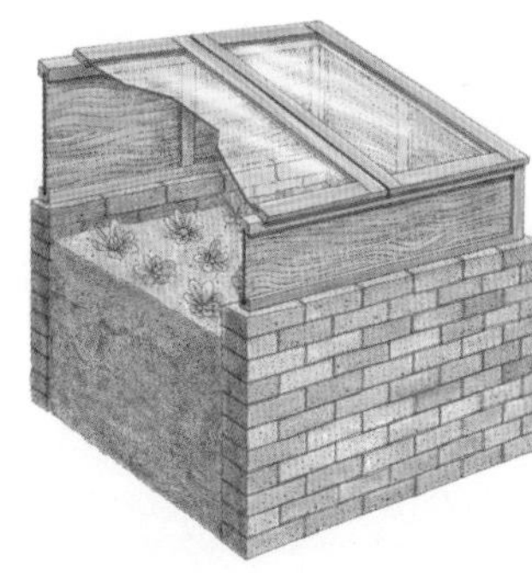

HOT FRAME
Enough heat to last from late winter right through spring comes from a thick layer of decomposing manure or compost. Cover with a layer of soil.

CARDBOARD BOX
A cardboard box painted black absorbs the sun's heat and aids germination.

PLASTIC SHEETING
A transparent plastic sheet will help germination and force on early vegetables.

Cloches

The first cloches were bell-shaped glass bowls, and were much used in France. They were simply inverted over the plants to be forced. These were replaced by continuous cloches, which are tent or bar-shaped glass sheds placed end to end to form long tunnels. These are much cheaper, which is a good thing, because if you are half as clumsy as I am, your cloche-managing career will be incessantly punctuated by the merry tinkling sound of breaking glass. If I just look at a glass cloche, it falls to pieces, so when you reflect that you have to hoe around crops, hand-weed, water (very necessary for crops under cloches as they do not get the rain), thin, inspect, and harvest, so cloches keep coming off and going back on each time you do such an operation, you will realize that cloche mortality can be very high.

CLOCHES AND A COLD FRAME
A cold frame is four walls with glass across them (top right). Cloches are portable: (above left to right) hard plastic cloche; glass barn cloche; soft plastic tunnel cloche; simple corrugated plastic cloche; glass tent cloche. A weighted-down plastic sheet "fleece" (top center) will also do.

Polythene tunnels supported by inverted U-shaped wires are all over the place now. They don't shatter, but can very easily be blown away in a gale, and blown to pieces. However, they do work, and many people use them now – market gardeners on a grand scale. Getting them on and off enormously increases the labour involved in growing a crop, but harvesting a couple of weeks early may well make the difference between profit and loss. PVC, by the way, retains the heat more efficiently than polythene, but is more expensive. And don't neglect the humble jelly jar. One of these inverted over an early-sown seed or plant of some tender species will protect it as well as any cloche. A sheet of any transparent plastic spread on the ground and weighted down on the edges with earth is fine for forcing on early potatoes and so on. When you do this sort of thing you must be careful to harden off the plants gradually.

Propagators

You can use a propagator to get very early seeds going. This is an enclosed glass box with soil in it and under-soil electric heating. It produces the condition known as "warm feet but cold head." Tomato seeds can be germinated in one in January in a temperate climate, but the air above it must be kept at 45°F (7°C) at least, as well as the soil being warm. A propagator is a good investment if you have the time and skill to grow your own tomato plants from seed.

Protecting from Pests

The weeds that grow so merrily in our gardens, in defiance of all efforts to wipe them out, are tough organisms, and well adapted to protect themselves from most enemies and diseases. They wouldn't be there otherwise. But our crops have evolved gradually through artificial selection so as to be succulent, good to eat, and productive of high yields. As a result, their natural toughness and immunity against pests and diseases have often been sacrificed to other qualities. We must therefore protect them instead; but avoiding attack by pests and diseases is not so easy. You will always get some losses, but they should not reach serious proportions. An organic farmer I know who farms a thousand acres with never an ounce of chemicals, and whose yields for every crop he grows are well above the national average, says that in his wheat he can show you examples of every wheat disease there is, but never enough of any one for it to make the slightest difference to his yield.

If you observe the principles of good husbandry, by putting plenty of animal manure or compost on the land, and by keeping to strict crop rotations (never grow the same annual crop on a piece of land two years running, and always leave the longest possible gap between two crops of the same plant), you will avoid many troubles. It's also important to encourage a highly diversified floral and faunal environment for balance between species: plenty of predators of various kinds kill the pests before they get out of hand. Destroy all forms of life with poisonous chemicals and you destroy all the predators, too. So when you do get a plague of some pest there will be no natural control, and you will be forced to use chemicals again.

> A few pests on healthy crops do very little harm.

Nevertheless, there will be times when, no matter how organically you farm, some infernal pest or disease gets the upper hand and something must be done if you are not to lose the crop.

WORKING WITH NATURE NOT AGAINST IT

Nasturtiums repel cucumber beetle and Mexican bean beetle.

Toads will eat nasties such as slugs, aphids, and mosquitoes.

Thrushes eat snails which would otherwise damage your plants.

Moles eat pests, including millipedes, that like potatoes.

Mint with its smell keeps white fly off beans.

Lacewings and their larvae destroy aphids.

Centipedes eat slugs' eggs and are the gardener's friend.

Ladybugs aren't just pretty. They consume aphids by the thousand.

Chemical pest control

Orthodox gardeners will say use poison. You can indeed use some poison, and maybe sometimes you will have to; but surely it is far better and more skillful gardening practice to save your crops without using poison? Any fool can keep disease at bay simply by dousing his crop with chemicals, but what of the effect on other, benign, forms of life? If a chemical is poisonous to one thing, you can be certain it will be poisonous to other forms of life too – including human life – and will do damage even if it doesn't end up killing someone.

The only chemicals I use are Bordeaux mixture against blight in potatoes. To make a Bordeaux mixture, I dissolve 4 lb (1.8 kg) copper sulfate in 35 gallons (160 liters) of water in a barrel, or in plastic garbage cans. Then slowly I sake 2 lb (0.9 kg) freshly burned quicklime with water and make it into 5 gallons (23 liters) of "cream." I slowly pour this cream through a sieve into the copper sulfate solution. Make sure that all your copper has been precipitated by putting a polished knife blade in the liquid. If it comes out coated with a thin film of copper you must add more lime. Burgundy mixture is even stronger and more drastic. It has 12½ lb (5.7 kg) washing soda instead of lime.

These mixtures must be used fresh, because they won't keep long. Spray with a fine spray very thoroughly. Soak the leaves above and below too. All the spray does is prevent spores getting in. Do it just before the haulms (tops) meet over the rows and again, perhaps a week later. An alternative is to dust with a copper lime dust when the dew is on. Blight attacks vary in date: it needs warm, moist, muggy weather.

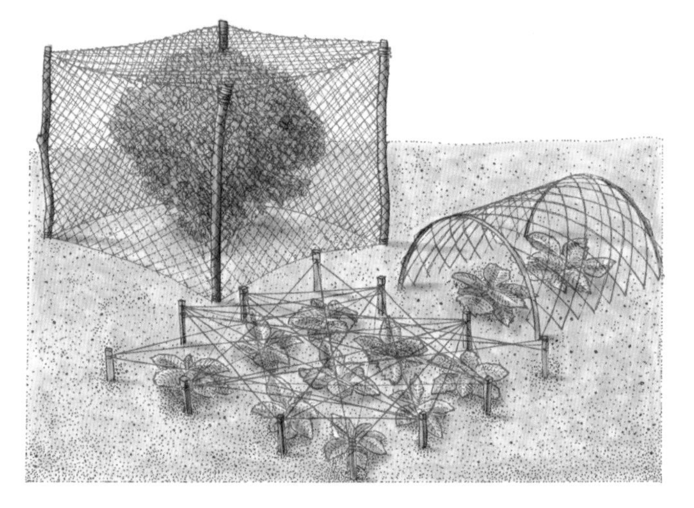

WIRE AND STRING PROTECTION
Young plants and bushes need protection from birds. Four sticks and some soft netting can cage in a growing bush effectively. Cover seedlings with wire netting stretched across hoops, or with a mesh of string wound on wooden pegs.

INTERCROPPING WONDERS
Carrots and onions, for example, repel each other's enemies.

KEROSENE-SOAKED SAND STRIPS
Strips of sand soaked in kerosene between rows of onions will deter onion fly.

RHUBARB VS. CLUBROOT
A piece of rhubarb under a brassica seedling frightens off clubroot.

THE BEER TRAP FOR SLUGS
Lure them from underground by sinking a saucerful in the ground in mid-summer.

I have also tried various poisoned baits against slugs, and rotenone or pyrethrum or a mixture of both against caterpillars and aphids. Rotenone and pyrethrum are plant-derived and nonpersistent in the environment, but they are toxic to fish and some mammals and should be used carefully. I have tried calamine (mercuric chloride) against clubroot, but it was ineffective.

Biological pest control

Comparatively little research has been done into natural, or biological, means of defense, simply because there is no money to be made out of doing such research. No big company will look into ways of controlling pests and diseases which aren't going to make it any profit (and which will even operate against the profits it already makes by selling poisonous chemicals).

Here are some tips recommended by Garden Organic (formerly Henry Doubleday Association) in England, as well as other sources. Many are merely confirmations of old and tried methods that have been used by farmers for centuries.

- Tie sacking strips or corrugated cardboard around fruit trees in late summer, and then burn complete with weevils, codling moth grubs, and other nasties.
- Put a very good old-fashioned grease-band around tree boles to catch nasties coming up. Most predators fly.
- Cut off all dead wood from stone fruits in early summer and burn as a guard against silverleaf and dieback.
- Spray dormant oil on fruit trees in winter – only if needed, for it kills useful predators as well as nasties.
- Use plenty of potash to prevent chocolate-spot in beans.
- Grow winter-sown broad beans instead of spring-sown to avoid blackfly. Pick out the tips of broad-bean plants at the first sign of aphid attack.
- Avoid carrot fly by interplanting with onions. The smell of the one is said to jam the smell of the other; thus you avoid both carrot and onion fly. Putting sand soaked with paraffin around carrot or onion rows may be more effective.
- Rigorously get rid of every brassica weed (wild mustard and shepherd's purse) so as not to harbor clubroot.
- Drop bits of rhubarb down each hole before you plant out brassica seedlings, or better still, water seed beds and seedlings with rhubarb-water. The smell of the rhubarb is said to deter the clubroot organism. This is an old remedy.
- Sink basins full of beer into the ground to trap slugs. Or save the beer and use milk and water instead.

My own experience is that, except for potato blight, if you don't spray occasional plagues of caterpillars on brassicas, and occasional aphid attacks, there is no need to worry as long as you work with nature, not against it. A few pests on healthy crops do very little harm – certainly not enough to worry about.

Maintaining a Healthy Plot

If you follow the basic tenets of the self-supporting gardening, working with nature not against it, feeding the soil and recycling everything possible, you will not be exposed to the same pest and disease problems as the monoculture gardener planting the same plant in the same place year in, year out.

Certainly we are all fixated with the notion of magic bullets to cure all ills. You will indeed find many promises of such in garden centers. In fact, much of their brightly colored, heavily promoted, and often nasty products are simply offshoots from chemical warfare. Most selective weedkillers, defoliants, insecticides, and fungicides are deadly poison. Suffice it to say we do not want to pollute our own small havens of the natural world with by-products of chemical warfare or, at the very least, chemicals whose effects we know very little about. So what is the answer?

First, it must be clear that in the natural world there is an enormous and very beautiful variety of healthy plants with all their attendant bugs and fungi. Nature itself does have a multitude of checks and balances which militate against epidemics and vegetative wipeouts. We can try to mirror some of these stratagems in our planting and management. We want variety: we do not want great big plots with uniform cropping, which lends itself to the spread of pests or disease. Smaller fields or plots will help minimize the dangers. We want to avoid large areas of single-species planting. We want to arrange our plantings so there is a mix of perennials and annuals. Perennials provide excellent winter shelter for valuable black beetles and other insect predators. I like to think we have no annuals in the garden which are more than 15 ft (4.5 m) from a perennial. We want areas of wilderness close by. We want birds and insects in profusion. We want invertebrates, dragonflies, frogs, and toads. We want a vibrant and healthy soil with plenty of compost added annually; this is the best guarantee of strong, healthy plants. Regular cultivation of your soil, especially by rototilling, will also discourage the breeding of many pests. Good organic soil conditioners such as seaweed, dried blood, and bonemeal will also help.

> Sink basins full of beer into the ground to trap slugs. Or save the beer and use milk and water instead

Good soil, wise garden layout, effective garden hygiene, and sensible precautions against ineffective composting – these are all crucial. Making regular garden bonfires is the number-two priority, and having proper sheds and buildings with easily cleaned concrete floors is number three. Be ruthless about tearing up and composting or burning diseased material, always use good seed, and never try to store anything other than top-quality produce.

My preference is for a six-year rotation in the vegetable garden. Pests such as nematodes (worms like wireworm, eelworm, and many more) can wreak havoc if crops are grown too frequently in the same plot. One way to minimize damage on plants you want to harvest is to plant others that the pests may favor but which you do not want to harvest. I even make a dummy seed bed some years to attract the local cats, while I put rabbit wire around my real seed beds on a temporary basis.

CONSTANT TRAFFIC

Domestic pets and unsupervised children not to mention wildlife can play havoc with your land. Learn to control them or your months of hard work might be in vain.

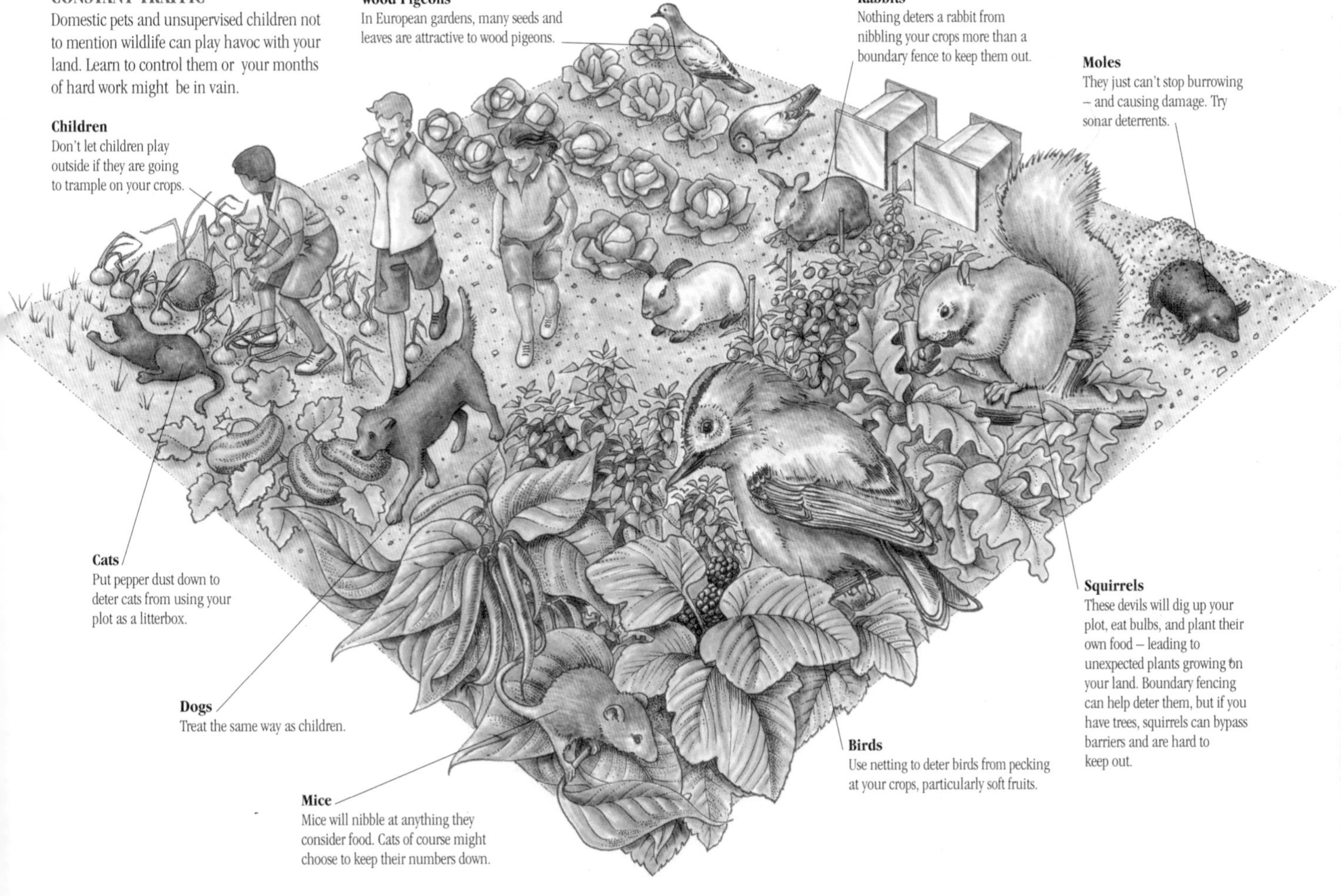

Children
Don't let children play outside if they are going to trample on your crops.

Wood Pigeons
In European gardens, many seeds and leaves are attractive to wood pigeons.

Rabbits
Nothing deters a rabbit from nibbling your crops more than a boundary fence to keep them out.

Moles
They just can't stop burrowing – and causing damage. Try sonar deterrents.

Cats
Put pepper dust down to deter cats from using your plot as a litterbox.

Dogs
Treat the same way as children.

Mice
Mice will nibble at anything they consider food. Cats of course might choose to keep their numbers down.

Birds
Use netting to deter birds from pecking at your crops, particularly soft fruits.

Squirrels
These devils will dig up your plot, eat bulbs, and plant their own food – leading to unexpected plants growing on your land. Boundary fencing can help deter them, but if you have trees, squirrels can bypass barriers and are hard to keep out.

FRIENDS TO THE GARDEN

Birds, beetles, bugs, bees, and many other insects and animals can be your greatest allies. Even chickens and ducks will help keep pests at bay in the orchard. Your own well-behaved dog can keep away the neighbors' marauding cats, whose scraping, defecating, and rolling will devastate your seed beds. (Make sure no one is allowed to throw sticks for your dog in the garden – smashed plants and mangled seed beds are sure to follow.) Here are some of the main allies.

Bees

Not only do bees supply us with copious quantities of honey, but they also provide a vital service in pollinating our garden crops. Make sure you have a healthy bee population in and around your garden.

Birds

Although some birds cause us trouble by robbing fruit and nibbling vegetables, there are many which eat insects, so we would be wise to encourage these. Blackbirds, robins, starlings, and thrushes constantly search out insects, caterpillars, and slugs. You can encourage birds by feeding in winter and by providing water in summer.

Centipedes

These are fast-moving little hunters who must not be confused with the millipede, which is slow and has more legs. Centipedes eat mites, bugs, and slugs.

Frogs and Toads

These require water for breeding and are extremely sensitive to poisons. Both eat insects in large quantities. They will travel all over your garden, provided you have areas of long grass or shade for them to lurk in.

Ground Beetles

There is a large family of beetles, mostly large black ones, that live on the ground and eat other insect pests, including the root fly larvae. These beetles need cover to survive the winter, hence the importance of perennial crops and hedges.

Hedgehogs

This little fellow is the great consumer of slugs in British backyards. Encourage him if you can with a bowl of bread and milk. He will need rough hedges and leaves to make his winter hibernation bed.

Hoverfly

Looking like small wasps, these pretty insects have larvae with a voracious appetite for aphids. The larvae are nasty-looking little creatures with a pair of nippers to hold their aphid prey. Encourage hover flies by growing flowers in your vegetable garden – they seem particularly fond of yellow flowers.

Lacewings

These delicate insects so beloved by trout are encouraged by water. Their larvae, which are flattish with a brown body, have a great appetite for aphids.

Ladybugs

The famous ladybug is the best-known predator for aphids. The adult and larvae both eat aphids. The larvae are gray in color and are very active killers.

Worms

Earthworms and manure worms are the two species of worm that we most want to see in our gardens. Earthworms are the great soil builders, constantly aerating the soil and bringing new soil to the surface as worm castes and dragging organic material down. If you have ever wondered why Roman remains are buried under several feet of earth, you only need to watch what happens on your garden lawn. I have taken soil plugs from my lawn where you can see clearly the depth of various dressings I have applied over the years. It is as plain as a pikestaff that these layers get deeper by about 1 in (2.5 cm) every 10 years. They get deeper as the worms push out new soil above them – so 1,000 years of worm activity would represent about 8 ft (2.5 m) of earth! Yes, it really does happen – worms are constantly digging under those old ruins and pushing up new soil all around them. Manure worms, on the other hand, are thinner and redder than earth worms. They rapidly turn organic material into compost and are the essential basis of worm composting. Buy them from bait shops as "brandlings" and you can build your own worm composter very easily. Manure worms like warm, wet places and will avoid material that is drying out.

INSECT PESTS

And here are some of your foes.

Aphids

Aphids come in all shorts of shapes, colors and sizes and affect a huge range of plants. Aphid damage will be limited if your plants are strong and healthy. Believe it or not, these plants will almost instantly create their own chemical defenses to limit the attacks. If your plants are weak and your garden has few natural aphid predators, then you will have to resort to other control methods. Soft soap mixed with warm water and then sprayed on will reduce small infestations. Alternatively, you can brew up your own homemade deterrents, such as boiling up rhubarb leaves or wormwood with water. The most lethal solution can be made from the deadly poison nicotine, which you can extract from old cigarette butts immersed in hot water.

Beetles

There are a range of beetles that are harmful to the garden – mostly through the appetites of their larvae. The most common are the chafer beetle and the flea beetle. Chafer beetles feed mainly on the leaves, flowers, and fruits of plants, while the grub destroys the roots, making the leaves wilt and the plant die. Continuous cultivation and good weed control are the main preventive measures. As you cultivate you may see and be able to gather up the grubs you find near affected plants.

Flea beetles eat small, round holes in the leaves of plants; their grubs tunnel into stems and eat roots. Control the beetle by making sure soil is clear of debris in the winter to deprive them of wintering quarters. Keep seedlings growing fast in dry weather by watering. Dust seedlings with calcified seaweed when the dew is still on the leaves in the early morning.

Big Bud Mite
This small mite attacks blackcurrants and sometimes red or white currants. As the name implies it creates "big buds" in early spring – these contain the mites and can be broken off and burned. You can spray with a solution of lime sulfur, but only when the buds have opened at the time when the plants are just showing full leaf. Use 1 pint (0.5 l) of lime sulfur to 7 gallons (4.5 l) of water and spray every 3 weeks.

Capsid Bugs
Similar to aphids but smaller and more virulent, capsid bugs cause small brown patches to appear on leaves, making them distorted and causing them to fall off. Keep the bottoms of your fruit trees well cleaned out during winter and replace mulches to prevent overwintering. Dormant oil sprays are helpful but the only effective summer control is by spraying with nicotine.

Caterpillars
The white butterfly is the great creator of caterpillars – and is a pretty but unwelcome guest in our summer gardens. The main control is to net seedlings with lightweight wire frames. Then, when plants are too large for the frames, remove the caterpillars by hand each day and destroy them. If your plants are really badly affected, they are better off being destroyed than abandoned.

Cutworm
Cutworms are the caterpillars of any of several moths, which feed at night on the stems of young plants, cutting them off at the ground. They attack the stems of seedlings at ground level. The damage is similar to slugs but without the slime. Keep weeds down to discourage cutworms. You can collect them by hand and then destroy if attacks are serious.

Nematodes
These worms are very small, even microscopic, but they breed in immense numbers and can do considerable damage to a range of crops. Prevention by good rotation and hygiene is the best remedy. Affected leaves may show brown discolorations between the veins. There is no really effective cure, although affected leaves and stems may be removed and burned. Potato nematode is a major problem if good rotation is not practiced. Leaves turn yellow before dying off, and when lifted the tubers will be marble-sized. The roots are attacked, creating small white or yellow cysts that can be seen with a magnifying glass. Each crop of potatoes should be at least six years apart on the same piece of land. Affected plants should be burned. Root-knot nematodes affect a range of plants, causing deformities in the roots and small galls, which may run together and cause general swelling. The affected plants die and there is no cure – plants must be burned and the same crop not planted in that area for at least six 6 years.

Rootfly
There are a number of important plants which are attacked by their own particular rootfly. Cabbage and carrot are the most common. Affected plants will discolor and wilt before they die. Cure is by prevention. Attack is most likely after cabbage seedlings have been transplanted. Make sure these are well-watered and earthed up.

In carrots, the attacks are encouraged by even the minutest damage to plants when thinning or weeding. Great care should be taken to remove all thinnings immediately – thin when the ground is damp and make sure the remaining plants are well covered with soil at ground level. If your carrots are continually affected, cover the whole bed with a store-bought fine-mesh netting, burying the edges carefully to prevent the flies from gaining access.

Red Spider Mites
These tiny mites look (under a magnifying glass) as their name suggests, and the main types attack greenhouse plants and fruit trees. Mites and larvae live on sap from leaves, which first have yellow spots and then turn brown. Keep plants cool and moist to avoid attack by spraying with water twice daily. There are biological controls available which can be bought and used commercially in greenhouses. With fruit trees control is difficult – remove and burn affected leaves.

Slugs
These gray, black, and orange plant munchers are the gardener's constant companions. Keep weeds and grass controlled to minimize their habitat – good garden hygiene plays a major role in prevention. Slugs can devastate your vegetables and have particular preferences, such as runner beans and basil. You can use piles of old leaves as hiding places which you can pick up and compost – old newspaper or planking placed on grass will also attract slugs. You can prepare slug traps using jelly jars set into the ground and filled with sweetened beer and water. Or, finally, as a last resort, you can go out at night with a flashlight and collect the little blighters. Dressing your soil with calcified seaweed or fresh wood ash will also limit attacks, as slugs dislike traveling over sharp dry material. Soot also works well but it will damage plants if it touches them.

Weevils
The larvae of weevil beetles attack a wide range of plants – particularly apple blossom, peas, beans, and turnip. In the orchard the pest can be controlled by catching the pupating larvae in bands of sacking around the trunks in June – then burning later. Keeping the soil clean, free from debris, and full of fertility will also reduce damage, as will good crop rotation.

Wireworms
These destructive worms inhabit grassland and can be very destructive when it is first cultivated. They are the larvae of the click beetle and live as brown wiry worms about 1 in (2.5 cm) long for four or five years before pupating. They are particularly destructive in potatoes in late summer. Newly cultivated grassland may be affected for up to 3 years – so you can plant resistant crops such as peas and beans. You can catch wireworms and destroy them by punching holes in a tin can, filling it with potato peelings, and burying it in the ground. Lift the can every three or four days and then tip out the peelings into a bucket of water to drown the wireworms. A green manure of mustard dug into the soil can help reduce the pest, but there are no effective sprays.

Vegetables

If you grow just a few of the vegetables listed below, you can eat your own fresh produce from early spring to late fall. And, if you grow the right things and store them properly, or if you set yourself up with a greenhouse, you can have your own vegetables year-round and need never again suffer a flabby lettuce or a tasteless tomato.

ARTICHOKES

Use As perennials they are a long-term proposition. I would not recommend them as the crop to feed a hungry world, but the object of the self-supporter should be to have a rich and varied diet. Basically, globe artichokes are huge thistles, and we eat their flower heads – and not even all of these; just the little bit at the base of each prickly petal and the heart, which lies under the tuft of prickles that are immature petals. Globe artichokes are delicious beyond description. Just boil the whole flower head, pull off the petals, and eat with just-warmed butter or an oil and vinegar mix.
Sowing In spring, plant the artichoke suckers from an existing plant, each with a piece of heel of the old plant attached. Plant them 4 in (10 cm) deep in well-manured and drained soil at 3 ft (1 m) intervals.
Aftercare Keep them well hoed.
Harvesting Spare the artichokes the first year but pluck the heads the second and each ensuing year. After five or six years, dig out and plant a new row somewhere else. If you plant a new row every year and scrap an old one, you will never have a year without artichokes to eat. Muck well every year and cover in winter with a thick mulch of straw.

JERUSALEM ARTICHOKES

Use These are a useful standby in winter as a substitute for potatoes. They can be lightly boiled or fried in slices.
Planting Just like potatoes, Jerusalem artichokes grow from tubers planted in early spring and are very easy to grow. They need only a little extra lime if your soil requires it. They are rarely attacked by pests.
Aftercare Hoe until the foliage is dense enough to suppress weeds.
Harvesting Dig up as you need them. They can be left in the ground throughout winter. Save a few mature tubers to plant next year. Cardoons are annuals but just like globe artichokes. The flowers can be eaten but in spring you can eat the stems like celery.

ASPARAGUS

Use Asparagus takes three years to get established, but are well worth the wait. They come very early – just when you need them – and are delicious and nutritious, perhaps one of the most valuable crops you can grow.
Soil They like a deep, light, well-drained loamy fertile soil. They will grow on sand if it has plenty of muck. Get rid of perennial weeds in your future asparagus bed: quack

grass or thistles can ruin a bed because they cannot be eliminated once the asparagus grows. The roots will get inextricably intertwined. I like a raised bed with three rows of plants – it tends to get higher because I put so much stuff on it. In autumn cover it thickly with seaweed.
Sowing Muck really heavily in autumn; in spring buy or beg three-year-old plants and plant 18 in (45 cm) apart, measuring from their middles. The plants look like large spiders. Don't let them, or the few inches of soil you pile on top of them, dry out.
Treatment Don't cut any the first year – not a single stick. In late autumn, cut the ferns down to the ground and muck well again. The following spring you can feed well with fish meal, mature chicken dung, seaweed, or salt (yes salt – asparagus is a seashore-plant), and weed again. Delay cutting till June. Muck again in the late autumn, and feed again in the spring.
Harvesting The third year, cut them just below the ground. You can cut away fresh asparagus ready to eat every two or three days (until later June); they soon shoot up again.

EGGPLANT

Use A delightful Mediterranean food, eggplants have an exotic taste and can be used for stews, ratatouille, and moussaka, or grilled on their own.
Sowing Sow seeds indoors in early spring. Sow them in compost and try to keep the temperature close to 60°F (16°C). Pot out into peat pots or soil blocks about a month later.
Planting Plant them out in the open in early summer. Protect them with cloches if you live in a cool climate. When you plant them, pinch out the growing points to make them branch. You can sow seeds under cloches in late spring to get a late crop.
Harvesting Pick them when they are deep purple and glossy. Pick before frost sets in.

BEETS

Use Beets are a very rich source of betain, which is one of the B vitamins. Beets therefore keep you healthy, particularly if you grate it and eat it raw, but it tastes a lot better cooked, although tiny immature beets are good raw.

Soil Beets likes light, deep loam, but most soil will do.

Treatment It doesn't like freshly manured

land, and wants a good fine seed bed.

Sowing In early summer sow your main beet crop very thinly; you only need a couple of seeds every 6 ins (15 cm). The seeds are multiple ones and you will have to thin anyway. Sow 1 in (2.5 cm) deep in rows 12 in (30 cm) apart.

Aftercare Thin and hoe. You can eat the thinnings raw in salads.

Harvesting Leave them in the ground until needed or until the heavy frosts set in. Otherwise lift in fall. Twist (don't cut) the tops off, not too near to the roots. Clamp or store in sand in a cool cellar.

BROAD BEANS

Use You can pick off the tops off fall-sown broad beans and cook them. You can eat the seeds when they are green, or you can dry them for winter. Rub the skins off winter-dried beans to make them more tender.

Soil They will grow in most soil.

Treatment Treat as you would peas. Lime well and use plenty of mulch.

Sowing I like to sow broad beans in late fall, but you can plant in early spring on light, well-drained soil. The later you sow, the more trouble you are likely to have from aphids. Sow 3 in (8 cm) deep, each seed

8 in (20 cm) from the next, in two rows that are 8 in (20 cm) apart. Common sense will tell you to stagger the seed in the rows. Each pair of rows should be 30 in (75 cm)away from the next pair.

Aftercare In spring, as soon as the aphids attack, pick the tender tops off and eat them.

Harvesting Continue to hoe the soil as well of course. Pick your broad beans as they are ready and pick as hard as you can. Dry any that are left after the summer.

HEARTING BROCCOLI OR WINTER CAULIFLOWER

Use Hearting broccoli are like cauliflower. They are a damned good winter and early spring standby, and you can have heads from late summer one year until early summer the next year if you plant successionally and use a number of different varieties.

Soil Hearting broccoli likes good, heavy, firm soil, but will grow in most soils as long as it is well manured.

Treatment Like all brassica, broccoli needs lime and doesn't like acid soil. It likes deeply cultivated, but very firm soil.

Sowing Start sowing in seed beds in late spring and go on for four or five weeks.

Planting Plant out as soon as the plants are ready and you have the ground. Seedlings are ready when they are a several inches high and you can see at least four leaves. Plant 2 ft (60 cm) apart and use rows 30 in (75 cm) apart.

Aftercare Hoe regularly until the weeds stop growing in the autumn.

Harvesting Fall varieties can be cut in September and October; winter varieties from January to March; spring varieties can be harvested up to April. To get late heads, protect the curds (the white cauliflower heads) by bending leaves over them. Always cut when ripe and don't boil, just steam lightly. (Don't "steam launder" any brassica, as hospital kitchens and schools do. This boils the life out of them.) Steam lightly until soft but still firm.

SPROUTING BROCCOLI, PURPLE OR GREEN.

Use These are quite different from hearting broccoli. Purple sprouting broccoli is very hardy and a fantastic standby in late winter and early spring when there is not much other winter vegetables around. Basically you can have an early or late purple sprouting crop. Green broccoli or calabrese is delicious for fall use.

Treatment The same as for hearting broccoli (see above), except that green broccoli is planted in midsummer. You pick and eat the purple or green shoots when they appear. Don't pick the leaves until the very last moment, and then you can eat them, too.

BRUSSELS SPROUTS

Use Brussels sprouts are the most useful and delicious winter green vegetable. You simply cannot have too many of them
Soil Sprouts like deeply worked rich loam, but they will give a crop when planted in most soils as long as it is deeply worked and made very firm.
Treatment Put on compost or muck in the previous fall, or plant after a well-mucked crop. If your soil is lime-deficient, plant after a limed crop.
Sowing Sow out in the open in seed beds during early spring. If you want late sprouts, sow again in a few weeks' time.

Planting Plant them out in early summer in rows that are 3 ft (90 cm) apart. It is useful, especially in windy places, to give each plant a stake so that it can be supported and kept straight as it grows taller.
Aftercare Hoe when required. Intercrop, that is plant in alternate rows, with lettuce if you like, or another quick-growing catch-crop, because the spaces are wide. Keep free of slugs and caterpillars. If you didn't stake the plants in spring, in fall earth up the stems to give support and to encourage the growth of new roots.
Harvesting Early sprouts are ready in late summer but look on them, that is, if you live in a reasonably temperate climate, as a winter standby. In some nations, Christmas dinner without sprouts is a travesty and they should keep you going until spring. Pick off the leaves only after they have gone yellow. Use the tops of the plants after you have picked the sprouts.

CABBAGE

Use Cabbage is the most reliable of all the brassicas. It is not fussy about soil and treatment, yields a heavy crop per acre and some varieties can be stored in clamp, cellar, or sauerkraut vat. There are three kinds: spring, summer and autumn, and winter.

Spring cabbage
Soil Light soil is ideal.
Treatment They like fertile soil which is not acid, and it needn't be particularly firm.
Sowing Sow in the summer in a seed bed.
Planting Plant spring cabbage in fall, 1 ft (30 cm) apart in rows 18 in (45 cm) apart.
Aftercare Hoe regularly, and top-dress with nitrogen if you think they need it.

Harvesting Use as spring greens in the hungry gap – early spring – or leave a few to heart for eating in late spring and early summer.

Summer and fall cabbage
Soil They are not very fussy.
Treatment See Spring cabbage.
Sowing Sow in late winter in a cold frame or outdoors in spring.
Planting Plant a few where there is room in early summer.
Aftercare See Spring cabbage.
Harvesting You don't need many cabbages in summer, but pick them when you feel like a change.

Winter cabbage
Soil They like a heavy loam.
Treatment See Spring cabbage.
Sowing Sow in seed beds in April and May.
Planting Plant 2 ft (60 cm) apart in rows also 2 ft (60 cm) apart in midsummer.
Aftercare Hoe regularly. Don't bother to top-dress.
Harvesting Where winters are not too severe, leave them in the ground until you want them. Where there's lots of snow and ice, cut in fall and store or make sauerkraut.

Red cabbage
Treat the same as winter cabbage. Pickle or cook in oil and vinegar with spices. Cook it for some time because it is tough stuff.

CARROTS

Use Carrots have more vitamin A than anything else we are likely to grow. And of course they help you see in the dark. Carrots store well through the winter and are a most useful source of good food for the self-supporter. They can be eaten raw in salads or cooked with absolutely anything.
Soil Carrots like a deep, well-cultivated sandy loam. They grow well in very light soil, almost sand in fact.
Treatment Like most roots they fork if planted in soil which has recently been heavily manured with muck or compost, although well-matured compost doesn't seem to affect them so much.
Shakespeare compared Man to a forked carrot. So don't plant them after fresh muck. They don't like sour ground (a pH of about 6 is fine). The land must have been deeply dug and then worked down into a fine tilth.

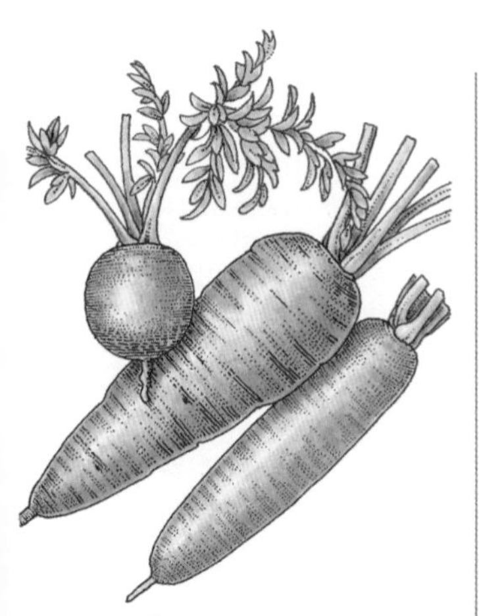

Sowing There is no point in sowing carrots until the ground is dry and warm, say, in the late spring. Carrots need a fine seed bed and will not thrive on acid soil so you may have to lime. Sow very shallowly, as thinly as you can, in rows 1 ft (30 cm) apart and tamp down rows with the back of the rake afterward. Some people sow a few radishes in with them to show where the rows are before the slower carrots emerge. Then they pull the radishes for eating when they are ready. Some people intercrop with onions, in the belief (and I support this) that the carrot fly is put off by the onions, and the onion fly is put off by the carrots.

Aftercare If you sow in dry weather, it is good to water the rows to start germination. Hoe the soil frequently and carefully so as not to damage the carrots, and be prepared to get down to hand-weed as well. Suffer not weeds to exist in your carrot rows. The crop takes a great deal of labor in hand-weeding as it grows slowly, far slower than the weeds in fact. To get a heavy crop, thin to about 3 in (8 cm) apart, then harvest every other carrot so as to leave them 6 in (15 cm) apart. This is best for big, tough carrots for winter storing. But, for summer and fall use, don't bother to thin at all. When you do thin, try to do it when it is raining (to thwart the carrot fly) After thinning, draw the soil around the plants and then tamp down so the scent of bruised carrots will not attract that beastly carrot fly.

Harvesting Pull them young and tender whenever you feel like it. Lift the main crop with a fork before the first severe frost of winter, and store in sand in a cool place such as a root cellar. You can clamp (see p.152) them but they sometimes go rotten in the clamp. Washed carrots won't keep whatever you do. They rot almost immediately.

CAULIFLOWER

Use Eat your cauliflower in summer and fall, as hearting broccoli are apt to take over during the winter. Cauliflowers yield well but in order to grow them successfully, you need skill and good land. They are not a beginner's crop.

Soil Cauliflowers want deep, well-drained, well-cultivated soil that has been well manured, and given ample water. They won't grow on bad land or under bad conditions.

Treatment They must have non-acid conditions, like all brassicas, so you must lime if necessary. Two weeks before planting, fork on or harrow in a good dressing of fish manure or such like. They will also need some potash.

Sowing Sow under cold glass in September or sow in a warm greenhouse in January or February. Sow outdoors in the late spring. Plant 24 in (60 cm) apart in rows 30 in (75 cm) apart.

Planting Fall and winter-sown plants go out in the spring; spring sown cauliflowers in summer.

Aftercare Hoe, of course. Ensure there is always plenty of moisture, as they can't withstand drought. Top-dress with nitrogen if you have any. Keep them moving – in other words, don't let them stop growing.

Harvesting Cut them when they are ready, early in the morning if possible. Don't boil them to death. They are nice boiled and then dipped in batter, fried, and eaten cold.

CELERIAC

Use You can grate the big swollen roots and eat them raw. Or you can peel and boil, or boil and then fry.

Sowing Sow, prick out, and plant out just like white celery.

Aftercare When you hoe, draw the soil away from the plants instead of earthing them up as you would for celery.

Harvesting Begin harvesting in fall. Earth them up in the middle of November for protection against winter frosts.

CELERY

White celery

Use It is said that celery is best after the first frost has been on it. If you are lucky it will keep going until a few weeks after Christmas, until the really filthy weather, provided that you ridge it well. Then it gets soggy and you'll get fed up with it. Celery is a most delicious and useful winter vegetable, whether eaten raw, as the blanched stems should be, or cooked in stews as the tops should be.

Soil It loves deep, fertile soil that is very moist but not swampy. The best celery is grown in soil that is high in organic matter and retains moisture. Whatever you do, don't let the soil dry out.

Treatment Celery prefers acid to alkaline conditions, so never give it lime. It needs plenty of humus so dig in muck or well-rotted compost where it is going to grow.

Sowing Sow celery under glass between 60°F and 65°F (16°C and 19°C) in spring, or buy plants from a nursery (we bought ours from a neighbor). The seedlings must be kept moist. Spray with water at least twice a day.
Planting Early summer is the usual time to plant. Plant very carefully 1 ft (30 cm) apart in trenches with muck underneath. Soak the plants well with water.
Aftercare You can grow catch crops such as lettuce or radish on ridges between the furrows. When these catch crops have been harvested, earth up the celery. Cut off the side shoots. Then hold the plants in a tight bunch and earth them up. Do this so that only the tops of the leaves are above the new ridges. Always keep ground moist. Never let it dry out. To prevent leaf blight, spray with Bordeaux mixture once or twice, as you would spuds. If you want to extend the eating season, in the winter protect the plants with straw, bracken, cloches, or what you will. You can also heel them in dry ground in a protected position if you fear very hard frost, but it makes harvesting difficult.
Harvesting Dig them out whenever you want them and eat them fresh.

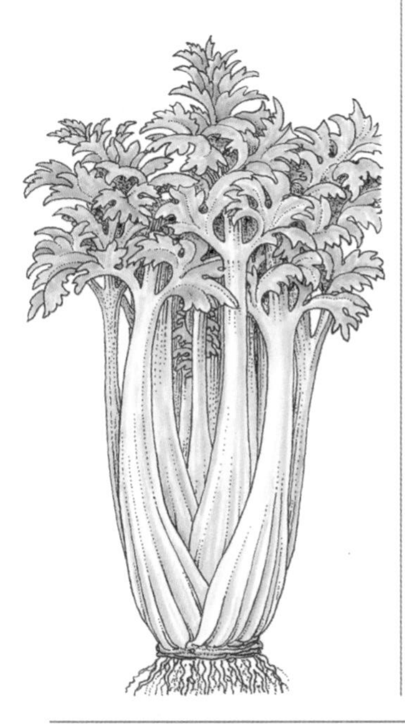

SELF-BLANCHING CELERY

You can grow this on the flat in the same conditions as ordinary or white celery but you don't need to earth it up. It gets used before the white celery and must be finished prior to hard frosts begin as it is not frost-hardy. It is not as good to eat as white celery but is a good autumn standby before white celery is ready.

CHICORY

Use Chicory is a good winter salad ingredient.
Sowing Sow the Witloof type of chicory in early summer in a fine tilth and thin to 1 ft (30 cm) apart in rows about 18 in (45 cm) apart.

Aftercare Cut down to just above the crown in November. Lift and plant in pots and keep in the dark at 50°F (10°C) or thereabouts. They will then shoot.
Harvesting Break the shoots off just before you need them. They should grow again every four weeks or so. Keep picking.

CORN SALAD

Use If you like eating salad in the winter this is an ideal crop for you. It produces leaves that taste like tender young lettuce.
Sowing Sow in drills 1 ft (30 cm) apart in late summer.
Harvesting Cut it when it's short with just three or four leaves. Don't let it get lanky.

CUCUMBERS

Use You can grow ridge cucumbers and pickling cucumbers, both of which are fine pickled, out of doors. Frame cucumbers, which are better looking and better tasting when fresh, are grown in frames or under cloches. A heated greenhouse is even better because you will get your cucumbers earlier.
Soil Cucumbers will grow on light soil if the soil has plenty of manure in it. They must have plenty of moisture, and they don't like acid soil.
Treatment Dig plenty of mulch in during the previous fall.
Sowing Frame cucumbers can be sown under cover in early spring – ideally start them off in a heated greenhouse, keeping the temperature at about 60°F (16°C). Outdoor types can't be sown until early summer unless you protect them for the first month. In wet climates plant six seeds of an outdoor variety on a small hill, 4 in (10 cm) high, and later thin out to the three best plants on each hill. In dry climates use the same method, but plant in a small depression that has had plenty of muck or compost dug below it the previous fall.
Planting Outdoor cucumbers just continue to grow where you have planted them. Frame cucumbers can be hardened off in early summer.

If you grow cucumbers in a greenhouse, pot them in peat pots as they grow big enough to handle, then plant them, pot and all, in the greenhouse soil when they look about to outgrow the pot. Always water them with warm water. Make sure you keep the greenhouse humid and well aired.
Aftercare They must have plenty of water and never be allowed to get dry. It helps to soak muck in the water. Ridge cucumbers should have all the male flowers pinched off them so that the female flowers that produce the cucumbers don't get fertilized. If they do, the fruit will be bitter. Ridge cucumbers should also have the growing points nipped out when the plant has seven true leaves.
Harvesting Pick them regularly while they are young and they will go on cropping. Pickle the last lot before the first frosts.

ENDIVES

Use A plant related to chicory, the crisp, curly, or broad leaves are used in salads during winter instead of lettuce.
Sowing Sow in mid-summer; place cloches over in late summer. Whitewash the cloches to keep out the light and the endives will blanch and make good winter salad fare. Blanching also helps to reduce the bitter flavor. For summer endives, sow out in the open from spring onward and eat in salads.

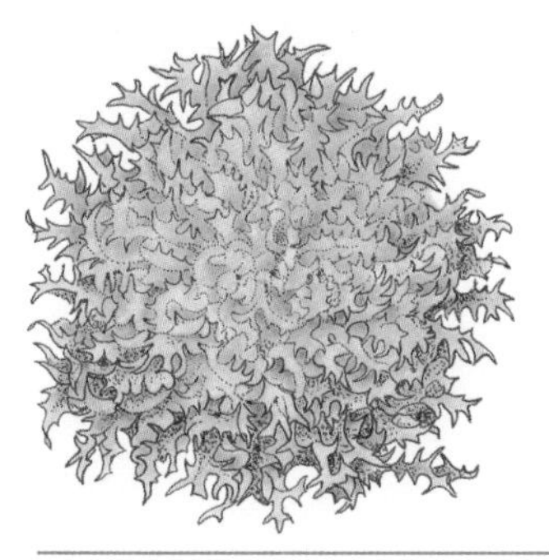

FRENCH BEANS AND DRIED BEANS

Use Haricots are ripe French beans that have been dried for winter use. Butter beans and Lima beans are specifically for drying and using in the winter. For vegetarians, such dried beans are really necessary, because they are about the only source of protein readily available to them in winter time. French beans can be eaten green, pods and all, just like runner beans.
Soil They all like lightish, well-drained and warm soil. It's no good trying to grow them in heavy clay or on sour land.

Treatment Like all the legumes, they grow best after a heavily mucked crop. Lime the soil well if necessary.
Sowing In temperate climes, sow in early summer. They are all very frost-tender, and won't thrive if sown in cold, damp ground. Sow in a wide drill, about 2 in (5 cm) deep, in two staggered rows, so the beans are about 6 in (15 cm) apart.
Aftercare Hoe well, and draw the soil around the plants. Dwarf varieties don't need sticking but high varieties do. Any arrangement of sticks, or wire and string supported on poles, will do.
Harvesting If the beans are for drying for the winter, let them get quite ripe and then pull the plants intact. Hang them upside down from the roof of an airy shed. Thresh them as required. If you are eating them green, pull them and pull again. The secret of having plenty of them, young and fresh, is to keep on picking.

KALE

Use Kale is very hardy and so is an excellent winter green standby. When I first grew it I put down marrow-stem and hungry-gap and planting out from a seed bed was a laborious process. The hungry-gap was indifferently successful: the marrow-stem good. Kale will grow in both cold and wet climates where there is little other greenstuff in winter and early spring. In the Highlands of Scotland the "kale yard" has often been the only source of greens in the harsh winters.
Soil Kale is not at all fussy but the richer the soil, the better the crop.
Treatment See Spring cabbage.
Sowing Sow in late April and early May in colder climes and early April in warmer ones.
Planting Sow the seed *in situ*, then thin instead of transplanting them, unless you need the land.

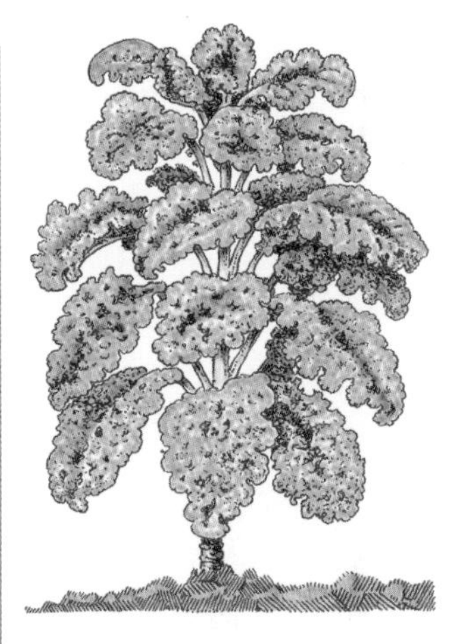

Aftercare See Spring cabbage.
Harvesting Leave until you really need it, that is, after the Brussels sprouts have rotted, the cabbages are finished, the slugs have had the rest of the celery, and the ground is 2 ft (60 cm) deep in snow and only your kale plants stand above it.

LEEK

Use In cold, wet areas this is one of the most useful plants, because it stands the winter as well as providing good food and vitamins in those months when perhaps little else has survived except kale. Onions are hard to grow and to keep but leeks are an easy substitute. It's hard to have enough of them and the Welsh are very sensible to have this excellent plant as an emblem and not some silly inedible flower or a damned thistle. There's also a nice creamed leek recipe on p.182.
Soil Leeks grow on pretty well any soil as long as it is not waterlogged.

Treatment Heavy manuring of leeks is advantageous. Most people plant them out on land from which early potatoes have been harvested and which has been heavily mucked for that purpose. However, if you can't lift your earlies before midsummer, this is too late. You must plant on other well dug and manured ground.
Sowing Sow the seed in the general seed bed 1 in (2 cm) deep and sow in rows about 1 ft (30 cm) apart in spring.
Planting The traditional way to plant leeks is to chop the bottoms off the roots and the tops off the leaves of the little plants and just drop the plants in small holes and leave them. If you do this they grow and make leeks, but I now believe that this is a silly idea and it is better not to mutilate the plants and also better to plant them properly. Why not try both methods and compare? Draw drills 3 in (8 cm) deep with a hand-hoe or a wheel-hoe and plant the leeks 5 in (13 cm) apart in the furrows. Create a biggish hole for each leek and plant carefully, making sure the little roots aren't doubled up. Don't press down as with onions. Just water them in and this will wash a little loose earth into the hole round the roots.

Aftercare Hoe and ridge them, raising the ridges from time to time so as to blanch the lower parts of the stems.
Harvesting Leave them until you really need them, and then toward the end of the winter dig them out and heel them in on another small piece of ground. Heeling in means opening a slot in the ground with a spade, putting the leeks in quite thickly, and heeling the earth back on their roots. They won't grow any more like this but they will keep alive and fresh until you need them.

LETTUCE

Use Lettuce is the firm base of salads all the fair months of the year, and with a little glass protection we can even have it through the winter if we feel we must. It is not a brassica so we needn't worry about clubroot.
Soil It likes good soil but will grow on most soil, especially if it is richly manured. Lettuce likes it cool and will stand shade, but will not grow well near trees. It likes a moist climate.
Treatment Dig in well-rotted muck or compost for summer lettuce, but not for winter, as winter lettuce doesn't like too much fresh manure: it gets botrytis. Work down to a fine seed bed.

Winter lettuce

Sowing and planting Sow about 1 inch (2 cm) deep in late summer and then expect to protect them with cloches or something over the winter. Of course, in very cold

climates, winter lettuce is out. You can sow winter lettuce in seed beds with the intention of planting them out in early spring to get an early crop. And of course you can get lettuce all winter in a heated greenhouse. There is a thing called lamb's lettuce which is a great standby for salad stuff in the winter time – true lettuce can be a bit of a dead loss then.

Summer lettuce

Sowing and planting Sow thinly starting in the spring with about 18 inches (45 cm) between rows. Thin the plants out to over one foot apart and transplant the thinning elsewhere because they transplant easily. Don't sow too much at one time; instead try to keep on sowing throughout the summer.
Aftercare Hoe and hoe and water whenever necessary. Keep eating.

SQUASHE, PUMPKIN

Use They can be kept for the winter and are rich in vitamins and highly nutritious.
Soil Nothing is better for these than to grow them on an old muck heap, and that is what we often do. They love a heavy soil.
Treatment If you don't plant on a muck heap, dig in plenty of muck or compost in the autumn.
Sowing Sow seeds *in situ* in late spring under cloches or better still, under upturned jelly jars. Otherwise sow in soil blocks or peat pots under glass. Harden plants off gradually in early summer by propping the jelly jars up in the day, for example, and putting them down again at night. Remove the glass, or plant the potted plants out in the open a few

weeks later. Plant three seeds to a station and have the stations about 6 ft (1.8 m) apart because these thing like to straggle.
Aftercare Hoe of course, and water when necessary, also mulch if you can, and beware of slugs.
Harvesting Keep cutting them when they are young and tender and you will get more. Young zucchinis are particularly good.
In late summer leave some to ripen and store

them out of the frost in a cool place, preferably hung up in a net. In southern Africa, where you don't get enough frost to mention, pumpkins are thrown up on corrugated iron roofs and left there all winter. They dry out in the winter sun, become delicious, and form the chief winter vegetable of that part of the world.

MELONS

Use Melons grow outdoors in warm climates and can be grown in cool climates outdoors as long as you start them off under cloches after the last frost. But they are best grown under protective frames in cooler climates.
Treatment Treat them exactly like cucumbers but don't remove the male flowers. Plant them on small hills 6 ft (1.8 m) apart.

ONIONS

Use Good food is inconceivable without onions.
Soil Onions are demanding: they like medium loam well drained, deeply dug and richly composted.
Treatment The soil must not be acid, so if necessary lime it in the fall. Dig deeply in the fall months and incorporate manure or compost. Get it down to a fine tilth in the spring and then get it really firm because firm soil is a necessity for onions to grow well.
Sowing You can sow in midsummer and leave in the seed bed until spring. Or you can sow in early spring, or as early as the ground is dry enough to walk on without it caking. Sow very shallowly, and very thinly in rows of about 10 in (25 cm) apart, if you intend to thin the onions and grow them *in situ*. But you can have the rows much closer together if you intend to plant them all out. Rake the seed in very lightly and firm the soil with the head of the rake.
Planting Plant very firmly in firm soil, but don't plant too deeply. Plant summer-sown seedlings in early spring – whenever the soil is dry enough. Inter-rowing with carrot is said to help against onion fly, and I believe inter-rowing with parsley is even better.
Aftercare Growing onions means a fight against weeds, which seem to love onions, and the onions have no defense against them from broad, shading leaves as many crops have. Now I know that some people say onions will grow well in a mass of weeds, but my experience is that you must keep them free of weeds in the early months of their growth. It is true that if large annual weeds grow among them for, say, the last month, they may still grow into good onions. I like to keep them weed-free and mulch them well with pulled-out weeds in their later stages. If you are growing onions *in situ* in the seed bed, single them in about 4 in (10 cm) apart. If you have sown very thinly you might like

to try not thinning at all. You will get smaller onions but they will keep better.
Harvesting When the tops begin to droop, bend them all over to the ground. This is said to start the onions ripening, and possibly it also stops them from growing up and going to seed. After a few days pull the onions and lay them down on bare soil or better still on a wire netting frame to keep them clear of the ground. Turn them occasionally. The more hot sun that falls on them the better. Before the fall string them and hang them up, or hang them in net bags, or lay them on wire netting in a cool and drafty place. The air must be able to get between them. They don't mind some frost, but can't stand lack of ventilation.

Shallots

Sow the bulbs in late winter and you get lots of little onions that grow around the first bulb next summer. You can then go on picking until fall. Keep some of the best bulbs to plant next year.

Tree onions

These onions are perennial so once you have planted them they will grow year after year. Each year, when the plant grows, little onions will form at the tips of the stems. When this happens you must support the weight of the plant on sticks. Plant 6 in (15 cm) apart in rows 18 in (45 cm) apart. You can use the onions that form underground as well as those on the leaf tips.

Pickling onions

These like poor soil. Broadcast the seed in spring and lightly rake it in. Hand-weed but don't thin. Pull and pickle when ready.

Salad onions

Sow these like ordinary onions in late summer and again if you like in early spring. Don't thin, and pick to eat as required.

Onion sets

These are the lazy man's way of planting onions. Sets are immature bulbs, with their growth arrested by heat treatment. Plant them early in the spring very firmly, and replant any the birds pull out. Then treat them like ordinary onions. They are much easier to grow.

PARSNIPS

Use Parsnips make the best of the root wines, and, properly cooked and not just boiled to death, are a magnificent vegetable, very rich in vitamins A, B, and C.

Soil Parsnips will grow on any soil, provided it is deep and not too stony. As with all root vegetables, don't use fresh manure.

Treatment Parsnips like potash, and the ground must be deeply dug. To grow really big ones, make a hole as if for a fence post, and fill the hole with peat and compost, or a potting compost, and sow on this.

Sowing Drill to 1 inch (2.5 cm) deep and 14 in (36 cm) apart in early spring or as soon as the land is open and dry enough. They take a long time to grow, so sow some radishes with them, as these declare themselves first and enable you to side-hoe.

Aftercare You can intercrop with lettuces for one lettuce crop. Then hoe and keep the ground clean.

Harvesting Leave the parsnips in the ground as long as you like. They are far better after they have been frosted. If you want them during hard frost, when it would be difficult to dig them out, pull them before the frost and leave them in a heap outside or in a shed. You can boil them in stews, but they are far better baked around a roast in fat, or partly boiled and then fried in slices. There are gardeners in England who devote half their gardens to rhubarb and half to parsnips. And the whole harvest of both crops goes to make wine! Parsnip wine is one of the best in my book.

PEAS

Use Eaten green, peas are delicious and extremely nutritious. Allowed to dry, they can be kept through the winter and cooked like lentils. It is better to have fresh green peas in their season, and only then, so that you come to them every year with a fresh and unjaded palate. Freezing them is a bore.

Soil They like a medium loam but will grow on most soils. Like all legumes (and brassica) they don't like acid ground. They like to be kept moist.

Treatment If you want a bumper crop, dig a trench in the autumn, fill it with muck, compost, or any old thing so long as it's organic, and bury it. Lime the soil well. Plant in what is left of the trench in the spring. But this is very laborious. Put your peas in after your spuds and your land should be well mucked already.

Sowing I personally sow peas thick in a little trench dug about 3 in (8 cm) deep with a hoe. And I eat a hell of a lot of peas. Plant each pea 2–3 in (5–8 cm) from its neighbor. Cover and firm the soil over the peas. It helps a lot to have soaked the peas for two or three days first, to get them germinating so they sprout early. Birds are a menace to peas; wire pea-guards are an answer, and so is a good cat.

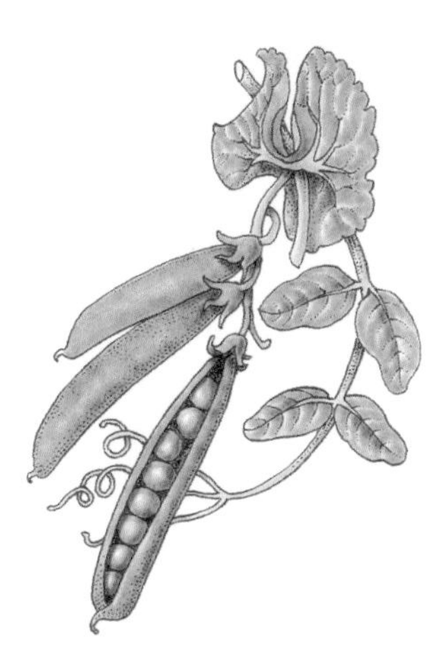

You can sow some round-seeded peas in November in mild climates, and some more in February. For this the land must be light and dry. Of course if you cloche them it helps. You will thus get very early pickings, but for most of your crop sow from mid-March onward, in successional sowings, going on right into July.

Finally, for your last sowings use early varieties (paradoxically). They will ripen quickly before the frosts cut them down.

Aftercare Hoe until the pea vines themselves smother the encroaching weeds. Also, mulch does wonders with peas, for it keeps the ground cool and moist, which is precisely the sort of conditions peas like.

Harvesting Pick them young to eat raw in salads, and then when the pods are tighter packed, pick for cooking. Keep picking as hard as you like, and if you have more than you can eat green, let them ripen on the vines and harvest properly. In other words, pull the vines when they are dead ripe (but before fall) and hang them up in the breeze but out of the rain. Thresh them in due course, stow them in jars, and eat them in soup.

PEPPERS

Use Peppers are either round and mild, or thin and long, and very much hotter! Peppers and chilis (the capsicums) spice up the blandest of meals and can be grown successfully under polytunnels.

Sowing and planting Sow seed indoors in early spring, and plant out in the garden on well-mucked ground at least two weeks after the last possible frost; under cloches if you

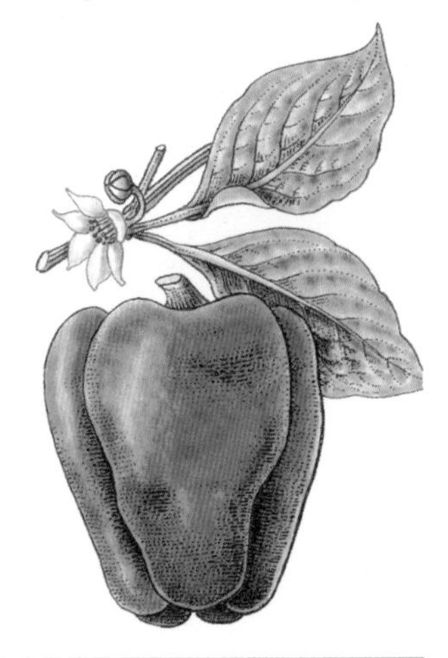

have them in cold climates. Plant 2 ft (60 cm) apart in rows 3 ft (90 cm) apart. After the ground has really warmed up, mulch. Peppers need moisture but not too much or they will die off. In a wet climate plant them on the tops of ridges.
Harvesting Harvest when they are green, or you can leave them to turn red.

POTATOES

Use Quite simply you can live on them. They are one of the best storable sources of energy we can grow, and are our chief source of vitamin C during the winter.

Soil Potatoes are a vegetable that likes good, strong soil. They will grow in clayey loam, they love peat, and they are one of the few crops that not only tolerate but like acid soil. If you lime before planting they will get scabby. They want plenty of muck and grow naturally in good manure.
Treatment Better to dig deeply in the fall and dig again in the spring, this time making ridges and furrows. They don't want a fine tilth but they want a deep one. Throw lots of muck or compost into the furrows before planting. Plant the spuds straight on top of it.
Planting Put your first earlies in when other people in your locality do, or two weeks earlier under cloches or transparent plastic. The slightest touch of frost on the leaves blasts them and they have to start all over again. If you want early potatoes, chit your seed potatoes, that is, lay your early seed in trays, on shelves, or in old egg cartons, in the light and not in the frost: 40°F–50°F (5°C–10°C) is right. When you plant potatoes, be careful not to knock off all the shoots. Leave two on each tuber. Don't chit the main crop. Put them straight in, in the late spring, but not before. Plant earlies only about 3 in (8 cm) deep, 1 ft (30 cm) apart in rows some 18 in (45 cm) apart. Plant the main crop 18 in (45 cm) apart in rows also 18 in (45 cm) apart, but less deep at about 5 inches (13 cm) deep for best results.
Aftercare As soon as leaves show, band earth lightly over the potatoes. Three weeks later, earth up some more, and, with the main crop, earth up again in another couple of weeks. Hoe between the rows. Spray with Bordeaux mixture (when the weather gets warm and muggy).
Harvesting If you have plenty of early potatoes in, don't deny yourself a meal or two when they are quite tiny. Then go on digging earlies until they are finished. If you have second earlies, go on to them. Your main crop will then take over for immediate eating, but don't lift the bulk of the main crop until the haulms (tops) have completely withered away. Then fork them out carefully and let them lie on the ground for a day and a half to set their skins (more than two days and they might start turning green, in which case they tend to become poisonous). Then clamp them, or put them in a root store in the dark. Potatoes must never be allowed to be affected by frost or they will go bad, which is a waste.

RADISHES

Use Radishes grow just about anywhere. Add to salads for extra flavor, crunchiness, as well as color.
Sowing Sow the large seeds in drills and pick them when they are ripe, after about six weeks. They are brassicas, but grow so

quickly that they don't get, or perpetuate, clubroot. Put in successional sowings all through the spring and summer so as to have a constant supply of tender young ones. Don't let them get old and go to seed.

RHUBARB

Use Rhubarb is a hardy perennial, and once you have planted it, or inherited it, you have it for good.
Soil Pretty well any soil is fine.
Treatment Put on plenty of muck.
Planting Buy or cadge crowns and plant them in late autumn. Leave about 3 ft (90 cm) between plants and 4 ft (1.2 m) between rows, and put some nitrogenous fertilizer on top to turn it into self-activating compost pile. Put upturned pots or buckets over some of the plants in spring to force them on early.
Aftercare Cover the beds with deep straw in fall.

Harvesting Pull what you want when the stems are thick and tall. Leave what common sense will suggest, so as not to rob the plants too much.

RUNNER (POLE) BEANS

Use These come later than the drying beans described below. They yield very heavily, are tougher and have a coarser, and I think better, flavor. They need more care in planting and must have tall sticks. Salted, they are a great standby for the winter.

Soil They like good, rich, deep soil.

Treatment Double dig a deep ditch in early spring and incorporate plenty of compost or muck in the bottom of it. If you have comfrey leaves, dig them in, because they are rich in potash, which all beans like. As they come in your bean break, you will already have limed the ground, if you had to, the previous autumn.

Sowing Sow runner beans in the early summer in a wide but shallow trench 2 in (5 cm) deep, in two staggered rows with the seeds about 9 in (23 cm) apart. Leave at least 5 ft (1.5 m) between stands of beans. Put in tall sticks early enough for the beans to get a good start.

Otherwise, you can pinch the growing tops out and let the vines straggle on the ground, but you won't get much of a crop, and in my opinion it's a poor way of growing these magnificent climbing plants, which can be about the most beautiful and productive things in your garden.

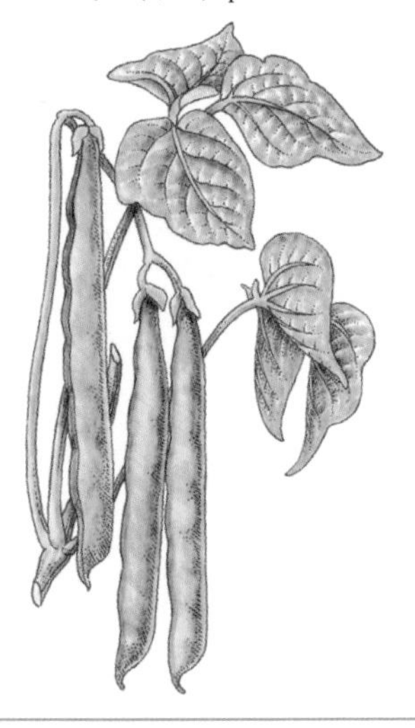

Aftercare Hoe and keep well watered in dry seasons. When they start to flower, make sure they have plenty of water. Mulch with compost if you can, and spray the flowers with water occasionally, because this "sets" the flowers in the absence of rain.

Harvesting Just keep on picking. If you can't cope with the supply, and you probably can't because they crop like hell, just pick anyway. String the beans, slice them (you can buy a small gadget for this), and store them in salt (see p.166). Pick them and give them to the chickens rather than let them get old and tough. Keep some, though, to get ripe for seed for next year.

SOYBEANS

Use Soybeans have been grown in Asia for centuries. They came to the West less than 200 years ago – and are now proving to be a very worthwhile crop to grow in warm areas because of their high protein value. They do need a long, warm growing season though – at least 100 days. They can be eaten green like peas, or the beans can be left to ripen and then dried for use all through the winter. The beans can also be ground into a nutritious flour.

Preparation Dig the ground in fall and add plenty of lime.

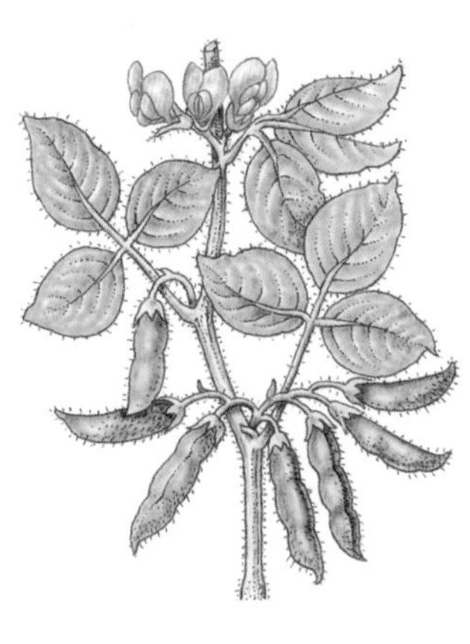

Sowing Sow in the late spring about 1 in (2.5 cm) deep, and 3 in (8 cm) apart in rows 2 ft (60 cm) away from each other.

Harvesting Pick the beans for eating green when they are young, certainly before they turn yellow. It's easier to remove the beans from the pods if they are boiled for a few minutes first. If the beans are for drying or for flour, leave them on the plants to ripen, but they must be picked before the pods burst. Be guided by the color of the stems on the

SPINACH

Use There are several kinds of spinach – New Zealand spinach, spinach beet, a leaf beet known as perpetual spinach, as well as seakale beet – but treat them all as one. Slow to start but ultimately a good pick.

Soil Like nearly everything else, spinach likes a good, rich loam, so give it as much muck as you can. It will do well on clay, but is apt to run to seed on sandy land unless you give it plenty of muck.

Sowing Sow 1 in (2.5 cm) deep in drills 1 ft (30 cm) apart. Later thin the plants in their rows to 6 in (15 cm) apart.

Aftercare Hoe, mulch, and water during the summer.

Harvesting Pick the leaves when they are young and green, raking only a few from each plant, leaving the smaller ones to grow bigger. Don't boil spinach. Wash it in water and put the wet leaves in a saucepan and heat over a fire. When you harvest seakale beet, pull off the stems as well as the leaves. Eat the stems like asparagus.

RUTABAGAS AND TURNIPS

Use Rutabagas and turnips can be eaten young and tender in the summer and fall and clamped for winter use. Turnips will survive in the ground until severe frosts begin, maybe till Christmas in temperate climates. Rutabagas are much hardier and will live in the ground all winter. All the same, it is handier to pull them and clamp them so you have them where you need them. They are cruciferous, which means they are subject to clubroot, and should therefore be part of the brassica break so that this disease is not perpetuated. You want to leave the longest possible gap between crops that are prone to clubroot. Kohlrabi (*Brassica oleracea Gongylodes* group), or cabbage turnip, is much like turnip and is grown in the same way.

Soil Light, fertile loam is best. Keep it well-drained but not too dry. But turnips, particularly your main crop for storing, will grow on most soils.

Treatment In heavy rainfall areas, say over 35 in (90 cm) a year, it is a good thing to grow turnips and rutabagas on the tops of ridges to aid drainage. So ridge up your land with a ridging plow, or on a small scale with a spade, and drill on the ridges.

If you want to grow them on the flat, just treat the land as you would for spring cabbages (see p.60).

Sowing Very early sowing can be done in the early spring or a week or two before the last probable frosts, but you can sow turnips and rutabagas right up until August. Sow the seed shallowly in drills about 9 in (23 cm) apart. Cover and press down.

Aftercare Beware the flea beetle. These are little jumpers that nibble tiny holes in the leaves. You can get rid of them by dusting with an insecticide, or you can trap them with a special little two-wheeled arrangement. The sticky underside of a board goes along just over the plants and a wire brushes the plants. The beetles jump and get stuck to the board. Thin to 4 in (10 cm) apart in the rows while they are still quite small. Hoe at least twice again afterward.

Harvesting Eat when they are ready (after two months), or leave until early winter and pull, top, and clamp.

SWEET CORN

Use Sweet corn is corn that has not been allowed to get ripe. The seeds are still fairly soft and milky, and the carbohydrate is mostly in the form of sugar. It will grow in the hottest climates; in temperate climates grow hardy varieties.

Soil Sweet corn will grow in most good well-drained soils, but it is a greedy feeder, likes plenty of muck and a pH of about 6.5.

Sowing A long growing season is essential but sweet corn can't stand frost, so if we plant it a week or two before the last likely frost under upturned jelly jars, or little tents of plastic, or cloches, so much the better.

In warm climates you can sow it right out in the open in early summer, but if your summers are a long time coming, you would do better to sow it in peat pots indoors in late spring and then plant it out. Sow the seed about 1 in (2.5 cm) deep, 15 in (28 cm) apart in rows 30 in (75 cm) apart. And try to sow in blocks – nothing narrower than four rows, for example – because corn is wind-pollinated, and if it is sown in long, thin lines many plants will not get pollinated.

Planting If you have grown it in pots, plant it out very carefully, because it doesn't like being disturbed anyway. Plant out when it is about 5 in (13 cm) high, and preferably plant peat pot and all. Water well after planting. It is a lot better if you can sow them in their final position.

Aftercare Hoe and top-dress with nitrogen about a month after planting sweet corn, if your soil is not as rich as it should be to keep the plants growing.

Harvesting Break the cobs off in the milky stage after the tassel has begun to wither and turn brown. To test, pull the leaves off part of a cob and press your thumbnail into the grain. It should be milky. They say you can walk down to the garden to pick your corn, but you must run back to cook it; it must be absolutely fresh. This is because the sugar starts turning into starch as soon as you pick it. If you have too many cobs, you can dry them (see pp.152-155 for harvesting and storing). The straw makes good litter for chickens, or material for the compost pile, and it is a valuable crop for this reason alone.

SWEET POTATOES

Use Sweet potatoes can be your staple food in a dry, warm climate, but you won't get much of a crop in a damp, cool environment. They are very frost-tender.

Soil They grow in sand, or sandy loam, and they don't like rich soil.

Treatment Just dig deeply. Add nothing.

Planting Plant tubers just like potatoes (if you are sure they haven't been sprayed with a growth-inhibitor). Plant them 16 in (40 cm) apart in rows 2½ ft (75 cm) apart. Don't plant them anywhere in the world until two weeks after the last frost.

Aftercare Just hoe.

Harvesting Dig them up very carefully at least two weeks before the first frost. Cure them by laying them carefully on hay and leaving them out in the sun for about ten days. They don't turn green because they are no relation of real potatoes.

After harvesting, turn sweet potatoes from time to time. If there isn't enough sun, keep them somewhere with 90 percent humidity between 80°F (27°C) and 90°F (32°C) for ten days. Store them packed lightly in straw in an airy place at not less than 50°F (10°C).

TOMATOES

Outdoor tomatoes

Use Outdoor tomatoes are a dicey business in any cold, wet climate. What they need is a warm, dry ripening season in late summer, and that is what, where I live, they don't get. But green tomatoes make excellent chutney or relish and if you store them well they sometimes get ripe in store, although they never taste like sun-warmed fruit picked off the vine and eaten right away. But if you can grow them, they are an enormously valuable crop for canning to keep your family healthy during the dark days of winter. They really are preserved sunshine.

Soil The soil must be well-drained, and in a sunny but sheltered position in cold climates.
Treatment I ridge the land in fall, put well-rotted compost or muck in the trenches in early spring, split the ridges over it, and then plant the tomatoes on the new ridges.
Sowing The most luxurious tomatoes I ever saw growing were on the overspill of a sewage plant, which leads one to think that it would be better to eat the seed before we plant it. But failing such extreme measures, sow thinly under glass in any seed compost, including the kind you make yourself. If you sow in the late spring in a temperate climate, the plants will grow even if you have no heat in your greenhouse, but if you do have a little heat, so much the better. If you have no heat put thick newspapers over the seedlings at night to keep them warm: 55°F (12°C) is right. Water diligently with lukewarm water but not too much. Don't drown them. Or you can sow direct, *in situ*, a week or two later, under cloches in warmer climates, or just outdoors in hot climates.

Planting Most people plant twice. First, when they have three to four true tomato-type leaves, they plant in either soil blocks or peat pots or in compost in small flowerpots. These pots can be put into cold frames and the plants gradually hardened off. Then plant out in the first fine warm weather in early summer. Plant very carefully, retaining as much of the compost on the roots as you can, and plant a little deeper than they were before. Plant on the mucked ridges described above. Give each plant a tall stake for support as it grows bigger and heavier.
Aftercare Hoeing and mulching, within reason, do help, and with low fruiting varieties. Pick out all side-shoots. These are little shoots that grow between the fruiting branches and main stem, rather as if you had another little arm growing out of your armpit.

You cannot pamper tomatoes too much. Water them whenever they need it (soak muck in the water so that you feed the plants as you water them). As they grow taller, tie them carefully to the stakes with raffia or string. Spray them with Bordeaux mixture to protect from potato blight. (The tomato is so closely related to the potato that it's almost the same plant.) Allow the plants to set about four trusses. To ripen tomatoes in dull climates try laying them down flat on clean straw and placed under some old clothes.
Harvesting Home-grown tomatoes are so good to eat (much better than commercially farmed tomatoes bred for a long shelf life, i.e. not for flavor) .

Indoor tomatoes

Use If your greenhouse is heated, you can sow seed in early winter and get ripe tomatoes in spring.

Sowing Sow in November at 70°F (21°C). Never let it fall below 60°F (16°C) in winter. If you can't maintain 70°F (21°C), sow in February and keep at 60°F (16°C). Sow in compost made of two parts sifted loam, one part leaf mold, and a little sand. Cover with glass to prevent evaporation. Keep moist.
Planting When the plants have two rough leaves, place singly in 5-in (13-cm) pots. Use the same compost but add well-rotted muck. When the first truss of flowers is formed, move into pots about double the size.
Aftercare As for outdoor tomatoes, but you can let them set up to ten trusses.
Harvesting Pick as soon as red.

WATERCRESS

Use Watercress is one of the richest sources of vitamin C likely to come your way. It makes a superb salad, or it can be cooked.
Sowing Sow seed or rooted cuttings in a damp, shady spot in late spring or midsummer. Dig the soil deeply and work in some peat if you can get it. Rake the bed, flood it, and sow thickly when the water has drained away. You can grow it in an unpolluted stream.

Herbs

Herbs are a very cheap and easy way of improving the flavor of food; they also make it more digestible and do you good at the same time. In ancient times they were valued as much for their healing properties as for their culinary ones. The coming of the Industrial society saw a decline in the use of herbs, and up to a time only parsley, mint and – in enlightened circles – horseradish were being much used in the North American or British kitchen. Now, the revival of a flourishing international cuisine has once again made people eager to experiment with a variety of new tastes. Consequently, growing fresh herbs to add natural enhancement to food is becoming an increasingly attractive proposition for everyone.

Even people without gardens can grow them in pots. A drift of borage or a sea of thyme look splendid from the kitchen window. There is really no reason why herbs should not take the place of inedible flowers in beds near the house instead of being relegated to an inaccessible patch at the back of the garden. But unless you are planning to become a herbalist, it is better to concentrate on a few herbs that will have a culinary or medicinal use to you, rather than cultivate scores of varieties, most of which you will end up neglecting.

If you want to grow herbs just remember that herbs divide fairly straightforwardly into two groups: perennial (grows year on year without re-seeding) and annual (grows, seeds, and dies in one year), with just the odd biennial (grows in the first year and seeds in the second) to complicate matters.

Harvesting your herbs

Most herbs prefer a light, well-drained soil and plenty of sun, although a few prefer the shade. All respond to constant picking.

You dry herbs in order to keep the color and aroma of a fresh herb in a dried one. It is a delicate operation, because it requires both speed and care, but most herbs can be dried and stored.

As a general rule, harvest the herb leaves and stems just before the plant flowers, on the morning of a fine, hot day after the dew is gone. If you are going to preserve the herbs, take them to a drying rack immediately. Do not over-handle them. They bruise easily, and every minute you waste means the loss of more volatile oils. These are what give herbs their flavour and quality.

Tie the herbs in small bunches and hang them in an airy place. Ideally you dry them at a temperature between 70˚F–80˚F (21˚C–27˚C), in the strongest possible draft of air. You can leave them hanging up indefinitely, but they will collect dust. A better thing to do is to rub leaves off the stem when they are quite dry and brittle (but you hope still green), crumble them up and store in sealed glass or pottery jars in the dark. If the air is too damp to get them dry, lay them in a cool oven at 110˚F (44˚C) on sheets of paper overnight. Or you can hang them in a solar drier (see p.210) which is ideal for drying herbs, but in that case watch the temperature by using a thermometer.

Over the next few pages, I describe many of the herbs that the self-supporter might find most useful for flavoring food – who could imagine lamb without rosemary? – or fortifying the spirit, or even, at a pinch, banishing ailments.

Angelica archangelica
ANGELICA
Biennial

Use Once thought to cure the plague, angelica-scented leaves make a fine tisane. The roots and stems can be candied or they can be crystallized.
Soil Angelica needs a rich, moist soil and a shady position.
Sowing The seeds must be fresh or they won't germinate. Plant in midsummer as soon as they are ripe, in drills 1 in (2.5 cm) deep.
Planting Transplant seedlings or young plants in the autumn and thin to 6 in (15 cm) the first year, 2 ft (60 cm) the following year. In the third year distance them 5 ft (15 m) apart. They grow very tall and their leaves are spreading.
Harvesting Leaves should be cut in early summer while still a good color. Pick stalks and leaves in late spring or they become too hard for candying. Roots should be dug up in the first year in fall before they really get too woody. Wash thoroughly, then plait and dry as quickly as possible.

Pimpinella anisum
ANISE
Annual

Use Anise has valuable digestive properties. The fragrant seeds can be used to impart a slight licorice flavor to breads, cheeses and also desserts.
Soil Needs a moderately rich and fairly dry soil to thrive.
Sowing Sow *in situ* in late spring, and thin later on to 8 in (20 cm) apart. Take care when thinning, as the herb is fragile and easily upset.
Harvesting The seeds will mature the first year after 120 days, as long as they are exposed to full sun. Harvest when the seed heads turn gray-brown and thresh them when they have dried out thoroughly.

Melissa officinalis
BALM
Perennial

Use The leaves impart a fresh lemony flavor to soups and summer drinks.
Soil Balm likes a fairly rich, moist soil in a sunny, sheltered spot. If it is too shady the aroma will be stifled; if too dry, the leaves turn yellow.
Sowing Grows easily from seed which it self-sows profusely. Sow in spring or early summer in a cold frame. It should germinate in thee to four weeks. Pick out and plant in the garden when 4 in (10 cm) high or sow the seed in your garden in midsummer and plant seedlings out in the early summer of the following year.
Planting Keep 10 in (25 cm) between the rows and 1 ft (30 cm) between the balm plants. Balm is susceptible to frost, so protect your plants by earthing them up or giving them a light cover of manure, peat or leaf mold.
Harvesting Harvest just before the buds flower and then again in the fall. Balm bruises easily, so keep your hands off it as much as possible. Dry in the dark with plenty of ventilation, then store in stoppered jars in the dark.

Ocimum basilicum
BASIL
Annual

Use A fine, pungent herb, basil is superb in sausages, spaghetti, and stuffed tomatoes.
Soil Basil needs dry, light, well-drained soil and a sunny, sheltered position.
Sowing A hardy perennial in hot countries, basil is a delicate plant in colder climes, where it has to be grown annually from seed. Sow indoors in early summer.
Planting Seedlings should not be planted until the soil is warm. Plant 8 in (20 cm) apart in rows 1 ft (30 cm) apart.
Harvesting Basil needs plenty of water to keep the leaves succulent. The leaves can be picked off as soon as they unfurl. Cut down for drying in late summer or early fall. Basil needs a longer drying time than most herbs; it is also very sensitive to light and heat, and it bruises easily, so handle it as little as possible.

Laurus nobilis
BAY
Evergreen

Use Once used to crown poets in ancient Greece, bay leaves are now more often used in casseroles.
Soil Bay is amenable to any reasonable soil. Give it shelter from harsh winds; it will grow in the shade, though it likes the sun. Intense frost will kill it; in colder climates bay is almost always grown in tubs so that it can be moved indoors in winter.
Planting It propagates rapidly from hardwood cuttings of half-ripened shoots. Don't let it dry out; feed manure occasionally.
Harvesting The leaves can either be dried (at a low temperature, which helps retain their natural color) or picked fresh all year

Borago officinalis
BORAGE
Annual
Use Tradition has it that borage will stimulate the mind and fortify the spirit. Add a sprig or two to your wine and you will certainly notice a difference. The flowers can be used raw to garnish salads and the leaves

can be chopped into soups and stews.
Soil Borage needs sun and a well-drained loamy or sandy soil.
Sowing Seed is best sown in spring in drills about 1 in (2.5 cm) deep, 3 ft (90 cm) apart, three seeds to a station. Later, thin to one plant per station. Seeds will germinate early and thereafter sow themselves and need only to be kept weeded.
Harvesting Leaves are ready for use in approximately eight weeks; only the young leaves should be picked. The herb is ready for harvesting as soon as it flowers but it needs quick-drying at a low temperature.

Poterium sanguisorba
SALAD BURNET
Perennial
Use Young, tender salad burnet leaves lend a

cucumber flavor to iced drinks or salads. They provide the perfect accompaniment to cream or cottage cheese. The dried leaves make a good burnet vinegar.
Soil Salad burnet grows well in dry, light, well-limed soil.
Sowing Sow from seed in early spring and thin to 1 ft (30 cm) apart. You can also grow burnet from cuttings. Full sun is essential; seed should be sown annually if a constant supply of fresh leaves is required.
Harvesting The plant is hardy in most climates. Pick young leaves frequently for salads or for drying.

Carum carvi
CARAWAY
Biennial

Use As well as using caraway seed for cakes and breads, sprinkle the ground seeds on liver or roast pork, or cook them with goulash and sauerkraut. Leaves can go into salads, and the roots make a good vegetable if you boil them and serve them like parsnips.
Soil Caraway likes a fertile clay loam and a sheltered position. It is winter-hardy, and thrives in cool temperate climates.
Sowing Sow from seed in midsummer, and it will flower and seed the following year. Protect flower stalks from the wind to prevent the seedheads from shattering before the seed is ripe.
Harvesting Cut off the flower heads as the seed turns brown, and dry the seed in an airy place before threshing.

Matricaria chamomilla
CHAMOMILE
Annual

Use Sometimes used in flower borders, this herb is grown chiefly for medicinal purposes. Chamomile tea is a cleansing aid to the digestion, and an infusion of two teaspoons of flowers to a cup of boiling water makes for a splendid gargle, or a soothing cure to help with toothache.
Soil Any good garden soil with full sun suits chamomile admirably.
Sowing Sow the very fine Chamomile seeds mixed with sand or wood-ash on a humid day in early spring. Thin later to 9 in (23 cm) apart. The seeds self-sow easily. Watering is advisable during germination.
Harvesting The flowers appear and are ready for picking eight weeks after sowing. Pick often, but only on sunny days, because that is when the oil content of the flowers is at its highest. Try not to touch the Chamomile flowers too much.

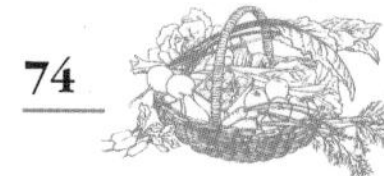

Anthriscus cerefolium
CHERVIL
Biennial

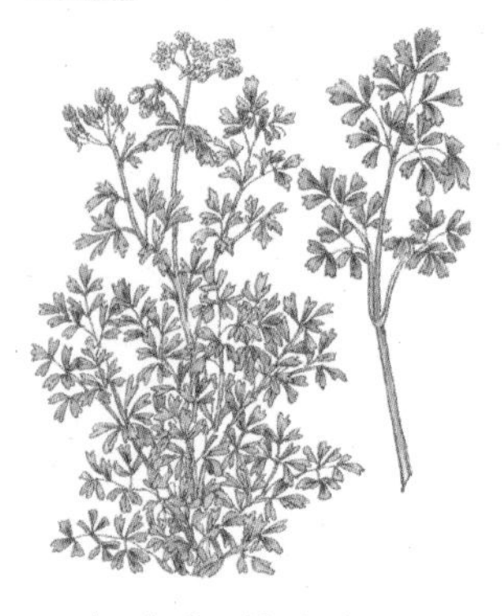

Use Chervil is famed for the flavoring it imparts to soups and sauces. Use it as a garnish, or make that classic warming dish – chervil soup.
Soil Chervil will grow in most soils but it will not thrive in a heavy, badly drained soil.
Sowing Sow from seed in early spring out of doors and in the greenhouse at over 45°F (7°C) all winter. Sow in drills 1 ft (30 cm) apart. After that it will self-sow easily. Chervil does not transplant well so sow where you want it to grow. Seedlings should be thinned out when 2–3 in (5–8 cm) high. Keep beds weeded and moist.
Harvesting You can eat chervil six to eight weeks after sowing. Always pick leaves from the outside to allow it to go on growing from the center. Don't allow it to flower – this takes away the flavor. Chervil is a difficult herb to dry, needing a constant low temperature, but as it is available fresh all year this shouldn't really be a problem.

Allium schoenoprasum
CHIVES
Perennial

Use Related to onions, chives add a less tear-inducing flavor and make a green, fresh difference to salads, soups, or any savory dish. Snip into scrambled eggs, cream cheese and mayonnaise for potato salad. The bulbs can be picked like small onions. Non-flowering stems tend to be sharper in flavor.
Soil Chives like a warm, shady position, and will grow in almost any soil, but they must have humidity. So plant them near a pond or water tank if you can.
Sowing Sow from seed in spring in drills, 1 ft (30 cm) apart. Chives will thrive on doses of strong humus, and then need careful, frequent watering.
Harvesting Chives are ready for cutting about five weeks after spring planting. Plants that are sown in a greenhouse in winter at 80°F (27°C) will be ready in two weeks. Cut close to the ground.

Coriandrum sativum
CORIANDER
Annual

Use An important ingredient in Indian cooking, coriander can be grown successfully in cold countries. Use the seeds crushed or whole in curried meats or stuffed vegetables; add some to marmalade to make an exotic change. Seeds are sometimes sugar-coated and eaten as candy.
Soil Coriander needs a sunny, well-drained site in fairly rich soil.
Sowing Sow in late spring in drills 1 ft (30 cm) apart, and thin seedlings to 6 in (15 cm). They will grow rapidly to a height of about 2 ft (60 cm).
Harvesting Cut the seedheads when the pods are ripe, and allow the seeds to dry thoroughly before using, as they will taste bitter if they are still green. Thresh and store in the usual way.

Anethum graveolens
DILL
Annual
Use The name comes from the Norse *dilla* meaning to lull to sleep, and at one time the seeds were called "meeting house" seeds, for they were taken to church to be nibbled during endless sermons. While dill seed is the soporific ingredient in colic water, the leaves can enliven your cooking. It is good with fish, roast chicken, vegetables, and chopped up raw and added to salads and sauces.
Soil Dill needs a well-drained medium soil in a sunny spot.
Sowing Sow consecutively through late spring and early summer in rows 1 ft (30 cm) apart and later thin to 9 in (23 cm). Keep plants well watered.

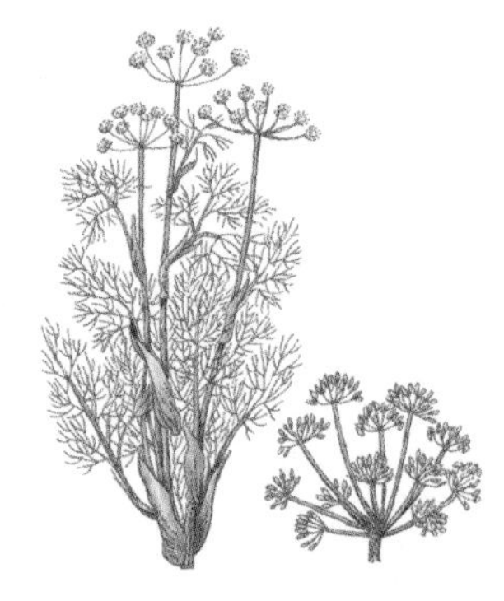

Harvesting Leaves can be used six to eight weeks after planting. Cut dill for drying when 1 ft (30 cm) high, before the plant flowers. For pickling seed, cut when both flower and seed are on the head at the same time. If seeds are wanted for sowing or flavoring, leave them longer, until they turn brown. Seedheads should be dried and then shaken or threshed. Never dry the leaves in a temperature higher than blood heat or you will cook them and they will lose their strong flavor.

Foeniculum vulgare
FENNEL
Perennial

Use Fennel's sharp-sweet flavor is specially suited to the oilier sea fish. Chop the leaves in sauces, salad dressings, and marinades. The broad base can be sliced into salads or cooked whole with a cheese sauce. The seeds can be put into sausages, bread, or apple pie.
Soil Fennel needs sun, a rich, chalky soil, and plenty of sunshine.
Sowing Seeds should be sown in spring in stations of three to four seeds 18 in (45 cm) apart. If you want to get seed you will have to sow earlier under glass and in heat. If propagated by division, lift the roots in spring, divide and replant 1 ft (30 cm) apart in rows 15 in (38 cm) apart.
Harvesting Leaves can be used through the summer months; seedheads are ready for drying in the fall. Harvest the seeds when they are still light, green, and dry, in a very low temperature, never in direct sunlight. Lay in thin layers and move often as they sweat. Harvest the whole fennel when it takes on a gray-brown hue.

Allium sativum
GARLIC
Perennial

Use Garlic is the basis of good health and good cooking. Unhappy are the nations who have to do without it. Use it liberally and use it often. Take no notice of foolish injunctions to "rub a suspicion" around the salad bowl. Chop a clove or two and put it in the salad.
Soil Garlic needs a rich soil, plenty of sun, and a reasonable amount of moisture. If your soil is light, enrich it with manure.
Planting Plant individual cloves in spring just like onion sets to a depth of 2 in (5 cm), 6 in (15 cm) apart. They will be ready for eating in the fall. Plant again then, and you will have garlic all year round.
Harvesting When the leaves have died down, lift the crop. Allow to dry in the sun for a few days, then plait and hang in bunches under cover in a dry, airy room.

Cochlearia armoracia
HORSERADISH
Perennial

Use Shred roots finely and use as it is or mix into a paste either with oil and a little vinegar, or grated apples and cream. Horseradish sauce is delicious with roast beef; it is also good with smoked trout and ham.
Soil It needs a rich, moist soil and a fairly shady position.
Sowing The horseradish plant grows furiously and spreads large taproots with equal abandon. So give it maximum space. Plant the roots in early spring. Dig trenches 2–3 ft (61–90 cm) deep, throw about 15 in (38 cm) of topsoil in the bottom, dig in a layer of good compost on top of this, and fill with the rest of the soil. Take 3-in (8-cm) pieces of root, plant roughly 12 in (30 cm) apart. And keep it weeded. Seed can also be sown in early spring and plants thinned to 12 in (30 cm) apart.
Harvesting The roots will be ready for eating nine months after planting. Use the larger ones in your kitchen and the smaller roots for replanting.

Hyssopus officinalis
HYSSOP
Perennial

Use Mentioned in the Bible for its purgative properties, monks now use hyssop to make green Chartreuse. You can try sprigs of it in salads, or chop it into soups and stews. Its slightly minty flavor is pleasant in fruit pies. I like it with fat mackerel. Use it sparingly.
Soil Light, well-limed soil and a sunny plot.
Sowing Grows easily from seed and often self-sows. It can also be propagated by division, from cuttings taken either in the spring before flowering or in the autumn after flowering. Sow from seed in drills ¼ in (0.5 cm) deep and then plant out seedlings 2 ft (60 cm) apart when they are 6 in (15 cm) high.
Harvesting Cut back the plant tops often to keep leaves young and tender. Cut for drying just before flowering.

Origanum onites
MARJORAM (POT)
Perennial

Use Pot marjoram has less flavor than sweet marjoram; it goes well in sausages as well as stuffings.
Soil Pot marjoram prefers a dry, light soil, and it needs sun.
Sowing Grow it from seed in spring in shallow ½-inch (1-cm) drills, 8 in (20 cm) apart. When the seedlings are big enough to handle, transplant to 1 ft (30 cm) apart. Alternatively, grow it under glass from cuttings taken in the early summer and plant out later, allowing 2 ft (60 cm) between plants and between rows.
Harvesting Harvest as for sweet marjoram. For marjoram seeds ripen in late summer or early autumn. Cultivated pot marjoram can last for years.

Origanum majorana
MARJORAM (SWEET)
Annual

Use Sweet marjoram lends a spicy flavor to sausages, and to game and poultry stuffings.
Soil It needs a medium-rich soil, plenty of compost and a warm, sheltered spot.
Sowing Sow sweet marjoram in pots under glass in early spring and then plant out in early summer 1 ft (30 cm) apart.
Harvesting Leaves and flowers are best collected just before the bud opens toward the end of summer. Dry in thin layers, at temperatures not over 100°F (38°C).

Origanum vulgare
OREGANO
Perennial

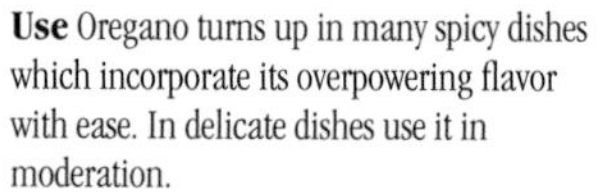

Use Oregano turns up in many spicy dishes which incorporate its overpowering flavor with ease. In delicate dishes use it in moderation.
Soil It needs a warm, dry place to grow, and prefers a chalky or gravelly soil.
Sowing Sow from seed in early spring. The distance between plants should be as much as 20 in (50 cm); if you sow in drills you should thin to 8–12 in (20–30 cm). Like pot marjoram, it can be grown from cuttings.
Harvesting Harvest as for sweet marjoram. Seeds ripen in early fall.

Mentha species
MINT
Perennial

Use There are several kinds of mint, with different properties and flavors, but they can be treated similarly. For mint sauce use Bowles mint rather than garden mint if you want a stronger flavor. A few sprigs of peppermint make a fine tisane. Mint added to any fruit dish or drink peps it up.
Soil Mint has a rampant root system and is best planted away from all other herbs.

Grow mint in the sun and it will have a fuller flavour, but it needs a moist, rich soil and plenty of water.
Sowing Plant mint in fall or spring from roots or runners. Lay horizontally in drills 2 in (5 cm) deep, 1 ft (30 cm) apart. Hoe frequently during the first weeks and compost liberally.
Harvesting Mint for drying should be harvested at the beginning of the flowering season (midsummer), but fresh leaves can be cut at any time. Frequent cutting helps the plant to grow. Don't cut for drying in damp, rainy weather, for the leaves will only blacken and turn moldy. Keep peppermint leaves whole when drying for tea. Rub them and they will have a totally different taste.

Tropaeolum major or *minus*
NASTURTIUM
Annual

Use The round, hot-flavored leaves are delicious tossed in rice salads. They are a healthy alternative to pepper. The flowers are good with cream cheese. Pickle the young green seeds and use like capers. They are excellent with roast lamb.
Soil Given a light, sandy soil and plenty of sun, nasturtiums will grow almost anywhere. Plants grown for leaves need a ground rich in compost.
Sowing Sow the seeds *in situ* in late spring. If they are planted near other plants, they are said to protect them from pests.
Harvesting The highest vitamin content is found in the leaves before they flower in midsummer, so harvest then. Chop or dry, then rub or shred. The leaves dry well, but eat the flowers fresh.

Petroselinum crispum
PARSLEY
Biennial

Use There are several varieties of parsley, including curly leaf and flat leaf, and all are rich in vitamin C, iron, and organic salts. Chop it up into tiny pieces and use lavishly as a garnish, as well as in cooking; it's especially complementary with fish.
Soil Parsley needs rich soil with a fine tilth.
Sowing Sow parsley fresh every year as it runs to seed. Sow in early spring and later in midsummer at a distance of 8–12 in (20–30 cm) in drills 2 in (1 cm) deep. Cover thinly and water well, especially during the five-to eight-week germination period. When the seedlings are 1 in (2.5 cm) high, thin to 3 in (8 cm) and finally to 8 in (20 cm) when mature. Keep it well watered. Curly parsley can often be sown three times a year: sow in a border in early spring, on open ground in early summer, and in a sheltered spot in midsummer.
Harvesting Pick a few leaves of parsley at a time. Bunches should not be picked until the stem is 8 in (20 cm) high. Pick for drying during the summer and dry quickly. Plain parsley is the only herb requiring a high drying temperature; it must be crisp and brittle before you start rubbing it.

Rosmarinus officinalis
ROSEMARY
Perennial
Use This evergreen shrub was used by the Greeks to stimulate the mind. We use it to stimulate meat, fish and game dishes. It's a very hardy plant except in severe winters, but it does require plenty of sunshine.
Soil Rosemary can grow to well over 5 ft m (1.5). It likes a light, dry soil in a wind-sheltered position, and it needs plenty of lime to thrive.

Sowing Sow seeds in early spring in shallow drills 6 in (15 cm) apart. Transplant seedlings to a nursery bed at a few inches high, keeping 6 in (15 cm) distance between plants, and finally plant out 3 ft (90 cm) apart. Cut in midsummer so shoots have a chance to harden off before winter sets in. Then cover the soil over the roots with leaf mold and sacking for the winter.
Harvesting Leaves can be picked from the second year on, at any time of the year, although late summer is the best time for drying purposes. Rosemary flowers should be picked just before they are in full bloom.

Salvia officinalis
SAGE
Perennial

Use Although now better known for its presence in stuffings (think roast turkey with sage dressing), sage was for centuries regarded as one of the most versatile of all healing remedies. Narrow-leaved sage is better for cooking, while broad-leaved sage is much more suitable for drying.
Soil Sage grows to around 2 ft (60 cm) and needs a light, dry chalky soil. It can take plenty of organic matter. Sage loves the sun.
Sowing For narrow-leaved sage, sow seed in late spring in humid soil and cover lightly. Germination then takes 10–14 days. Transplant the sage seedlings 15–20 in (38–50 cm) apart in the early summer. Broad-leaved sage is always propagated from cuttings taken in very late spring. When rooted plant out 15–20 in (38–50 cm) apart in rows 2 ft (60 cm) apart.
Harvesting Second-year plants are richer in oils and give a better harvest. Broad-leaved sage is best cut in midsummer and again a month later to prevent it from becoming too woody. Don't expect it ever to flower in a temperate climate. Cut narrow-leaved sage in early fall. Sage leaves are rough and need a longer drying time than most herbs.

Satureja hortensia
SAVORY (SUMMER)
Annual

Use Summer savory is known as the "bean-herb" and brings out the innate taste of all beans. Savory has the added benefit of attracting bees to your garden.
Soil Being a bushy plant, growing about 1 ft (30 cm) high, it flourishes best in a fairly rich, humid soil, without compost.
Sowing Sow in late spring or early summer, in rows 1 ft (30 cm) apart. Thin seedlings to 6 in (15 cm). You will get two cuts from this sowing, one in midsummer and another smaller one in fall.
Harvesting Cut shoots for drying shortly before flowering occurs (from midsummer through to fall). Harvest seeds as soon as they are brown.

Satureja montana
SAVORY (WINTER)
Perennial

Use Winter savory has a strong flavor and goes well with sausages, baked fish, or lamb.
Soil More erect than the summer variety, winter savory makes an ideal herb garden hedge, preferring a chalky, well-drained soil and plenty of sun.

Sowing This is one of those plants that is germinated by light, so make sure you don't cover the seed. Sow in late summer in drills 12–15 in (30–38 cm) apart, and propagate by cuttings in spring, planted out 2 ft (60 cm) apart. Plants will continue to grow healthily year on year in the same spot.
Harvesting Cut the shoots and the tips from early summer of the second year onward. If you want to get the oils at their peak, you will need to cut winter savory before it flowers.

Rumex acetosa
SORREL
Perennial
Use Pick young leaves and eat them raw or cook like spinach. Sorrel's acid taste combines well with rich stews and fish. Sorrel soup is a speciality of France.
Soil Sorrel needs a light, rich soil in a sheltered, sunny spot.
Planting The herb is best propagated by the division of roots in spring or fall. Plant out about 5 in (38 cm) apart. When the plant flowers in early summer, cut it back to prevent it from going to seed.

Harvesting Pick your sorrel three to four months after planting when it has four or five leaves. Harvest shoots and tips for drying in the early summer before flowering starts.

Artemisia dracunculus
TARRAGON
Perennial
Use An important cooking herb, tarragon is a classic for shellfish and is also delicious with chicken and buttered vegetables (especially zucchini). It also goes well in homemade vinegars.The strong taste of its young leaves adds zest to salads (the flavor of the leaves wanes as the plant matures). There are two types, French and Russian, and both are hardy though the latter, as its name suggests, is able to withstand harsher weather. The French variety needs protecting from frost.
Soil Drainage is important if you are to grow tarragon well. Slightly sloping and sunny ground is also preferable.
Planting The roots will spread out about 4 ft (120 cm), so give it growing room.

The best way to establish tarragon is to buy plants from a nursery and plant out 18–24 in (45–60 cm) apart after the last frost of winter. Add a light mulch cover of straw or bracken to protect the French tarragon from a late spring frost. Pull underground runners away from the main plant for propagation in late spring. Transplant cuttings in either spring or fall. Both types can benefit from a replanting after four years to retain vigor and flavor in the plants.
Harvesting Fresh leaves can be picked all summer long and this will encourage new ones to grow. Harvest the leaves for drying at the beginning of the flowering period for best results, but they will still tend to lose their delicate aroma.

Thymus vulgaris
THYME
Perennial
Use Garden thyme is one of the stronger tasting herbs and so is ideal with any roast meat, or in soups and stuffings. Adding a sprig inside slow-cooking game brings out a superb flavor, but be careful not to use too freely, as it can drown other tastes. It also has the welcome attraction of luring bees to the garden.
Soil Thyme has low, carpeting leaves and thrives in a dry, well-drained position, with light soil. It's pretty hardy and can be sat or trodden on without doing too much harm, not that I would recommend this as part of your good husbandry routine.
Planting Seeds can be sown in late spring ¼-inch (0.5-cm) drills 2 ft (60 cm) apart, but the herb is generally grown from cuttings taken in early summer. Side shoots can be layered in spring. Transplant the rooted

cuttings or layers 1 ft (30 cm) apart in rows 2 ft (60 cm) apart. Keep beds well watered and free from weeds.
Harvesting In the first year only one cutting should be made. Two cuttings can be taken from the second year on, the first in early summer, just before flowering, the second in midsummer. Do not cut stem from the base of the plant; cut shoots about 6 in (15 cm) long. Trim the plant after flowering to prevent it from growing leggy. For drying purposes you can cut the young healthy leaves before the plant comes into flower. As with other herbs, tie the stems in small bunches and hang upside down in a dry, airy shed. Avoid any tight or rough handling of the leaves as the essential oils will evaporate and the aroma will be lost. Eventually you can crumble the dried leaves into an airtight jam jar.

Vegetables through the year

Exactly the same principle of crop rotation applies to the garden as to field crops, but in the garden there are two main considerations to take into account: you want the biggest possible gap (at least three years) between brassica crops to prevent clubroot disease from building up, and the biggest possible gap between potato crops to guard against nematodes. You should also take into account that potatoes don't like freshly-limed ground, which makes them scabby, whereas beans and peas do. Brassica prefer limed ground, but after the lime has been in it a few months. The root crops don't like land too freshly mucked or dunged.

You can pander to the needs of all these plants if you adopt a four-year rotation something along the lines explain below:

Manure the land heavily and sow potatoes. After the potatoes are lifted, lime the land heavily and the next year sow peas and beans. Once the peas and beans are lifted, set out brassica immediately from their seed bed or their "holding bed" (see p.78). The brassica will all have been eaten by the next spring and it will be time to put in mixed crops. These will be onions, tomatoes, lettuce, radishes, corn, and all the gourd tribe (squash, zucchini, pumpkins, and cucumbers). Follow these with root crops such as

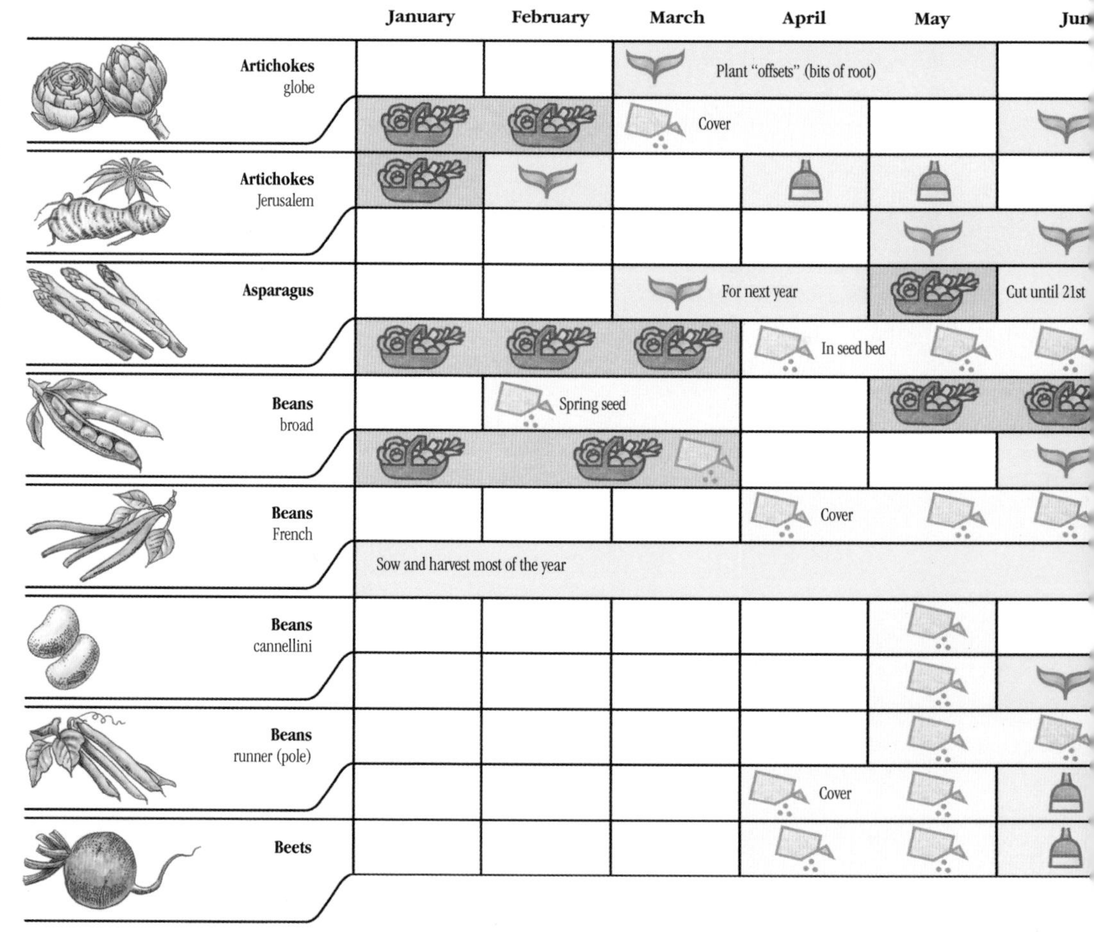

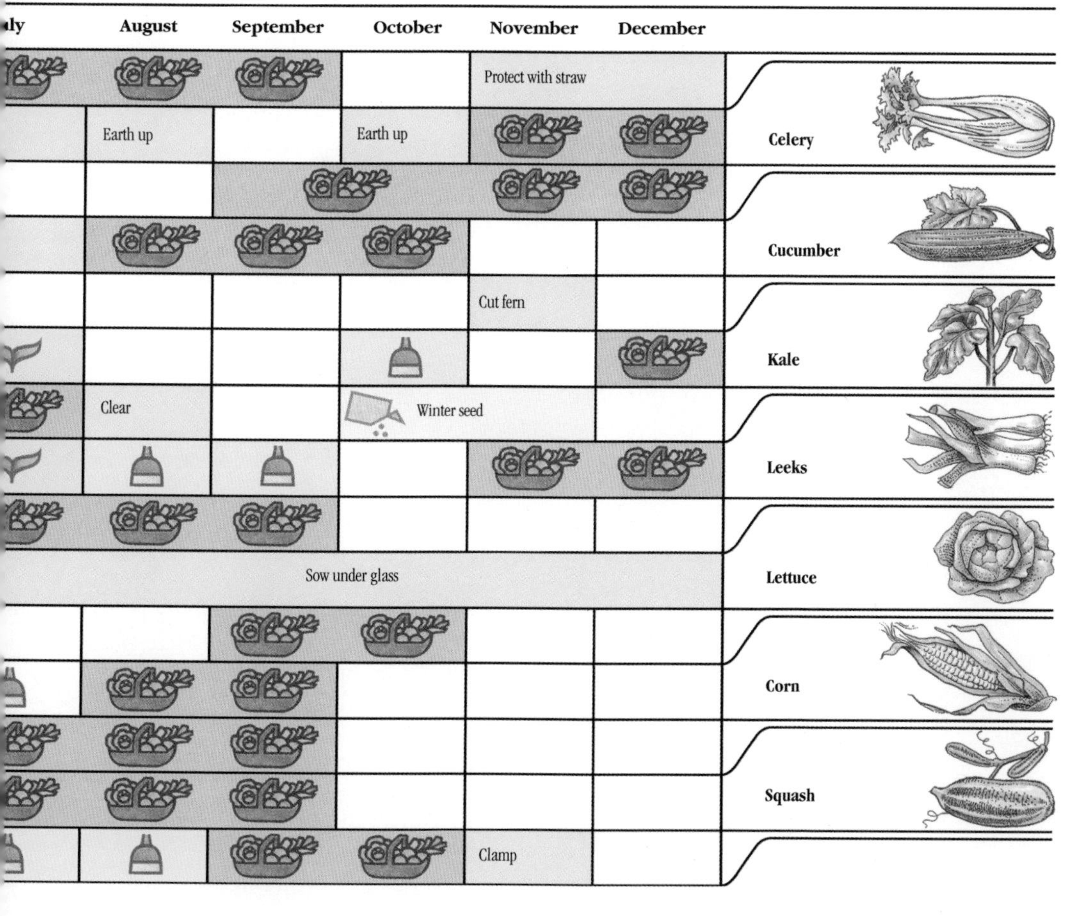

carrots, parsnips, beets, and celery. (Mixed crops and root crops can be very interchangeable.) Don't include turnips or rutabagas which suffer from clubroot and therefore must go in the brassica rotation (if you have a large plot and aren't already growing them on a field scale, which suits them better). Then back to spuds again, which is where we started.
The garden rotation outlined on these pages will work well with a garden in a temperate climate with a fairly mild winter. (Snow doesn't hurt the garden much unless it is extremely deep, but intense frost stops you from having anything growing outside in the winter at all.)

A VEGETABLE CALENDAR
The chart here and overleaf shows you when you can sow, plant out, hoe, and harvest for vegetables you might grow in a temperate climate.

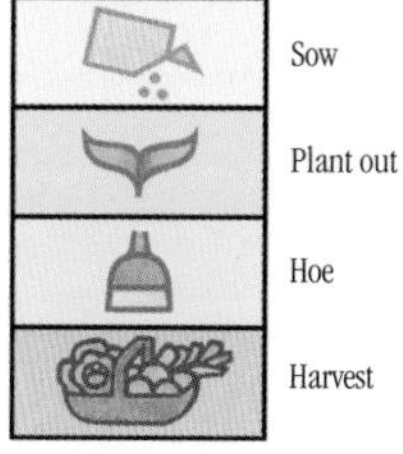

Probably no one would stick to my suggested four-year rotation slavishly. I know that there are idiosyncrasies in it, but I also know that it works. For example, I cram the brassica break in after the peas and beans, and clear the land of brassica the subsequent spring: this may be crowding things a bit, but two main crops are being produced in one year. To do this (and personally I find it a very good thing to do) you must sow your brassica seed in a seed bed, preferably not on any of your four main growing plots at all but in a fifth plot, which is for other things such as perennials. Then you must plant out the little plants from your crowded seed bed to a "holding bed" (a piece of clean, good land, in which these small brassica plants can find room to grow and develop). It will be late in the summer before many of them can go in after the just-harvested peas and beans, and it would be fatal to leave them crammed in their original seed bed until that late. So cramming five main crops into four years requires a holding bed as well as a seed bed. We can then look upon such quick growing things as lettuces, radishes, and early peas (which are actually best sown late) as catch-crops, ready to be dropped in wherever there is a spare bit of ground. Perhaps you think that radishes are brassica and therefore should only go in the brassica break? Well, we pull and eat ours so young that they don't have time to get and perpetuate clubroot.

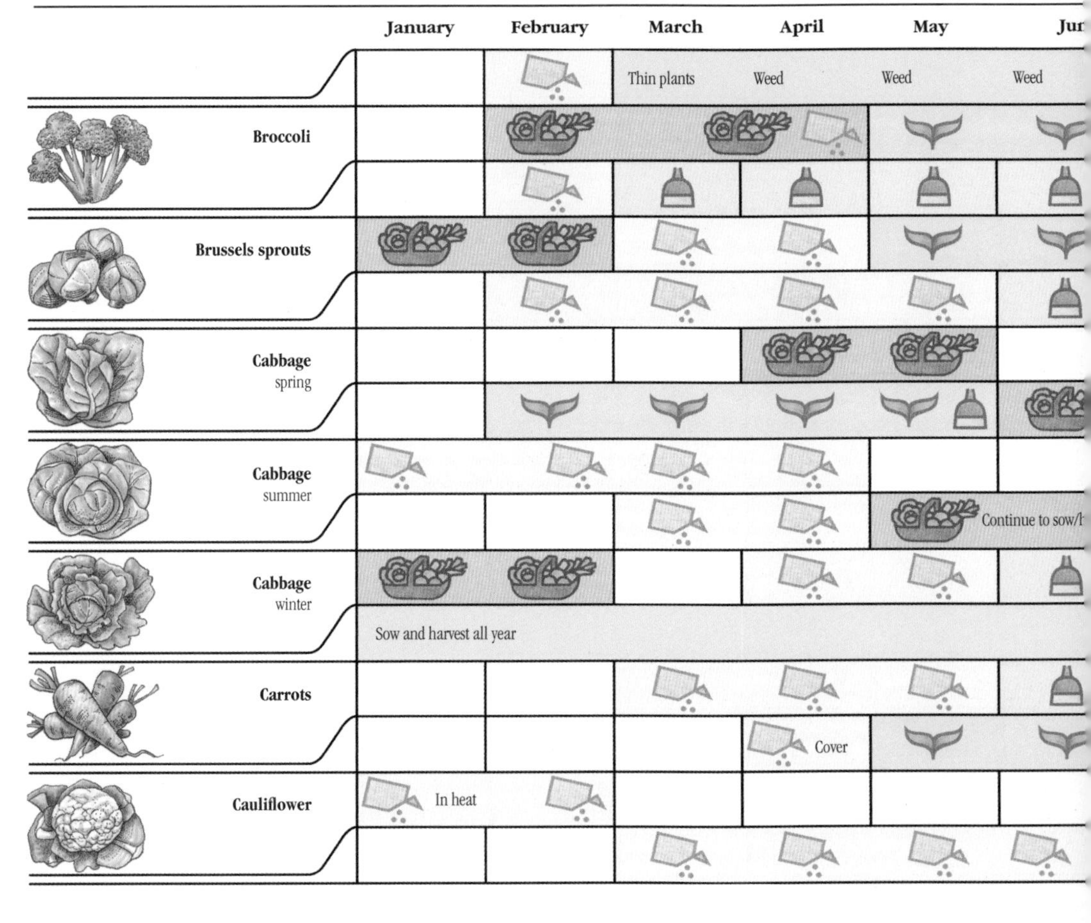

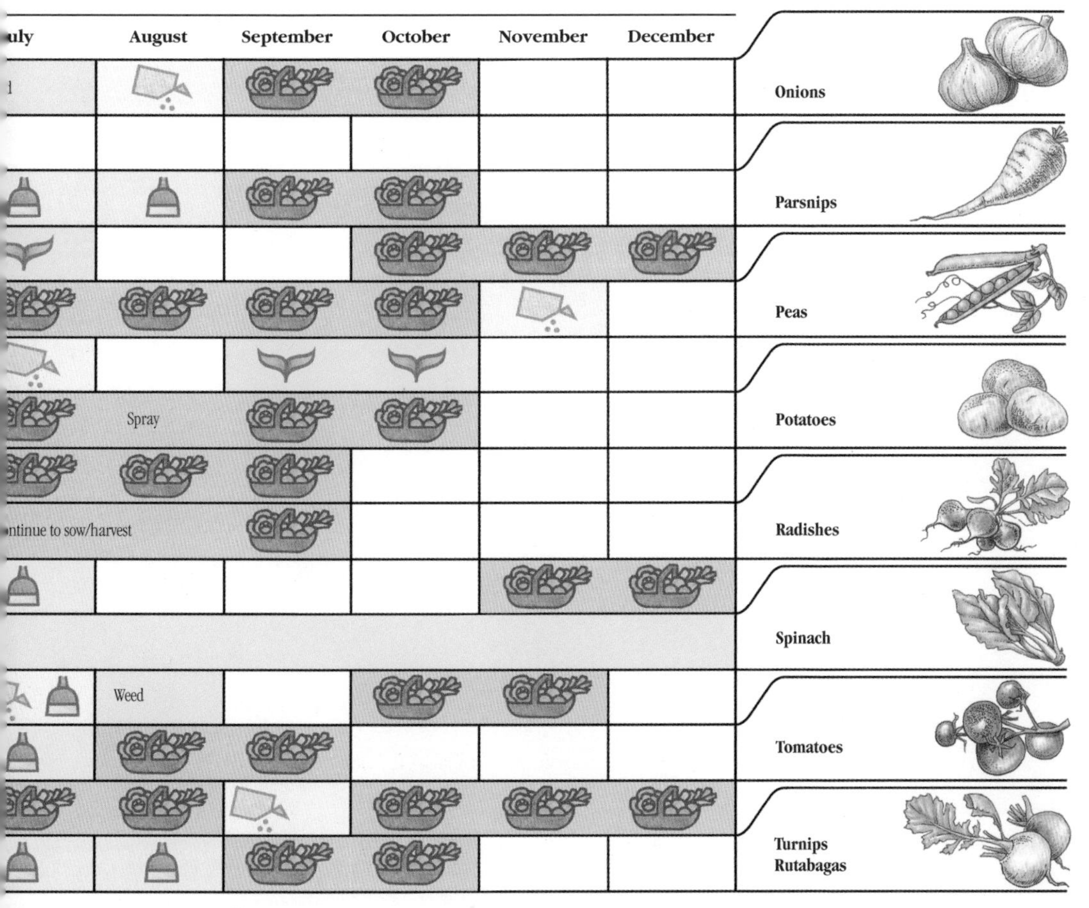

But don't leave them in to get too old and go to seed, or they will spread this rather nasty disease. Provided you keep brassica crops three years away from each other, you won't go far wrong. Climate is all-important, and for the seasonal plans on the next pages I have taken as the norm a temperate climate, which will support brassica outdoors all winter but will not allow us to grow subtropical or Mediterranean plants outdoors. In a climate with no winter frosts we could get three or four crops a year, provided we had enough rain or enough water for irrigation. In climates too cold for winter greens outside, we would have to devote the summer to one plot of brassica for storage during the winter.

A VEGETABLE CALENDAR

Shown here are ideal timings for a temperate climate. As a tip, check first what your neighbours are growing; the climate where you live could make up to a month's difference.

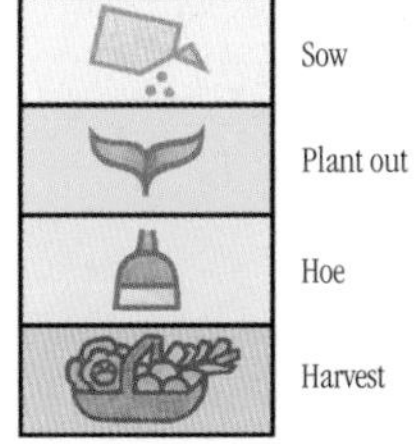

Winter

Winter is a time for building and repairing, for felling timber and converting it, for laying hedges, digging drains and ditches, building fences and stone walls. If the soil in the garden is heavy clay, it is best to keep off it as much as possible, because digging or working such soil in winter only does harm to it. On lighter land the same inhibition does not apply. In cold climates the land may be deep under snow anyway, and all the crops that have been harvested will be safe in a clamp or root cellar, or stored away in jars or bottles, crocks and barrels. Your varied food store should see you through the dark months.

GREENHOUSE AND PERENNIALS

In the greenhouse, it is time to clear winter lettuce, and the enriched soil that grew tomatoes last year goes out to the garden, with fresh soil barrowed in and mixed with compost. Tomato and cucumber seed are sown in the heat of the greenhouse. Hot beds can be built up in the cold frames. Mature compost is emptied on to your potato patch and the rest goes into an empty bin to aerate it, so a new compost heap is begun. Perennial plants protected from the winter cold by straw and seaweed are resting, before their spurt of growth in the spring.

PLOT A

This plot will have been very heavily mucked after the potatoes were lifted last fall. A small part of it may well be winter-sown broad beans this year if the winter is mild. The rest will go under winter rye or another winter green crop, which will stop the loss of nitrogen, and keep it ready to dig in as early as the land is dry enough to work in the spring. The plot was limed last fall after the spuds had been lifted, and this will also benefit the peas and beans that are to follow and the brassica crop which will come after them. A small part of this bed will have been planted with spring cabbages last autumn, and there will be a bed of leeks, ready to pull.

PLOT B

This should be full of big brassica plants – Brussels sprouts, hearting broccoli, big hard-hearted winter cabbage, and the like. There may well be a few rows of rutabagas if these haven't already been harvested and clamped. Turnips must be in the clamp or root cellar by now, for they can't stand the winter as swedes can. This plot will provide most of the greens during winter, helped by the leeks in plot A. Shallots can be planted out, as this plot becomes the next "miscellaneous" break.

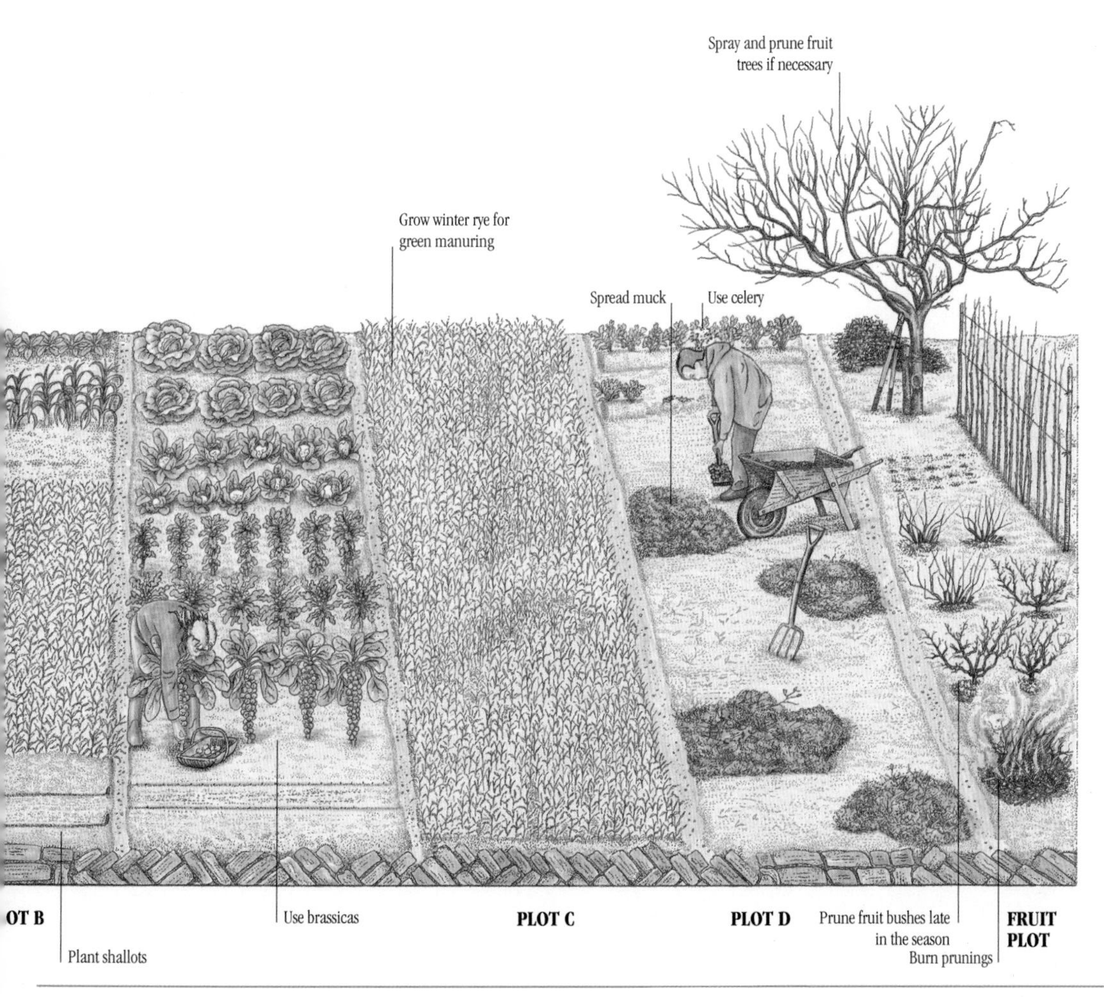

PLOT C

This plot is under green manure such as rye or other winter crop. Last year it bore the miscellaneous, short-lived crops. As soon as the land is dry enough to work, the green manure can be forked in, and begin to rot down. There is no hurry as this plot is going to be "roots" this year, and most of these will not have to be planted out very early.

PLOT D

Lying fallow, or under green manure (if the roots were harvested late last year, there may not have been time to sow this). It is time to barrow out compost or muck for the future crop of spuds. It is easier to push the barrow if barrowing is done in heavy frost. It also does the ground less damage. There may be a row of celery left undug; this can be remedied as during the winter.

FRUIT PLOT

Fruit trees only need spraying with a winter wash if pests have afflicted them badly: 2½ lb (1.1 kg) of caustic soda (lye) dissolved in 10 gallons (45 liters) of water was the old-fashioned remedy, but most people now buy commercial winter washes. Pruning starts from mid-February. Currants may have been pruned in the fall. Muck or compost is barrowed and dumped around trees and bushes, and the ground between soft fruit bushes is forked lightly. Burn all prunings.

Spring

There's so much to do in spring that it is difficult to get going fast enough. For a start, the green manure crops are turned in (a rototiller helps a lot), the seed beds prepared and seeds sown. Don't be in a rush to sow seeds, because they can't grow in half-frozen ground, and wet ground is cold ground. You're better off sowing a week or so later, in dry, warm soil, than earlier, in wet, cold soil. Some plants, like parsnips, need a very long growing season, and can be put in early. In March I have a big sheet of transparent plastic over February-planted early potatoes. The soil under it feels warm to the touch, while the soil outside is freezing.

GREENHOUSE AND PERENNIALS
Some plants are best started off early, but under glass – cloches also will warm the soil for early sowing. In a heated greenhouse, corn is sown in peat pots and green peppers in seed boxes. As the tomato and cucumber plants become big enough they can be planted out in pots or greenhouse soil. Cucumbers can be sown in the hot bed. With herbs it is time to lift, divide, and replant the perennial such as mint and thyme if needed. The seaweed covering should be removed from the asparagus bed, and the seaweed put in the compost heap. Rhubarb is forced under dark cover. Globe artichokes should be progressing well. Seeds are sown in the seed bed ready for planting out later: onion, broccoli, cabbage, cauliflower, Brussels sprouts, and leeks. Lettuce can also be sown in the seed bed if space is wanting in the main garden and lettuce plants are wanted ready for replanting later when there is room.

PLOT A
The leeks are cleared and eaten as the spring advances. The winter-sown broad beans will be growing well, but if there aren't enough of them spring-sown varieties may be planted early in the season, when early peas will also go in. After this, peas will be sown in succession. However many are grown, there will still never be enough! Early turnips, soybeans, and rutabagas should go in this plot, which will be brassica next winter. The row of spring cabbage will do for fresh greens, and will get eaten as spring advances.

PLOT B
Spring is more of a hungry-gap than winter, but the late hardy brassica, together with the leeks, tide things over. The brassica are nearly finished, but maybe a few Brussels sprouts and broccoli are still standing. As the plants are finished, they must be pulled out, the stems smashed and put on the compost heap.

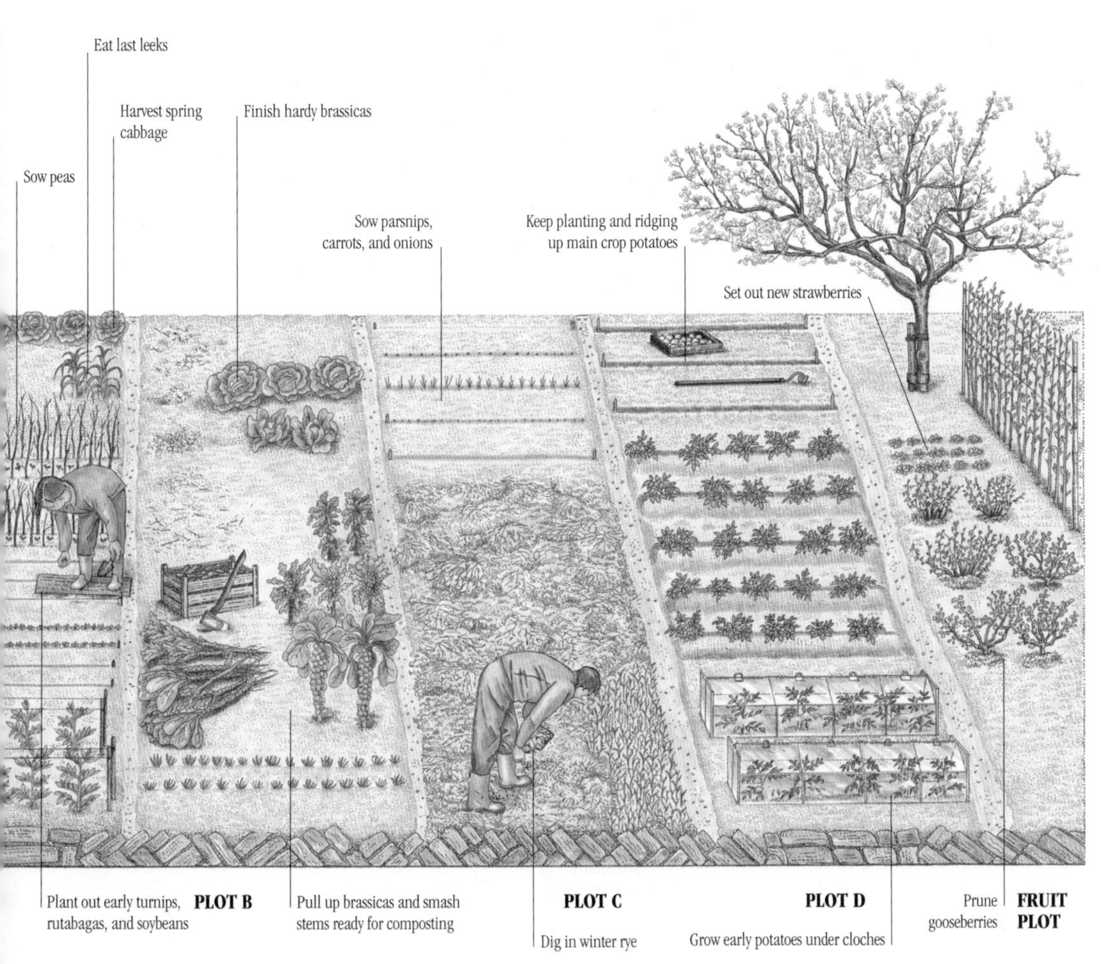

PLOT C

By now the winter rye sown last year as a green manure crop should be dug in, to make way for the roots to be sown later in the year. The only root crop sown early on is parsnip, but as spring progresses onion seed and carrots are sown in the bed. It is time to plant out onion sets and autumn-sown onions. If there is no garlic in the herb garden, it must be put out here early in spring. As spring turns into early summer more and more crops go into this root break bed.

PLOT D

A row of early potatoes could be growing under cloches or plastic, perhaps planted in March if winter is severe. The main crop won't go in until mid-April. The earlies get planted shallowly but the main crop go in deep furrows, both with ample muck compost. They are ridged up as they grow.

FRUIT PLOT

Prune gooseberries early in the season. Some people set out strawberry plants in March or April. The ground around soft fruit such as currants and raspberries should be kept hoed and cultivated to prevent grass from growing. Keep alert for pest attack. Grease bands put around fruit trees will catch crawlies climbing up. Don't spray insecticides on flowering trees, as they kill the beneficent bee.

Early Summer

Successional planting must go on unabated with crops in April, May, and June. Expect a constant supply of fresh peas, lettuces, radishes, and French beans from planting these short-lived plants little and often. Fresh young turnips should be available all summer too. Hoe hard in early summer, as this is when the weeds are raring to get a foothold and, if they do, say goodbye to fresh food. Onions and carrots must be meticulously hand-weeded. If some radish seed is sown along with parsnips, radishes will be clearly visible before the slow-growing parsnips have declared themselves, and can be side-hoed with safety.

GREENHOUSE AND PERENNIALS

Asparagus can be cut and eaten until the end of June, when it must be abandoned and allowed to grow. Herbs will thrive on frequent pickings. Artichokes are growing fast. The seed bed is kept weeded. If flea beetle appear on brassica seedlings, they can be dusted with pyrethrum. A good airing inside is vital during the day, but cold air must be kept out at night. The air is kept humid by spraying the floor and plants. The top glass should be lightly shaded with whitewash. Tomato plants are fed with water in which muck has been soaked. Brassica plants are pricked out into a holding bed. The lids on cucumber frames should now be propped open. Forcing of rhubarb continues.

PLOT A

Peas are sown in succession and given sticks to twine around as they need it. More turnips and rutabagas can be sown. May, or June in later districts, is the ideal time to sow out French and runner (pole) beans on previously prepared well-composted beds. Weed and water frequently, especially in a dry season. Harvest the broad beans (if you'd seen any signs of aphids earlier, you should have snapped off the tops immediately and cooked them. Once finished, cut them down and sow French beans in their place.

PLOT B

Now cleared of last winter's brassica, this is the new miscellaneous bed for outdoor tomatoes, zucchini, melons, pumpkins, squashes, radishes, lettuce, ridge cucumbers, spinach, and corn. As all these things – some reared in the greenhouse or cold frame – become ready, and the weather warms up, they are planted out, and should be watered and tended. A good mulch of well-rotted muck or compost will do them all good and revive the soil.

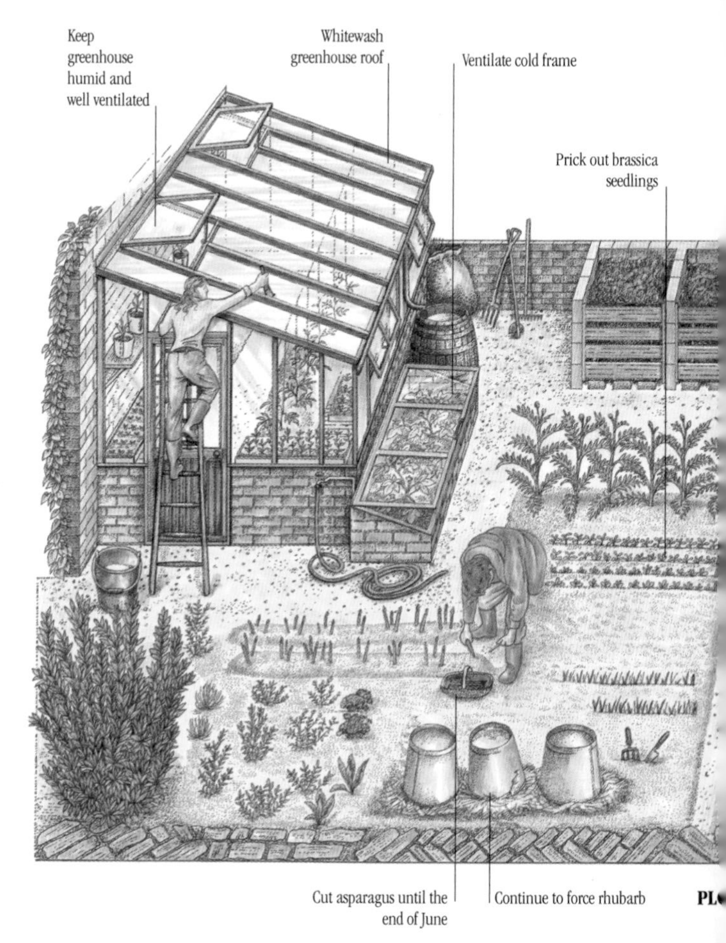

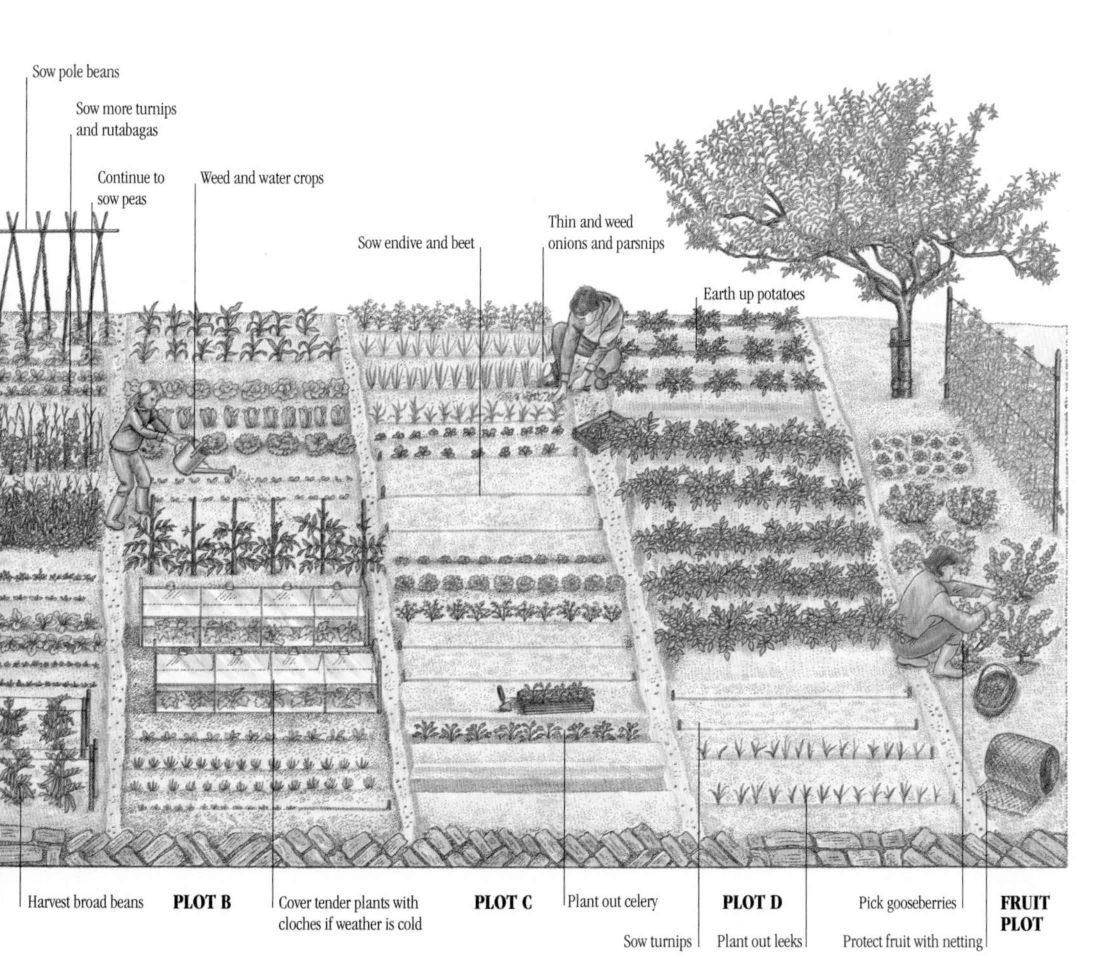

PLOT C

Onions in the root break plot should be growing well and in need of weeding and thinning. The carrots should be thinned if they are wanted for winter storing but not if intended for summer eating. The wily carrot fly must be avoided. Carrots should only be thinned when it is raining; otherwise, the tops should be protected with floating row covers. Parsnips are thinned and weeded. Endive and beet are sown. Celery should be planted out before the end of May in a previously prepared celery trench, and never allowed to dry out at all.

PLOT D

Start to earth up the already planted potatoes – very early morning, or late evening, when the leaves don't lie down and sprawl. Turnips can be sown to come up in the brassica break when the early potatoes are out. Leeks can only be planted after spuds have been lifted, if the spuds are early ones. Earlies are being eaten by June, so leeks can be transplanted when rows are clear.

FRUIT PLOT

Bird-free nets go over strawberries, straw underneath them. Soft fruit can be picked. Insects and various blights must be kept at bay. The ground between soft fruit bushes is hoed, and a mulch of compost put on. It is vital on light land.

Late Summer

Earlier labor will start bearing fruit in earnest – so think of giving away or bartering this harvest. The surplus of French or runner beans can be stored in salt, and cannellini beans and peas prepared for dry storage. As fast as they are harvested and cleared, the space is filled with well-grown brassica plants. Fitting the main brassica crop in as a catch crop after clearing peas and beans is possible because of the "holding bed," which now comes into its own. Hand-weeding must go on incessantly; weeds that are too big to hoe must be pulled out before they have time to seed: one year's seeding is seven years' weeding.

GREENHOUSE AND PERENNIALS

With the lid now taken off the cold frames, the cucumbers will run riot. Tomatoes, cucumbers, and peppers will be bearing, and will want watering, feeding, and plenty of ventilation. In the seed bed early spring cabbage seed can be sown. The herb and asparagus beds are kept weeded and the rhubarb needs to be regularly pulled. Soon the flowers of globe artichokes will be eaten; they should not be neglected, because uncut plants will not produce any more. However, leave a few for their brilliant blue flowers.

PLOT A

The peas and beans are watered if they need it, and runner (pole) bean flowers sprayed with water every evening, to help the flowers set. Peas, French beans, and runner (pole) beans galore are now ready to be picked. So are the turnips. As each row passes its best, it must be ruthlessly cleared out of the way, and the space planted up with well-grown brassica plants from the holding bed. When the runner beans begin to yield, they must be picked and picked again and never allowed to get old and tough. A great many are salted in anticipation of the dark days of the winter.

PLOT B

Any straggling vines of melons, pumpkins, and squashes must be cropped. Tomatoes must be staked, side-shoots picked out, and the plants stopped when they have four trusses. Water well if dry. In a damp climate, lay tomatoes down by end of August and cover with cloches so that more may ripen. Outdoor cucumbers must be picked so as not to get too big and bitter. All male flowers must be picked off. Lettuce should not be allowed to go to seed. Successional plantings of both lettuce and radishes continue. Sweet corn is high, in a block to facilitate wind pollination. The shallots can be harvested.

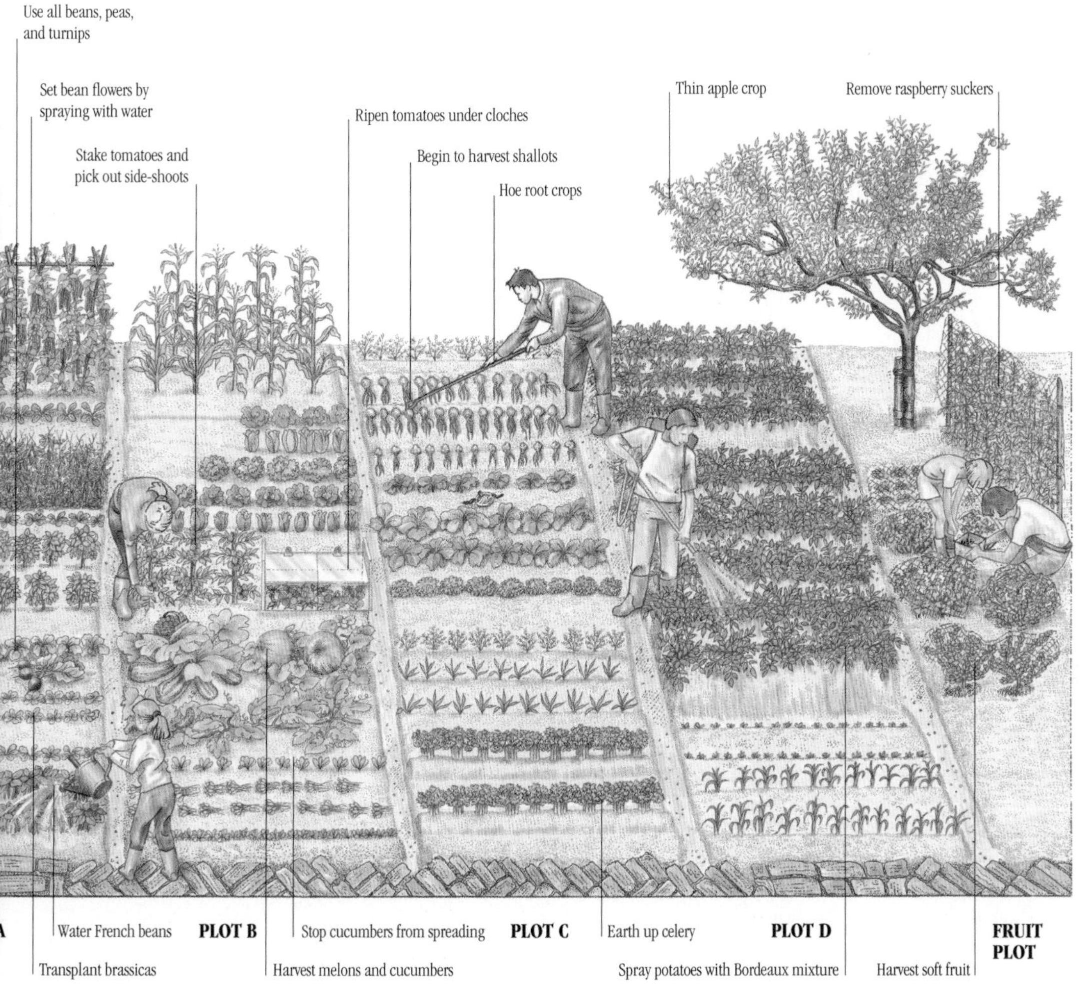

PLOT C
Just hoe all the root crops, keep the weeds down, and deter any lurking slugs. This is by far the best time of the year to clear all the weeds in the garden. Celery can be earthed up and sprayed with a Bordeaux mixture in preference to leaf-spot. Start harvesting the onion tribe now.

PLOT D
Early potatoes are gradually being eaten, and the second lot (if any) started on. The main crop must not be lifted yet, but can be sprayed twice with Bordeaux mixture, if blight is feared. Warm, muggy weather is the enemy. The main crop must be well earthed up, but when the tops meet across the furrows it won't be possible or necessary to hoe any more, though the big annual weeds should still be hauled out. Turnips and leeks should be establishing themselves.

FRUIT PLOT
Cut suckers from the base of raspberry plants. Thin immature apples where they are too thick on the tree (the "June drop" may have done this naturally) and summer-prune fruit trees. Eat plums and soft fruit while birds eat the cherries. August is the time to plant a new strawberry bed, so root the strawberry runners in small sunken pots. Hoe between soft fruits to keep the grass down and give the birds a chance to eat creepies.

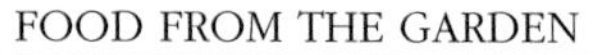

Fall

Fall is the season of mists and mellow fruitfulness according to Keats. It is also the real harvest time, when all the main crops have to be gathered in and stored for the dark days of winter. The good husbanding gardener will try to broadcast green manure seed wherever beds are left empty, although on very heavy soil, old-fashioned gardeners are fond of leaving it "turned up rough" after digging so that frost can get at it. Use annual weeds as a green manure if you like. After the first frost has touched celery and parsnips, it is time to start eating them, and time to think of parsnip wine for Christmas (or the Christmas after next, as purists would have it).

GREENHOUSE AND PERENNIALS

The frames and greenhouse can be sown with winter lettuce, spring cabbage, and summer cauliflower. The last two will be planted out next spring. Asparagus ferns are cut down and composted, thus defying the asparagus beetle. Potatoes may well be clamped near the house or put in the root cellar (or anywhere cold, dark, and frost-proof). Globe artichokes are cut as long as there are any left. Then they are abandoned, except for a covering of straw, as they die down, to protect them against frost. It is a good idea now to cover the asparagus bed with seaweed, or manure, or both. All perennial crops want lavish manuring.

PLOT A

Now it is time to clear away all the peas and beans, even the cannellini beans, soybeans, and any others intended for harvesting and drying for the winter. This bed will hold winter and spring brassica, planted late perhaps, but none the worse for that, as they have been growing away happily in their holding bed. The cabbages will benefit from the residual lime left by the peas and beans and the residue of the heavy manuring given to the previous spuds. When all weeds are suppressed, it is a good idea to mulch the brassica with compost, but slugs must also be kept down.

PLOT B

All the plants in this bed (which are plants with a short growing season) will have been harvested. After the bed has been cleared, it should be lightly forked over, and winter rye planted for green manure. Unfortunately, it is not much good trying a clover for this, because it is too late in the year; only a winter-growing crop such as rye will work.

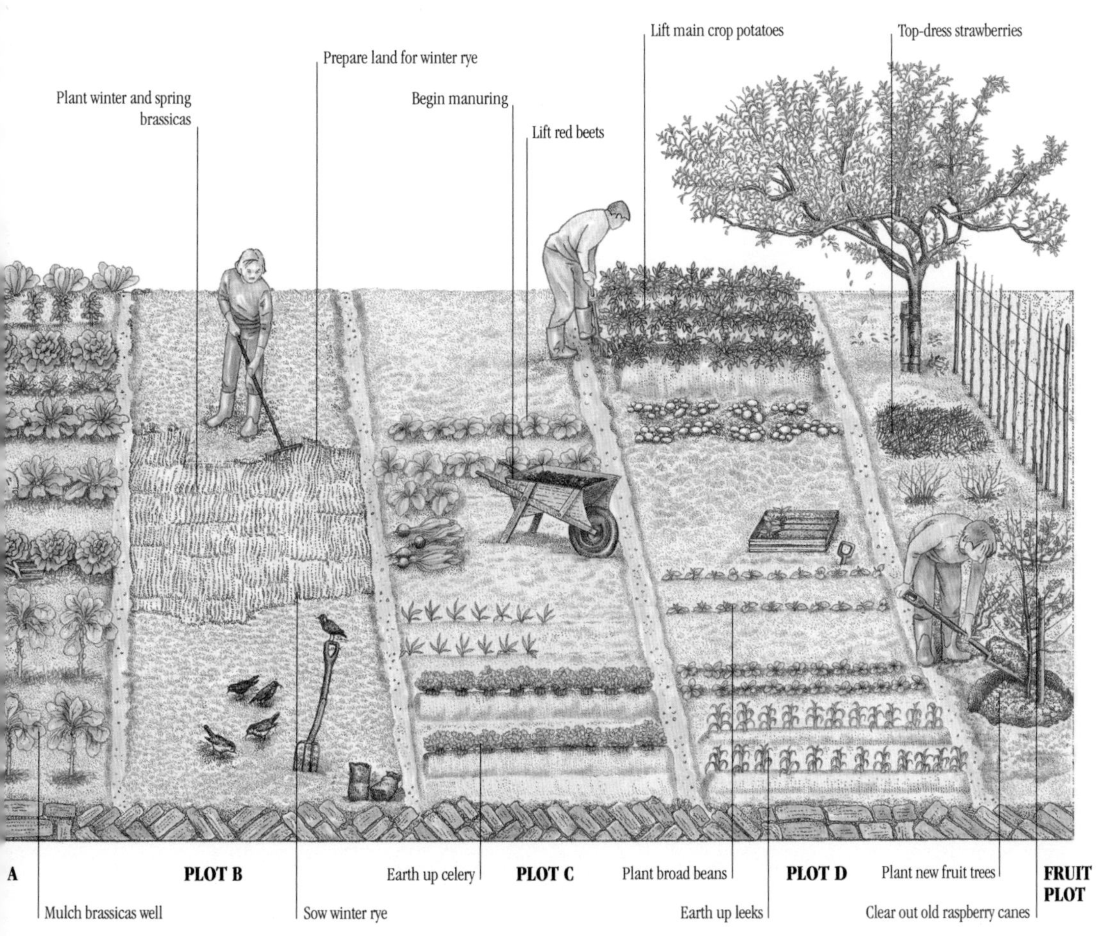

PLOT C

Once earthed up, parsnips and celery will also survive much of the winter. The rest of the roots are lifted in September and put safely in store. Red beets will bleed if lifted hurriedly. As the land is cleared rye can be sown in it until the end of September. This bed will be spuds next year, and manuring can begin.

PLOT D

Lift the main potato crop just before the first frosts are expected. This way the tubers will harden in the ground and keep better, and if blight is present there is less chance of spores being on the ground's surface to infect the tubers when lifted. The spuds should lie drying out on the surface for a day or so, while their skins set. Then they are clamped or stored away. The leeks are earthed up to be a great winter stand by. This plot will be the pea and bean break next year, so plant broad beans in October, or September if you have hard winters.

FRUIT PLOT

Runners are cut away from the strawberries, the ground cleared and given a good top-dressing of muck or compost. All fruit is harvested as it ripens; apples and pears are stored in a cool (not frosty) place, without touching each other. Old fruiting canes of raspberries are cut out, leaving the young wood. Prune currants in late November.

The Greenhouse

A basic greenhouse need only be a 3-ft (90-cm) high foundation of brick, concrete or stone, with a wooden framework containing heavy glass, a door, and four ventilators (two at each end, one high up and another low down). Inside you need removable staging for standing seed boxes on, and then in summer you can plant tomatoes in its place.

Unheated greenhouses

In temperate climates even an unheated greenhouse is enormously useful for giving plants like celery seed, corn, and early summer cabbage a flying start once the frosts are over. In the summer you can grow that magnificent plant, the tomato – a most desirable crop for the self-supporter. Expensive to buy yes, but they are easy to grow and they can well. Having a supply of them makes all the difference between some pretty dull food in the winter and *la dolce vita*. You can also nurture such luxury crops as melons, eggplants, green peppers (which turn into red ones if you leave them long enough), and cucumbers. Those grown inside a greenhouse taste much better than frame or ridge cucumbers grown outdoors, as does lettuce. Except by bringing along some early cabbage or some winter lettuce, a cold greenhouse will not help you much in the winter time, as the inside temperature, when there is no winter sun, may go well below freezing point.

> A hothouse enables you to grow practically anything that can be grown on earth.

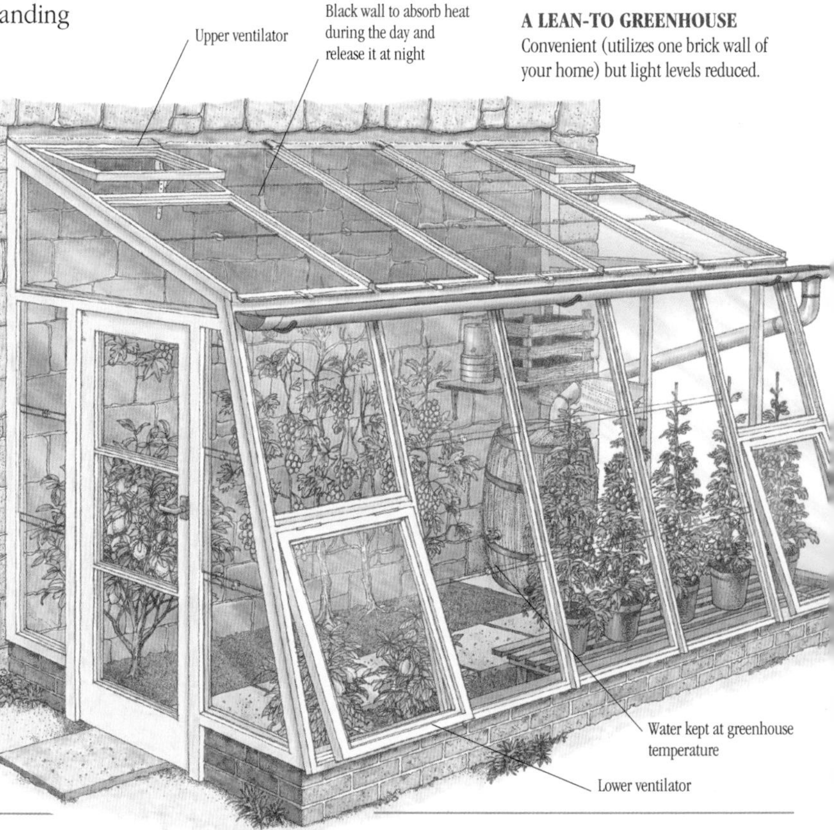

A LEAN-TO GREENHOUSE
Convenient (utilizes one brick wall of your home) but light levels reduced.

Heated greenhouses

If you can just manage – by hook or by crook, by oil or electricity, or wood-burning or coal – to keep the temperature of the air in your greenhouse above freezing all winter (and your greenhouse is big enough), you can have most Mediterranean fruits every year in any climate.

The self-supporter will like the idea of heating his greenhouse without buying fuel. This can be done possibly by harnessing an all-purpose furnace or by water or wind-generated electricity. Solar heating, properly used, has always been adequate to heat greenhouses in the warmer months of the year. A useful tip is to paint the masonry inside the greenhouse black, so heat is absorbed during the day and let out during the night to allay the frost.

Greenhouse temperatures

In the winter the temperature should be about 40°F (4°C) at night. The sun should bring this to about 50°F (10°C) on bright days. The day temperature should not be allowed to get too high, but it must not be kept down by admitting freezing air in its place, as this will inevitably kill the more tender plants. So cool the air by letting the boiler fire go out, but get it going again in the afternoon. In this way the temperature can be kept up at night. During the day, have the leeward (that is, the side away from the wind) top ventilator open. Then as spring gets into its stride, open both top ventilators a little more. Eventually, open one of the bottom ones as well. In spring and summer sprinkle water on the floor occasionally in order to keep the air humid. Ensure that proper guttering channels rainwater from the roof into a rain barrel.

Greenhouse soil

If you mix very good compost, good topsoil, and sharp sand in equal parts, and add a scattering of ground rock phosphate and a little lime, you will have a very good soil for your greenhouse. You can put this soil in raised beds, or right on to the existing soil of the greenhouse. The more you rotate crops inside the greenhouse, the better, but if you are driven to growing the same crop year after year then you may have to remove the old, or spent, soil bodily and replace it with new soil. Tomatoes are especially prone to suffer from disease if grown for too many years in a row on the same soil.

Greenhouse crops

A cold greenhouse means you can grow a slightly greater range, more reliably than you could outdoors. A hothouse enables you to grow practically anything that can be grown on earth. For my part the greenhouse is mainly for winter lettuce and other salad greens; seed sowing in flats or seed boxes in the early spring of celery, tomatoes, peppers, melons, eggplants, corn, and cucumbers; and my greenhouse crop is tomatoes, which go on all summer. I know you are supposed to be able to grow tomatoes outdoors in a temperate climate, but it's difficult.

Don't overcrowd your greenhouse. It's better to grow plenty of a really useful crop, like tomatoes, in the summer, and another really useful crop, like lettuces, in the winter than to fill your greenhouse with exotic fruits and such. Make use of hot beds under cold frames, cloches, jelly jars, and sheets of transparent plastic and the like, out of doors.

Soft Fruit

Soft fruits are one of the most productive and problem-free plants for the new gardener. Even on newly-cultivated land they will cope well with weeds and can be heavily mulched to boost their yields. They should be one of the first plants you think of when starting a new garden. They will come into bearing quickly enough: strawberries planted one summer will give you a big yield the next, and bush fruit does not take much longer. Soft fruits will give you, besides a lot of taste pleasure, a source of easily storable vitamins. By far the best to plant, for my money, are blackcurrants. They are hardy, prolific, extremely nourishing (about the richest source of vitamin C you can grow) and easily preserved. You can be sure of an ample source of delicious fruit right through the winter gap. Bottled they taste nearly as good as fresh, and seldom seem to have a crop failure. Raspberries are hardy, thrive in wet and cold latitudes, and are far easier to grow than strawberries, as well as being a treat for jam. They have a long picking season and children can be turned out to graze on them. Blueberries and their ilk are grown by people who are hooked on their flavour. They are so laborious to pick in any quantity that they must be viewed as a luxury. But they are useful in cold climates.

BLACKBERRIES / BRAMBLE FRUIT
Use I live in countryside where brambles are a blasted nuisance, and as we pick bushels of wild fruit from them, I wouldn't dream of planting blackberries. But cultivated brambles provide a heavier crop of bigger, sweeter fruit, and are very hardy. They also make good prickly hedges.

Planting If you want a hedge of tame blackberries, make sure the ground is completely clear of perennial weeds such as couch grass. Dig in muck or some phosphatic manure, or both. Then plant small plants every 1.8 m (6 ft). Each plant must have a bit of stem and a bit of root, and each stem and root should have been shortened to about half its length. Provide them with a wire fence and they will climb along it. In fact, they will spread at quite an amazing rate, so keep a close eye on which direction they are growing.

Pruning If you inherit wild brambles, and want to improve them for fruiting, cut the big patches into blocks by clearing rides, or paths, through them. Cut a lot of the dead wood from the bushes, clip the long straggling runners, and fling in some phosphatic manure if you really want to make a meal of it.
Aftercare Keep the rides clear, and you will greatly improve both the yield of that bramble patch and the ease of picking the fruit. Do not forget to watch for stray shoots growing up nearby.

BLACKCURRANTS
Use Blackcurrants are by far the best soft fruit you can grow, and make the best wine.
Soil They thrive on a cool and rather heavy soil, even on clay. The land should be limed the previous autumn if it is under about pH6.

Planting Take your cuttings from existing bushes in late autumn in the ordinary course of pruning; remove the tops and bottoms with a very sharp knife. Cuttings should be about 25 cm (10 in) long. The lower cut should be just below a joint. Make a slot in the soil with a spade, put a little sand in the bottom, and if you are a perfectionist, stick the cuttings into it with about 30 cm (1 ft) between each. Cover with leaves or compost to protect against frost heaving the soil up during the first winter. Nurserymen in cold climates make the cuttings from prunings in November, tie them in bundles and heel them in until March. Then they plant them. Next November lift the young rooted plants carefully and plant them 30 cm (1 ft) apart in rows 45 cm (18 inches) apart. At the end of the second year, lift them and transfer them to their permanent quarters, 1.8 m (6 ft) apart.

Pruning Blackcurrants, unlike red or white currants, fruit on new wood, so, if you can, cut out all the wood that was fruited on last year. But you will often find that you are faced with a long, old branch with a new branch growing on the end of it, so you will end up retaining some of the old wood. Do not worry if that is the case.

Pests "Big-bud" is the worst pest. It's caused by a mite, and causes swollen buds. Pick off all such buds and burn them. Another disease they can get is "reversion" when the leaves go a weird shape like nettle leaves. Pull these bushes right out and burn them.

Harvesting Some lazy people cut fruiting branches off, take them indoors, and strip the berries off there! Well, you kill two birds with one stone because you should prune out those already fruited branches that winter!

BLUEBERRIES

Use Blueberries aren't much good in warm climates, but people living in cold northern regions should consider them very seriously, for they are basically mountain fruit.

Planting Blueberries prefer acid soil to alkaline, so don't put lime on them. They stand up to intense cold and like a rather shallow water table so their roots are near the water. They can't grow in a swamp unless they're on a hummock. They will grow well on mountain peatland and prefer a pH value of about 4.5, which is very acid. Propagate from cuttings, or buy some three-year-old plants, and then plant them 1.8 m (6 ft) away from one another.

Pruning When the plant is four years old (the first year after planting three-year-olds), cut out most of the flower clusters and cut away the suckers, the shoots that come up from the roots. Do this for two years. Limit suckers to two or three for each bush. From then on cut away old wood from time to time. Don't pick the berries until they come off very easily, or they will have little taste.

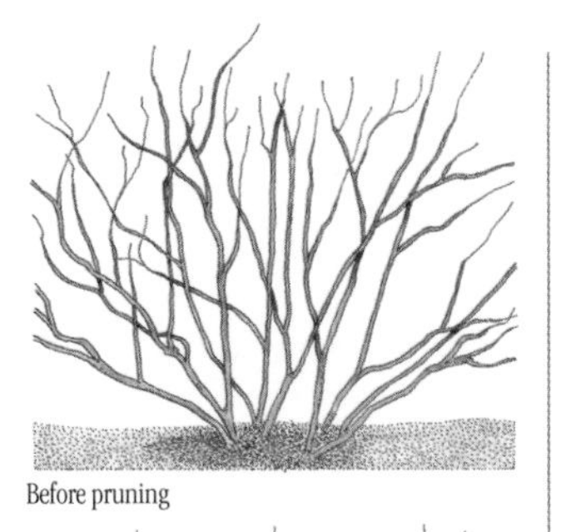

Before pruning

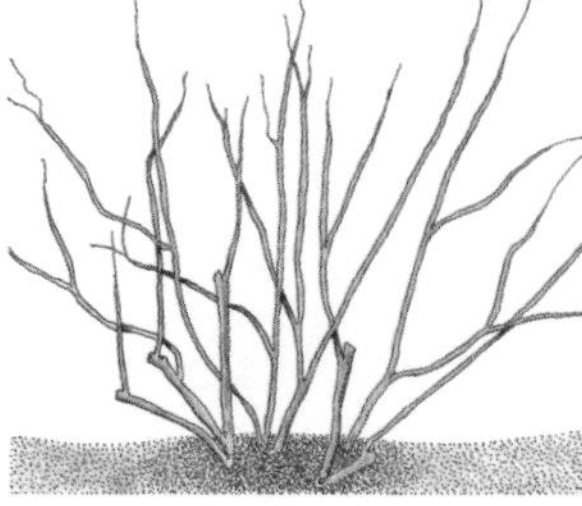

After pruning

CRANBERRIES

Use These fruits are most commonly used to make cranberry sauce, which is traditionally eaten with turkey and goes well with game. They will only grow under carefully controlled conditions; for this reason they are rarely grown in gardens.

Soil Cranberries grow in very acid soil. They must be well-drained yet well watered in summer, and then flooded in winter.

Planting Cuttings go in spring time in a 8-cm (3-in) layer of sand on top of peat.

Harvesting After at least 3 years of weeding, watering, and protecting, the plants may begin to fruit. The fruits are hand-picked.

GOOSEBERRIES

Use Gooseberries are a very useful source of winter vitamins and they bottle and cook well. You can't have too many of them, and for my part these and blackcurrants and raspberries are the only bush fruit really worth bothering about.

Soil They like a good, deep loam, but you can improve clay for them by digging sand in, and you can improve sand by digging clay in, and of course you can improve all soils by heavy mucking.

Propagation Treat as for blackcurrants except that you rub out, with your fingers, all the lower buds on the cutting, leaving only four at the top. They also layer well – peg a low branch to the ground and it will root. Cut it off and plant.

Pruning Prune hard the first year or two to achieve a cup-shaped bush (open in the middle, but with no branches straggling down). Then shorten the stems to 8–10 cm (3– 4 in) every winter, cutting out all old

branches that don't fruit any more. Always keep the middle open so you can get your hand in to pick the fruit.

Remember, however, never to prune gooseberries in frosty weather.

Aftercare Muck or compost mulch every year. Bullfinches have a history of destroying every bud during the winter if they can, so build a fruit cage if you have to. Leave the cage open in the summer until the fruit can form in order to let friendly birds in to eat the pests, but close it in the winter to keep baddy birds from eating the buds. The bullfinch plague in England and other places was due to gamekeepers. They destroyed all the predators, like owls and hawks, and small birds became a pest.

Diseases A horrible aphid sometimes lives inside gooseberry leaves and makes them curl up. Pick the curled leaves off and burn them. American gooseberry mildew can be sprayed with 55 g (2 oz) of potassium sulphide dissolved in 23 litres (5 gallons) of water. You can recognize it by a white felt-like growth over leaves and fruit.

Harvesting Just pick them when they are ready. You will find them good for bottling or for wine.

GRAPES

Use Grapes don't mind how cold the winter is, provided the summer is warm enough and there is enough sunshine. They will grow as far north as Suffolk, England. I grew some 90 outdoor vines there and got plenty of grapes. The pheasants ate all the grapes but I ate all the pheasants, so that was all right.

Soil Grapes need a very well-drained, warm soil, rich in humus, and they want plenty of sun and air. A south-facing hillside is fine. A pH of 6 is good, so you may have to lime. They can also be grown in a greenhouse and left to climb all over the place.

Propagation They grow well from soft fruit cuttings. Plant rooted cuttings out in lines 1.8 m (6 ft) apart in cold climates, and maybe more in warm. Grapes will fruit better in a cold climate if you keep the vines small and near the ground.

Pruning Have two horizontal wires, one at 30 cm (1 ft) from the ground and the other 75 cm (30 in). Vines fruit on this year's wood, so you can always prune last year's off, provided you leave two or three buds which will produce this year's shoots. In cold, damp climates, don't be too ambitious; leave three shoots to grow. One is a spare in case something happens to one of the others and you cut it off when the other two are established. Train the two you leave in the same direction along the two wires by tying them. In warmer climes, leave five shoots. Train four along the wires, two each way, and keep one spare. Prune in late winter. Cut the shoots off after they have made some six buds.

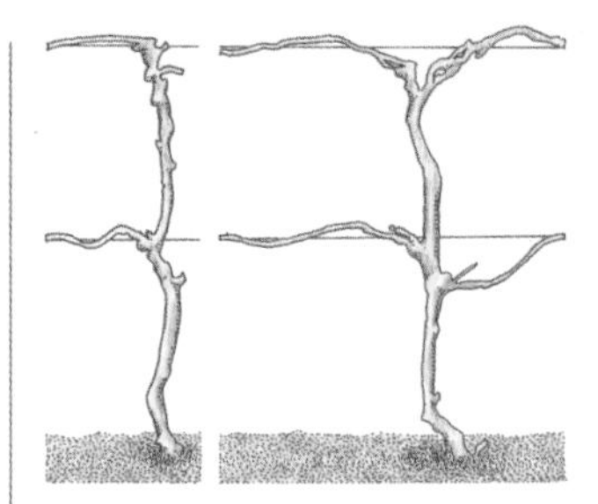

Aftercare Mulch heavily every year with compost. Keep down weeds, and spray with Bordeaux mixture in June.

Harvesting Cut the bunches of grapes off with secateurs. Never tear them off roughly.

RASPBERRIES AND LOGANBERRIES

Use Both taste excellent with fresh cream, and store well as jam.

Soil These soft fruit like a heavy, moist soil and will thrive in cold northern regions better than most soft fruit. They tolerate shade and a northern aspect. Get rid of all perennial weeds, and muck very heavily; they will thrive if you give them plenty.

Propagation Buy these young berry plants from a nursery, and then raise them from layers, or just dig them out from the ground near existing raspberries.
Planting Plant them quite shallow, 60 cm (2 ft) apart, in rows 1.5 m (5 ft) apart. Establish a fence for them to climb up, or to contain them. I just have three pairs of horizontal wires and make sure the canes grow between these, but some people tie them to the wires to give the canes extra support and to keep them closer.
Pruning Let them grow but don't let the first shoots flower – cut them down before they do that. The second generation of canes

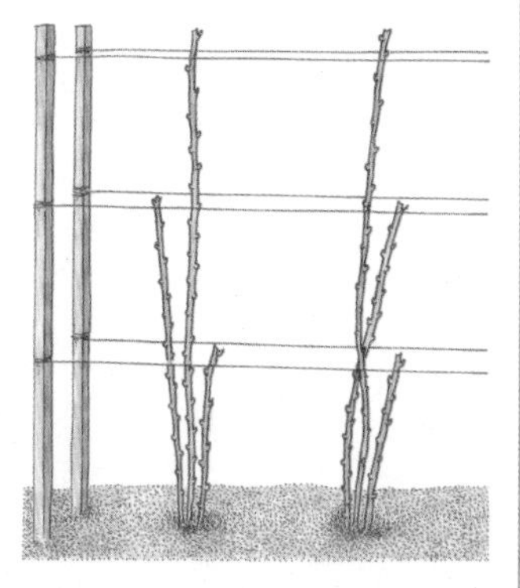

will fruit. Cut the canes out after they have fruited, and just keep three new canes to fruit the next year. Cut out all the weak canes. As the years go on, leave more canes to grow, maybe up to about a dozen. Suppress suckers, or dig them up to plant elsewhere. Cut the tips at different levels because that is where they fruit and you want fruit to thrive at all levels on the plant.

RED AND WHITE CURRANTS

Use Not as useful as blackcurrants, but good for making jelly.
Planting As with blackcurrants.

Pruning They fruit, not on the leaders like blackcurrants, but on spurs like apples. So cut back the first leader, or new shoots, to half their length the first winter. Then cut all the main leaders back to half their length, and cut out all subsidiary leaders to within 1 cm (½ in) of where they spring. Fruiting spurs will form at these points. In fact, keep

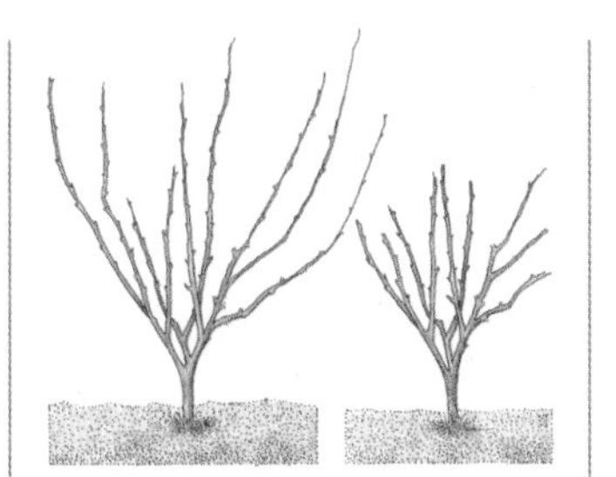

as much older fruiting wood as possible, while cutting out much of the new wood.
Aftercare Otherwise treat them just the same as blackcurrants. They don't get "big-bud" or "reversion".

STRAWBERRIES

Use This fruit is a very good source of vitamin C, rashes in some small children, and income for homesteaders. Strawberries are very labour-intensive, but they yield about

the highest income per acre of anything you can grow. If you grow different strains, you can have strawberries all summer.
Soil They are a woodland plant so they need tons of muck and slightly acid soil: no lime.
Propagation Strawberries make runners which root, and you can dig these out of the ground. Or you can make the runners root in little buried flower pots with compost in them. Then when they are rooted you can cut the runners, remove the pots, and plant out.
Planting Put little plants in during August and then transplant them.

30 cm (1 ft) apart in rows 45 cm (18 in) apart. Don't plant them deep and spread the roots out shallow.
Aftercare Hoe and weed constantly or your bed will become a mess, and mulch heavily with peat or compost. Keep an eye out for slugs. If you haven't any peat, put straw below the plants to keep the berries clean. If you get botrytis (grey mould), dust with flowers of sulphur.
Harvesting It is best to let strawberries fruit for three years, then scalp them. Establish a new bed every year for a constant supply.

Tree Fruit

Happy is the homesteader who inherits a holding that has plenty of established fruit trees. But this is a rare event and usually the newcomer has to plant from scratch and wait... and wait. If space permits, go for a mix of standard or half-standard hard fruit trees; otherwise espalier or cordon hard fruit trees, or else dwarfed trees, which generally yield a much heavier crop much more quickly than full-size trees; and some soft fruit. The latter will give you fruit in three years, or less if you plant two-year-old bushes. The big or half-standards, will eventually give you a great bulk of fruit, annually, and enough apples for cidermaking. However, if you have a very small garden, you had better not grow too much top fruit (that is, fruit grown on large trees), because trees take up a lot of space and sterilize the ground underneath them by drying out the soil, extracting nutriments from it, and shading it from the sun. When you site your orchard, consider water and air drainage: no fruit trees will thrive with their feet in water, and frost runs downhill and therefore a basin is a "frost pocket." Thus you don't want a hedge below a sloping orchard because this will impede the flow of cold air downhill, creating frost, which will impair the quality of your soil.

APPLES

Use Quite simply apples are the most useful fruit of all for cool and temperate climates. By having both early and late varieties, and long-keeping varieties, you can have prime apples nearly all the year, with maybe a little gap in summer when you have plenty of soft fruit anyway. A raw apple a day can be one of the most valuable items of your diet.

Soil Good, deep loam, but they grow in most soils with added muck. They don't do well on acid soil so you may have to lime. Land must be well-drained and not in a frost pocket.

Preparation Cultivate well and get rid of all perennial weeds. Dig holes bigger than the tree roots are likely to be, and if you can get it, throw some lime construction rubble in the bottom of the hole.

Planting If you buy from a nursery, go for three-year-old trees, but if you take immense care with planting you can have an almost ready-made orchard with seven-year-old trees.

Varieties There are at least a thousand varieties, so you need to get local advice on the best varieties to grow in your area, and make absolutely sure that varieties that need other varieties to pollinate them have their mates nearby. Otherwise they will remain fruitless old maids.

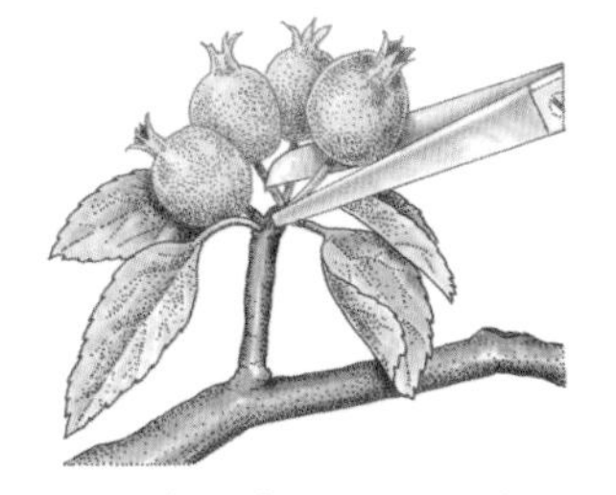

Pruning This is of vital importance if you want large fruit, but don't prune until the middle of February (to guard against rot spores). If your apples are "tip-bearers" – and you must find this out from the nursery – the only pruning you should do is to cut out some main branches, and in fact cut out the odd complete branch to keep the tree open and not too densely crowded. But most other apples you will have to prune more scientifically. Cut all leaders (the long shoots which you want to leave to form new branches) to a third of their length, and cut to about ½ in (1 cm) beyond an outward-facing bud. This is because the last bud you leave will turn into a branch next year and you want the branches to grow outward away from the center of the tree. Try to aim for a cup-shaped tree, open in the middle, with four or five nicely-shaped main branches growing out from the trunk at about 45°. Don't let it get too crowded with minor branches. So for the first year or two remove all young shoots that are not required for leaders to create the final shape of the tree. Cut them off ½ in (1 cm) from where they join the trunk. The aim should be to encourage fruiting spurs and discourage too much non-fruiting wood. If you cut off young shoots within ½ in (1 cm) of their base, a fruiting spur will probably grow in their place. So, on each small branch, cut the middle, or main, leader back to half its length but cut all the subsidiaries back to within ½ in (1 cm) of their bases so that they will form additional fruiting spurs. Prune lightly in midsummer, too. Don't prune leaders, but cut all subsidiary shoots that have grown that year down to within about 4 in (10 cm) of their base. In later years you may have too many fruiting spurs. In this case you must cut some out. And if a tree bears a lot of small fruit one year and none the next, thin the flowers out. If, during a good year, your tree appears to be supporting excessive amounts of fruit, thin out some of the tiny apples to make sure that the fruit left grows to a good size.

Aftercare Try to keep the ground directly around your trees free of weeds and grass; annual heavy mulching with whatever waste vegetable matter you have, plus muck or compost, helps this. However, don't put too much highly nitrogenous compost on. Try keeping a few hens under fruit trees because the birds scrap out a lot of wicked insects, but chicken dung is no good for apple trees.

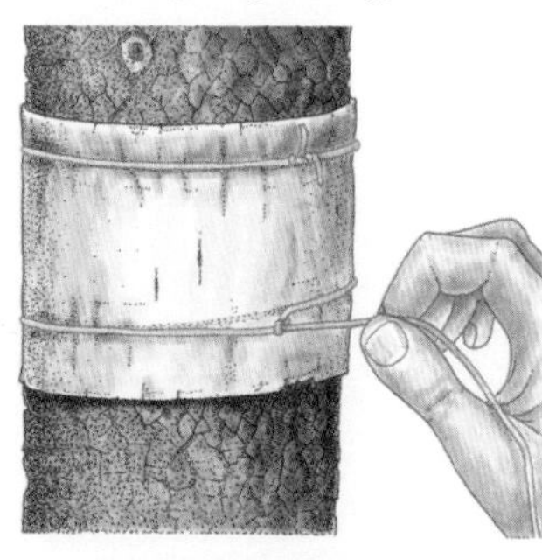

Grease-banding (*above*) is a good, old-fashioned pest control. Just stick bands of greasy material around a trunk or stem and the bugs will get stuck on it as they climb up.

CITRUS FRUIT

Use If I could only grow one citrus fruit tree – in other words if I only had room for one tree in a greenhouse – I would grow a lemon, because you could not hope to produce a significant amount of oranges off one tree,

whereas one lemon tree would keep a family in lemons, and without lemons a good cook is lost. You can, of course, grow oranges or lemons in tubs, kept indoors in the winter and put outside in the sunshine in summer, but you will get very little fruit like this.

Soil and climate Citrus fruit will grow well outdoors in subtropical climates. Lemons are slightly more frost tender than oranges: 30°F (-1°C) will kill the young fruit and 26°F (-3°C) may kill the tree. Oranges will put up with a degree or two colder. The best soil is sandy loam, pH between 5.5 and 6.2, and good drainage is essential.

Planting Plant like any other fruit trees.

Aftercare Keep the ground constantly moist for several weeks after planting. After the second year, if you are using irrigation, they should have at least 20 gallons (90 liters) of water a month. They don't need much

pruning, except for rootstock suckers and diseased wood. They like plenty of compost mulch but keep it from touching the trunk's foot – if you do not, foot rot may result.

Harvesting Fruits are harvested in winter and can be left on the trees quite safely for many months. So leave them until you want them and then pick them while fresh.

CHERRIES

Use The two distinct species of cherry, *Prunus avium* and *Prunus cerasus*, have given rise to the many varieties now

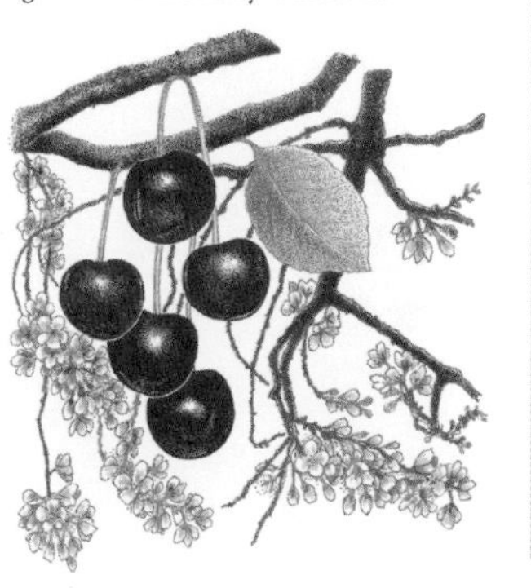

cultivated. The former are sweet, the latter sour, but hybrid breeds are common.

Soil Successful cultivation depends mainly on a favorable climate. An unexpected late frost will kill the crop without fail. Good water and air drainage is crucial. On well-drained soil trees can send their roots down as far as 6 ft (1.8 m) at which depth they are not in danger of suddenly drying out. Sweet cherries like a dry, friable loam; sour cherries prefer a clay soil that is more retentive of moisture.

Planting Plant in fall, and the first buds will appear early in spring. A thick mulch applied soon after protects the tree.

Aftercare Cherry trees bear their crop early in the season, so if a good mulch is maintained, spring and winter rain will give enough moisture.

Harvesting Picking cherries with their stems is not simple, for it is easy to damage the fruiting twigs. The small farmer with the single tree may find it easier to pick cherries without stems, although the fruit must then be used at once, before any bacteria have time to enter through the break in the skin.

FIGS

Use Fresh figs, sun-warmed, are a unique Mediterranean fruit that you can grow out of doors in cooler climates, as long you have well-drained, water-retentive soil and a south-facing wall to capture the sun.

Climate and soil In the northern US the Brown Turkey fig is the one to grow. It is best grown against a south-facing wall, and in rainy and fertile land the roots should be confined in some way. A box a cubic yard in size is ideal. Concrete walls are best and the floor should be soil with broken stone on it.

Soil for figs The reason for having a protective stone wall and stone broken up in the soil is that figs grown unconfined in moist and fertile places put on too much leaf and branch growth and not enough fruit. An eccentric parson of my acquaintance confines the roots of his fig trees with tombstones of the long deceased.

The fig will thrive in most soils but a light or sandy loam is held to be best. In fact, the fig is very much a fruit of poor soils.

Planting Figs grow well from cuttings. Take two- to three-year-old wood of under 1 in (2.5 cm) in diameter in winter, cut to 10-in (25-cm) lengths, plant almost completely buried in the soil, and keep moist. In places where figs grow well a fig tree can do with about 20 ft (6 m) of space. In colder climates, train a fan-shape up against a wall.

Aftercare Figs need little pruning unless fan-trained. If their roots are not enclosed and they do not fruit, root-prune them severely. An interesting thing about some figs, particularly the Smyrna fig, is that they can only be fertilized by a certain very slim wasp (*Blastophaga psenes*) that can crawl into the fig's neck. The fig is not a fruit, but a piece of hollow stem that has both male and female fruits inside it. When the Smyrna fig was taken to America, it was not understood why it would not fruit until it was discovered that the fig wasp was needed, and these were imported in a certain wild fig called the Caprifig. The Brown Turkey fig, which is the one to grow in northern climates, does not need *Blastophaga* to fertilize it. Figs can be dried, and make a very nutritious and easily stored food for the winter.

OLIVES

Use Where you can grow it, the olive is the most valuable tree imaginable, for it produces the best edible oil in the world besides the most delicious and nutritious fruit. In fact, one could live on good bread, olives, and wine, and many people have.

Soil and climate Olives suffer damage at -18°F (8°C) and very severe damage at 10°F(-12°C) so they are not suitable for cold climates. But they don't worry about late frosts above these temperatures because their

flowers don't come until late spring or early summer when such frosts will probably not occur. They will not grow at altitudes over 2,600 ft (800 m) unless they are very close to the sea, but near the sea they suffer from fumagine (a sooty mold disease). If you are able to provide these ideal conditions, grow them on a slope if you can, because they cannot stand having their roots in stagnant water. On the plus side, they will put up with practically any soil at all. If they are growing on sandy soil in a semi-desert climate, they will survive with as little as 8 in (20 cm) of rain annually. In clay soils farther north they will need 20 in (50 cm) or more. The best soil of all for olives is sandy soil interspersed with clay layers. They need rain in the summer period and if there is none you must irrigate profusely and regularly.

Propagation If you take cuttings in late summer and plant them in a mist propagator, you can grow trees from these. There are three ways you can do it: you can plant small cuttings of ¾ in–1½ in (2–4 cm) diameter and 10–12 in (25–30 cm) long vertically in the ground; you can plant larger cuttings 1½ in x 10 in (4 cm x 25 cm) below the ground horizontally; or you can plant root cuttings (taken from a tree growing on its own roots, of course, not from one grafted on a wild olive root stock) either in a bed or in the position you want your new tree. Professionals grow trees from seed, then graft them on wild olive stocks, but this is a very tricky business. If you are going to grow olives on any scale – and you are fortunate to have a sizeable farm – you should plant about 250 trees to the acre. Plant them any time between late fall and early spring. Trees may begin to fruit at five or six years old, be producing heavily at 10–15 years and go on for a hundred. Mature trees will give 90–150 lb (40–70 kg) of fruit and some 18 pints (10 liters) of olive oil.

Aftercare Olives must be heavily pruned, and this is a complicated job which really must be learned from somebody with plenty of experience.

Harvesting You can harvest from the end of November right on through the winter. If you are going to eat your olives you must carefully pick them by hand. If you want them for oil you should shake them down into a sheet.

PEACHES AND APRICOTS

Use Peaches and apricots are perhaps most appreciated in temperate climates where they are not so easy to grow. Increasingly, they are found frozen or canned, so it is well worth growing them fresh.

Soil and climate These fruit like light soil, sandy or gravelly loam. Paradoxically, peaches and apricots need both heat and cold. If they don't get cold in winter, say 40°F (4°C) or below, they don't have their winter

sleep and exhaust themselves. On the other hand, one late frost after flowering will wipe the crop out, and they need real heat and sunshine in summer. Most people who tried to make a fortune growing outdoor peaches in England after World War II gave it up.
Planting Best planted in spring except in climates where winters are very, very mild.
Aftercare Prune right back when you transplant the tree. Prune sensibly in the early stages to shape the tree, and nip out half the fruit if it is too crowded. If they get leaf curl disease, spray with Burgundy mixture in early spring, just before the buds swell.
Harvesting Peaches and apricots are ripe when all the green in the skin gives way to yellow. Be careful not to bruise the fruit when picking, as they then degenerate very rapidly. You can store them for up to two weeks.

PEARS

Pears like a more sheltered spot than apples and they are not quite so hardy; but otherwise treat exactly the same as apples. Plant a succession of varieties. Give copious top-dressings of manure, but see that it doesn't touch the stem, or roots will grow out from the scion instead of the stock. Incidentally, if you graft pear scions on wild

hawthorn bushes they will grow and produce pears! And remember, pears don't keep as well as apples do.

PLUMS

Use A number of very different species are all known as plums. They range from sweet dessert plums to tart damsons exclusively

used for jam. Prunes are varieties of plum which have so much natural sugar that they do not ferment while drying out with the pit still inside the fruit.
Varieties Plums are not always self-pollinating, so you must make sure that the varieties you plant are capable of pollinating each other or you won't get any fruit at all. If you only want to plant one tree, find out if any of your neighbors have plum trees and choose a variety which can be pollinated by any of them.
Pruning Don't prune plums for the first three years you have them, and then don't prune them until early summer or disease might get into them. Then take out any over-crowded branches, and, if the tree is too luxurious, shorten leaders to 1 ft (30 cm) and side-shoots to 6 in (15 cm). This will slow them down and make them fruit. In early summer make sure you always cut out any "die-back" (branches that are dying from the tips) and paint the wound with paint. Never prune plums in winter.
Aftercare Silverleaf disease is a bad disease of plums to get. If you get it, the leaves will

turn silver and the insides of the twigs brown. To remedy, cut off the twigs until you get into clean wood, and (this is an old remedy)

slit the bark with a knife right from the cut you have made down the trunk to the

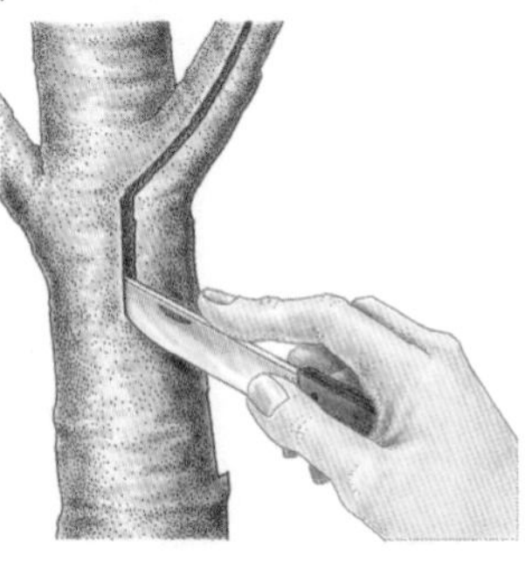

ground. Of course, burn all affected parts to prevent the disease from spreading.
Harvesting Plums for preserving can be picked as soon as a bloom appears on the skin, but if they're to be eaten fresh they should be left to hang for a while longer. Their flavor is best when they look and feel over-soft to the finger.

Caring for Fruit Trees

Planting

All fruit trees are planted in the same way. If your climate allows, it is best to plant during the winter months when the sap is not moving around the tree. Normally you would buy three-year-old trees to plant from a nursery, but get the nursery to prune them before they deliver them. If you take enormous care with planting, you can have an almost instant orchard by planting even seven-year-old trees. But these trees would be much more expensive, and you really need to know what you are doing when you plant them. You would have to put a bag around the root ball to keep the soil in, dig right below and all around the roots, plant with immense care, and keep watered for a month. So anyone inexperienced should stick to three-year-old trees.

Grafting

If you buy trees from a nursery they will already be grafted: that is, the cuttings from the fruit tree that you think you are buying will have been grafted on to another kind of tree. The latter will be some hardy, near-wild variety: for example, it will be a crab if the fruit tree is an apple. Thus you have the advantage of a hardy variety for the all-important root and trunk, and a highly-bred, high-yielding variety for the fruit. Very few amateur gardeners do much grafting, but there is no reason why they shouldn't, as it is easy enough. It is no good grafting on to an old diseased tree, or one that is prone to, or has had, canker (rot in the bark or wood). A very useful exercise is the top-grafting of old established fruit trees, which are of a poor variety, or are neglected, badly pruned, and in need of reviving. The growing tree you graft on to is called the stock, and the tree you graft on top of it is called the scion. Scions can be made from winter cuttings. Heel in the cuttings (plant them in a cool place) after you have cut them off an existing healthy young tree of the type you want, just as if they were ordinary cuttings. Then, in spring, cut all the branches of the old tree you wish to revive down to about a foot from their point of union with the trunk, for top-grafting. Trim the edges of the saw cut with a super-sharp knife, and go about grafting your scions on to each branch.

There are several ways of grafting, according to what sort of branch you are grafting on, but the principle is the same, and involves bringing the cambium (under-bark) layers of stock and scion into close contact. It is in this layer just under the bark that growth and union of tissue start.

Aftercare

Grass the space in between the trees if you don't want to intercrop with something else, but above all keep the grass close-mown all summer and don't remove the cut grass. Leave it there to rot and for the worms to pull down. Don't start spraying. If you obey all the books you read, you will swamp your trees with deadly poisons (some growers spray once a month, drenching trees, fruit, and soil with persistent toxins) and you will kill all the predators, the insects and arachnids that feed on your insect enemies, as well as your enemies themselves. Planting buckwheat near fruit trees is said to be good, for it attracts beneficial hoverflies.

PLANTING A TREE

When planting out a tree or a bush put yourself in its place. Consider the shock to the roots, accept that the tree is delicate, and treat it accordingly. Start by digging a hole much bigger than the root ball of the tree.

Drive a stake into the bottom of the hole before you put the tree in. You train the tree up the stake. Then put the tree in and prune off any broken roots or very long ones.

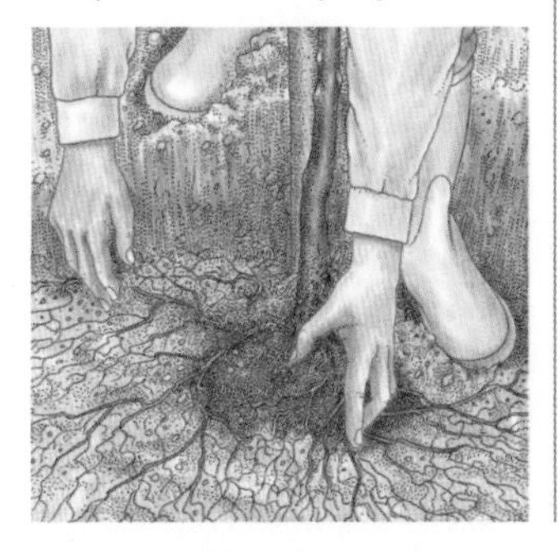

You will of course only be transplanting the tree in winter when it is dormant; but even so you can minimize the shock. Put a heap of rich loam in the middle of the hole and spread the roots round it. Make sure that you plant the tree at the same depth as it was before. Sift in more loam round the roots with your fingers, and rub the soil gently into them. Continue filling the hole until the roots are in close contact with the soil.

As the tree grows it will need a good supply of nutriments below it. So the soil under the tree and all round it must be firm; if the soil caves away under the roots and leaves a cavity, the tree will die. You should firm each layer of soil as you plant, making sure it is broken up finely. When you have installed the roots to your satisfaction (as well as the tree's), throw more soil in on top and stamp gently but firmly around it.

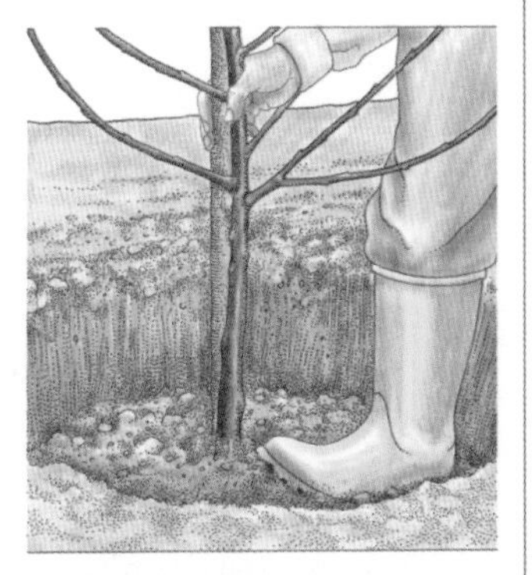

Do not stamp heavily as this will tear delicate roots. When the hole is completely filled in, and the soil heaped up a little, you can stamp harder. The stake ensures that no movement

disturbs the roots of the tree once growth begins. A tree must also have moisture after it has been replanted. So water it really well, and then put a good thick mulch of organic matter on the soil around the tree to conserve that much needed moisture.

Tie the tree to the stake with a plastic strap and buckle. Do not overtighten. Regularly check the strap and loosen it as the trunk grows and thickens.

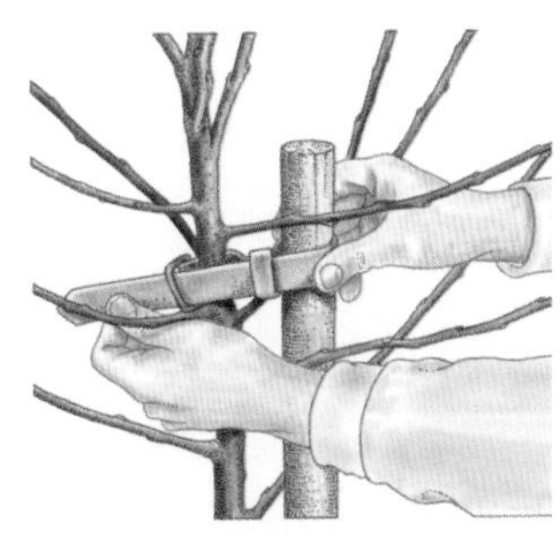

As a final tip, just stick bands of greasy material around the tree above the ground. Grease-banding really is a good old-fashioned safeguard against the many horrid things trying to climb up the trunk.

WHIP GRAFTING

This is a form of grafting which is used when the stock and the scion are approximately the same size. The stock is the branch on to which you graft the scion; the scion is a shoot that you have cut in winter, and then "heeled in" to a cool place until needed for grafting. Prepare the scion by making a cut just behind a bud at the lower end of the scion so that it slopes away to nothing at the base. The cut might be 2 in (5 cm) long.

Near the top of this cut make another small one upward, without removing any wood, so that a small tongue is formed. Cut the tip off the scion leaving from three to five buds. Now you can make cuts on top of the stock branch to correspond with those you have already made in the scion.

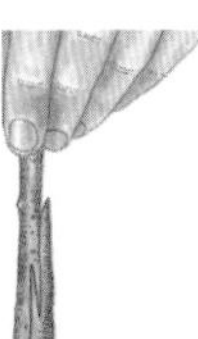

Fit scion to stock, slipping one tongue down behind the other. The two cambium layers must be in contact with each other.

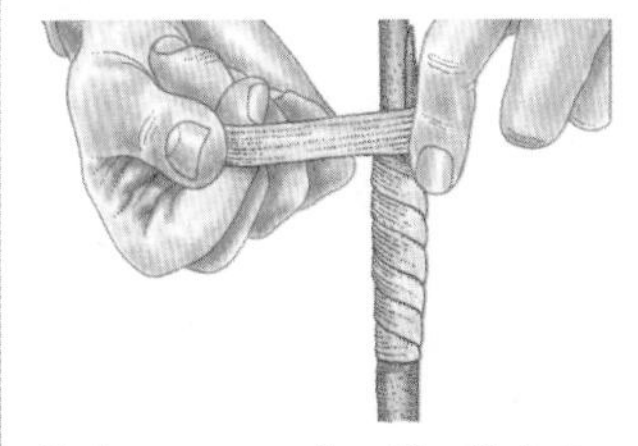

Tie the two parts together with raffia (cotton will do) and cover the whole joint with grafting wax.

TREE SHAPES

Train your young fruit trees into a variety of decorative shapes. This can save space, and in some cases can considerably increase your yields.

Cordons

Train a young fruit tree up a post-and-wire fence at an angle of about 45°, and limit it to one stem and no long laterals.

Fans

Train a maiden (which is a single-stemmed, one-year-old tree) along a wall or fence, with the help of canes tied to wires 6 in (15 cm) apart (*as above*). Prune so that the two opposite shoots grow from the main stem.

Espaliers

Stretch horizontal wires 1 ft (30 cm) apart between posts. Train the central stem vertically upward against a wall or fence and the lateral shoots at 90°, tying them to canes fastened to the wires. Keep spread below 5 ft (1.5 m) and no higher than 8 ft (2.5 m).

Dwarf pyramids

The advantages of choosing dwarf trees (*left*) are that they take up less space than full-size stock, while at the same time bearing as heavy fruit yields as full-size trees. Dwarf trees also give you an eye-catching free-standing tree shaped, as its name suggest, like a pyramid (with lower branches longer than the upper ones). Restrict the growth of a young tree to 7 feet (2 m). Keep sideshoots short. Dwarf trees fruit earlier, but do not live as long as full-size stock. Fine for apples, pears and plums.

BUDDING

This method of grafting is much used by rose-growers, although it can also be done with fruit trees just as effectively. In summer select a strong healthy scion (a cutting or twig for grafting) about 1 ft (30 cm) long and put it in water.

1 Cut a T-shaped slit along the back of your stock.

2 Peel back the two flaps of bark formed by the cut.

3 Take your scion out of water and slice out a shield-shaped piece of bark which contains a bud within a leaf axil.

4 Insert the shield into the T-shaped cut. Remove any of the shield sticking out above the T-shaped cut; put back the flaps on each side. Bind with raffia or tape after insertion. As the bud grows you can cut off any stock above the bud-graft.

Clearing Land

Unless your property is big and you plan to farm a proportion of it on the "dog and walking stick" principle, one of your first priorities will be to see if you can gain any extra usable land by clearing overgrown wood and bush land. Such land is definitely worth clearing as long as it is not on a ridiculously steep slope, or irretrievably swampy or covered in rocks and boulders. Clearing land is hard but rewarding work, although it can be extremely expensive and time-consuming.

Self-supporters with a pig have the best pioneer. They can concentrate pigs in bush land and the pigs will clear it for them with no effort on their part at all. Pigs won't, of course, remove trees, but all brambles, gorse, and undergrowth generally will yield to their snouts and they will manure the land at the same time. If there are any stubborn areas of thicket, throwing some corn into them will soon get the pigs rooting them out.

Goats will kill small trees, and big ones too if they are concentrated, by barking them, and they will prevent trees from coming back. They will not, of course, get the trees out, any more than pigs will. You will have to do that.

Clearing woodland

It is essential to have a gasoline-powered chainsaw for this work (of course you could hire a mechanical excavator, which is another consideration of cost against time, plus the back-breaking slashing of usable timber when the wood is green). A chainsaw is a lethal, noisy monster and you'll have to learn to use this with great care. (Courses in chainsaw safety are available and you should ask your supplier about this.) First cut off all light branches that are no good for firewood, then cut logs from timber that might serve as good firewood (this includes sections of large roots when the stumps are pulled out). Take all this away to your woodshed for cutting up and splitting later. You can then get a few helpers – kids often love this job – to take all the brashings (small branches) to make a bonfire. Make this in a corner somewhere where the flames will do no harm and you can then leave it for a couple of months until a cold dry winter day makes a good occasion for a bonfire party.

If you leave the tree stumps reasonably high, say at about 2–3 ft (50 cm–1 m) this will make it much easier to lever them out. A good digger driver can clear a big area in a day at a reasonable cost. Have the stumps piled up in a corner for burning a few months later when they have dried out. It is cheaper to haul stumps out with a tree-jack or monkey-winch. You might rent or borrow one of these. Alternatively, you can dig stumps out with spade and mattock, but this is very laborious.

A more accessible method is sodium chlorate, which is a common weed killer, much used by terrorists for the manufacture of their infernal machines. If you drill holes in the stump and fill them with sodium chlorate, put some cover over the holes to stop the rain from getting in, and wait a month, you will find that the stump has become highly inflammable. Build a small fire on the stump and it will burn right away. A more organic option might be filling the holes with sugar, buttermilk, or dried milk powder to encourage decomposition.

Gorse, broom, and brambles

Areas covered with gorse, broom, and brambles can be cleared very effectively with a bow saw and a sharp scythe. Make sure you have a good pair of leather gloves and you can remove gorse fairly quickly with a small bow saw. A chainsaw is noisy and will quickly blunt when cutting gorse near to the ground (which is what you want to do). Your scythe will easily cut brambles if it is sharp and you always pull away from the roots. Cutting thorny brambles from a distance with a scythe is very effective: use a pitchfork to pile them up in a heap for burning. Once you have cleared an area, you may need to pass over it with your scythe once or twice every year for a few years after to keep down the prickly shoots that are re-emerging.

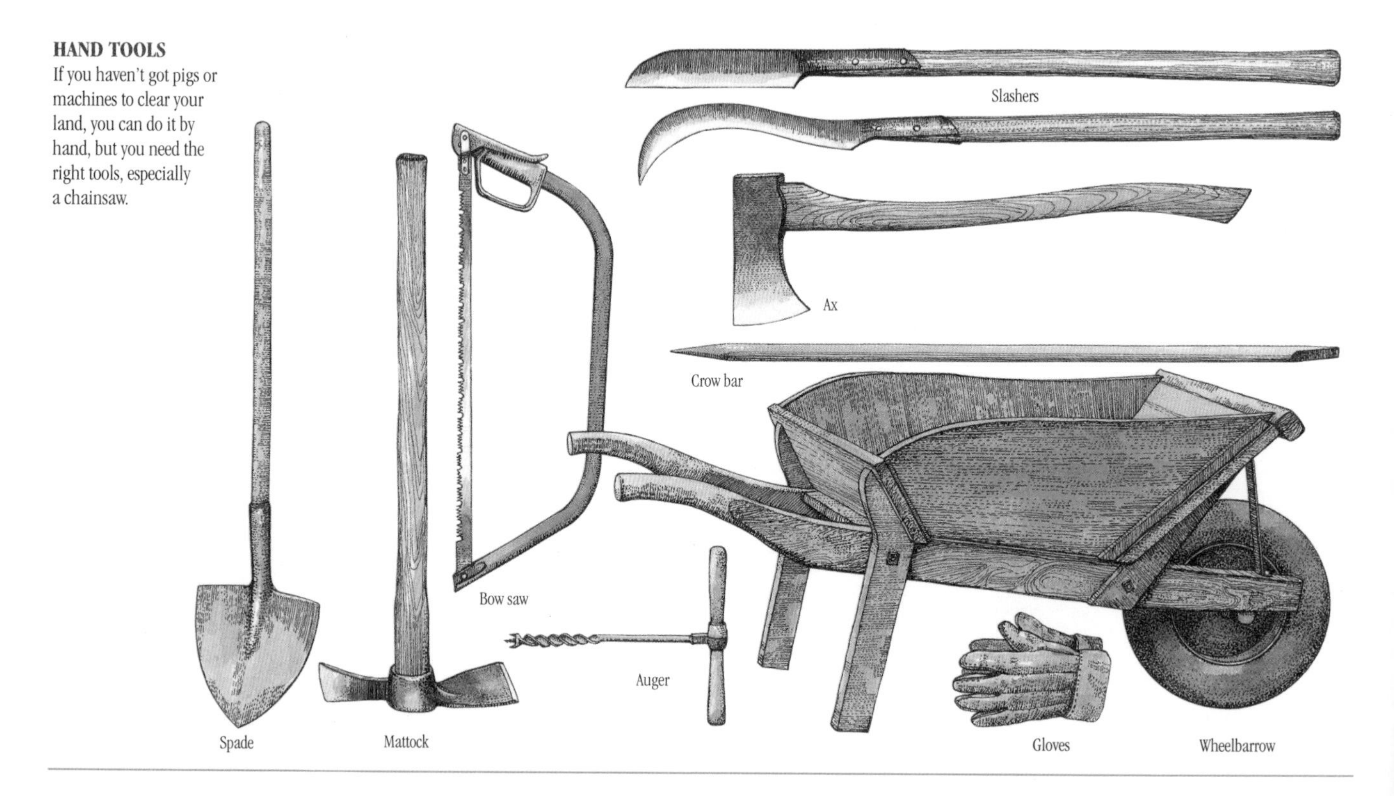

HAND TOOLS
If you haven't got pigs or machines to clear your land, you can do it by hand, but you need the right tools, especially a chainsaw.

Removing rocks

Rocks can be very obstructive, particularly on boulder-clay or glacial till in which boulders have been left by the retreating ice in a completely random fashion. Again, a mechanical excavator can deal with these if they are not too big, hauling them out and dozing them to the side of the field. You can lift quite large rocks, of several tons or more, with levers. Dig down around the rock, establish a secure fulcrum at one side of it – a railroad tie will do, or another rock – insert a long beam of wood or a steel girder (a length of railroad track is ideal) and raise that side of the rock a few inches. Now pack small rocks under the big rock, let the latter subside, and apply your lever to the other side. Do the same there. Continue to work your way around the rock, raising it again and again the few inches made possible by your lever and packing small stones under it each time you have gained a bit. You will eventually work your rock to a point above the surface of the surrounding ground.

Once you have got a boulder out you may be able to roll it to the side of the field, again using levers. If it is too big for this, you can try lighting a big fire under it, heating it right through, and then throwing cold water on it. This should crack it.

Don't forget that clearance is not the only option. It is perfectly possible to renovate old woodland by judicious felling and replanting. You can then leave the old stumps to rot *in situ*. When the timber is more mature the wood will make an ideal holding ground for poultry or pigs. Or consider if it would not be better to replant old woodland as new woodland and farm it as forest.

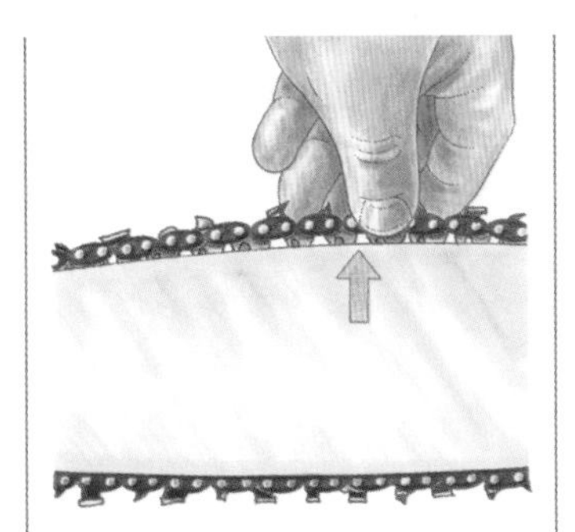

CHAINSAW TENSIONING
Check the chain tension is right by pulling with your thumb, and make sure the chain lubrication is filled up and working properly.

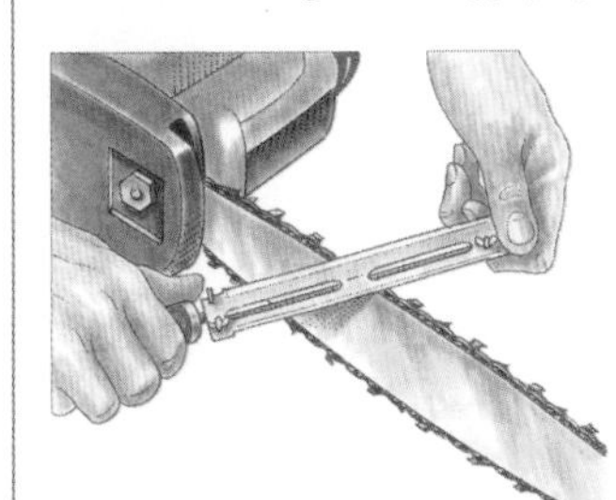

SHARPENING A CHAINSAW
With a file holder leave the chain on the bar and lock it with the hand guard. Always file from inside to outside with the cutter in a horizontal fashion.

LEVERING UP A BOULDER

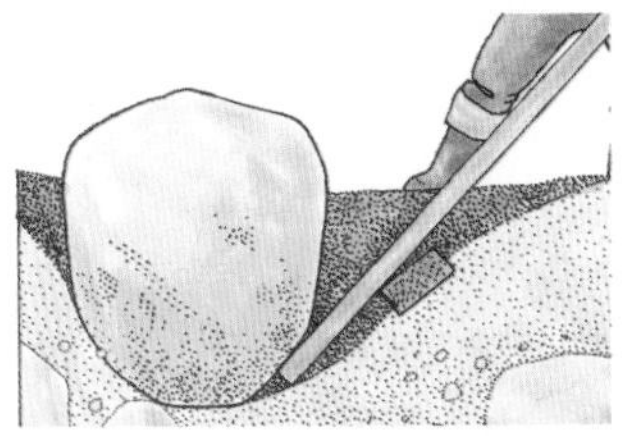

1 Use a rock or a chunk of wood as a fulcrum. Work a lever down beside the boulder.

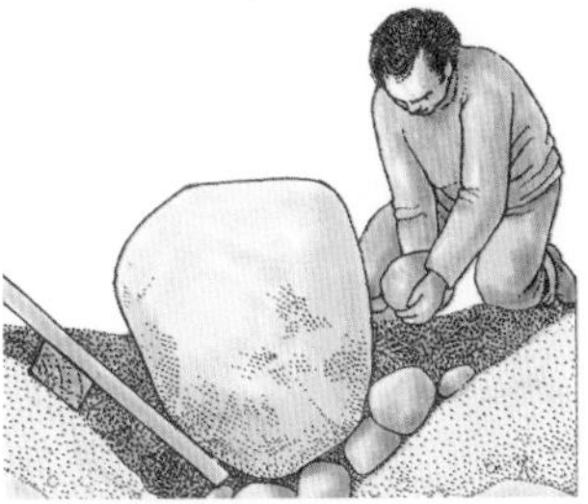

2 Raise the boulder as far as possible. Prop up with stones. Take the lever and fulcrum to the other side.

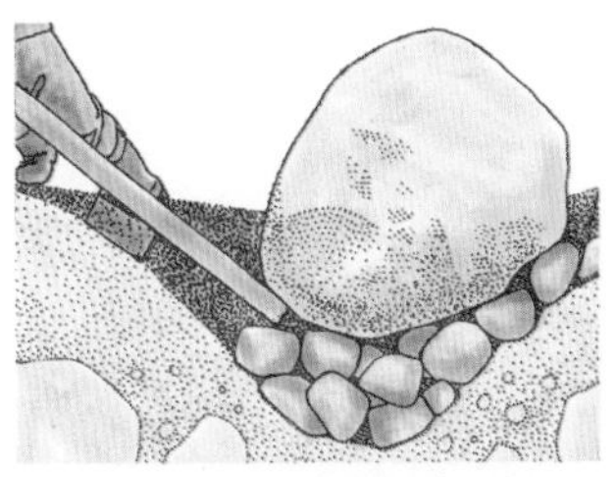

3 Repeat the process over and over to gain a few inches each time. Once the boulder is out, roll it off your field.

Making Use of Trees

The most useful trees for the self-supporter are, in order of importance: sweet chestnut (the best tree in the world for timber), oak, ash, and larch. In North America you would add hickory, sugar maple, and black cherry. If you have a saw bench capable of ripping down trees, then softwoods or any of the timber hardwoods are useful, too.

Hardwoods and softwoods

When considering timber for purposes other than fuel, you should look out for: a fairly quick rate of growth, hardness, and resistance to rot, and what I like to call "cleave-ability" or "split-ability." It is often better to cleave wood rather than rip-saw it (that is, saw it along the grain). Cleaving is quicker, cheaper, the resulting wood is stronger, and lasts longer. Why is this? Because when you rip-saw you inevitably cut across some of the grain, or wood fibers. When you cleave, your cleavage always runs between the grain, which avoids "cross-graining" and leaves undamaged grain to resist the weather. Sweet chestnut cleaves beautifully. It is fast growing, straight, hard, and strong. It also resists rot better than any other tree. Oak cleaves well, too, but not as well as chestnut.

THE FORESTER'S ESSENTIAL TOOLS
Fell your tree with ax and saw. Use hammer and wedge, or club and froe, for splitting. Adze and draw-knife are for stripping and shaping.

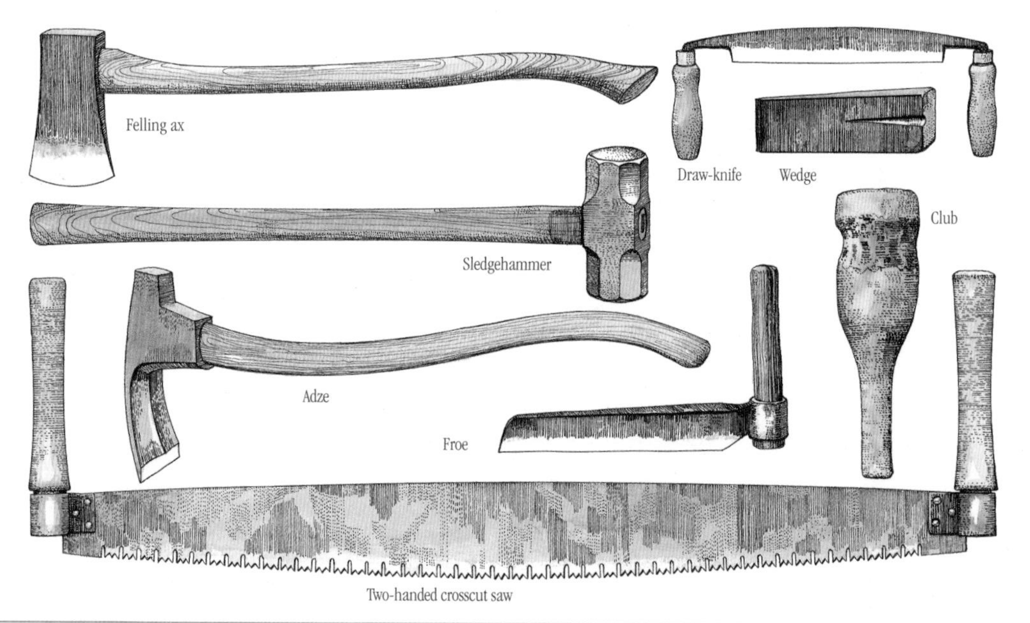

Oak is extremely slow-growing and needs good soil to grow. The heart of oak is as hard and lasts as long, but the white sapwood on the outside – most of a small tree – is useless. Ash, however, is tough and resilient, but will rot if put in the ground. It is straight, grows fast, and splits well. Above the ground, but exposed to the weather, ash will last a long time if you apply a preservative every now and then. It makes good gates or hurdles. Larch is unusual in that it is a conifer but not an evergreen. It is very fast-growing and is the best conifer for lasting in the ground, with help from preservative treatment. All other conifers, or softwoods, are hopeless in the ground if not treated with preservatives, and even then they don't last many years.

Cherry and all other fruit woods are hard, and make fine firewood. They are good for making cog teeth in water mills, for example. Hickory is the best wood for tool handles. It doesn't grow in Europe (why? I don't know), and so is either imported or else ash is used, which is a pretty good substitute. Elm – alas virtually killed off by Dutch elm disease – is good for any purpose where you want a non-splittable wood, such as for wheel hubs, chopping blocks, and butcher's blocks. It is great under water. Maple and sycamore are good for turning on a lathe, and making treen (carved objects). Walnut is a king among fine woods, and fit to harvest in just a mere 150 years, though 350 years is better if you have the patience to wait for it!

As for firewood, trees are undoubtedly going to be your best and most likely source of solid fuel. If you are fortunate enough to own even an acre or two of woodland, you will find that, with proper management, the trees in it will grow faster than you can cut them down for your fire. A good piece of woodland is the most efficient solar heat collector in the world, in my opinion.

A piece of woodland is the most efficient solar heat collector in the world.

Ash is the best of all firewoods. "Sere or green, it's fit for a queen!" The loppings of felled ash are excellent. It burns as well when newly cut as when mature. Oak, when seasoned, is a fine and long-burning firewood, but it grows far too slowly to be planted for this purpose. Silver birch is good for firewood, though not for much else. It burns very hot when seasoned, and it grows fast. Conifers aren't much good for firewood. They spit a lot and burn very quickly, but in the frozen north, where there's nothing else, that's what people have to use. Birch is better as firewood, and it will grow further north than any other tree. All the weed woods, like alder and pussy willow, are very sluggish when green, but can be burned when dry, though even then they don't burn well or give out prolonged heat. But what else is there to do with them? Any wood in the world will burn. But if you are planting trees especially for firewood, plant ash, and then coppice it.

Coppicing & planting

Coppicing means cutting down all your trees when they are about 9 in (23 cm) in diameter, and then letting them grow again. They will coppice by putting up several shoots from each bole. Cut these down again in about twelve years and they will grow once more. This twelve-yearly harvesting can go on for aeons, and help harvest the greatest possible quantity of firewood from a woodlot.

Plant trees very close together and they will grow up straight and tall, reaching for the light: 5 ft (1.6 m) by 5 is fine. When they become crowded, you thin them and get a small preliminary harvest. In winter, plant trees at least three years old. You can buy them from a nursery, or the Forestry Service, or you can grow them yourself from seed. Keep the grass and yard waste down every summer for three or four years, so the trees don't get smothered. Saw off low branches from the growing trees to achieve clean timber without knots. Feed with phosphate, potash, and lime if needed. A scythe is ideal for clearing around young trees.

In existing woodlands uproot the weed trees (alder, pussy willow, thorn) to give the other trees a better chance. Wet land favors weed trees, so drain if you can. Keep out sheep,

TREES TO PLANT
These trees are among the most useful that you could grow on your land: **1** Ash **2** Larch **3** Silver Birch **4** Elm **5** Walnut **6** Sweet Chestnut **7** Shagbark Hickory **8** Oak

cattle, and goats to give seedlings a chance. Cut out undergrowth if you have time.

Stack the planks as they come out of the log, with billets of wood in between to let the air through. Kiln-drying is a quick way of seasoning, but time is better. Some wood, for example ash, can be laid in a stream for a few weeks to drive the sap out. This speeds seasoning, but some trees do take years to season. If you want woods for cabinet-making, for example, there must not be any subsequent movement. But for rough work, gates, or even timbers for rough buildings, seasoning is not so important. Always remember to treat trees as a crop. Don't hesitate to cut mature trees when they are ripe, but always plant more trees than you cut down.

FELLING A TREE

Use an ax to trim off all roots to cut a face in the side of a tree.

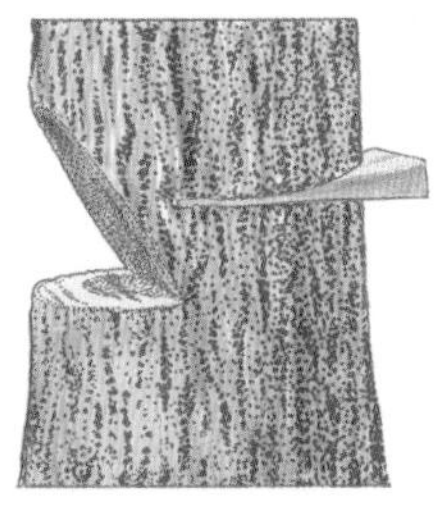

A "face" is a forester's term for a deep, V-shaped notch and you cut it in the side toward which you want the tree to fall. Now begin sawing from the other side, making your cut a few inches above the deepest part of the face. When the tree sits on your blade, so that you can't move it, use your sledgehammer to drive a wedge in behind your saw. Continue sawing until you are close to the face.

The tree should feel like it is about to fall. Now pull out your saw, bang the wedge further in, and over she goes. A jagged piece of wood, called the "sloven," will be left sticking up from the stump. Trim it off with your ax.

RIVING WITH WEDGE AND SLEDGEHAMMER

Wedges and a sledgehammer are the best tools for riving, that is splitting, large logs.

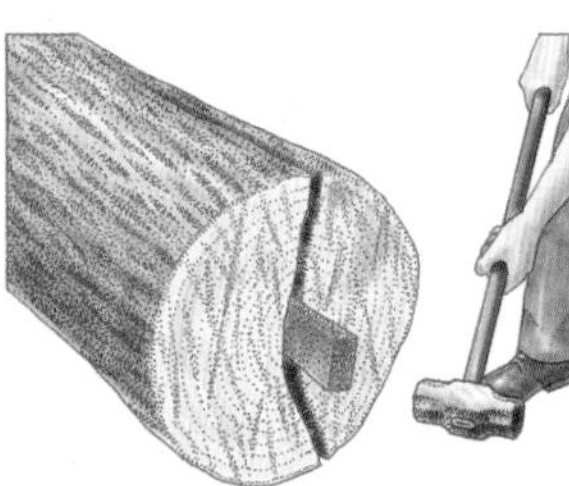

Use the sledgehammer to drive a wedge into the end grain of the log. Then drive more wedges into the cleft thus made until the log splits right down its length. Never use an ax as a wedge. The handle will break.

RIVING WITH FROE AND CLUB

For riving smaller wood the ideal tool is a froe. Whack the blade into the end grain with a club.

Or use a mallet. Now work the blade further into the wood by levering sideways with the handle of the froe.

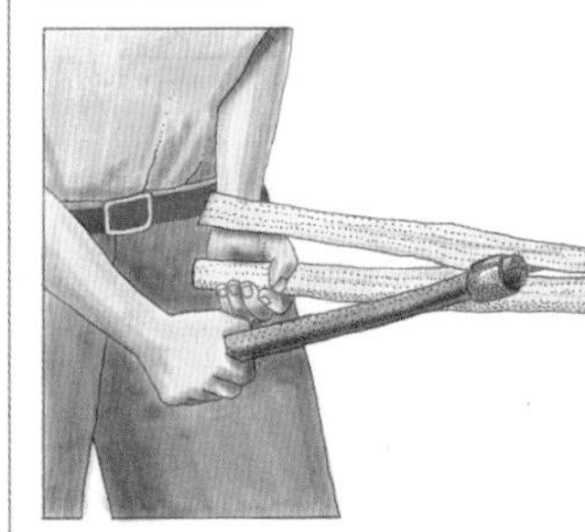

You won't get very far before the wood splits down its length. This is much quicker than using wedges.

SAWING PLANKS

A pit saw is a time-honored tool for sawing logs into planks. One man stands on the log; the other is down a pit dodging the sawdust. Band saws and circular saws are easier but more expensive.

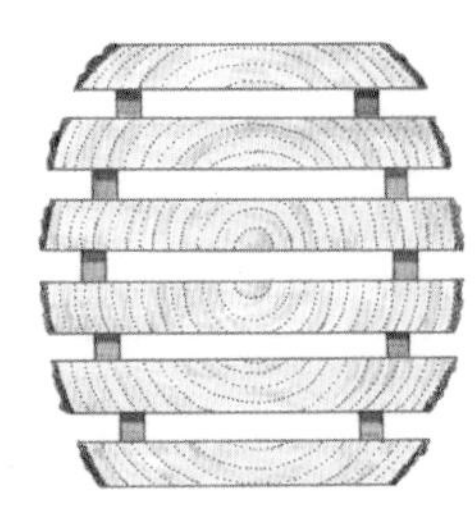

SEASONING PLANKS

Stack planks as they leave the log with spacers to let air through. Leave them for at least 18 months.

Hedging and Fencing

Fences and hedges help you compartmentalize and manage the different facets of your self-supporting labors – that is, your vegetable plots, fruit trees, cottage gardens, boundaries – as well as providing shelter and privacy. Fences will also relieve self-supporters with animals of the time-consuming task of herding, but will also give them a useful tool for the better husbanding of their land. Without the fence they cannot concentrate pigs on rooting or even keep goats and chickens out of the garden.

Quickthorn hedge

The cheapest and most natural barrier you can build is a quickthorn hedge. Quick means alive, and such a hedge is established by planting thorn bushes, generally whitethorn (may), close enough together in a long line. Seedling thorns, about 6 in (15 cm) high, can be planted in two lines, staggered, 9 in (23 cm) between the two rows but 18 in (45 cm) between the plants in the rows. You can buy the plants from nurseries or grow them yourself from haws, the seeds of the hawthorn. But the hedge must be protected from stock for at least four years, and this is what makes a quickthorn hedge so difficult to establish. Animals, particularly sheep and even more particularly goats, will eat a young quickthorn hedge. Therefore, some other sort of fence – probably barbed wire – must be established on both sides of a new quickthorn hedge: an expensive business.

> “The invention of galvanized steel was the answer to the fencer's dream.

Laying a hedge

But once the quickthorn hedge is established it is there, if you look after it, for centuries. You look after it by laying it. That means that every five years or so, you cut most of the bushes' trunks half way through and break them over. The trunks are all laid the same way – always uphill. They are pushed down on top of each other, or intertwined where possible, and often held by dead stakes driven in at right angles to them. Sometimes the tops of these are pleached (intertwined) with hazel or willow wands twisted through like basketry. In due course the pleaching and the dead stakes rot and disappear, but the hedge puts out new growth and can be very stockproof.

The quickthorn hedge is a labor-intensive way of fencing, but labor is all it uses, and it lasts indefinitely. Also it looks nice, gives haven to birds and small animals, and serves as a windbreak (very important in windy regions). In days of old it supplied, with no extra work, wood for heating bread ovens and other purposes, to say nothing of blackberries. You can often restore old hedges to efficiency on a new holding by laying them, judiciously planting here and there an odd thorn bush to fill in a gap.

Dry-stone wall

If there is freestone (stone that cleaves out of the quarry easily in fairly even slabs) in your area, you probably already have dry-stone walls. “Dry” means no mortar.

If you have dry-stone walls, you will need to maintain them. If you haven't, but you have the stone on your land, you can build some. It is backbreaking but costs nothing. For dry stone walls you need tons of stone – much more

USING STONE
A well-maintained dry-stone wall is even more stockproof than an established hedge. You need stone that comes in even, flattish slabs. Dig down about 9 in (23 cm) and make a level foundation trench. Lay the stones, neatly fitting them together. Make sure the sides are vertical and all joints are broken. If you can get hold of large, round stones, you can make a sort of stone hedge. Build two stone walls leaning toward each other about 1 ft (30 cm) apart. Plug the gaps between the stones with turf and the space between the walls with earth, and plant a hedge on top. To be really stockproof, reinforce with barbed wire to ensure that sheep don't walk straight over it, at least until the hedge is mature.

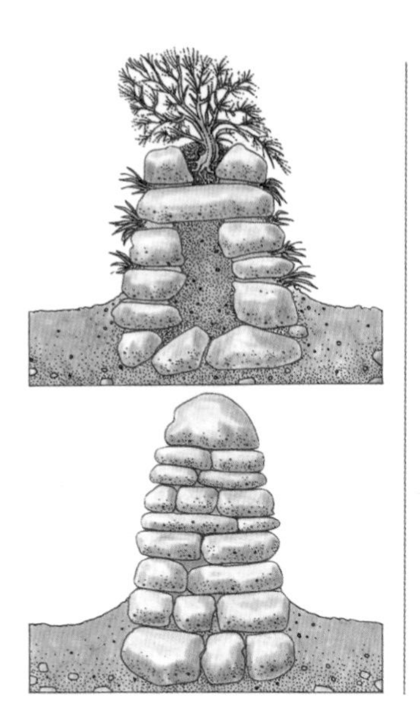

BUILDING A HEDGE
Cut stakes out of your hedge so as to leave strong bushes at intervals of about 12 in (30 cm). Wearing a leather hedging glove, bend each trunk over and half-cut through the trunk near the base with a bill-hook. Force the half-cut trunk down to nearly horizontal and try to push the end under its neighbor, so

than you think you are going to need – and a good hand and eye. Dig a level foundation trench first, then lay the stones carefully, breaking all joints, keeping sides vertical, and fitting the stones in as snugly as you can. Dry-stone walls can be quite stockproof, but they are enormously expensive in labor and need repairing from time to time.

Stone hedge

It is possible to build a cross between a wall and a hedge. You find these in areas where the natural stone is rounded or boulder-shaped, not the rectangular slabs which are found particularly in limestone country. Two stone walls are built with a pronounced batter – that is, they lean inward toward each other. The gaps between the stones are filled in with turf, and the space between the two walls is filled in with earth. Finally, A quickthorn hedge is then planted on top of the earth.

After a year or two, you'll find that grass, weeds, and scrub will start to grow from the earth and the turf. The wall becomes quite green and is not, to be quite frank, very stockproof. If you look at a hundred such hedges I'll warrant you'll find a discreet length of barbed wire or two, or even sheep-netting, along ninety of them. The truth is that these wall-hedges aren't really much good at the job unless you take the extra step of reinforcing them with barbed wire.

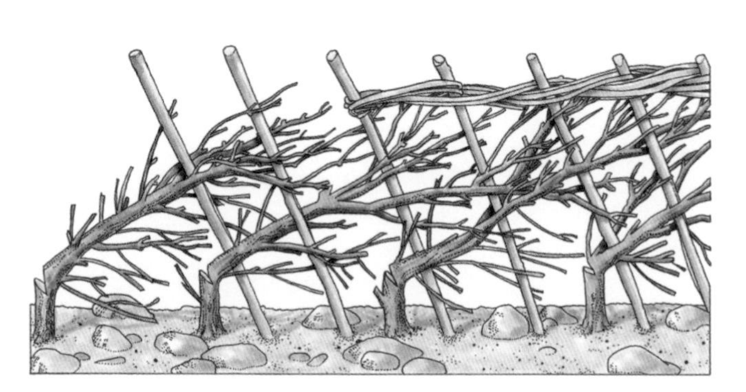

keeping it in position. Be sure not to break it off. Take the stakes you have just cut and drive them in roughly at right angles to the trunks, and interweave them with the trunks.

Intertwine the tops of the stakes with pliable growth (e.g. hazel, willow). The stakes will rot but the living hedge will be secure.

OVERGROWN HEDGES
Tame a runaway hedges with a slasher (*left*). Clear the undergrowth with a bagging hook (*above*), but also hold a stick – or you might lose a finger or thumb.

Wattle-hurdle

If you can get stakes from your own trees, a wattle-hurdle fence is free except for labor, and fairly quick to erect, but it doesn't last long. You drive sharpened stakes into the ground at intervals of about 9 in (23 cm) and pleach, or weave, pliable withies (willow branches), hazel branches, holly, ivy, blackberry, or other creepers between the stakes to make a continuous fence. The material dries out and cracks and gets rotten and you have to ram more in. The stakes, unless of chestnut or heart-of-oak or other resistant wood, rot after a few years and break off. Where stakes or posts are expensive, it is an extravagant form of fencing.

Post-and-rail

A post-and-rail fence is stronger and, unless you are able to grow your own wood, more economical. It consists of strong stakes, either of resistant wood or else softwood treated with preservative, driven well into the ground, with rails of split timber nailed on to them. Abraham Lincoln, we are told, started his life as a rail-splitter. The rails he split would have been for post-and-rail fences, for in his day that wonderful invention, wire, had not begun to encompass the world, and yet the new settlers heading west over North America had to have fences on a large scale. Today we have the benefit of simple but highly effective post-hole diggers.

Two people may be needed to use one of these tools, but a single self-supporter can drive posts into what seems like extremely unlikely soil (see p.116).

Steel wire

The invention of galvanized steel wire was the answer to the fencer's dream. It can be plain wire (often high- tensile), barbed wire, or netting. Plain wire is effective only if stretched. Barbed wire is more effective if it is stretched, but often a strand or two attached somewhat haphazardly to an old unlaid hedge is all there is between animals and somebody's valuable crop.

Netting is very effective but still terribly expensive. Square-meshed netting is strongest for a permanent situation, but is awkward to move very often: diamond-meshed netting is much weaker, but stands being repeatedly rolled up and moved and is therefore ideal for folding sheep.

Stringing wire

If you buy a wire stretcher you can see easily enough how to use it, but there are several very effective ways of improvising one.

TEN ANCHORS IN A FIELD
Every stretch of stretched wire fence needs an anchor, and one anchor can only take a strain in one direction. Thus each corner of your field will need two anchors, and you will need one on each side of the gate.

THE BOX ANCHOR
A fence is only really secure if its wires are stretched, which means they can take a pull of two tons. Half a dozen stretched wires will pull your corner posts straight out of the ground unless they have good anchors. The box anchor is the best of all. Heavy soft wire (generally number 8 gauge) goes from the buried rocks to the second post. A cross-piece morticed in this supports the two corner posts on which the wires are held.

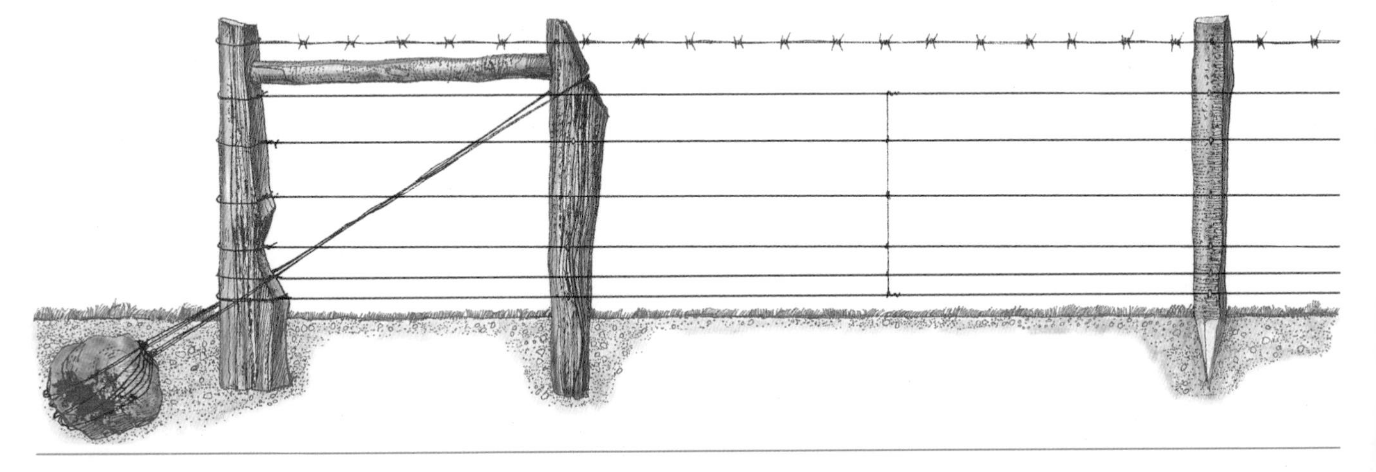

A tensioning tool often used in Africa consists of a forked stick 2 ft (60 cm) long, with a 6-in (15-cm) nail fastened with staples along its length just below the fork. The wire to be stretched is inserted under the nail and then wrapped twice around it for firmness. The slack is taken up by twisting the stick, using the fork as a handle. Then the final stress is put on by turning the stick around the corner post, using the stick as a lever. You can get short lengths of wire tight enough like this, although if you are stretching extremely long lengths at a time, you will need a store-bought wire stretcher, unless you have a tractor on hand and use it to pull the wire taut.

Stretching tips

If you stretch wires on a post on a cold winter's day, you may well have to strain them again on a hot day next summer. Heat makes metal expand. Often, in practice, you can apply strain to wire by hauling it sideways – out of the line of the fence – to, say, a suitable tree with another snatch of wire. This is frowned upon by many farm managers but is often useful just the same, especially when you are trying to make a fence stockproof down in the depths of the woods on a pouring wet day.

If you can't get a wire stretcher, you can exert quite a bit of tension by using a post as a lever, or by using a block and tackle, or even by using a horse or a tractor. Many farmers use the tractor method. But do not strain wire too much. It breaks the galvanizing and takes the strength out of the wire. Always use common sense.

A stretched fence is only as good as its anchor posts. A wire stretcher, such as you can purchase, or easier still borrow from a neighbor, can exert a pull of two tons, and this, multiplied by the number of wires you have in your fence, will pull any corner post out of the ground, unless it is securely anchored.

You can anchor a fence with a kicking post, a post placed diagonally against the corner post in such a way as to take the strain. The kicking post itself is secured in the ground against a rock or short post. Alternatively the strain can be taken by a wire stretched taut around a rock buried in the ground. A refinement of this, the box anchor, is the most efficient of all (*see opposite*). Remember, if you anchor wire to any tree that is not fully mature, the tree will gradually lean over and the fence will slacken. It is bad practice to fasten wire to trees anyway: the staples and lengths of wire get swallowed up by the growing tree and ultimately break some poor devil's saw blade. Not that many of us are quite innocent in that respect.

Electric fencing

The electric fence provides marvelous control over stock and land, making possible a new level of efficiency in farming. You can get battery fencers, which work off 6-volt dry batteries or 12-volt accumulators, or fencers that work off the main electrical supply and will activate up to 20 miles (32 km) of fencing! One strand of hot wire will keep cattle in – it should be at hip height – and one wire 1 ft (30 cm) from the ground will keep pigs in if they are used to it. Until they are, use two wires. The wires needn't be strong, or stretched, just whipped around insulators carried on light stakes, and the whole thing can be put up or moved in a couple of minutes or so.

Hurdles

Except for electrified wire-netting, which is expensive and hard to come by, sheep won't respect an electric fence. So when we wish to fold sheep on fodder fields we make hurdles. It's cheaper than buying wire netting. Some wood that rives (splits) is necessary: ash or chestnut is fine. If you use ash you should treat it with preservative. To erect hurdles, drive a stake in at the point where the ends of two hurdles meet, and tie the hurdles to the stake with a loop of binder twine. To carry hurdles, put as many as you can manage together, shove a stake through them, and get your shoulder under the stake. A fold-pritch is the traditional implement for erecting hurdles, and you can hardly do the job without it.

You can make wattle-hurdles out of woven withies or other flexible timber. These are light, not very strong, don't last long, but good for windbreaks at lambing time. To make them you place a piece of timber on the ground with holes drilled in it. Put the upright stakes of your hurdle in the holes and then weave the withies in, basket-style.

WATTLE-HURDLES

Wattle-hurdles can be made of split hazel or willow withies woven on to uprights. Put a balk of timber with appropriate holes drilled in it on the ground to hold the uprights while you are weaving.

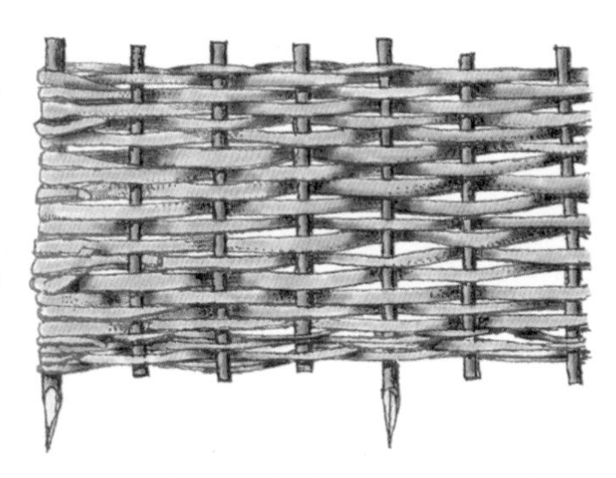

USING A POST RAMMER

Metal post rammers are popular with British homesteaders, since they are the simplest and easiest way to drive posts into the ground. First you need to get the post embedded upright in the ground; you might need someone to help you. Use a mallet to drive the pointed end of the post into the ground. Your aim needs to be accurate here, or you may split the timber. Once the post feels secure, drive the posts in with the post rammer. You just hold the heavy rammer at head height above the post and let go so that the sheer force and weight of the hollow cylinder drives the post down into the earth. Quick and strong work!

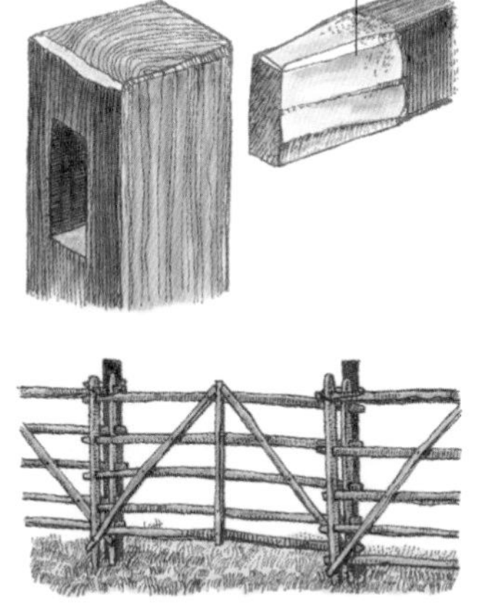

HURDLES

Hurdles are movable fences which you can easily make yourself from any wood that splits. Use mortices to join the horizontals to the pointed uprights. Be sure that the ends of the horizontals are tapered in such a way that they apply pressure up and down and not sideways, otherwise the uprights will split. You can drive thick nails through the joints to hold them, or else use wooden dowels. Nail the cross-braces. Drill all your nail holes or you will split the timber. To erect your hurdles, drive stakes into the ground and fasten the hurdles to them with string.

A FARM GATE

A cattle-proof gate for a field or farmyard is best built of split ash or chestnut. Use bolts to join the four main timbers to make up the frame, and also bolt the hinges on. Use clenched 15-cm (6-in) nails for the other joints. Drill holes for the nails as well as the bolts and pour creosote through all holes. If you have a forked timber use the fork as the bottom hinge, but you must put a bolt through the throat to stop it splitting. The diagonal timbers hold the thing in shape; fit as shown.

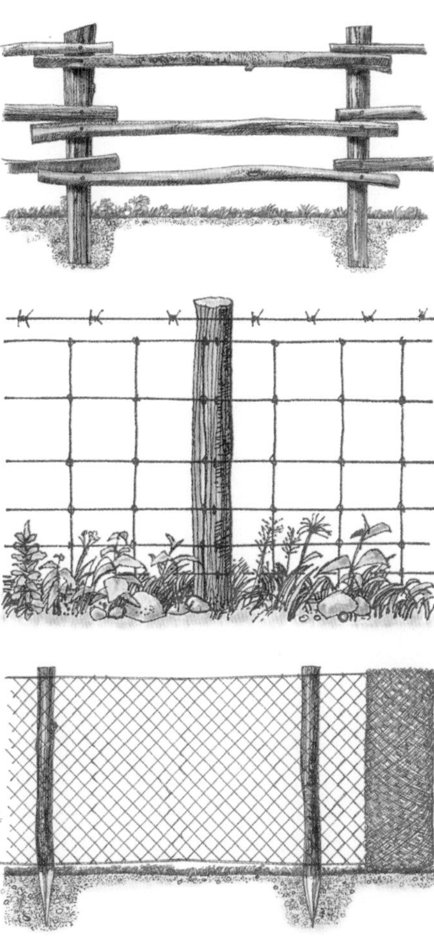

POST-AND-RAIL FENCING

Strong uprights must be well tamped into the ground. Drive all nails right through and clench them.

WIRE NETTING

Wire netting is often convenient but always expensive. Square-meshed netting makes an excellent permanent fence, and coupled with a strand of barbed wire is completely stockproof. Diamond-meshed netting is weaker, but it can be rolled up and reerected wherever you want it. You just need your posts with pointed ends and a heavy mallet or post rammer to drive in the posts. Then use galvanized staples (see p. 228) to secure the wire to the post to make an excellent chicken run. This fencing is also what you need for folding sheep.

Scything

The traditional scythe consists of a long blade of sharpened spring steel which is fixed by a simple ring and wedge to an ash frame – and a well-swung, sharp scythe is a thing of great beauty. There is little that can beat the wonderfully satisfying scrunch of this tool as it cuts the grass and magically peels it away to form a windrow. There are three quite distinct skills involved in scything: setting and sharpening; perfecting a smooth stroke; and planning.

Traditionally the set of the scythe was adjusted to suit the user's size by the local blacksmith who could heat up the fixing pin and bend it to just the correct alignment. The objective is to have the blade of the scythe running parallel to the ground and lying comfortably on it when held in the scything position. Make sure the blade is very firmly fixed to the handles by getting a good fit between the wedge and the steel ring. You hammer down the wedge by turning the scythe over and resting the handle on the ground. The short stay should be a tight fit, being fastened to the frame by a single screw.

A good scythe blade is quite literally as sharp as a razor and will cut paper with ease. The only time you will have to touch it is when you're feeling for burrs, followed by stropping with the stone, to take off the burr. You will see the area you are sharpening become bright as the tarnished metal is worn away. But your scythe is nowhere near sharp until the bright area stretches all the way to the edge of the blade. In tough grass you may have to sharpen the blade every 20 or 30 strokes – but you will waste much less time

SHARPENING A SCYTHE

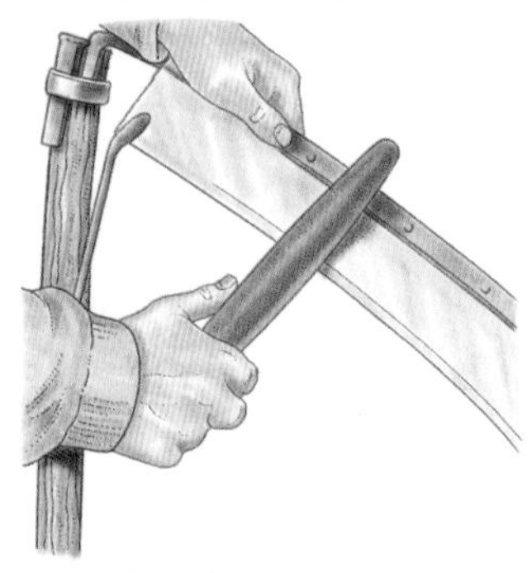

1 Test the scythe upside down; grasp the back of the blade firmly in your left hand so the sharp side is facing toward your right hand. Press the sharpening stone firmly against the blade.

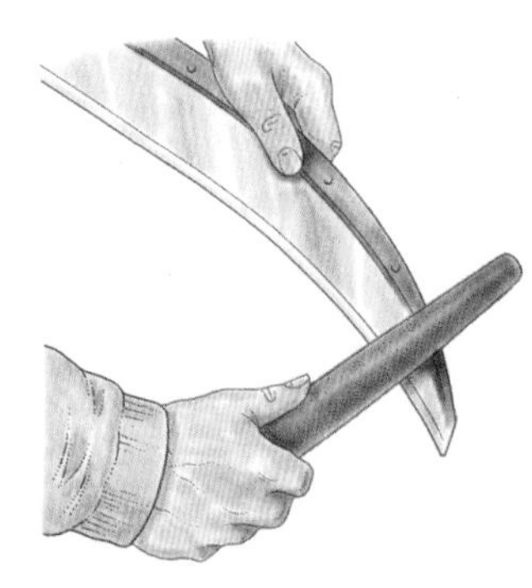

2 Sharpen at the shallowest possible angle so the stone is just touching the band on the outside of the blade. Move the stone along the blade in small circles, from tip to handle.

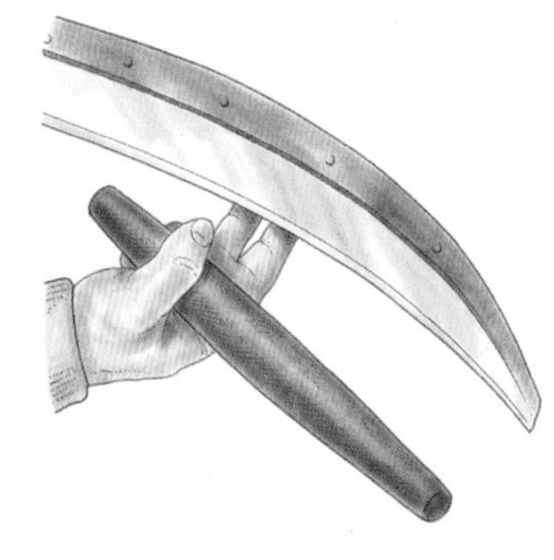

3 The result is a slight burr or sliver of metal pushed down off the blade's edge. Feel for this carefully by pulling your fingers at right angles to the line of the blade across the underside.

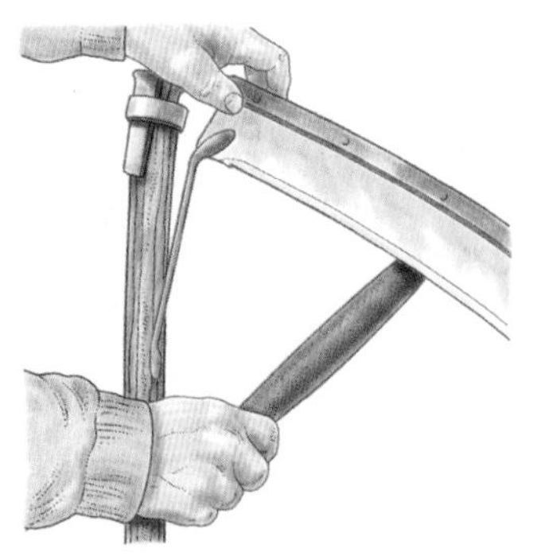

4 Swipe the blade back and forth quickly to remove the burr, along both sides of the edge in turn. When a tip breaks off you must grind down the end of your scythe to make a new tip.

if you do this frequently, rather than waiting until the blade is really blunt, when you will have a tough time getting it sharp again. It may take 20 minutes or more to bring up a good edge the first time you get to work on a new blade. Sharpening is a hard skill but the essence of good scything.

Cutting grass

Set your scythe so the blade runs parallel to the ground comfortably when you hold the handles. Take advantage of the lie of the grass produced by wind and rain. Every area is cut from left to right. It is best to experiment at the beginning with short, firm little strokes backward and forward to give you that first feeling of how a sharp blade will sweetly cut the grass. You should gradually extend the length of your stroke, always remembering to keep the back of the blade pressed against the earth. You can cut along grand by just scything across about 18 in (45 cm) of grass in each stroke, and by taking the next stroke just 1–2 in (3–4 cm) further on. You need to keep a firm grip of both handles and avoid any temptation to chop.

USING A SCYTHE

1 Test the sharpness of the edge by resting the blade on the ground as if to cut. Gently press down and move backward and forward. It should cut even the shortest grass easily.

2 The scythe is pulled around in a short arc with the back of the blade in firm contact with the ground. Do not use as a chopper, and remember it does not need to move fast to cut.

3 Throughout the stroke you must keep the tip of the scythe up and the heel of the scythe pushed firmly down using the right hand. You are looking for a gentle rolling action.

4 The outside of the blade is blunt, so slip the point between vegetation and a chosen tree and then slide the blade forward. Continue around the plant until you clear a full circle.

CHAPTER THREE

FOOD FROM NATURE

"...collecting wild food, whether from the fresh or salt water, the fields or the woods, or the air, takes time; and we do not do as much of it as we would like to. It is, however, part of our pleasure. If we go for a country walk, we keep our eyes open for fungi. Mushrooms we get in the autumn, if we have the initiative to go and look for them...these we eat fresh of course. But we dry a lot in the hot cupboard and they keep the winter through. When we used to have a van we always carried a sack or two in the back for anything that looked edible and didn't belong to anybody. Chestnuts for example. Or crab apples. And a day's or night's fishing is a relaxation: one must get away from the spade or the plough sometimes, and if one's pleasure leads to good food – how useful."

John Seymour *The Fat of the Land* 1976

Pigs

The pig fits so well into the self-supporter's economy that the animal almost seems designed with that in mind. It is probably the most omnivorous animal in the world and will thrive on practically anything. It is even more omnivorous than man, because a pig can eat and digest grass and we cannot. A pig will not thrive on grass alone, but it can make it a substantial part of his diet. And it will convert virtually anything you grow or produce on your land into good meat.

We do not breed pigs on our smallholding at Killowen. We simply do not have enough land to justify keeping a sow and a boar; anyway the market for young piglets (weaners or bonhams as they are called) is very limited nowadays and we certainly could not eat all the progeny. Our routine is a simple one of buying in a couple of piglets from one of our neighbours during April or May. We keep them in a well-built concrete pigsty with occasional forays into virgin turf under the control of a portable electric fence. They really are the most cheerful and pleasant animals to have around – although you may want to site your pigsty downwind of the main dwelling! Pigs will always be delighted to see you, they never seem to get depressed and we have never had one get ill. They grow as the garden grows, and are nicely ready to become bacon as soon as the first frosts drive away the blow flies.

Housing

The housing you need depends to some extent on the breed of pig you are fattening. The old traditional breeds are much hardier than modern commercial breeds and they will do better on a less intensive feeding regime. On the

TYPES OF PIG

DUROC
A breed of hogs with its origin in the eastern United States and in the Corn Belt. Compact, attractive colour and good for fleshing out.

GLOUCESTER OLD SPOT
A fine and beautiful English breed evolved originally for living in apple orchards and woodlands. It is hardy, prolific, and a fine baconer.

WESSEX SADDLEBACK
Also known as the British Saddleback, this is a hardy outdoor breed popular for crossbreeding.

WELSH
A popular commercial breed because it's white, long, and lean. It is a reasonable outdoor breed.

other hand they tend to put on a lot of fat when you try to feed them up quickly and this, when you come to butcher, is an awful waste of food as well as being difficult to dispose of sensibly. So, attractive as traditional breeds are, we have tended to go for a more commercial modern pig that will make more of our good food into pork and bacon.

Pigs need secure and storm-proof housing. It needs to be waterproof and, if possible, the floor and roof should be insulated against the cold. Pigs are extremely strong and always want to dig, dig, dig. They will easily lift gates off their hinges and can even undo bolts on the outside if they are easily accessible. Our concrete sty is about 6 sq m (20 sq ft) with the covered area covering about one quarter of this. The floor slopes down to a drain at the front for easy cleaning, and there is a small area set aside at the back which the pigs always use for their personal hygiene. We have a robust "on demand" water trough bolted to the wall and a concrete trough with drain hole in the front corner for feeding. Each year our pigs manage to dig through the concrete floor – quite amazing really. We feel it is very cruel to ring them so they cannot do this and we always tip in a good load of weeds, old turf, leaves or grass cutting as frequently as we can as they love to sift through all this for the odd tit bits.

Fencing

When we run the pigs onto fresh ground we use a portable electric fencer as it is the only effective way to control them. Have one wire about 23 cm (9 in) above the ground and another about 46 cm (18 in) higher. But watch out – pigs will dig up the soil right up to the fence and very easily short circuit the high voltage on their way to freedom and a good root about in your garden. If they escape they are well designed to cause trouble and can be very difficult to catch as they are quick, and do not have ready-made handles to grab hold of! A bucket of tasty food is generally the best approach to lure them back into captivity.

Feeding

With a small area of land it is not realistic to expect to grow all your pig food yourselves. Even with our half acre of very productive garden we buy in rolled barley and dried milk powder as a staple for the pigs – supplemented, of course, by a large amount of sub-standard or damaged vegetables and fruit from the garden. You can easily make a good mash by adding boiling water to a mixture of rolled barley and milk powder: leave it to cool either overnight or over the day for the evening feed. We use about one-fifth as much milk powder as barley and the pigs themselves soon tell us how much to give them. The rule of thumb is that they should take about ten minutes to finish their food. If it takes less then they probably do not have enough; if it takes more you are going to have very fat pigs to butcher at the end of the season.

Pigs need enough good protein in their diet if they are to produce high quality meat. Milk powder from the agricultural merchants is convenient but fish meal, soya meal or any other high protein supplement will do. We like to buy what the merchants call "straight" foods for all our animals – the alternative of buying ready made-up pellets always worries us (perhaps unnecessarily) because we are never quite sure we can trust what might be in them.

The pig bucket

Now I must touch on the high art of the pig bucket. As I have said before, nothing should be wasted on the smallholding and the dustman should never have to call. We keep a pig bucket in the kitchen for all the non-meat food scraps (meat scraps go to the dog or are cut up for the chickens). You can supplement your pig's diet very well by boiling up vegetable peelings and all sorts of odds and ends left over from cooking. Scrape in all the scraps of food from your plates before you do the washing up – all the grease and assorted nutrients are most excellent food for your pigs. We have a separate bucket for the compost and the chickens, and keep all of them in floor-level cupboards to avoid attracting flies. Naturally they are emptied every day so keeping them clean is not a problem.

Slaughterhouse and butchering

The modern slaughterhouse is a formidable operation. Literally thousands of animals pass through its machinery every day – big articulated lorries coming in at one end with live animals and other big articulated lorries leaving at the other with plastic packs of meat for the supermarket. The old local slaughterhouses have been forced out of business by over-regulation and specialization. It is legally required in most countries that domestic animals are slaughtered in a government-approved commercial slaughterhouse where they can be inspected by vets and (we hope) humanely killed. In some countries, a herd number or other form of registration is required so you need to check on this. You may also have to notify the authorities before you move animals from your holding.

EDIBLE PARTS OF A PIG

After visiting the slaughterhouse, you will want to butcher the pig yourself. This way you can have the cuts of meat as you want them and not have the risk of this beautiful healthy meat being dumped into some great vat of pickling chemicals and so emulate the flaccid bacon you can pick up in any supermarket. Real dry salted bacon is a different (and wonderful) article altogether.

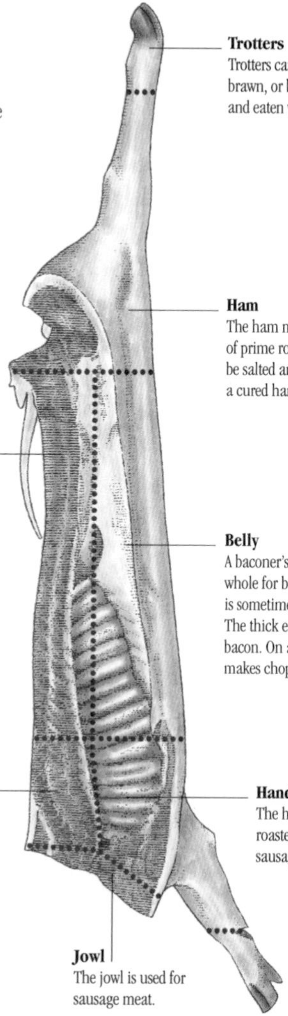

Trotters
Trotters can be cooked up for brawn, or boiled separately and eaten with vegetables.

Ham
The ham makes a huge joint of prime roast pork, or it can be salted and smoked to make a cured ham.

Back
A large pig's back can be cured as bacon. On a smaller pig it may go for chops. On a large baconer it can be cut into good roasting joints.

Belly
A baconer's belly can be salted whole for bacon. The thin end is sometimes pickled in brine. The thick end makes prime bacon. On a porker the belly makes chops.

Spare ribs
The spare ribs can be roasting joints or cut into chops. The shoulder can make a joint, or it can be cured to make second-rate bacon.

Hands
The hands can be roasted, or cut up for sausage meat.

Jowl
The jowl is used for sausage meat.

You will need to contact a slaughterhouse well in advance to arrange a day to take your pigs in. Sometimes the factories will have set aside special days to do over large pigs or "house" pigs as your pigs may be called. Be warned they may not be able to book you for a month or so later – so check up in good time. Your pig will become much more expensive to feed in winter without the help of the garden and with cold weather adding to its appetite. The slaughterhouse will want to know how big your pigs are, by weight ideally. You can get around this simply by giving the age of the animals – so they know what to expect.

Although it would be ideal in many ways to kill, bleed and scrape your pig on the smallholding (so avoiding all the stress of transport and factory), there are some big advantages in taking the animals to the slaughterhouse. The biggest bonus is that their machinery can kill, scrape and split your pig extremely quickly and economically. And if you take my advice then make sure they only split it and do not turn it into joints or bacon (*see illustration, left*).

Jointing your pig

When you pick your carcass up from the factory your pigs will be in two halves. My advice, by the way, is never take more than two pigs to slaughter at any one time. It will take you four hours at least to joint each pig – so an eight-hour stint will make an exhausting day's work and you do not want a butchered carcass to be hanging around for too long in an un-refrigerated shed. You will need a very strong clean work top at least 1.8 m (6 ft) long on which to lay out one half of each pig at a time for jointing. You could need help carrying the carcass from the transport to the work surface – a heavy dead body is not easy to move around!

Buy yourself a new sharp woodsaw from the builder's merchants, get a good sharp cleaver if you can find one, and make sure you have one large knife and one smaller pointed knife. Your knives must be very sharp and I always keep a steel and sharpening stone on the shelf above the work surface so I can re-sharpen regularly. Make sure you have an ample supply of strong freezer bags to hand and, if you are dry salting for bacon, make sure you have some clean wooden boxes and salt ready for the flitches of bacon. You will also need a large wooden chopping board to cut down onto and avoid damaging your worktop.

Now I generally cut off the ham first, using the saw and a sharp knife. It's a matter of judgement and practice where to cut, but my advice is not to try to make the ham too big. Remember that you want to have a very straight, clean surface without scrappy pieces hanging down – this is the best way to ensure your ham will cure well. You will then need to decide whether you want to take the pig for pork joints like chops and joints on the bone, and whether the carcass is too small and would be better simply turned into bacon. Generally I cut the side of meat into two halves as soon as I have taken off the ham; this makes it easier to handle. The "chops" around the top of the ribs may well be big enough to joint out on the front half but too small on the rear. There are advantages in taking out the bone simply so you don't take up so much space in your deep freeze. You will find the hip and shoulder joints very complicated to butcher unless you simply cut them into reasonable sized joints with the saw. Once cooked the meat comes away easily and this is much the easiest way to deal with them.

Poultry

CHICKENS

All hens should be allowed access to the great outdoors except in the winter in very cold climates. Not only is it inhumane to keep chickens indoors all the time, it leads to all the diseases that commercial flocks of poultry now suffer from. Some poultry-keepers go to such extremes of cruelty as keeping hens shut up in wire cages all their lives.

Sunshine is the best source of vitamin D for poultry, as it is for us. Hens evolved to scratch the earth for their living, and to deny them the right to do this is cruel. They can get up to a quarter of their food and all their protein from freshly growing grass and derive great benefit from running in woods and wild places. They crave, and badly need, dust-baths to wallow in and fluff up their feathers to get rid of the mites. In well over 20 years of keeping hens running out of doors, I have yet to find what poultry disease is, with the exception of blackhead in turkeys. Our old hens go on laying year after year until I get fed up with seeing them, and put them in the pot.

Feeding

Hens running free out of doors on good grass will do very well in the summer time if you just throw them some grain. In the winter they will need a protein supplement. You can buy this from a corn merchant, or feed them fish meal, meat meal, soya meal, other bean meal, or fish offal. I would actually recommend soya meal most of all, because soya is the best balanced of any vegetable protein. So if you live in a region where soya beans can be grown with reasonable success, the problem of your protein supplement is easily solved. But soya must be cooked, as it contains a substance which, when raw, is slightly poisonous. Sunflowers are good too, particularly if you can husk the seed and grind it, but they're quite good just fed as they are. You can also feed the hens lupin seed (either ground or whole), rape seed (but not too much of it), linseed, groundnut or cotton seed (but this must be cooked first), crushed or ground peas or beans, lucerne or alfalfa, or alfalfa meal. These all contain protein.

> In 20 years of keeping hens running out of doors, I have yet to find what poultry disease is.

From ten days old onwards, all chickens should have access to fresh vegetables, and after all, this is one thing we can grow. So give them plenty of vegetables whether they run out on grass or not. My method of feeding hens is to let them run outdoors, give them a handful each of whatever high-protein meal or grain I have in the morning, and scatter a handful each of whole grain in the evening. Wheat is best, or kibbled maize. Barley is very good, but it should be hummelled – banged about until the awns (spikes) are broken off. An equally good method is to let them feed both protein and grain from self-feed containers. These should be placed out of the reach of rats.

If you allow hens to run out of doors, or to have access to a good variety of foods, they will scratch and peck away to their hearts' content, balance their own rations, and not eat more than they need to anyway. But if hens are confined indoors, there are several ways you can balance their rations, such as the following self-made mashes:

Laying mash

50 kg (1 cwt) wheat meal
50 kg (1 cwt) maize meal (preferably yellow maize)
50 kg (1 cwt) other grain meal (oats, barley, or rye)
50 kg (1 cwt) fish meal
13.5 kg (30 lb) dried milk
9 kg (20 lb) ground seashells
2.3 kg (5 lb) salt

Give them free access to this, and a handful each of whole grains to scratch out of their straw or litter.

Fattening mash for cockerels or capons

Barley meal is the best fattener for any poultry, but can be replaced by boiled potatoes. Skimmed milk is also ideal:

150 kg (3 cwt) barley meal
50 kg (1 cwt) wheat meal
25 kg (½ cwt) fish or meat meal
13 kg (30 lb) dried milk; plus some time (ground sea shells) and salt

Little chick mash

13 kg (30 lb) meal (preferably a mixture of wheat, maize and oats)
5 kg (12 lb) fish meal or meat meal
5 kg (12 lb) alfalfa (lucerne) meal
0.9 kg (2 lb) ground seashells
0.5 kg (1 lb) cod liver oil
0.5 kg (1 lb) salt
plus a "scratch" of finely cracked cereals

If you give your chickens plenty of milk (whole preferably, but skimmed is nearly as good) you can forget all but a little of the cod liver oil, the alfalfa meal, and half, if not all, the fish meal or meat meal.

As far I'm concerned though, if you have food that is free to you, or a by-product of something else, it is better to use that (even if the books say it is not perfect) than give your chickens something you have to end up paying for. As with other areas of self-sufficiency, I have always been a great believer in making the best of what is available.

CHICKEN BREEDS
Commercial breeders breed hybrids for egg production and nothing else, so you will have to search for those marvellous old-fashioned breeds which can live outdoors, lay plenty of eggs, go broody and hatch their eggs, rear their chicks, and make good table birds as well. You want breeds like the Rhode Island Red, a good dual-purpose hen, meaning it is a good layer and a good table bird; the Light Sussex, an Old English breed, again dual purpose; or the Cuckoo Maran, which is very hardy and lays large, deep-brown, high quality eggs, but not in prolific quantities. US breeds like the various Plymouth Rock and Wyandotte fowl are good for eggs and meat.

COOPS

TRADITIONAL ARK
This is made of sawn timber and weather-boarding, is well creosoted, has a night-house with perches, a row of nesting boxes accessible from outside by a door, and a run. It is strong but easily moveable by handles at each end.

BROODY COOP
Individual sitting hens need a broody coop. It must have a rat-proof floor and slats in front to confine the hen, if needed, but also admit her chicks.

HOME-MADE ARK
The homesteader should try to make his gear for nothing, and used fertilizer bags are free. We made this ark for nearly nothing. Thatch would work as well, and would look better.

SELF-FEED HOPPER
You can buy galvanized hoppers, but you can make them yourself, for free, by hanging up an old oil-drum, bashing holes round its base to let the hens peck food out, and hanging the cut-off base of a larger oil-drum underneath to catch spilled food. Hang above rat-reach.

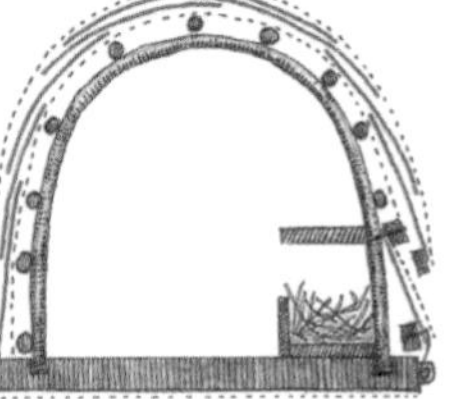

"FERTILIZER-BAG" ARK
A layer of wire-netting over the overlapping bags keeps them from flapping. The bags can be supported underneath by closely spaced horizontal rods of hazel or willow. An inspection door for nesting boxes can be made by hanging up fertilizer bags weighted with a heavy batten across their bottoms.

Free range

If hens run completely free range, it is often better to keep them in their houses until midday. They generally lay their eggs before that time, so you get the eggs before you let them out, instead of losing them in the bushes where the rats get them. Hens will do a pasture good if they are not too concentrated on it, and especially if their houses or arks are moved from time to time over the pasture.

We tend to forget that the chicken is a woodland bird, and hens always thrive in woodland (if the foxes don't get them). They can also be run very advantageously on stubble (land from which cereals have just been harvested). Do try to keep them out of the garden, picturesque though it may look, or you will rue the day.

Limited grass

If you have fresh grassland it is a great advantage if you can divide it into two (a strip on each side of a line of hen houses, for example), and let the hens run on each strip in turn. As soon as they have really eaten the grass down on one strip, let them run on the other. In the summer, when the grass grows so quickly they can't cope with it, let them run on one strip long enough to let you cut the other strip for hay. Or alternate hens with geese (or a sheep, or a goat if you have one). Poultry will eat any grass provided it is kept short, but ideally it should be of the tender varieties like timothy or the meadow grasses. There can also be clover with it, although the hens will provide enough nitrogen in their own droppings.

> I am a great believer in making the best of what is available.

The Balfour method

This is suitable for the "backyard poultry-keeper" or the person who only has a small or limited garden. You have a pen around your hen house in which you dump plenty of straw, bracken, or whatever vegetation you can get. In addition, you have two (or three if you have the space) pens which are grassed down, and which can be approached by the hens from the straw yard. The hens will scratch in the straw yard and so satisfy their scratching instincts and spare the grass.

Now let the hens run into one of the grass pens. Change the chickens into another pen after, say, a fortnight or three weeks. They will get a bite of grass from this, and the grass in the first pen will be rested and have a chance to grow. The straw yard will provide half a ton of good manure a year from each hen. The old "backyard poultry yard" which is a wilderness of scratched bare earth, coarse clumps of nettles, rat holes, and old tin cans, is not a good place to keep hens or anything else to speak of. And when it gets damp and turns into a quagmire, forget it.

Housing

The ordinary commercially produced hen house, provided it is mobile, works perfectly well. If used in the Balfour or limited grassland methods described beforehand, it doesn't even have to be mobile, unless you intend to move it from time to time into another field. Utter simplicity is fine for a hen house. Hens need shelter from rain and wind, some insulation in very cold climates, and perches to sit on. Make sure the perches are not right up against the roof, and are placed so their droppings have a clear fall to the floor.

The nesting boxes should be dark, designed to discourage hens from roosting in them and roofed so hens don't leave droppings in them. You should be able to reach in and get the eggs easily. There are patent nesting boxes which allow the eggs to fall down to another compartment. I think these are a very good idea; they prevent the eggs getting dirty. If you want eggs in the depth of winter is not a bad idea to confine some birds in a house with electric light. Give the birds, say, 12 hours of light and they will think it is summer time and lay a lot of eggs; otherwise they will go off laying as soon as the days draw in.

We have hen arks with an enclosed sleeping area and a wire-netted open run. They hold 25 hens each and cost nothing but a handful of nails, some old torn wire netting, and some free plastic fertilizer bags. They are moveable with a bit of effort, but I've seen some adapted to wheels which is a great idea and makes moving far less back breaking.

Rearing chickens

It is always a good idea to keep a rooster among your hens, and not just to wake you up in the morning. The hens will lay just as many eggs without a rooster but the eggs won't be fertile. Also if each batch of hens has a cockerel to marshal them and keep them together out of doors, they fare better and are less likely to come to harm.

If you leave a hen alone, and the fox doesn't get her, she will wander off into the hedgerows and wander back again in a few weeks with a dozen little chicks clucking at her heels. These chicks, being utterly naturally reared, will be the healthiest little chicks you will ever see. Alternatively you can watch your hens for broodiness.

KILLING AND PREPARING A CHICKEN

Grab the legs with your left hand, and the neck with your right hand so that it protrudes through the two middle fingers and the head is cupped in the palm. Push your right hand downwards and turn it so the chicken's head bends backwards. Stop as soon as you feel the backbone break, or you will pull the head off.

PLUCKING

Start plucking the chicken as soon as it is dead, while it is still warm; once it gets cold the feathers are much harder to get out. Be very careful not to tear the skin.

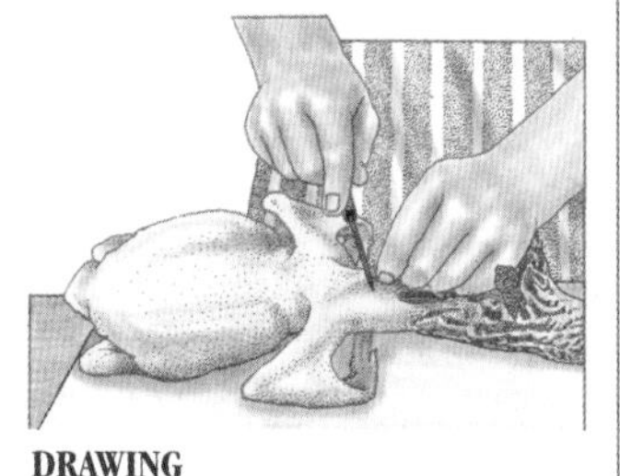

DRAWING

1 Slip the knife under the skin at the bottom of the neck and cut up to the head.

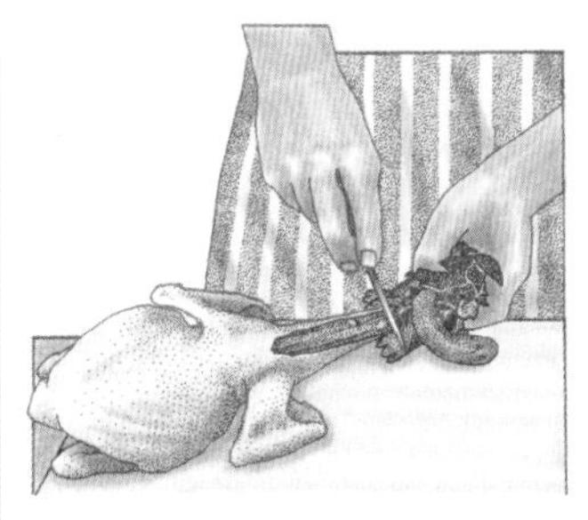

2 Sever the neckbone at the bottom end with secateurs or a sharp knife.

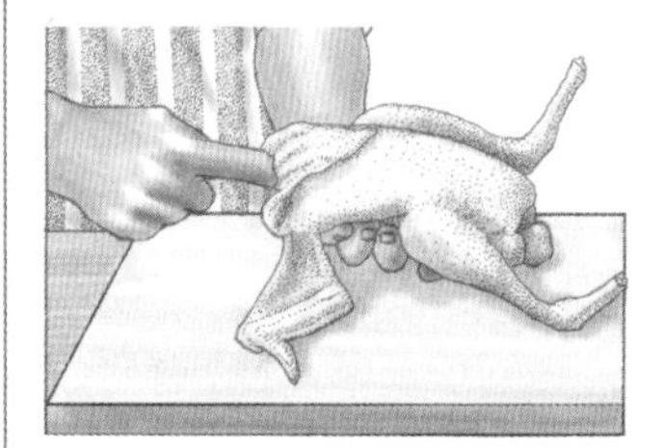

3 Remove the neckbone. Insert the index finger of your right hand, move it around inside, and sever all the innards.

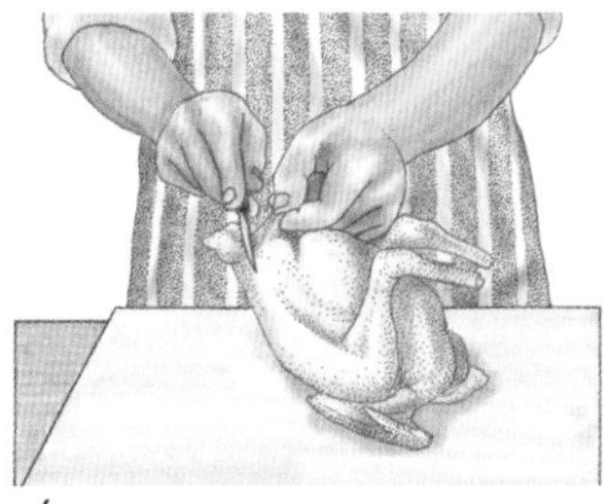

4 Cut between the vent and the tail, being careful not to sever the rectum.

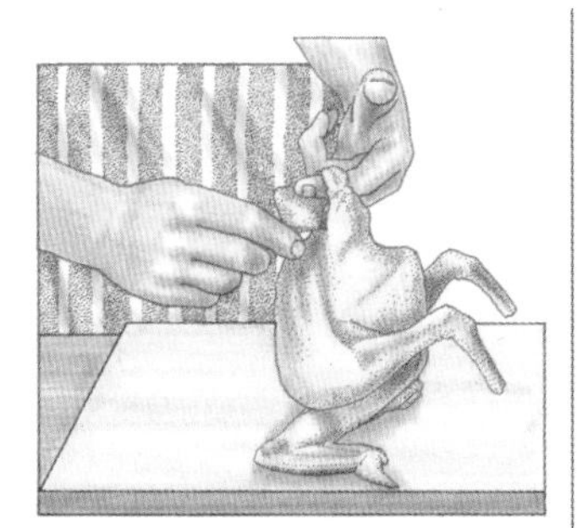

5 Cut all the way around the vent so that you can separate it from the body.

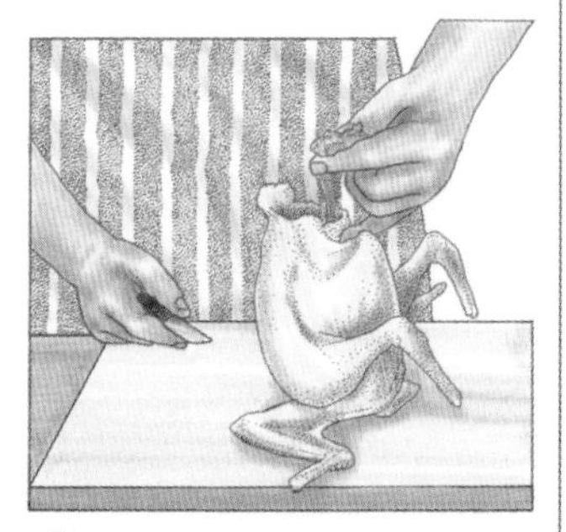

6 Carefully draw the vent, with the guts still attached, out from the tail end.

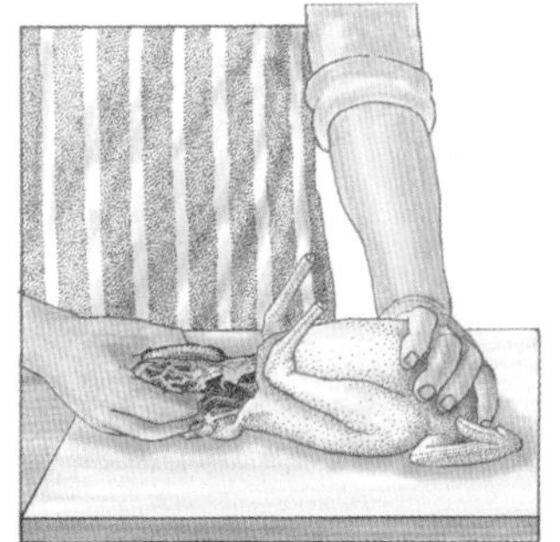

7 The gizzard, lungs, and heart will follow the guts.

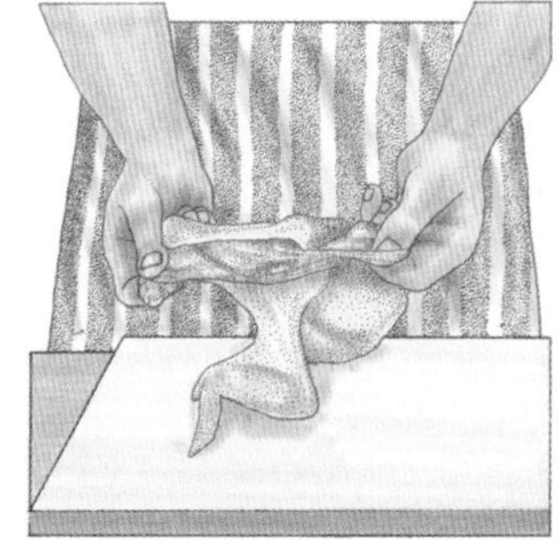

8 Remove the crop from the neck end of the bird.

TRUSSING

If you put the bird in the oven and cooked it, it would taste just the same as if you trussed it. But to make a neat and professional job it is worth trussing properly.

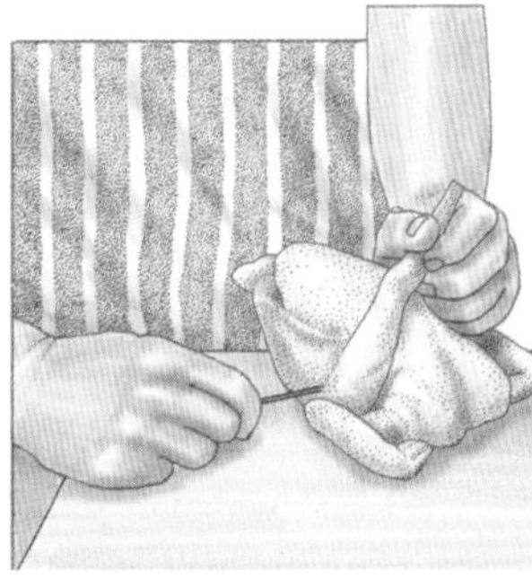

1 Thread a large darning needle, force the chicken's legs forward, and shove the needle and thread through the body low down.

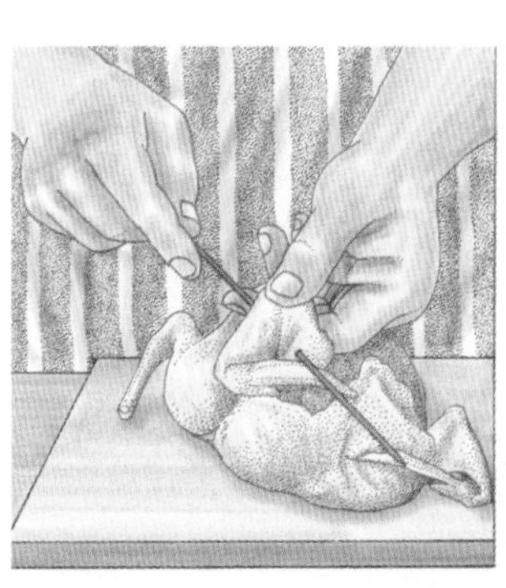

2 Push the needle through the wing and bring it across the skin at the neck.

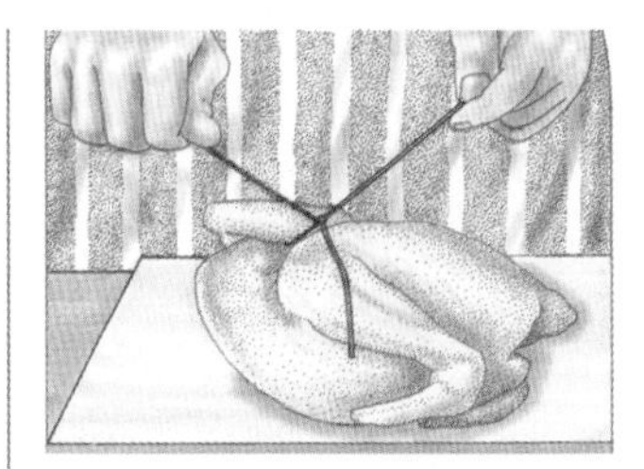

3 Push through the other wing and tie the ends of the thread together.

4 Re-thread the needle and pass over the leg, below the end of the breastbone and round the other leg.

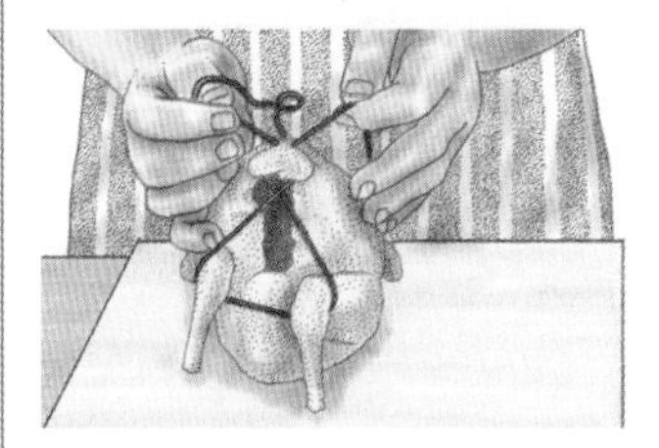

5 Cross the thread behind the hocks and tie around the parson's nose.

You can tell when a hen is broody by the way she squats tight on her eggs and makes a broody clucking noise when you try to lift her off. Help her by enclosing her in a broody coop (a little house with slats in front of it that baby chicks can get through and the mother can't). Give her nice, soft hay as a nest, and put a dozen fertile eggs under her. (They can be any kind of poultry egg you like.) See that she always has water and food: she will eat very little. Let her out once a day for a short walk, but get her in within half an hour or the eggs will get cold. Eggs should hatch out in 21 days from the start of brooding. As soon as the chicks are a few days old, you can let the hen out, and she will lead them around and teach them how to look for food. This is by far the best way to raise poultry, and beats any incubator.

If you are just starting with hens, you could order "day-old chicks" or "point-of-lay pullets" which are young females just about to lay. Keep such pullets as you need for your flock replacements and fatten the cocks for the table. Little chicks need a fairly rich diet of protein and finely ground meal. For the first few days add ground-up hard boiled eggs and milk by-products to their ration. Wheat meal mixed with milk is also a perfect food. Make sure chickens have access to enough lime, say in ground seashells, and to insoluble grit like crushed flint to ensure healthy shells.

Cockerels at 8 to 12 weeks are called "broilers", and should weigh from 1–1.5 kg (2–3 lb). Birds or table breeds should, at 12 or 14 weeks, weigh more – 1.4–1.8 kg (3–4 lb) – and in America are called "fryers". After this you may call them "roasters". At six or nine months old they are called "boilers"; so are old hens culled from your laying flock. An old hen can make good eating.

Good laying hens should have bright eyes, large, red, healthy-looking combs and wattles, wide-apart pelvic bones (fairly loose so eggs can get out) and a white, large, moist vent. If they have the opposite, wring their necks. They won't lay you many eggs and you should certainty not breed from them. Don't stop hens from going broody.

Finally, it goes without saying that eggs are much better eaten fresh, and it is quite possible to have your hens laying most of the year. Remember the old freshness test too: place an egg in a bowl gently; if it's really fresh it should sink and stay flat on its side. If it stands on its end at the bottom of the bowl then it's a few day's old but alright to eat. But if the egg floats, forget it.

GEESE

These are most excellent birds for the self-supporter. They are hardy, tough, self-reliant grazers and they make good mothers. The best way to start breeding geese is to buy eggs from somebody and put them under a broody hen. A hen will sit on five or six goose eggs and hatch them, but you want to make sure that she hasn't been sitting too long when you put the goose eggs under her, for goose eggs take longer to hatch than hens' eggs do (up to 30 days or even more). During the last week of the sitting, take the eggs out from under the hen every day and wet them with lukewarm water (goose mothers get wet but hen foster mothers don't). On the day when the eggs start to pip, wet them well. Some people remove the first goslings that hatch so that the foster mother doesn't think she's done her job, and then they replace them when the last egg has hatched. I've never bothered and always had good results.

Feed the goslings well for the first two or three weeks on bread soaked in whole or skimmed milk. If they are fairly safe where they are, let the hen run around with them. If you fear they will get lost, confine the hen in a broody coop. I prefer the hen to run loose. When the young geese no longer need the foster mother, she will leave them and start laying again.

Geese, though fierce and strong, are vulnerable to two enemies: rats and foxes. Rats will pull goose eggs out from under a sitting hen or goose, and they will kill baby geese if they get a chance. So do anything to get rid of them. These vermin are the enemy of everything wholesome on your plot. As for foxes, they just love geese. They will snatch a sitting goose off her eggs whenever they can. Foxes cannot really co-exist with the self-supporter. Shoot them at night if you have a gun license. If there are foxes in the area, you must confine sitting geese in a fox-proof place.

If you start reducing the goslings' food after three weeks, they will live on grass. As adults, they don't need any food except grass, but it is a good idea to chuck them some corn in January and February when you want to feed the goose up a bit to get her to lay well. Three weeks before you intend to kill them (generally Christmas), you should confine them, and feed them liberally with barley meal, maize meal, and milk. They will fatten nicely on this.

Geese pair for life, so I prefer to keep one goose and one gander together as a breeding pair, though many people keep a gander to two or three geese. They lay early: in February or March. If you leave them alone, they will sit on a dozen or more of their own eggs and hatch them with no trouble at all, but if you are greedy you can keep stealing their eggs and putting them under broody hens. But hens aren't always broody as early in the year as that.

When it's time to kill a goose, grab it by its legs with both hands. Keep the back of the bird away from you. Lower the head to the floor, and get someone else to lay a broomstick across the neck just behind the head. Tread on both ends of the broom stick, and pull the legs upwards until you feel the neck break. Hold the tips of the wings as well as the two legs, and the bird will not flap after it is dead.

DUCKS

To say that ducks don't need water is nonsense. Ducks do need water and cannot possibly be happy without it. It is inhumane to keep animals in conditions grossly different from the ones their species has evolved to live in. So give them access to water, but keep your ducklings away from it for their first week or two, until they have the natural protection of oil on their feathers. (You must give them drinking water, however.) Swimming water is better for ducks if it is flowing and renews itself. Many eggs get laid in the water, or on the edge, and if the water is stagnant, eggs (which have porous shells) can be dangerous to eat. So don't eat eggs that have been lying in filthy water, no matter how much you clean them.

If there is no natural water on your holding, my advice is not to keep ducks. You can, of course, create an artificial pond, out of concrete, puddled clay, or plastic sheeting buried in the ground, but if you do, make sure the water is renewable and does not become stagnant.

One drake will look after half a dozen ducks and enjoy it, but ducks make rotten mothers.

If you let ducks hatch their own eggs you must confine them in a broody coop, or they will kill the little ducklings by dragging them all over the place. Hens are much better duck-mothers than ducks are. Duck eggs hatch in 28 days and the baby ducks need careful feeding. Up to ten weeks feed them as much barley or other meal as they will eat. Add milk if you have it. Feed ducks about the same as you would hens when you are not fattening them. The duck is not a grazing bird to the extent that the goose is, but ducks get quite a lot of food from roaming around on water, or mud, and will eat slugs, snails, frogs, worms, and insects. Don't let breeding ducks get too fat, or they will produce infertile eggs. They like a mash in the morning of boiled vegetables, flaked maize, pea or bean meal, wheat meal and a little barley meal. Give each one half a handful for breakfast, and half a handful of grain in the evening. There are ducks (such as the Indian Runner) with very little meat on them that lay plenty of eggs, and table ducks (such as the Aylesbury) with plenty of meat but not many eggs.

TURKEYS

Compared to other poultry, these are very delicate birds. If they associate in any way with chickens, they get a fatal disease called blackhead, unless you medicate their water or food. If you want to have them without medicating them, you must keep them well away from all chickens. Turkeys do not seem to me to be a very suitable bird for the self-supporter, unless he wants to trade them.

AYLESBURY DRAKE
The best British table breed. It is large, heavy and very hardy, and its ducklings grow exceptionally fast.

EMBDEN GANDER
The Embden is a good table breed. Its feathers and down are pure white and ideal for stuffing cushions and eiderdowns.

WHITE TURKEY
These can grow up to 17 kg (38 lb). There is a small, quick-maturing form of this breed called the Beltsville White.

Rabbits

Rabbits are a very good stock for the self-supporting family to keep. They can be fed largely on weeds that would otherwise be wasted, and they make excellent meals. New Zealand Whites are a good breed to have because they are good meat and their skins are very beautiful when cured. Californians are also excellent. Such medium breeds tend to be more economical than very large rabbits (e.g. Flemish Giants) which eat an awful lot and don't produce much more meat. If you get two does and a buck, these should provide you with up to 90 kg (200 lb) of meat a year.

Shelter

In the summer, rabbits will feed themselves perfectly well on grass alone – if you either move them about on grassland in arks, or else let them run loose in adequate fenced paddocks. The wire netting of the paddocks should be dug 15 cm (6 in) into the ground to prevent them from burrowing. You can keep rabbits in hutches all the year round. They can stand cold but not wet, and they don't like too much heat but need a cosy nest box.

Breeding

Sexing rabbits is easy enough. Lay the rabbit on its back, head towards you: press the fingers gently each side of where its equipment seems to be and this will force out and expose the relevant part. It will appear as an orifice in the female and a slight rounded protrusion in the male.

If you are going to breed rabbits, always take the doe to the buck, never the buck to the doe, or there will be fighting, and always put a doe by herself when she is going to kindle (give birth). A doe should rear from seven to nine rabbits a litter, so if the litters are over 12 it is best to remove and foster them on another doe that has just kindled with a smaller litter. If you do this, rub the young with the new doe's dung and urine before you give them to her, to confuse her sense of smell. Then you can try to sell or give them away.

Feeding

Rabbits will eat any greens or edible roots. They like a supplement of meal: any kind of ground grain will do, but a pregnant doe should not have more than 115 g (4 oz) of meal a day or she will get fat. Assuming that rabbits are not on grass and that you are not giving them a great quantity of greenstuff, feeding should then be in the order of 85 g (3 oz) of concentrates a day for young rabbits over eight weeks old, plus hay ad-lib.

Killing

To kill a rabbit, hold it by its hind legs, in your left hand; grab its head in your right hand and twist it backwards. At the same time, force your hand downwards to stretch its neck. The neckbone breaks and death is instantaneous. Before the carcass has cooled, nick the hind legs just above the foot joint and hang up on two hooks. Make a light cut just above the hock joint on the inside of each rear leg and cut up to the vent (anus). Peel the skin off the rear legs and then just rip it off the body. Gut the rabbit by cutting down the belly and removing everything except liver and kidneys (known as hulking). Remove the gall bladder from the liver.

Bees and Honey

Bees will provide you with all the sugar you need, and as a self-supporter you shouldn't need much. A little sugar (or, preferably, honey) improves beer, and sugar is necessary if you want to make "country wines" (which I discuss on pp.190–194), but otherwise the part that sugar plays in the diet is wholly deleterious. It is such an accessible source of energy that we satisfy our energy requirements too easily, and are not induced to turn to coarser foods, whose valuable constituents are less concentrated and less refined. The ideal quantity of refined sugar in the diet is: nil.

Now honey will do anything that sugar can do and do it much better. Not only is it a healthier food, for beekeepers it is also free. It is sweeter than sugar, so if you use it for cooking or wine-making purposes, use about two thirds as much as you would sugar. And beekeeping is really a way of getting something for nothing. It is a way of farming with no land, or at least with other people's land. You can keep bees in the suburbs of the city, or even in the centre of the city, and they will make plenty of excellent honey.

The medieval skep

The medieval method of keeping bees was in the straw skep. You plaited straw or other fibres into ropes, twisted the ropes into a spiral, lashing each turn to the next, until you formed a conical skep. You placed this in a cavity left in a wall, so as to protect it from being blown over or soaked from above by rain.

> Beekeeping is a really good way of getting something for nothing.

In the autumn, if you wanted the honey, you either destroyed the bees you had in the skep, by burning a piece of sulphur under them, or you could save the bees by turning their skep upside down and standing another empty skep on top of it. The bees in the inverted skep could crawl up into the upper skep. More sensibly, you could stand an empty skep on top of a full one, with a hole connecting them, and the bees would climb up. When they had done so you removed the old skep which was full of honey and comb. If you dug this comb out, you could wring the honey out of it by putting it in some sort of strainer (muslin would do), squeezing it, and letting it drip.

If the skep-inversion method worked without killing the bees, it would be quite a good way of keeping them. You need no equipment save some straw, a bee-veil, gloves, and a smoker. You get nothing like so much honey out of a skep as you do out of a modern hive, but then you could keep a dozen skeps with practically no expenditure, whereas a modern hive, even at its most basic, is a fairly costly item. When hundreds of people kept bees in skeps, and probably every farm had half a dozen or more, there were a great many more bees about the countryside, and swarms were much more common than they are now in a new millennium. It was easy to find them and not so necessary to conserve the bees that one had.

Langstroth's method

In 1851, a Philadelphian named Langstroth discovered the key secret about bees, which was what he called the "bee space". This is the exact space between two vertical planes on which bees build their honeycomb without filling the space in between, yet still remaining able to creep through. This discovery made possible an entirely different method of keeping bees, and turned beekeeping from a hunting activity into a farming one.

The method Langstroth developed was to hang vertical sheets of wax down at the correct space apart. Instead of building their comb in a random fashion, the bees would build it on these sheets of wax. Then, with the invention of the queen excluder, which is a metal sheet with holes just big enough for the workers but not the queen to get through, the queen was kept down below in a special chamber (the brood chamber) so that she could not lay eggs in the cells above, which as a result were full of clean honey with no grubs in them. You could then remove the frames, as the vertical sheets of wax were called, with their honey, extract the honey without killing any of the bees or bee larvae, afterwards replacing the emptied frames for the bees to build up and fill once more.

Langstroth's discovery has affected the construction of the modern hive. This has a base to raise it, and an alighting board, with a narrow slit for the bees to enter. On top of the base is the brood chamber, with its vertically slung "deep" or "brood" frames.

THE SKEP
The original beehive, or skep, is made of twisted straw or rope sewn together into a conical shape with straw. If you use a skep, your honey will be full of brood, or immature bees, because the queen can lay eggs in every cell. There is no queen excluder as there is in a modern hive. You can strain the brood out, but you kill a lot of bees. It is also impossible for the bee inspector to check a skep to see whether your bees have any diseases.

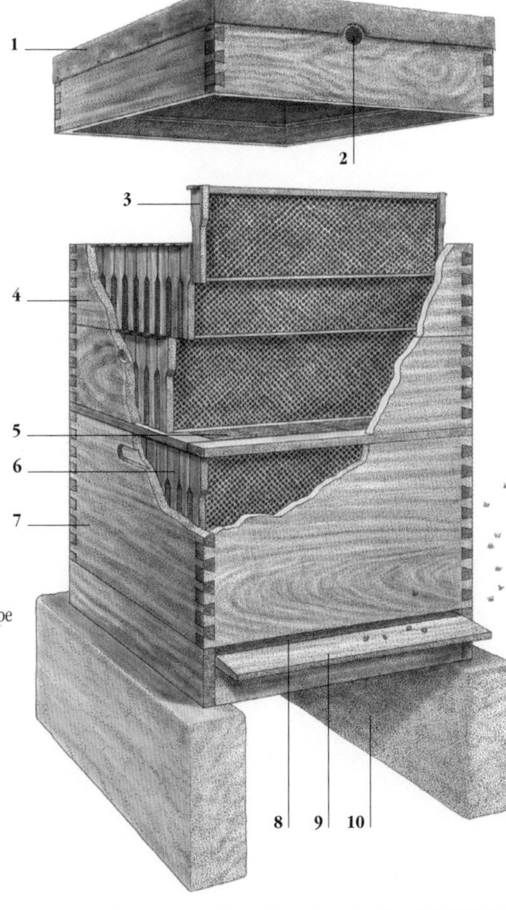

THE HIVE
1 Waterproof roof
2 Ventilator and bee-escape
3 Shallow honey frame
4 Super
5 Queen excluder
6 Deep brood frame
7 Brood chamber
8 Entrance
9 Alighting board
10 Base blocks

COLLECTING HONEY

Take the honey-loaded super out and bang, shake, and brush the bees out of it. Or else insert a clearing board the day before under the super, or supers, from which you wish to extract honey. The supers will then be free of bees when you want to take them out.

ROBBING

Smoke, which is best applied with a special "smoker" quietens bees and makes them fill with honey and sting less readily. Use a screwdriver to break the top super off.

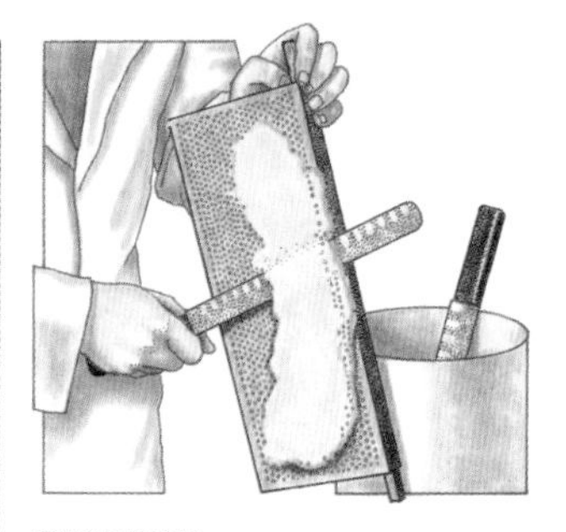

DECAPPING

To remove the honey, cut the wax capping from the comb with a hot knife. Use two knives – heat one while you use the other.

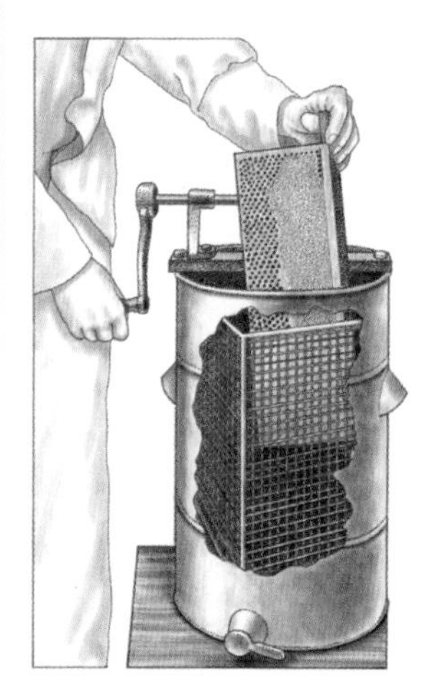

EXTRACTING

Put the decapped frames in the extractor. Spin very fast until the honey is all out of one side, turn the frames round and spin again.

THE HONEY TANK

This is useful if you have a large number of bees. Pour the extracted honey carefully through the strainer and let it settle before drawing it off into jars or containers.

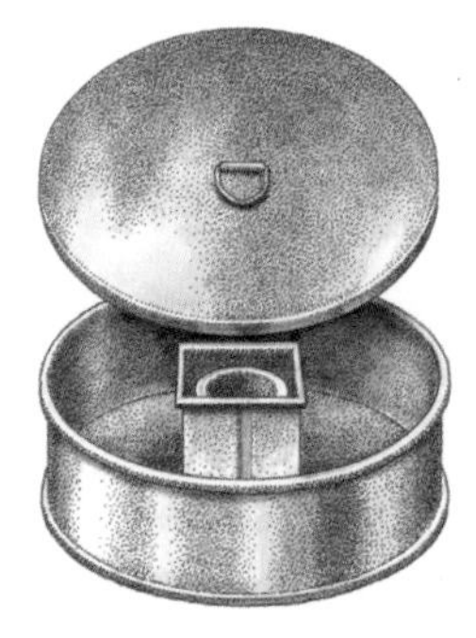

FEEDING

If you take all the honey from a beehive in the late autumn, you will have to feed the bees sugar or syrup. The feeder allows the bees to lick the syrup without getting drowned.

The wooden brood frames have foundation inside them, like canvas inside a picture frame. The foundation is sheets of wax that have been embossed by a machine with exactly the pattern made by comb-making bees. Above the brood chamber is a super, which is shallower. The queen excluder divides the two chambers. You may have two or three supers, all complete with frames fitted with foundation one on top of the other. On the very top is a roof.

The roof has a bee-escape in it, through which bees can get out but not in. There should also be a clearer-board, which is a board with a bee valve in it. This will let bees through one way but not the other. Then you should have a bee veil, gloves, a smoker, and an extractor, which you may be able to borrow. The extractor is a centrifuge. You put your sections full of honey into it and spin them round at great speed, which flings the honey out of the comb onto the sides of the extractor. It then dribbles down and can be drawn off.

Gathering the honey

As the frames get built up and filled with honey, and the brood chambers below with bee grubs, you may add a super, then a second super, and you may decide to take some honey. To do this take out one super, insert the clearer-board under it, and replace it. The next day, go and remove the super, which should be full of honey but empty of bees. Put the frames in the extractor and spin the honey out of them. You must first cut the capping off the combs with a hot knife. Each frame should be turned once to extract both sides. Then put the empty frames back in the super and return it to the bees so that they can start building on it again. Always work quietly and calmly when you work with bees. There is no substitute for joining a local beekeepers' group, or for making friends with a knowledgeable beekeeper and learning from him.

You should leave at least 16 kg (35 lb) of honey in the hive for the winter. I rob my bees only once: in early August. After that I leave them alone, with one empty super, and they make enough honey to last themselves the winter. My one hive gives me 9–18 kg (20–40 lb). The later honey in our case is heather honey which I could not extract anyway, because it will not come out in the extractor: it has to be pressed out. People who rob all the honey from their bees have to feed them heavily all winter on syrup or candy. In fact, some commercial honey nowadays is little more than sugar turned into honey by the bees. The honey you buy from small beekeepers is generally flower honey, though, and much more flavourful.

Wax

The cappings which you cut off the combs are beeswax, which is a very valuable substance: it makes polish and candles (the best in the world), and is good for waxing leatherwork and other purposes. Gentle heat melts the wax and it will run down a slope for you to collect, minus most of its impurities, in a container. The heat can be supplied by the sun, shining through a glass pane into an inclined box. It has been said that the reason why the monks of the Middle Ages were such a jolly, drunken lot was that they had to keep lots of bees to provide the wax for their ecclesiastical candles; what could they do with the honey except make mead from it?

Plants, Nuts, and Berries

There are wild foods aplenty growing in woods, fields, and hedgerows, but my advice would always be: find out what the locals consider good to eat in your locality and eat that. This is especially true for fungi and you really must know which ones are safe (see pp.146–147). Besides the common field mushroom, a few fungi both delicious to eat and easy to identify are: shaggy ink cap (boiled lightly in milk), giant puff ball, parasol, shaggy parasol, horse mushroom, cep, *boletus* (several species), morel, and chanterelle.

An enormous number of "weeds" can be eaten, as can all kinds of seeds, and of course a great many wild fruits, berries, nuts, and fungi. More "weeds" can be eaten than are a positive pleasure to eat, but a few that are excellent are: nettles, fat hen, and Good King Henry. Treat all three exactly as you would spinach: pick them in the spring when they are young and tender, cover with a lid, and boil. Some other wild substitutes for green vegetables are: shepherd's purse, yarrow, ground elder and lungwort. Common mallow can be pureed and turned into a good soup; chickweed can be cooked and eaten like spinach or used in salads; Jack-by-the-hedge is a mild substitute for garlic. You will find many other varieties in your locality, and don't forget the dandelion: it is delicious raw in a salad.

Of the edible nuts, walnut is king in temperate climates. After picking, leave the nuts for some weeks until the husks come off easily, then dry them well. You can pick hazelnuts green when they are nice to eat but won't keep, or you can pick them ripe and bury them, shells and all, in dry salt. Sweet chestnuts are simply superb. Pick them when they ripen in autumn. De-shell the prickly covers, and store in a dry place. Of course the finest way to eat them is to roast them in the embers of a fire, but prick them first to stop them exploding. Raw, they are bitter. Puréed, they taste marvellous, and turkey is unthinkable without chestnut stuffing.

> An enormous number of 'weeds' can be eaten.

Wild fruits

Of the wild fruits, the elderberry is perhaps the most versatile. The berries can be used for cooking in a number of ways. Mixed with any other fruit they improve the flavour; boiled in spiced vinegar they make an excellent relish or sauce which will keep well, if properly bottled when hot. The berries also make an excellent wine, as do the flowers, which add flavour to cooked gooseberries and also gooseberry jam. If you find blueberries or bilberries in the wild, do not ignore them: they make a wonderful pie. And if you find cranberries, you can preserve them but their flavour is nowhere better captured than in a fresh cranberry sauce. Mulberries and rowanberries make very good jam. And do not forget juniper berries, which can impart an agreeably tart flavour to all savoury dishes.

There are few people who realise that all around them are birch trees which can be the source of the most perfect country wine. Birch wine is made from the sap gathered in spring. Simply choose a good strong tree where the trunk is at least 30 cm (12 in) in diameter. Using a battery drill or brace and bit, drill a hole about 2.5 cm (1 in) in diameter into the tree at a point where you can conveniently hang a bucket. The sap will flow into your bucket.

BIRCH SAP
Betula pendula

Birch trees provide a most perfect country wine. Drill a 2.5-cm (1-in) hole in diameter into the tree at a point where you can conveniently hang a bucket. The sap will flow into your bucket.

CRAB APPLE
Malus sylvestris

Crab apples vie with sloes for the title of the bitterest of fruits (caused in part by tannin, in which they are rich). Their best use is, of course, crab apple jelly made by boiling and sieving through muslin.

ELDERFLOWER
Sambucus nigra

The secret of using elderflowers to make a delicious fruit cordial drink is never to put too many into your brew and always harvest on a fine, sunny day when the fragrance and nectar are at their height.

HAZEL
Corylus avellana

Hazel is a moody sort of tree which seems to grow like a weed in some places and can be completely impossible to grow in others. Hazelnuts are a wonderful addition to a winter diet.

SWEET CHESTNUT
Castanea sativa

With the right varieties and a good season, sweet chestnuts will stand you in good stead. More people should grow them, for the wood is also one of the best for furniture that is not liable to twist and shrink.

BLACKBERRY
Rubus fruticosus

Blackberry gathering is an enjoyable signal that autumn is near. A walking stick with a good crook is useful for pulling down the higher berries and even the smallest child can join in the fun.

ELDERBERRY
Sambucus nigra

Boiled in spiced vinegar, elderberries make an excellent relish. Elderberry wine is one of the kings of country wines – it matures well and can almost pass for a claret after three or four years in the bottle.

GORSE
Ulex europaeus

Few things can beat the spectacular show of colour of gorse in full flower. Collect the flowers for what is probably the most enticing and delicate of country wines. It is prickly but rewarding work.

SLOE
Prunus spinosa

Gather your sloes after the first frost. Take 228 g (½ lb) of sloes, prick them all over with a fork or pin before putting into the gin. Half fill a bottle with them; add sugar, fill with gin, and a fine liqueur awaits.

WALNUT
Juglans regia

For sheer volume of crop you cannot beat a good walnut tree. The nuts need to be separated from their green skins and well dried before you store them. Walnut oil is super for salads.

Mushrooms

Wild field mushrooms are well worth the search after a hot, late Indian summer spell has been followed by rain. The majority of edible fungi grow in the proximity of woodland and many have close symbiotic relationships with particular tree roots. But wild grassland can also harbour an excellent crop of fungi in autumn. Sadly the overuse of chemicals on the land and periodic ploughing up of pastures has seen a decline in wild mushrooms. The beneficent mycelium, the fungi spore, does not have time to establish itself. The edible parts of fungi are the fruiting bodies that are produced very dramatically by huge spreading masses of mycelia, which draw their nutrients as parasites from roots and decaying vegetation.

Mushrooms can be stored by slicing, and drying, or flash freezing. They taste fine sliced raw, and make great soup. There are many edible varieties: the parasol mushroom is a favourite of mine; it's stronger-flavoured than a field mushroom, and I think better. There are also many inedible and poisonous types: the fly agaric with its bright, red-and-white spotted cap is well known. The most toxin-ridden fungi is the death cap (*Amanita phalloides*). Usually it grows in woodland, often near oak trees. Similar in size to a field mushroom, it varies in colour, but its characteristic features are white gills on the underside and a "volval" bag at the base. (Any fungi growing from a "volval" bag are best left alone.) Avoid the "yellow stainer", easily confused with a field mushroom. It also noticeably turns bright yellow when bruised, or cut, and smells like disinfectant.

BAY BOLETUS
Boletus badius

Usually found in woodlands, this fungus is pale to brown in colour. It has light yellow pores on the underside and these stain blue if damaged, making the fungus easy to recognize. The stalk has no frills but is smooth from base to cap. The flesh also stains a bluish colour when cut.

PARASOL
Macrolepiota procera

Try dipping pieces of parasol in batter and deep frying. Usually found in open fields it has large brown scales in a symmetrical pattern around a pronounced central bump. The cap can grow up to 25 cm (10 in). The gills are white.

SHAGGY INK CAP
Coprinus comatus

Often growing in large clusters, these mushrooms make wonderful soup. The cap is covered with beautiful white scales and there is no veil on the stem when the cap opens to a bell shape with its dark black underside.

WOOD MUSHROOM
Agaricus silvicola

Only found in woodland, this is a delicate relative of the horse mushroom. It is only 10 cm (4 in) tall. The cap is a creamy-yellow that darkens with age. The flesh does not discolour when cut and the smell is slightly of aniseed.

GIANT PUFFBALL
Langermannia gigantea

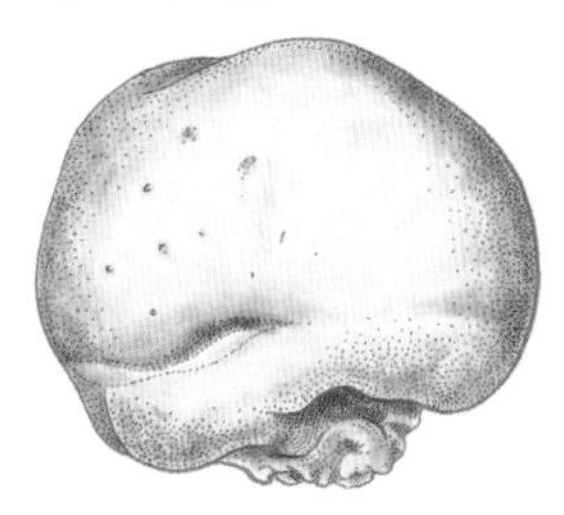

I have seen this mushroom well over 45 cm (18 in) across, which makes a major feast. They must be used young before the spores have time to develop and the insects taken their share. It is the easiest food to prepare as it cuts cleanly into firm slices, and is delicious fried quickly with butter and bacon.

HORSE MUSHROOM
Agaricus arvensis

Grows on old horses or cattle pasture. It has a slight aniseed smell and, unlike a field mushroom, does not shrivel up when cooked. The cap may be yellowy, but don't confuse it with the "yellow stainer" fungus, which will make you ill.

CHANTERELLE
Cantharellus cibarius

Much loved by the French, these fungi – up to 10 cm (4 in) across – are found in woodland clearings. They are yellow with a slight smell of apricots. The caps become like small, fluted trumpets as they age and the gills run down the stems.

ORANGE PEEL
Aleuria aurantia

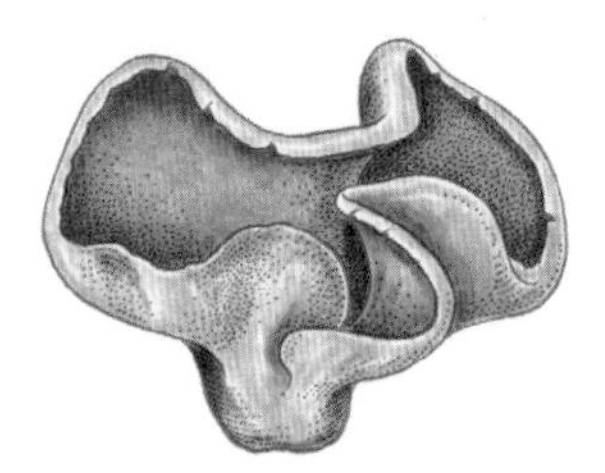

A brightly coloured and very striking fungus, the orange peel thrives in large clumps in grassland and on bare earth from autumn to early winter. The caps soon become wavy and are of fairly robust texture. Only up to 5 cm (2 in) in diameter, the fungus is bright orange on top and a lighter shade on the velvety underside.

PENNY BUN
Boletus eduli

Also called the "cep", this one has an unusual nutty flavour. When picking, cut the cap (which looks like freshly baked bread) in half to check for maggots. These work their way up in the stems. The underside will have yellow pores, not gills.

THE PRINCE
Agaricus augustus

A stocky version of the parasol, the prince grows to 25 cm (10 in) in woodland. It is too tough to make good eating unless cooked in stews. The top is flecked with brownish scales. The gills are off-white when young, turning dark brown. The flesh is strong and white.

HONEY FUNGUS
Armillaria mellea

This yellowy-brown fungus is a tree-killer – but highly edible for humans. The flesh is white and smells sweet. The gills are off-white to brown. The stalks are tough, often fused at the base with a white, cotton-like ring below the cap.

FIELD MUSHROOM
Agaricus campestris

The silky white caps grow up to 10–12 cm (4–5 in), the gills are pink. The ring around the stems is very fragile and often missing. Check stems for maggots. Pick after rainfall follows a hot spell. I like to store by flash freezing or drying.

CHAPTER FOUR

IN THE KITCHEN

"Our kitchen is not just an ordinary kitchen in which cans are opened and ordinary dishes cooked. It is a food factory. Large quantities of food of various sorts are prepared there for sorting, or bottling, or wine or jam making. There is a barrel of vinegar at one end of the dresser and bottles of our wine at the other. The larder shelves, in autumn and winter, are piled high with kilner jars and jam jars, and home-filled tins. I must say it is satisfying at the end of the summer to see shelf after shelf absolutely loaded with jars and tins full of good fruit and jam and other foodstuffs. It gives one a feeling of hope that at least one is likely to survive the winter. But – to come to the grand anti-climax – after all these romantic yearnings for the fine and the primitive we ended up with an Aga."

John Seymour *The Fat of the Land* 1976

The Storeroom

Rearing, growing, and brewing are the nitty-gritty of self-sufficiency, but good and effective storage is fundamental too. Sadly, this is often only learned by bitter experience, as wonderful produce from the garden becomes useless fodder for the compost heap long before it can be eaten. You simply cannot eat all the food you grow as you harvest it – and you wouldn't want to since the whole point of being self-sufficient is having home-grown produce all year round.

North-facing

It wasn't so long ago when houses were always built to include pantries, dairies, and cellars – the storerooms. But today "white goods" have supplemented them, so most self-supporters will have to improvise: and the north-facing storeroom is my way around the problem. If you cannot muster the resources to build such a space then you can at least make do with the smaller and simpler device of a "meat safe." My preference is to construct a storage area against the north wall of the house, or the east wall if there is no convenient north wall, to provide the following essential requisites for the ideal storeroom:

Temperature Good storage temperature should be cool, but without frost, and should not change quickly. This will work for wines, beers, jams, pickles, and all vegetables. A north-facing storeroom or traditional pantry may be warmer than we would like if the weather is hot but it will provide ventilation and protection from flies and rats.

2 Humidity If a place is too wet, then molds and fungus will thrive, string or muslin will rot, and paper will be worse than useless. On the other hand, if your storage is too dry, your vegetables will quickly shrivel up. In temperate climes the ambient air humidity is reasonable enough. If there are sufficient vegetables in the store, then they will also create their own humidity as water slowly evaporates from them.

3 Anti-pest Rats and mice get in through the tiniest of holes and they will also remorselessly gnaw away at wood, cement, or plastic when they scent the prospect of food. Avoid using plastic or wood for the base of doors, and try aluminum sheeting for a good resistant material to keep the pests out. Hanging food from a rafter is useless protection against mice, but if you hang from rings screwed into a flat, smooth ceiling then you will keep the beasts at bay.

4 Ventilation Plenty of fly-proof mesh is crucial. Make sure you have ventilation at the top and bottom of the store or in line with the prevailing wind to keep an air flow going through. Ventilation prevents mold and fungus even though it will tend to dry things out; so if the weather turns hot and windy you may want to cover some of your vents.

5 No flies zones Unless you plan to store uncooked meats, it doesn't have to be perfectly fly-proof. My preference would be to have a special "meat safe" kept specifically for this purpose and that should be as fly-proof as you would want. Obviously, the more you discourage flies, the better, and not just blowflies but also the moths that could lay eggs of vegetable-eating grubs on your produce. Cover individual items with muslin if you are worried about them.

6 Sunlight Direct sunlight creates unwanted warmth and discolors and drys out foodstuffs. Wines and beers should be kept out of the sun while they mature.

AN IDEAL STOREROOM

Your storeroom needn't be enormous; something like 6 sq ft (3.5 sq m) will be extremely useful. Moreover, it should not let in damp from the earth, so use a good quality plastic membrane under your floor. Make sure to keep the edge of its base (where the door opens) well above ground level to put off pests and prevent flooding in heavy rain. Use aluminum sheeting to make the door sill and base of the doors resistant to rats and mice. Your storeroom could be a walk-in one, depending on your space. I would recommend having shelving that can be taken in or out as the need requires – and all shelving should be easily cleaned (varnished wood or plywood is my preference). I also prefer to use brick, stone, or blockwork for the walls. Not only is this more resistant to pests, but the extra thermal mass helps to keep temperatures even.

MEAT SAFE

You cannot beat the simplicity of a meat safe for a multitude of uses. Essentially this is a fly-proof and well-ventilated box which can be fixed up anywhere out of the sun. It is ideal for storing recently killed game, for hanging game, and for storing cured meats of all kinds. It does not need to be especially large: 1 ft x 2 ft x 3 ft (30 x 60 x 90 cm) would be very useful. A simple yet effective way of storing all kinds of meat. It must be fly- and pest-proof and kept in a cool place.

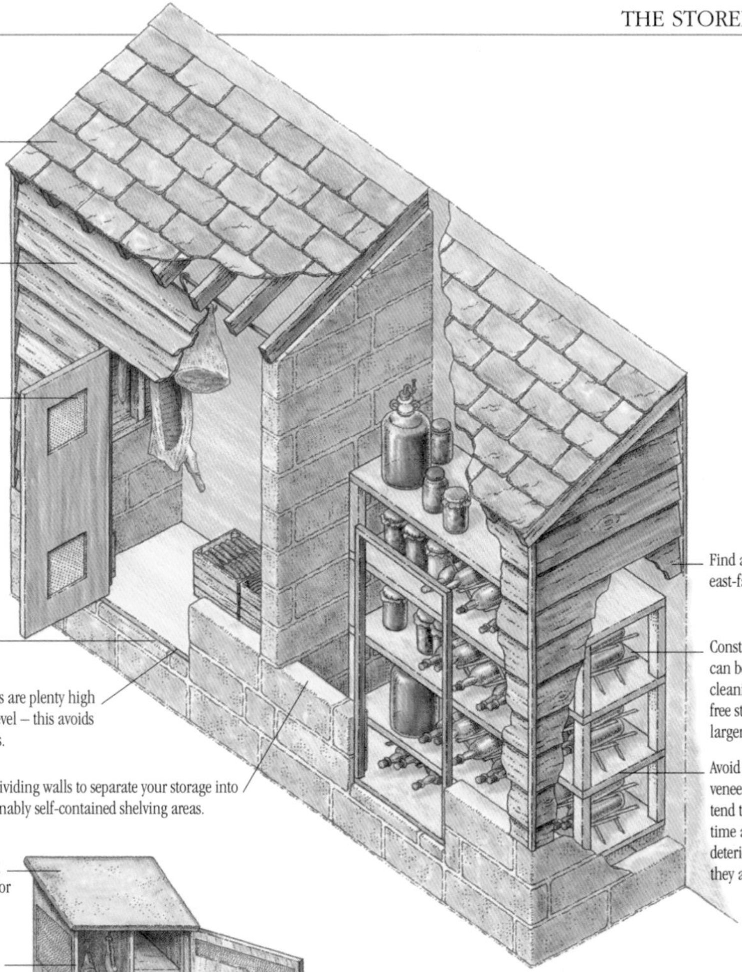

Use good quality slates, tiles, or felting to make a long-lasting and weatherproof roof.

Use clapboarding to provide additional insulation and soften the look of concrete blockwork.

Cover ventilation holes in fly-proof mesh and make sure all ventilation slots have fly-resistant mesh.

Use strips of aluminum or galvanized sheeting to make the bottom of your doors secure against rats and mice.

Make sure your door sills are plenty high enough above ground level – this avoids flooding and deters pests.

Use dividing walls to separate your storage into reasonably self-contained shelving areas.

Find a suitable north- or east-facing wall.

Construct shelves so they can be lifted out for cleaning or to allow more free storage space for larger items.

Avoid using plastic veneered boards as they tend to absorb water over time and their quality deteriorates, even though they are very easy to clean.

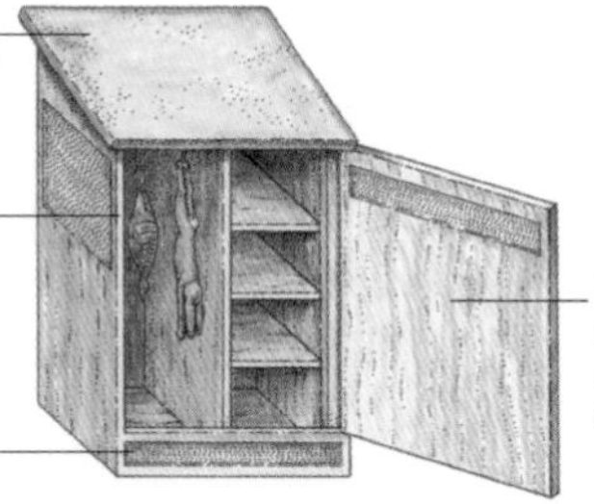

Use plywood plus felting or aluminum sheeting for your watertight roof.

Walls can be plywood or good quality tongue-and-groove. Varnish or paint as necessary.

Cover bottom vent below door with fly mesh.

Ensure the door is close-fitting and flush and constructed to a robust standard that will not warp.

Harvesting and Storing

Harvesting, processing, and storing are part of a seamless process, each dovetailing into the other and all useless without each other. In many ways the excitement of the harvest is often tempered by the realities of processing and storage. Here are a few golden rules that I suggest you follow when it comes to harvesting your hard-won crops. Don't harvest more than you can process or store, or it will simply be wasted unless you can barter or give it away and improve your social credit ratings. Be ever so careful not to damage the crop when you pick it or dig it. And finally never try to store substandard or damaged produce.

VEGETABLES

Clamping is the traditional way to store a variety of root crops. Basically you make them into a pyramidical pile covering with a good layer of straw or bracken and then covering with a 6-in (15-cm) layer of earth beaten flat with the back of a spade (see p.154). The problem for the small farmer is that this is not a very effective method for small quantities. That is why I suggested (on p.162) you try using an old nonworking freezer or two as a vegetable store. It can work surprisingly well, and it keeps out the rats. For beets and other roots, I have found burlap or stout paper sacks very good if kept in the confines of a good storeroom or cellar. Beans and peas should be dried and stored away in great quantities every fall. When they are thoroughly dried, threshed, and winnowed, store them in crocks, barrels, bins, or other mouse-proof places. Mushrooms and most fungi dry out at an ideal temperature of 120°F (50°C) so crumble them afterward into a powder and store them in closed jars. The powder is marvelous for flavoring soups and stews. Sweet corn is excellent dried: it really is a thing worth having. Boil it well on the cob, dry the cobs in a slow oven overnight, cut the kernels off the cobs, and store them in closed jars. When you want to eat them, just boil them.

> "Never store substandard or damaged produce.

FRUIT

As a rule the early-maturing varieties of apples and pears will not store well. So eat them as you pick them, and store only late-ripening varieties. Leave these on the trees as long as possible and only pick them when they are so ripe that if you lift them gently, they come off. Pick them and lay them carefully in a basket. Then spread them out gently in an airy place to let them dry overnight. The next day store them in a dark, well-ventilated place at a temperature of 35°–40°F (2°–4°C). Pears like it very slightly warmer.

Ideally each fruit should be wrapped individually in paper to isolate any molds or bacteria. Only perfect fruit can qualify for storing: so disqualify any with bruises, cuts, or missing stalks. If the floor is earth, stone, or concrete, you can throw water on it occasionally to keep the air moist. Storing fruit in a hot, dry attic is simply wasted effort. Apples may well keep until spring. If you feel like your apples won't keep long enough, you can dry them. Core them, slice thinly, string up the slices, and hang over a stove, or in a solar-heated drier (see p.210), at 150°F (65°C) for 5 hours. When crisp and dry put them in an airtight container and store in a cool place.

LIFTING POTATOES

Any damage to potatoes or other root crops, especially carrots, will be multiplied twenty-fold by storage – roots are so easily bruised. Always sort the crop carefully into three piles: the first for storage, these are perfect and large; the second for more immediate consumption, these may be damaged or too small to store; and the third for the compost heap or burning, these are diseased, too small or too damaged to use. Your crop must have time to dry out, preferably on a breezy day, before being put into storage. Also remember that the places you are going to store your crop must be scrupulously cleaned and dry – as must any straw.

STORING POTATOES

1 Use an old freezer for storing potatoes. First place a layer of clean, dry straw across the base.

2 Dump in several baskets of dry, undamaged tubers until you have a layer perhaps 1 ft (30 cm) deep. Then add a further layer of dry, clean straw.

3 Dump in the next layer of spuds. Then put a final layer over the top before closing down the lid on to a small shim to allow in air but keep out rats.

DIGGING CARROTS

When digging carrots for storage make sure your fork is well away from the roots. Put the fork right under and pull gently up with your hand grasping the foliage.

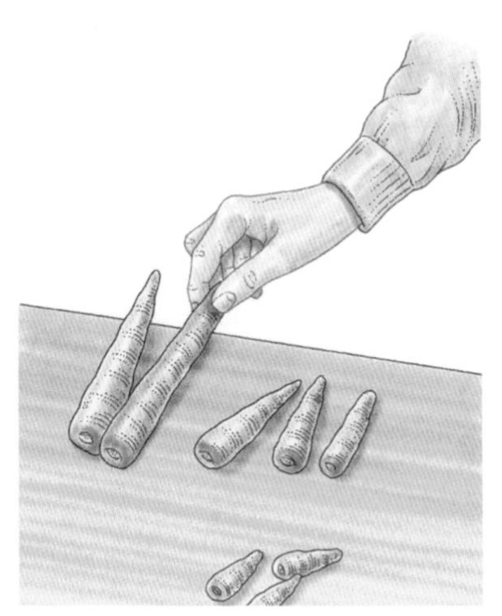

SELECTING CARROTS

Shake or brush the soil free, never wash in water, before you start selecting. Now sort the crop carefully into three piles: one to store, one to use, and one to dispose of.

CLAMPING

Clamping is a method of protecting root crops in the open, where diseases do not build up as they can in a cellar. But no clamp keeps out hard frost, so in very cold winters you must store indoors

1 When you pick potatoes for clamping you should let them dry for 2 or 3 hours first. Prepare the clamp by putting a layer of straw on the ground.

2 Heap the potatoes (or other root crop) up on top of the straw in the shape of a pyramid so that when it is finished, rain will drain off.

3 Cover with a layer of straw or bracken. Allow a period for sweating before covering with earth.

4 Cover with a layer of earth 5– 6 in (13–15 cm) thick. Beat the earth flat with the back of a spade.

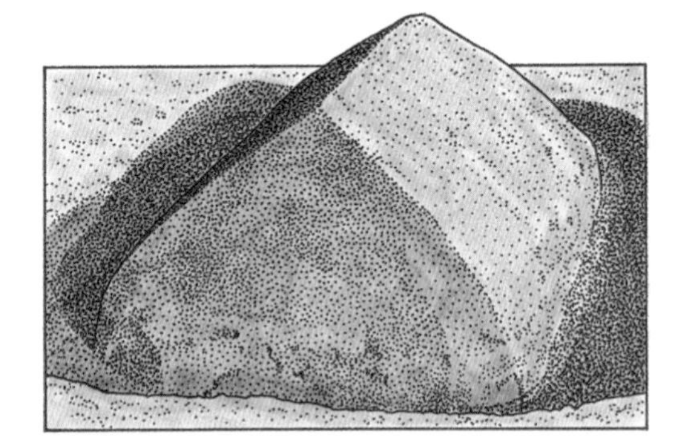

5 Make sure that bits of straw protrude from the clamp to admit some air to the crop inside.

STRINGING ONIONS

You can store onions on trays with slats, on polythene netting, or on a wooden stand. But the ideal way of keeping them is to string them up in a cool place with access to plenty of air. Before you store your onions, always remember to dry them thoroughly first, either by leaving them on the ground in the sun, or covered but in the wind if it is wet.

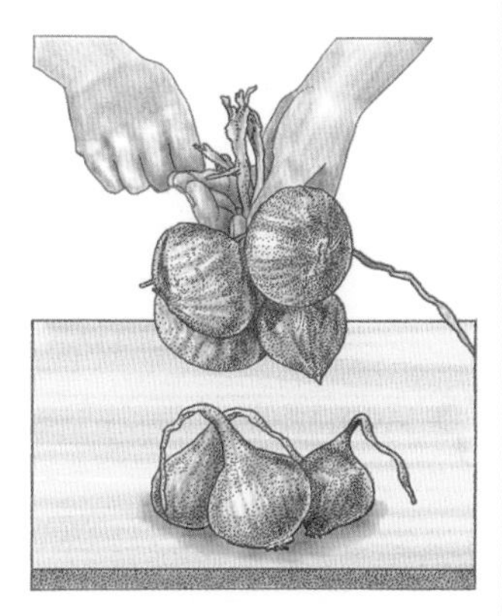

1 Make sure that all the onions you want to string have long stalks. Start by knotting four of them firmly together. Add onions one by one to the original four. Twist their stalks and knot them tightly around string or binding twine.

2 Continue adding individual onions to the growing bunch, ensuring that each one is securely tied on, and that the bunch does not become too heavy.

3 Plait the knotted stalks around the end of a long piece of string so that the onions hang evenly when you hold them up.

4 Hang the string up when you decide the your bunch is complete. The onions should keep indefinitely.

OTHER STORING METHODS

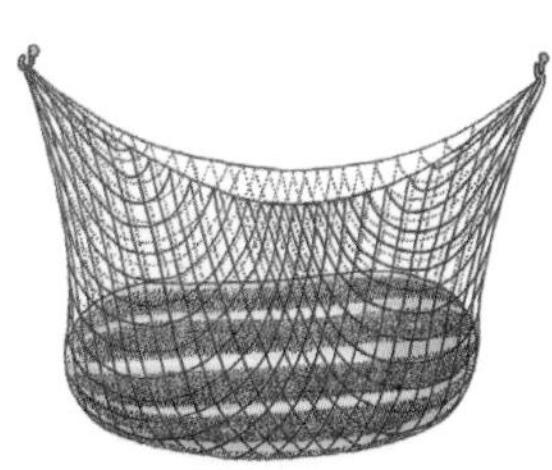

HANGING IN NETS

Squashes (including pumpkins) will keep best if hung in nets, although they can be stored on shelves, if turned occasionally.

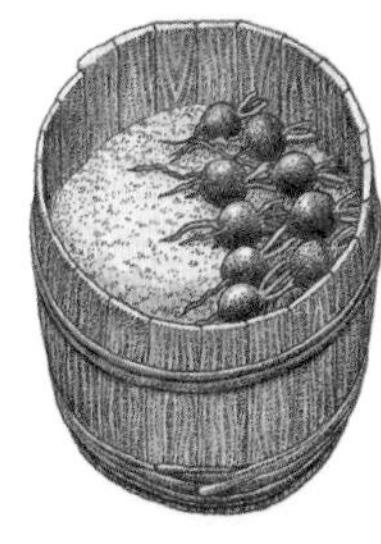

STORING BEETS

Use dry sand so that the roots don't touch and keep safe from frost.

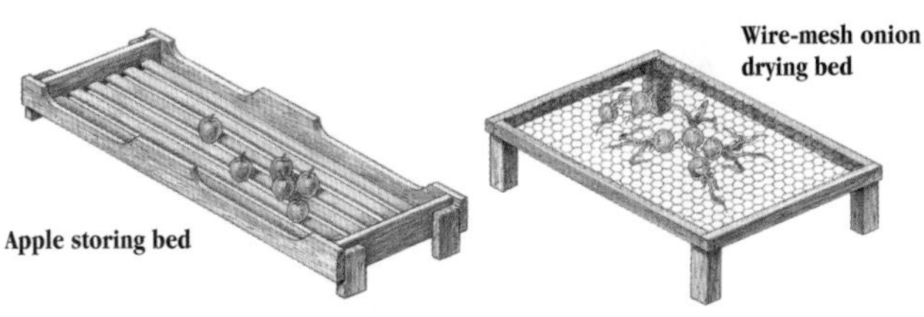

FLATBED STORING

Late-ripening apples last all winter if you keep them in a cool, dark place, but be sure that they aren't touching each other. A storing bed (above) is ideal for this. You could even wrap each one in paper also. Store onions on wire netting. If it rains, they should be in the wind, but under cover.

HEELING IN LEEKS

If you fear that your leeks, celery, and Jerusalem artichokes might be exposed to frost in the open, "heel" them into dry, sheltered ground near the house, where they will derive some protection from harsh weather. Otherwise they are generally best left in the ground until required.

Making Bread

There is white bread and wholemeal bread, and many gradations between the two. There is leavened bread and unleavened bread, and again many gradations. There is sourdough and soda bread, pita bread and flat bread, but the great thing for the self-supporter to remember is that whatever kind of bread you choose to make, and whatever kind of grain you make it from, the process is simple. It is also fun, and even the most ham-fisted cooks can take pleasure and pride in their efforts.

Undoubtedly the first breads were unleavened, and undoubtedly the first person who discovered yeast discovered it by accident. If you make a dough with flour and water without yeast or baking powder and then bake it, you will be left with something very like a brick. People got over this by rolling the dough out very thinly and cooking it that way. But no doubt one day someone mixed up some dough, didn't cook it immediately, and found the stuff began to ferment. What had happened was that wild yeasts had got into it and were converting the sugar (in the flour) into alcohol and carbonic acid gas. The alcohol evaporated, but the carbon dioxide blew the glutinous dough up into bubbles. This unknown ancient took up the bubbling doughy mass and placed it upon a hot stone or maybe into a little hollowed-out stone oven and made what was the first leavened bread.

It was then found that bread could be made not in thin sheets but in thick loaves, and was still good to eat. Furthermore, it was discovered that leavened bread stays palatable longer than unleavened bread: good home-baked wholemeal bread can taste fine for 5 days or more, while unleavened bread tastes very dreary unless you eat it when it is still absolutely fresh.

Yeast

How long it took us to figure out the true nature of that lovely stuff yeast, we will never know. But certainly the first self supporters must have found that if they were lucky enough to get a good strain of wild yeast in their dough, they could go on breeding it – simply by keeping a little raw dough back from each baking to mix in with the next batch of bread. The old pioneers in the Wild West were called "sourdoughs" because they made their bread thus. And even today, people out of touch with bakeries and yeast suppliers commonly make bread with sourdough.

If you live near a bakery, always buy your yeast fresh. It should be a creamy putty color, cool to the touch and easy to break, with a nice yeasty smell. Don't buy any that is crumbly or has dark patches. It will keep for 1 week to 10 days in a screw-top jar in the fridge. Or cut it into 1-in (2.5-cm) cubes and freeze it. Both yeast and bread freeze well.

If you cannot obtain fresh yeast, you can still make a perfectly good bread with dried yeast. This is widely available in packets, and it will keep for up to 3 months. But it is a good idea to test dried yeast if you have had it around for some time. Drop a few grains into a little warm liquid dough mix; if it is still "live" the water will froth in under 10 minutes. If you are using fresh yeast for any recipe specifying dried yeast, always double the quantity. Or halve it if the recipe in question asks for fresh yeast and you are using dried yeast.

Yeast flourishes in a warm atmosphere in temperatures between 48–95°F (9–35°C), but strong heat – over 140°F (60°C) – will kill it. Set your dough to rise in a warm place: on top of the stove, in the oven, or even under the quilt on your bed.

Kneading and keeping

A word about kneading. It's important because it releases the gluten and distributes the yeast right through the dough. Don't be afraid to treat your dough fiercely when you knead it. Push and pull it around until it seems to take on a life of its own, becoming silky and springy in your hands. Then leave it alone to prove, that is, to rest for a few hours until it has risen. When it has risen enough it should jump back at the touch of a finger.

If you don't have a freezer keep bread in a dry, cool, well-ventilated bin. Don't put it in an airtight container or it will turn moldy. Make sure the bread is quite cool before you stow it away or the steam in a warm loaf will make it turn soggy. Keep your flour in a dry, dark, cool cupboard.

Enjoy your bread

Bread at its most basic is simply yeast, flour, salt, and water. Add milk, butter, eggs, sugar, honey, bananas, carrots, nuts, and you will enrich your bread, change its taste and texture. Roll it in poppyseed, sesame, dill, celery, or caraway as you please. Brush it with milk, paint it with egg yolk. Knot it, twist it, plait it. Experiment, and you will find that your own bread is one of the great joys of the self-sufficient way of life.

> Home-baked wholemeal can taste fine for 5 days.

Be your own baker

For people who grow rye, barley, oats, corn, rice, sorghum, and the rest, it is useful and interesting to try some breads made with these grains, or with them mixed with wheat flour. It must be remembered that of all the grains, only wheat has enough gluten to sustain the gas generated by the living yeast sufficiently to make fairly light, or risen, bread. You can try a combination of two or three different flours, but it is usually worth adding some wheat flour. And always add salt. Oil, butter, lard, or margarine help to keep bread moist. Water absorption varies with the sort of flour. Here is a rundown of the different flours:

Wheat flour Wheat flour is rich in gluten, which makes the dough stretch and, as it cooks, fixes it firmly around the air bubbles caused by the leavening.

Rye flour Rye flour gives bread a nice sour taste, and can be used on its own, although a lighter bread will result if half or a third of the flour is wheat flour. Maslin, flour made from rye and wheat grown together and ground together, was the staple English flour of the Middle Ages.

Barley flour Barley flour alone makes very sweet-tasting bread. A proportion of a third barley flour to two-thirds wheat produces good bread. If you toast the barley flour first your bread will be extra delicious.

Oatmeal Oatmeal is also sweet and makes a very chewy, damp bread, which fills you up very nicely. Use half oat and half wheat flour for a good balance.

Cornmeal Bread made from cornmeal has a crumbly texture. Try half cornmeal and half wheat flour.

Ground rice Ground rice bread is a lot better if the rice is mixed half and half with wheat flour.

Cooked brown rice Like the whole cooked grains of any other cereal, cooked brown rice can be mixed with wheat flour to make an unusual bread.

Sorghum By itself sorghum (or millet) flour makes a dry bread. Add wheat flour and you get nice crunchy bread.

Soy flour Soy flour too is better mixed with wheat. The soya flour adds a lot of nourishment.

Making standard wholemeal bread

I never measure my flour because what really matters is getting the dough to the right consistency, and flour absorbs more or less water according to its fineness, quality, and so forth. However, if you must have a recipe, this is one that a baker friend of mine, who grows and mills his own wheat, uses:

2½ lb (1 kg) of wholemeal flour
1 oz (28 g) salt
½ oz (14 g) dried yeast
2 teaspoons soft brown sugar
1 ¼ pints (0.7 liters) water

Put the flour and salt in a large bowl. Put the yeast in another bowl, add the sugar and some warm water. Leave in a warm place to rise. When the yeast is fermenting well, add it to the flour and the rest of the water, and knead it till it is soft and silky in texture. Return it to the basin and leave it to stand in a warm place until it has about doubled its size. Knead it again for a few minutes and mold into loaves. Place in warmed greased and floured tins, and, if it is soft wheat flour, leave it to rise for 5 minutes. If it is hard wheat flour, allow longer, up to 20 minutes. Put in an oven of 425°F (220°C) for 45 minutes.

MAKING BREAD

If you can boil an egg, you can bake bread. There is absolutely nothing difficult about it. To make six medium loaves, take 4½ pints (2.3 liters) of water, warmed to blood heat, 2 oz (56 g) of salt, and the same amount of brown sugar, 1 tablespoon of fresh yeast (or half this amount of dried yeast). You can even use yeast from the bottom of your beer kive.

TEMPERATURE AND TIME

Bread rises (and yeast ferments) best at 80°F (27°C). Yeast will die at any temperature much over 95°F (35°C) and it won't multiply under 48°F (9°C). So the place where you set the bread to rise must fall within these temperatures. Usually the top of the stove is ideal. The oven should be – well, hot. Apart from the time you spend waiting for things to happen, you probably don't spend more than half an hour working the dough, and the result is six beautiful wholemeal loaves.

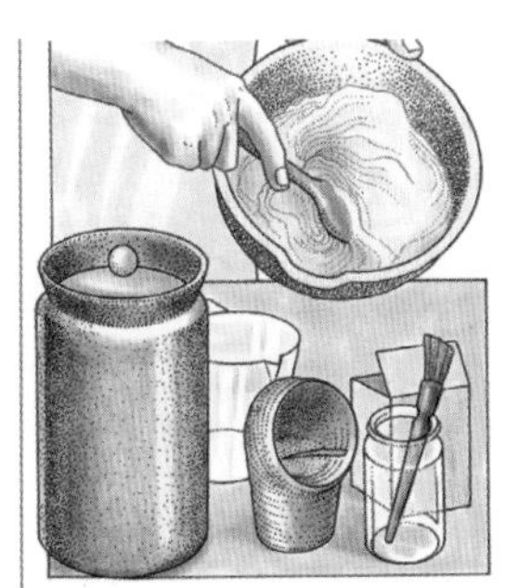

1 Put all the ingredients into a large mixing bowl. When the yeast has dissolved, pour in enough flour to make a fine, sticky mash. Stir this well with a wooden spoon. The spoon should stand just about upright. Cover dish with a cloth and leave it overnight in a warm place free from drafts.

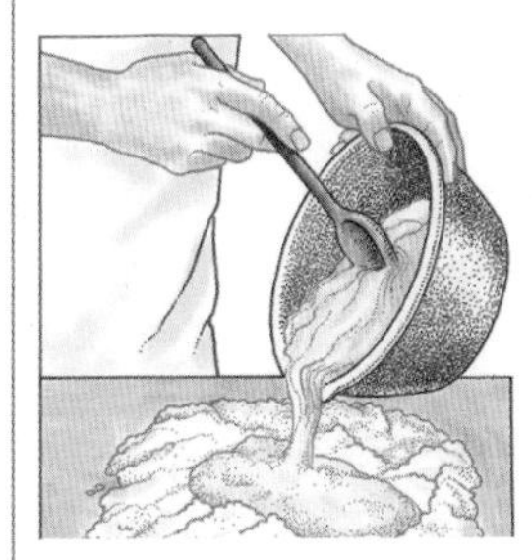

2 Come morning the yeast will have the dough spilling over with enthusiasm. Heap some dry flour on to a table and dump the dough into the middle of this.

3 Sprinkle dry flour on top of the dough and it is ready for kneading. Start by mixing the dry flour with the wet dough.

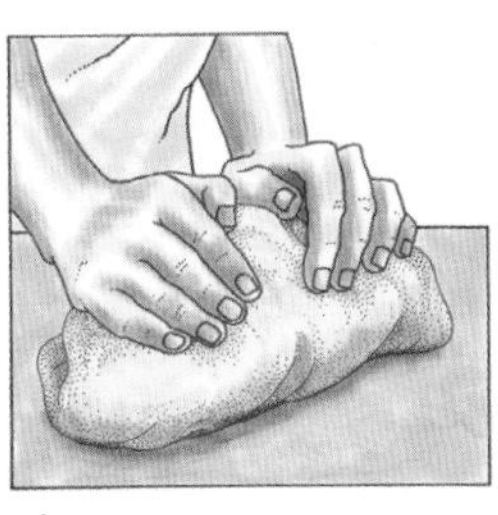

4 The aim is to make a fairly stiff dough, dry on the outside. You do this by pushing the dough away from you with the palms of your hands (above) and then pulling it toward you again (below). This is kneading and it is a very sticky process. When the dough sticks to your hands (and it will), fling on some flour. Whenever it feels sticky, sprinkle flour.

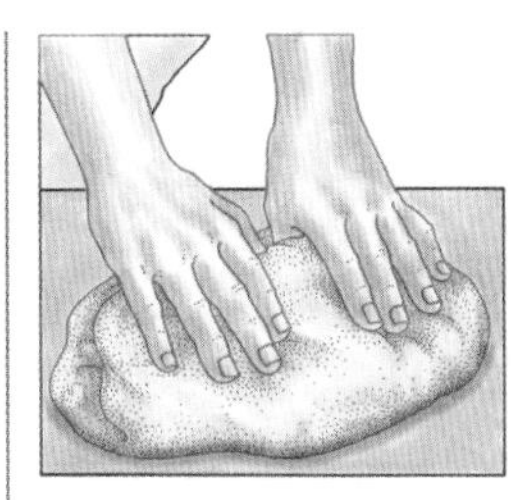

5 Kneading must be done thoroughly – you need to push and pull and fling on the flour until you have a dry, satisfying little ball. Roll it about to your heart's content and after 10 minutes it's ready for baking.

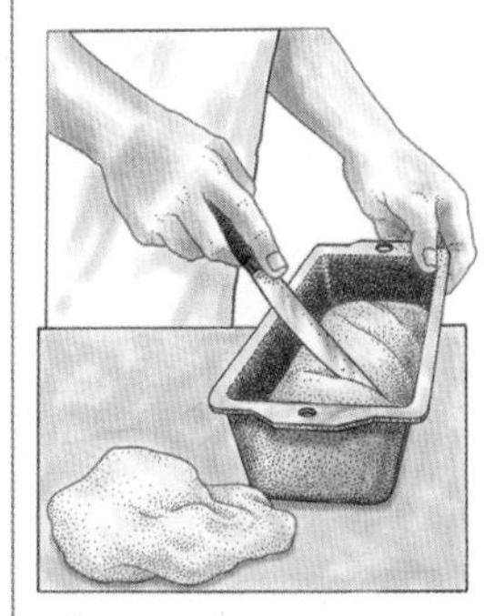

6 Divide the dough into six equal portions. Grease the baking tins and shape your dough. Fill the tins just three-quarters full. Score patterns on top with a knife and leave covered for about an hour in a warm place.

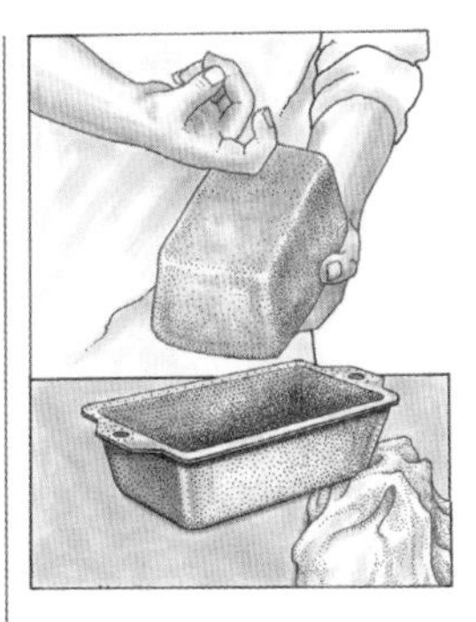

7 To test them, tap the bottoms. If they sound hollow they are done. Or push in a skewer – it should come out clean. If it doesn't put back for a bit longer.

8 When you are sure your loaves are good and ready, take them out and stand them on top of their tins to air.

Preserving

Few things can equal the pleasure of coming fresh to new green peas at the beginning of their season after 6 months of pea-abstinence. The palate, jaded and corrupted by months of frozen peas, or quick-dried peas masquerading as fresh garden peas, gets no real pleasure from these specimens. But true dried peas, cooked as pease pudding, or put in soups and stews, are quite another thing. They are a traditional time-honored way of preserving plant protein for the winter months, and eating them all winter does not jade the palate for the fresh garden pea experience in June.

At the same time there is, potentially, a vitamin shortage in the dark winters, and those dark, cold days should be enlivened by nice tastes and odors besides that of salt bacon. So the self-supporter will wish to preserve certain things, preferably by a process which improves their natural flavor, such as canning, pickling, chutneying, or wine-making.

There is a place for freezing, especially foods such as berries. Although it is an effective storage system, you may not improve any food by deep freezing, but you actually improve fruit and vegetables by making them into chutney, jam, and the like. Freezing meat is another matter: unless you are very hungry you cannot eat a steer before it goes bad. In more sensible times people killed meat and shared it with the community. Nowadays the whole principle of sharing with neighbors is forgotten and the cold of the chest freezer often replaces the warmth of neighborly relations.

> Those dark, cold days should be enlivened by nice tastes and odors.

Wine

Wine-making, much like beer-making, turns sugar into alcohol. Some fruits, such as grapes grown in a warm climate, have so much natural sugar in them that you don't have to add any. But many of the things you can make wine from are low on sugar. So you will have to add sugar if you want alcohol of a decent strength. And remember that weak wine won't keep, it just goes bad. Some "wine" described in books of wine recipes is simply sugar-water fermented and flavored with some substance. Most flower wines are made like this, and people even make "wine" of tea leaves – that sugarless substance!

Fruit wines have their own sugar, but usually not enough, so you must add some. The same goes for root wines. Parsnip, which is by far the best, has quite a lot of sugar. What country wines do is to preserve and even enhance the flavor and bouquet of the things they are made of. They cheer us up in the cold, dark days of winter and are very good for us too.

Chutneys and pickles

You make both chutneys and pickles by flavoring fruit or vegetables, or a combination of both, with spices and preserving them in vinegar. The methods of preserving, however, do not resemble each other. Chutneys are fruits or vegetables which have been cooked in vinegar, often heavily spiced and sweetened. They are cooked until all excess liquid has evaporated, leaving a thick pulp, the consistency of jam. The flavor is mellow. Pickles are put down whole or in large chunks in vinegar, but not heated in it. Anything which is to be pickled must not have too much moisture in it. So sometimes moisture must be drawn out first with salt. The resulting flavor is full and sharp.

Both chutneys and pickles are an excellent way of preserving things for the winter and of enhancing their taste as well. They are delicious with cold meats and meat pies, and also offset the taste of curries or cheeses.

Ketchups and similar sauces are strained juices of fruits or vegetables spiced and cooked in vinegar. These, too, if well made, can give a lift to plain food.

Canning

The principle of canning is very simple. Food is put in jars, and both jars and their contents are heated to a temperature which is maintained long enough to ensure that all bacteria, molds, and viruses are destroyed; at this point the jars are completely sealed to prevent any further pathogens from getting in, and then allowed to cool. Thus the contents of the jars are sterilized by heat, and safe from attack by putrefactive organisms.

Fruit cans very well. Vegetables are far more difficult, because they are low on acid, and acid makes food preservation easier. My own feeling about the canning of vegetables is don't do it. What with salted runner (pole) beans, sauerkraut, clamped or cellared roots or cabbages, and, in all but arctic climates, still quite a few things that will grow and can be picked fresh out of doors all winter, there is no need for the rather tasteless, soggy matter that canned vegetables become. But tomatoes (which aren't strictly speaking a vegetable) are a very good thing to can indeed. They are easy to can, you can grow a big surplus during their short growing season, and are rich in vitamins.

Freezing

Virtually all fruits, vegetables, and meat can be stored by freezing. Some freeze better than others, and you will discover just what you like and what you do not. Freezing preserves by making it too cold for bacteria and molds to function – but the downside is that ice takes up more space than water so the cells within foodstuffs are broken and the texture, and even the flavor, of foods can change.

You may think that by using freezing as a major method of storage we are courting disaster if your electricity supplier cuts off your power, or if the weather or other natural elements disrupt it. There are two remedies for this: the paper remedy is to take out insurance; the practical remedy is to organize yourself with a standby generator. You can buy reliable standby generators at a fairly reasonable price and the power requirements of a freezer are fairly minimal. We are so dependent on electricity, which is, after all, a very convenient power source for many things, that a standby generator is well worth the effort.

Frozen filing cabinets

As with all food storage, we should only process good quality raw materials. Be fussy about this. Damaged fruit and vegetables will not freeze well and you risk wasting time and space that could be better used for other things.

The chest freezer is like a bizarre frozen filing cabinet and, like all filing systems, it needs to be kept in order. Not only must you have your foods clearly labeled – with labels that do not come off when frozen – but you must also rotate your usage so the oldest items are used first. To give you some idea of how we manage, our farm has three fairly large chest freezers: one is kept for meat; the other two for fruit, vegetables, ice cream, and other delicacies we have a taste for. At least once each year we arrange to empty one of the freezers to give it a good defrosting – and almost every year we panic to use up or give away fruit we have been carefully hoarding through the winter because June has arrived and the next crop is due. Possibly we have links to prehistoric squirrel species.

TIPS FOR FREEZING

- Don't skimp on quality of raw foodstuffs.
- Use foods in rotation.
- Defrost freezers regularly.
- Use good-quality freezer bags.

The longer food is stored, the more moisture it loses; so, after much trial and error, we now use the expensive zipper bags because they are tough, they lie flat, and you can use them several times.

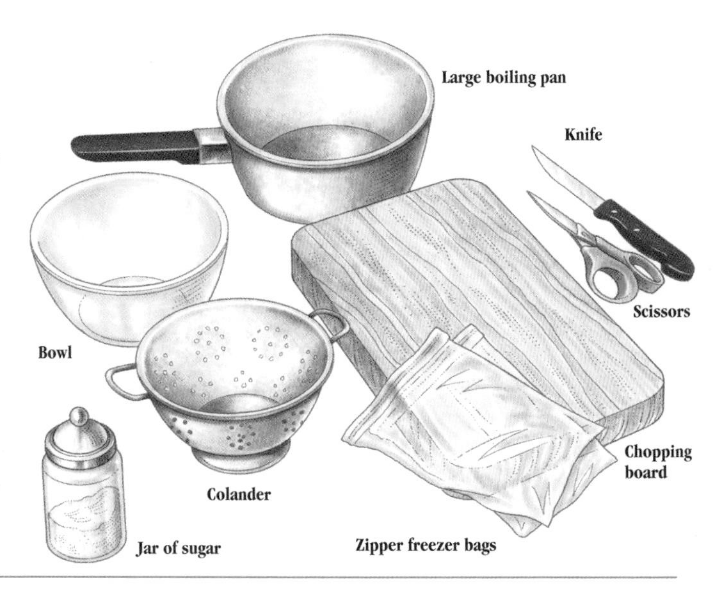

FLASH FREEZING

1 For best results many foods are best "flash" frozen, especially mushrooms and soft fruits. Spread the fruit on a tray or on newspaper and put straight into the freezer uncovered for 24 hours.

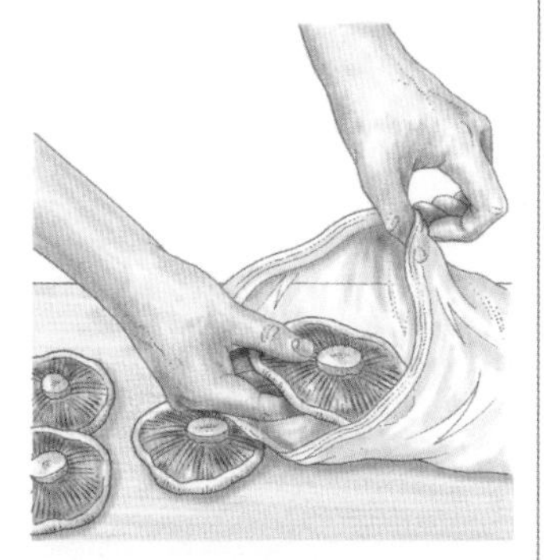

2 Put the frozen foods into plastic bags. As they are already frozen they will not stick together, making them more attractive when cooked.

FREEZING BLACKBERRIES

1 A freshly picked basket of blackberries is full of stalks, leaves, and bugs. Take out as much of this unwanted debris when you are picking and you will save time later.

2 Cut off stalks, take out leaves and debris, and toss bugs into the compost bin. This is actually a very pleasant job to do socially after supper on a fine summer evening.

3 Fortunately, fruit does not need any special treatment before being frozen. However, it is a good idea to spread out the fruit to be frozen so they don't touch before flash freezing.

4 Now put the fruit into good-quality plastic bags ready for storage in the freezer. Write the contents and date on the bag. Self-sealing or "tuck-and-lock" freezer bags are best.

Beans, Snow peas, and Sugar snaps

All these vegetables freeze very well and the basic approach to preparation and freezing is the same. First of all, harvest your crop when it is perfectly ripe. Check the crop regularly, for you do not want food that is stringy. This may mean picking every day. Get into a good routine of picking and processing a little every day as the crop progresses. Young and tender food is the essential aim and the more often you pick, the better the plant will respond by producing more. Different varieties of pea crop in different ways – there are dwarf varieties, which can crop for weeks on end, but others may produce almost the whole crop in just two or three pickings.

1 Sort and trim the pods, getting rid of unwanted leaves, damaged pods, and stalks. Top and tail by cutting off each end of the pods. You can slice three or four beans at a time but watch your fingers!

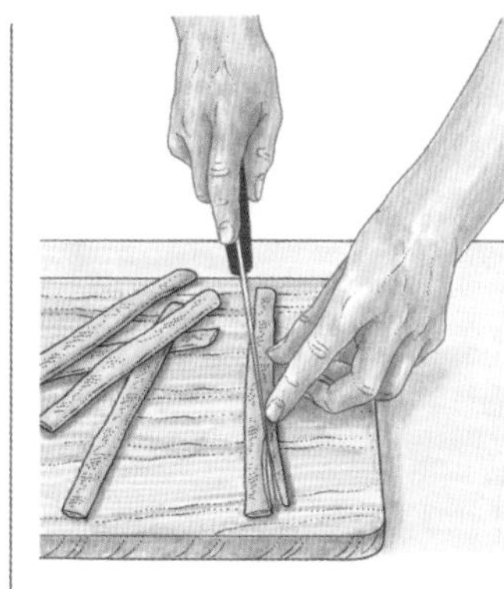

2 Beans must be sliced diagonally into thin slices with a sharp knife or by using a cunning bean slicer. Snow peas and sugar snaps are frozen whole.

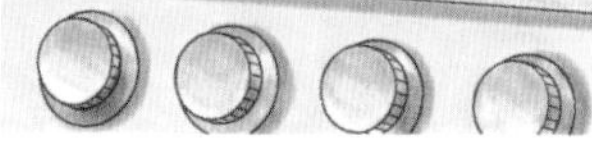

3 Put a large pan of water on the stove to boil and tip your pods into the boiling water. Leave for a minute or two until it comes back to the boil.

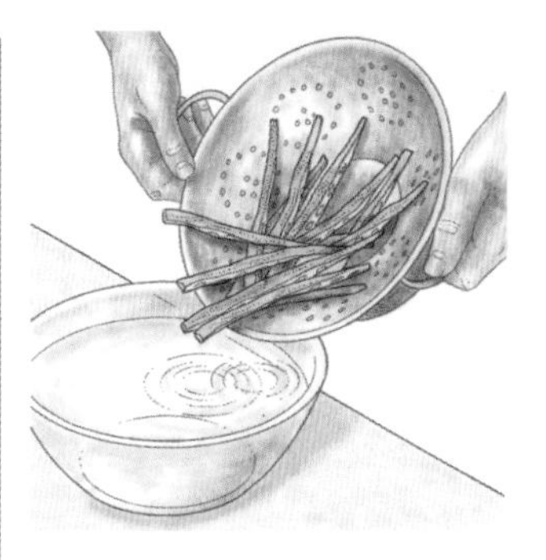

4 Drain off the pods after they have been "blanched." Plunge them quickly in cold water to stop them from cooking (you may need to do this a few times) and give them a good shake to get rid of any water and let them drain.

5 Once cooled, bag up the pods for freezing. Be careful to squeeze out all the air in the bag before you seal it. Purpose-made freezer bags with resealable tops and strong plastic that resists tearing are a great help for this.

Plums

Everyone looks forward to the plum harvesting season. After all, what can be better than a fragrantly fresh plum straight from the branch? I pick my plums by making sure the grass under the tree is well cut and cleared, then I simply give the tree or the branch a gentle shake. Ripe plums will rain down on your head – possibly with a few angry wasps to boot. Picking them up from the ground is a pleasant job – and if your turf is soft there will be little bruising. Watch out for dozy wasps and get the plums inside for sorting and processing as soon as you can. Plums keep reasonably well for a few days but the flavor definitely suffers over time.

1 Split each plum with a sharp knife and take out the stones. It's a great way to sit down with friends and enjoy a chat while working.

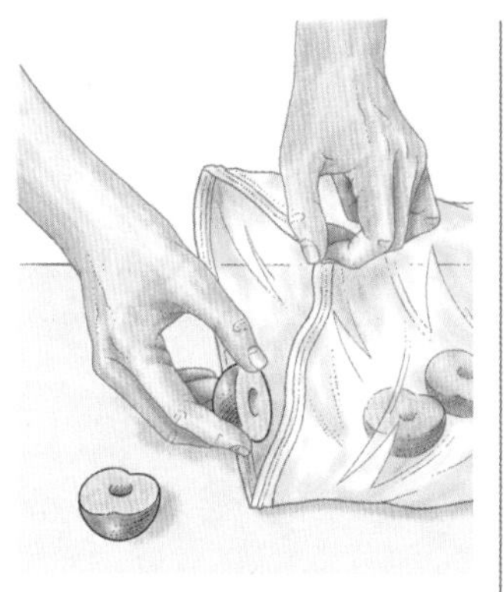

2 Put the halved plums straight into your freezer bags, making sure that no leaves or stalks manage to creep in, too.

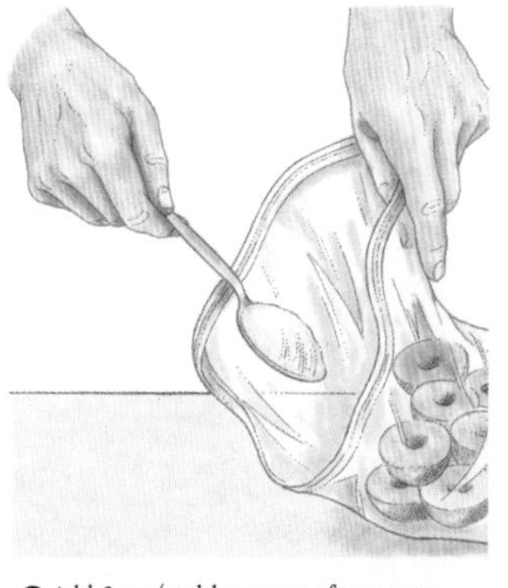

3 Add 3 or 4 tablespoons of sugar to each bag. Give it a shake to spread out the sugar, squeeze out the air, and seal for the freezer.

SNOW PEAS

Simply top and tail snow peas or sugar snaps with a sharp knife before you blanche them in boiling water. Try to remove any "strings" from the peas at the same time as you top and tail.

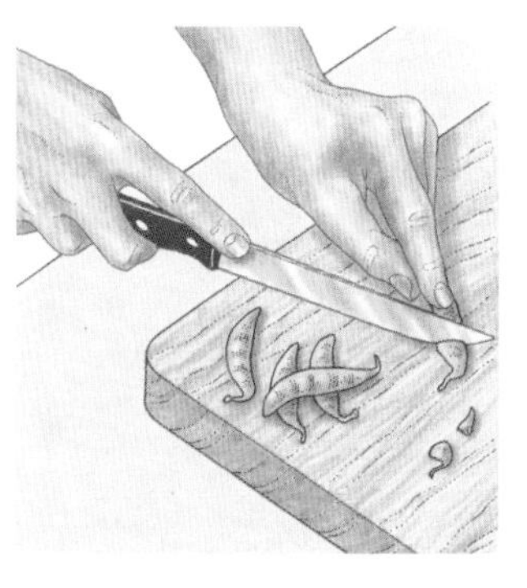

PEAS

Ordinary peas freeze very well. Pod the peas, take out any leaves or pod and blanche them before freezing. Have your pig bucket handy to put the "waste" in right away.

Canning

Glass jars for canning must have airtight tops, capable of supporting a vacuum, and arranged so that no metal comes into contact with the contents of the jar. If you examine the common Mason jar, or any of its rivals, you will find quite a cunning arrangement ensuring that the above requirements are met. A rubber ring compressed by a metal screw-cap forms an airtight seal, and only the glass disk inside the screw cap comes into contact with the jar's contents. Mason and other proprietary jars need the metal parts smeared with vaseline to prevent them from rusting, both when in use and when stored away. Keep the rubber rings in the dark, for light rots rubber.

To can you also need a container in which jars can be boiled. If you buy one it should have a false bottom, so that the jars are not too close to the source of heat. Alternatively, put a piece of cardboard in the bottom, or else just a folded towel. When canning fruit pack the jars as tightly as you can; tapping the base of the jar on the table helps to settle the fruit, and drives air bubbles out.

CANNING FRUIT

Cold water bath method

Put the fruit into jars of cold brine or syrup and put the jars in cold water. Take an hour to bring the water to 130°F (54°C), then another half hour to raise it to 165°F (74°C) for soft fruits (plus another 10 minutes); 180°F (83°C) for stone and citrus fruit (plus 15 minutes).

> Jars of bottles on your shelves in winter are a cheering sight.

Oven method

Fill the jars, not putting any syrup or brine in them yet, and covering them with loose saucers only. Put them in a low oven at 250°F (121°C). Leave them for 45–55 minutes for soft fruits; 80–100 minutes for tomatoes; and 40–50 minutes for stone and citrus fruit (at 300°F/149°C, putting hot syrup in before processing them). Take out and top up with fruit from a spare jar that has undergone the same process, then fill up with boiling brine or syrup, screw on the tops, and leave to cool.

Hot water bath method

If you have no thermometer, and no oven, use the hot water method. Fill packed jars with hot syrup or brine, put the lids on loosely, lower into warm water, bring to the boil – starting at 100°F (39°C) take 35–30 minutes to reach the required temperature of 88°F (190°C). Then simmer for two minutes for soft fruits; 15 minutes for stone and citrus fruits and 40 minutes for tomatoes – all at 88°F (190°C). For fruit other than tomatoes, use a syrup of sugar and water if you wish. Water alone will do, and if you pack the fruit tightly you won't need all that much. But if the fruit is sour, a weak syrup does help.

CANNING VEGETABLES

I'm not mad on the canning of vegetables, with a few exceptions. Ripening tomatoes for example can be dropped into scalding water for a moment so that the skin comes off, then put into Mason jars, top up with sugar, and salt, and spices, boil for an hour, screw up and leave. They give life, grace, and vitality to food dishes throughout the year.

CANNING TOMATOES

Jars of tomatoes on your shelves in winter are a cheering sight. They are easy to bottle and it even improves their flavor.

1 Remove the green tomato stalks, and nick the skins with a knife.

2 Put the tomatoes in a bowl and pour over boiling water. Leave until the skins have loosened.

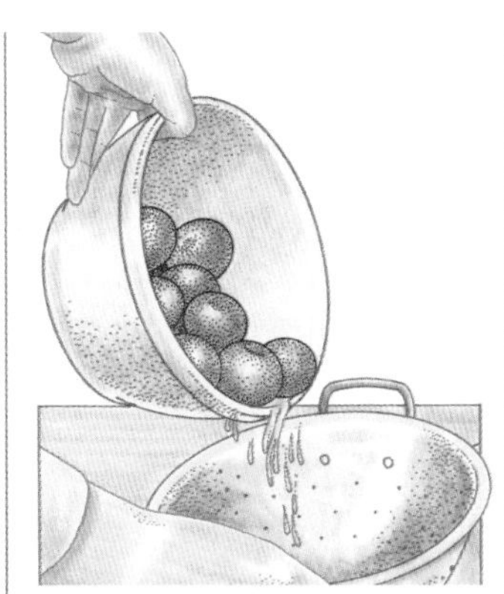

3 Drain and cover with cold water. Don't leave them very long or they will soon turn soggy.

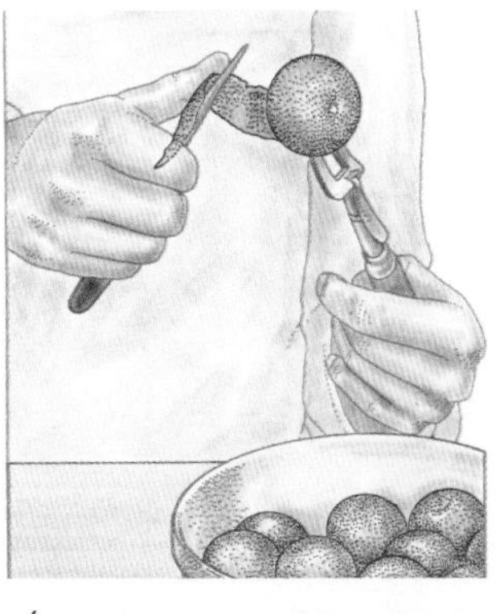

4 Peel off the skins carefully so that the tomatoes retain their shape and do not lose any juice. Make up a brine by mixing ½ oz (14 g) of salt to 1 liter (a quart) of water.

5 Pack tomatoes in jars very tightly. Push large fruit into place with the handle of a wooden spoon.

6 If sterilizing in water, fill the jars with brine, cover with sealing disks, and screw lids on loosely; if in the oven, add brine afterward.

7 Put jars in a pan of water, or stand on newspaper in the oven. Now cook.

8 When cool, try lifting the bottle by the disk only. The vacuum should hold.

If you must can your vegetables, you must heat in a pressure-cooker, as boiling at atmospheric pressure is not enough to make it safe. With sweet corn I used to pick them young, and the surplus beyond my daily requirement I boiled, scraped the grain off the cobs with a knife, dried it on a wire gauze thing over the stove or in the slow oven, then put it away in tin canisters. In the hungry gap, I soaked for 12 hours, heated in water and ate. Nearly as good as new. Alternatively, sweet corn can be canned: husk your corn, remove the silk, wash well, and cut the corn off the cob with a knife. If you force the cob onto a nail sticking up from a board at an angle, you will have it steady for slicing. Pack the corn in the jar to within 1 in (2.5 cm) of the top, add half a teaspoonful of salt to each pint of corn, fill up to ½ in (1 cm) from the top with boiling water, put the lid on loosely and heat in a pressure-cooker at 240°F (115°C), at 10 pound pressure, for an hour. Remove the jars from the cooker and seal.

Salting string beans

Use 1 lb (0.5 kg) of salt to 3 lb (1.4 kg) of beans. Try to get "dairy" salt or block salt; though ordinary salt will do. Put a layer of salt in the bottom of a crock, a layer of stringed and sliced beans (tender young French beans do not need much slicing, whereas runners always do) on top, another layer of salt, and so on. Press down tightly. Add more layers daily. Cover the crock with an airtight cover and leave in a cool place. The beans will be drowned in their own brine, so do not remove it. To use, wash some beans in water and then soak them for no more than two hours.

MAKING SAUERKRAUT

Winter cabbages (see p.60) can be clamped but, if greens are scarce, make a sauerkraut standby.

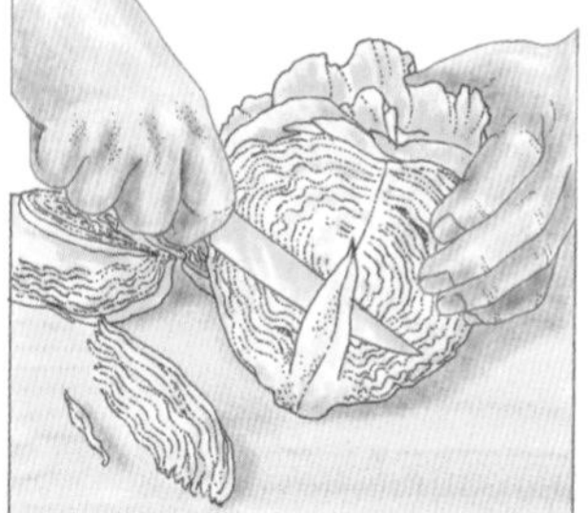

1 Shred hard white cabbage hearts finely, and estimate ½ oz (14 g) salt for each 1 lb (0.5 kg) of cabbage.

2 Pack layers of shredded cabbage into a stone crock or wooden tub; sprinkle salt between the layers.

3 Spread one big cabbage leaf across the top, put a cloth over it, and cover that with a plate.

4 Weigh the plate down and leave in a warm place. In 3 weeks put the cabbage in jars and sterilize.

Making Pickles and Chutneys

Pickles and chutney can preserve produce and add flavor to cold meats, meat pies, cheeses and curries. The principle of both involves flavoring fruit and vegetables with spices, and then storing them in vinegar. If you can't make your own vinegar, take time to investigate their varying strengths, flavors (and costs!) before purchasing.

Distilled or fortified vinegar is much the strongest (it is also the most expensive). Wine vinegar is the strongest natural vinegar, and more expensive than cider or malt vinegar. Remember that vinegar leaves its flavor in chutney, and even more so in pickles, so if you want to have the best-tasting accompaniments to your cold pies, you may find yourself paying for your vinegar. And the best-flavored vinegar is wine. However, when you make chutney, much of the liquid is evaporated during the cooking, so malt vinegar could be a more economic proposition.

Spiced vinegar

The vinegar is first steeped with spices and sometimes cooked with sugar, to improve and mellow its sharpness. To make a spiced vinegar suitable for a variety of pickles, you can add any spices you like. Ground spices make vinegar turn cloudy, so if you want the pickle to be attractively presented, and clearly recognizable, use whole spices.

The ideal way of making spiced vinegar is to steep all the spices in cold vinegar for a couple of months, after which time the liquid is ready to be strained and used. Since this is not always practicable, here is a speeded-up version. For two pints of vinegar take 2–3 oz (56–84 g) of spices and tie them in a little muslin bag. Include a piece of cinnamon bark, slivers of mace, some allspice, 6 to 7 cloves, likewise peppercorns, ½ teaspoon mustard seed; add garlic, or any herb, if you like the flavor, and for a hot taste add chili, ginger, or more mustard.

Now put the vinegar and spices into a jug or heatproof jar which can be covered with a lid or a plate. Stand it in a panful of water. Bring the water to the boil, then take it off the heat. Leave the whole thing to cool down for 2 hours, by which time the spices should have thoroughly flavored the vinegar. Remove the little bag and the vinegar is ready to use. You can pickle fish, eggs, fruit, and vegetables, and pickle them whole or in pieces. Moist vegetables and fish are usually salted first to draw out some of their water.

Crisp pickles like cucumbers, beets, cabbage, and onion are put straight into cold vinegar. Others, like plums, tomatoes, and pears, are cooked till soft in spiced vinegar; this is then reduced to a syrupy consistency before finishing. When adding sugar to sweet pickles, use white sugar: it keeps the pickle clear and light. Pickle jars need close sealing to prevent evaporation, and the vinegar must not come in direct contact with metal lids. Eat all pickles within 6 months; after this they are likely to soften.

Pickled eggs

For hard-boiled, new-laid eggs you need a quart (1 liter) of vinegar per dozen. Shell them. Pack them in jars and cover them with spiced vinegar. Add a few pieces of chili pepper if you like. Close tightly and begin to eat after 1 month.

Pickled onions

Choose small button onions, and don't skin them at once. Instead, soak them in a brine of salt and water using 4 oz (114 g) of salt to each liter (quart) of water. After 12 hours skin them. Put them in a fresh brine for 2 to 3 days, with a plate on top to keep them submerged. Drain and pack in jars or bottles with spiced vinegar. Add a little sugar to help the flavor. They are good to eat after 2 or 3 months.

Pickled apples

Use small apples (crabapples are good) for this sweet pickle. For 2 lb (1 kg) of apples use 2 lb (1 kg) of sugar and 1 pint (0.5 liter) of spiced vinegar. Cook the sugar and vinegar until the sugar is just dissolved. Prick the apples all over, using the prongs of a carving fork. If they are too big for the jar, cut them in half. Simmer in the vinegar-sugar mixture until they are soft but not falling apart. Put them gently in jars. Reduce the syrup to ½ pint (0.3 liter) by boiling. Pour it hot over the apples, but not so hot the glass cracks.

CHUTNEYS

Chutney is a concoction of almost any fruit or vegetable you like, flavored with spices and cooked with vinegar to a thick, jamlike consistency. Soft, overripe fruit and vegetables are ideal, as they turn into pulp quickly. Ingredients for chutney can be just about anything you like – squashes, pumpkins, rutabagas, turnips, peppers, onions, beets, celery, tomatoes, apples, rhubarb, blackberries, pears, damsons, gooseberries, plums, dried fruit, oranges, elderberries, cranberries, and grapefruit. The herbs and spices could be bay leaves, chili, cumin, coriander, cardamom, cinnamon, cloves, ginger, allspice, peppercorns, mustard seed, horseradish, garlic, or whatever. It is best to mince vegetables or fruit for chutney finely and then cook them slowly for a long time to evaporate the liquid. Sugar plays a large part in chutney. Most chutneys turn dark as they are cooked, so if you want an even darker one, use brown sugar, or even molasses.

Cooking and storing chutney

Use stainless steel or enameled pans. Vinegar eats into copper, brass, or iron pans, so don't use them. Simmer hard ingredients such as onion in a little water before mixing with softer ingredients such as squash, and before adding salt, sugar, and vinegar, which harden fruit or vegetables.

Put whole herbs and spices in a muslin bag, which you can tie to the handle of the pan so that you don't lose it in the chutney. Powdered spices can be added loose as you wish. Crush garlic and fresh ginger in a pestle and mortar before adding to chutney. Soak dried fruit in water before cooking it. Use sufficient vinegar just to cover the ingredients. Cook until the consistency is of thick jam, and there is no free liquid. Be careful it doesn't burn toward the end. Stir well while it cooks. Can while still hot in clean hot jars, cover and label.

Chutney improves with keeping, so store in a cool, dark place in glass jars. Make sure they are tightly sealed or the vinegar evaporates, leaving an dry, shrunken mess. Jam-cover style cellophane papers are not suitable. I use twist-on metal caps from old jam or pickle jars. Check that the metal from the lid is well lacquered or protected with a waxed cardboard disc, otherwise the vinegar corrodes the metal.

MAKING TOMATO CHUTNEY

The secret of good chutney is use contrasting ingredients. Here, spice and garlic offset tomatoes and apple. You need: 2 lb (1 kg) tomatoes, 2 onions, 1 cooking apple, raisins, 2 cloves garlic, ½ oz (14 g) fresh ginger, 2 oz (56 g) brown sugar, ½ pint (0.3 ltr) vinegar.

1 Skin the onions, peel and core the apple; chop up finely. Simmer onion in a small pan with a little water. Add the apple and raisins, cook until they soften.

2 Skin the tomatoes, then chop them up roughly into chunks. Have salt and some spices (for personal taste) handy.

3 Crush the garlic and fresh ginger in a pestle and mortar with salt. If you are using dried ginger instead, add ½ oz (7 g) to the bag of spices.

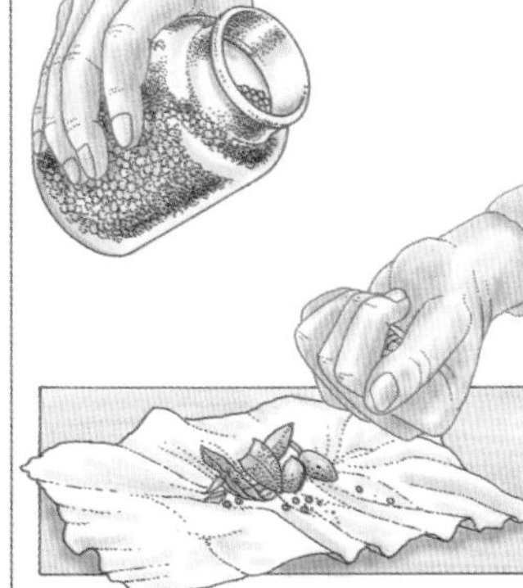

4 Tie up in a little muslin bag: 1 crushed bay leaf, 2–3 crushed dried chilies, ½ teaspoon mustard seed, 4–5 cloves; add cardamoms, cinnamon, coriander, peppercorns as you wish.

5 Tie the muslin bag to the handle of a large saucepan, so as not to lose it in the chutney. Pour the softened ingredients into the pan, then everything else.

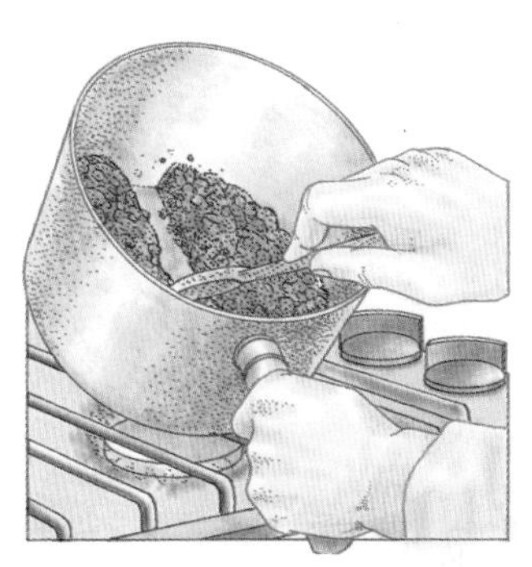

6 Cook on low heat for an hour or so, until mixture thickens, that is so when you draw a spoon through it you can see the pan.

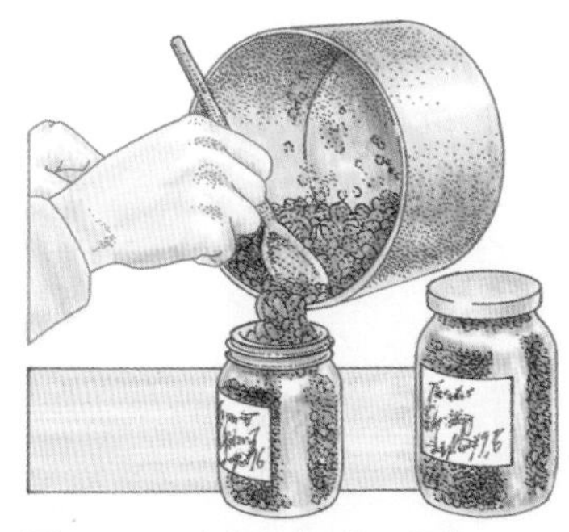

7 can at once in hot, clean jars. Seal and label. You can also use synthetic skins, or waxed paper circles underneath a greaseproof paper tie-on cover.

Making Jams and Syrups

Jams and conserves of all kinds are a very useful way of preserving fruit. Usually the fruit is cooked first without any sugar, to soften it and to release the pectin, which is what makes it set. (Some fruit has more acid and pectin in it than others. Fruit which is low in acid or pectin usually needs extra acid or pectin added to it, see below). Sugar is added next, and the whole thing boiled rapidly until setting point is reached. As long as jams are properly made, well covered, and kept in a cool, dry place, they keep for ages.

Fruit should be under- rather than overripe, and clean. Bruises on damaged fruit don't matter as long as they are cut out. It is important to weigh the fruit before you begin cooking, otherwise you don't know how much sugar to add. The sugar should be fine sugar, as this dissolves fastest. Brown sugars are okay, but bear in mind that they add a flavor of their own and in some cases are damp; therefore, adjust the weight.

Basic jam-making

Jam-making goes like this: clean, sort, prepare fruit. Weigh it. Cook it with sufficient water to make it tender. Put it in a large, wide pan, and when it is boiling add the required sugar. Stir until all sugar is dissolved. Bring to a rapid boil. Don't stir. Test from time to time to see if the setting point is reached. Stop cooking when it is, and allow to cool a bit so that fruit pieces will not float to the top of the jam in the jars. Fill hot clean jars to the brim with jam: cover, seal, label.

“Fruit should be under-rather than overripe.

Testing for pectin

Put into a little glass a teaspoonful of strained, cooled fruit juice from the cooked fruit, before you add the sugar. Add three teaspoons of denatured alcohol, and shake together. Wait a minute. Pour the mixture out into another glass. If the fruit juice has formed one solid blob, the pectin is good. If it is several blobs, it is not so good, so add less sugar. If it is all fluid, it is useless, in which case boil the fruit again. Even add commercial pectin at a pinch.

Testing for set

Put a little jam from the pan on a saucer to cool. If the surface wrinkles when you push it with your finger, it is done. Examine the drips from the spoon: if a constant stream flows, it is no good; if large thick blobs form, it is okay. The temperature of the boiling jam should reach 222°F (105°C). It is best to use all or at least two of these methods to be absolutely sure your jam is ready.

Canned fruits or conserves do not keep as long as jam, but because they are only cooked briefly the flavors are very fresh. It is not so necessary to worry about pectin with conserves, so you can make them with low-pectin fruit like raspberries, strawberries, blackberries, and rhubarb. Also, note that there is more sugar per pound in conserves.

Damson or plum jam

Much of the pectin in plums is found in the stones, so if you can, extract the stones first, crack some of them, and tie the kernels in a little bag. If this is difficult, never mind; they will float to the top when the jam cooks and you can skim them off with a slotted spoon at the end.

THREE-FRUIT MARMALADE

Make this from oranges, lemons, and grapefruit as a tasty change from the usual recipe of Seville orange marmalade.

1 Squeeze out the juice from eight oranges, two lemons, and two grapefruit. Strain it through a sieve and save the seeds for use later.

2 Shred the peel coarsely or finely, depending on how thick you like your marmalade. A course shred will make marmalade with a thick rind.

3 Using a stainless steel preserving pan, tie the seeds in a muslin bag and hang into the juice, and soak with peel and juice for a day in 10 pints (5.7 liters) water. Boil for two hours, stirring to ensure that nothing burns at the bottom of the pan.

4 Test for pectin by adding three tsp denatured alcohol to one of juice. Shake. The juice should solidify. Found in the skins and seeds of oranges, pectin, when boiled with sugar and the fruit's acid, helps it set as jelly.

5 Remove the bag of seeds from the pan. Boil the mixture, add 7 lb (3 kg) sugar and stir until dissolved. Again, make sure nothing burns at the base of the pan. Cook until it sets.

6 Let some marmalade drip from a spoon. If it falls in thick flakes it is properly set.

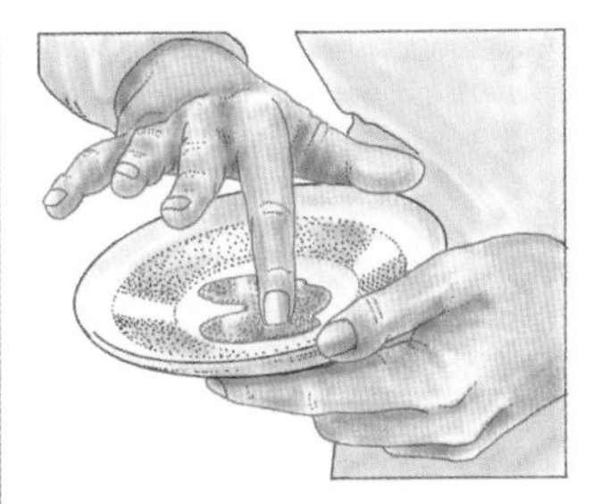

7 Alternatively, place a saucer in the freezer then spoon a little out onto the cold saucer. Put the saucer back into the freezer for a few minutes. It is set (that is, done) if the surface of the marmalade creases when lightly touched.

8 Put into hot, clean jars (you should warm the jars first in the oven, but be careful not to burn yourself when lifting out). Spoon into the jars then cover with greaseproof paper and cellophane seal, or screw-top jars if preferred, and label.

To make damson or plum jam you will need

6 lb (2.7 kg) damsons or plums
6½ lb (3 kg) sugar
½ pint (0.3 liter) water

Wash the plums, and cut them in half. Simmer with the water until tender. Add the sugar, stirring until dissolved, then boil hard until setting point. Remove floating stones, or if you put kernels in a bag, remove the bag. Leave the jam to cool a little before jarring so that the fruit will not rise to the top of the jars. Jar, seal, and label.

For raspberry conserve

4 lb (1.8 kg) raspberries
5 lb (2–3 kg) sugar

You can use damaged but not moldy fruit. Warm the sugar in a bowl in a low oven. Butter a large pan, put in the fruit, and cook over a very low heat. As the fruit begins to give up its juice and bubble, slowly add the warm sugar. Beat hard until the sugar is quite dissolved. It should remain a lovely bright color and taste of fresh raspberries. It should be quite thick. Pot and cover in the usual way, but examine for mold after a few months. Another way is to put sugar and raspberries in layers in a large bowl. Leave overnight, and bring just to the boil the next day, before jarring.

For lemon curd

4 oz (114 g) butter
1 lb (0.9 kg) sugar
4 eggs, plus 3 to 4 lemons depending on size and juiciness

This is not a jam, but a good way of using up eggs. Grate the rind from the lemons and squeeze out their juice. Put rind, juice, butter, and sugar into a small pan and heat until the butter melts and the sugar just dissolves. Let it cool. Beat up the eggs. Put them in a bowl which will just fit over a saucepan of simmering water, and stir in the juice. Beat over the saucepan of water, or use a double boiler, until the mixture thickens to curd consistency. Jar and cover. Lemon curd doesn't keep long, so use it up quickly. Don't make too much at a time. Richer curds can be made using eight egg yolks instead of four eggs. Also try oranges or tangerines instead of lemons, using less sugar.

For lemon and carrot marmalade

8 oz (228 g) thinly sliced lemon
8 oz (228 g) shredded carrot
2 pints (1 liter) water
1 lb (0.9 kg) sugar

Mix the lemon, carrot, and water. Cover and stand overnight. Cook in a covered saucepan, bring to boil, then simmer for about 30 minutes or until tender. Then add sugar, and simmer until it completely dissolves; boil rapidly until setting point. Try a bit on a cold plate to see if it jells; it may take 15 to 30 minutes. Pour into clean, warm jars, cover with waxed paper and seal. The flavor of carrot and lemon is very fresh and fairly sweet. Eat within three months.

Making fruit butters and cheeses

Fruit butters and cheeses are jams made from puréed or sieved fruit. Butters are softer than cheeses. Cheeses, if they are firm enough, can be turned out of their molds as little "shapes." Fruit butters and cheeses are delicious when they are eaten as desserts with cream or even spread on bread.

Blackberry and apple cheese

You will need equal amounts of blackberries and apples. Wash the apples but don't bother to peel or core them. Cut them up roughly. Pick over the blackberries and wash them if they are dusty. Put both fruits into a pan, just cover with water, and stew, stirring occasionally, until the apples have turned mushy. Sieve the cooked fruit. You should have a fairly thick pulp. Weigh it. Add 1 lb (0.9 kg) sugar to each pound of pulp. Boil together. Stir all the time as this burns easily. When it thickens enough for you to see the bottom of the pan as you draw the spoon across it, it is done. Can and cover like jam. It sets quite firmly, like cheese, and will last for ages.

Making jellies

Jellies are simply jams with all the solids strained from the cooked fruit. When the juice is boiled up with sugar it forms jelly, which can be used in the same way as jam.

Blackberry and apple jelly

This recipe will suit any high-pectin fruit, such as crabapples, currants, citrus fruits, quinces, gooseberries, sloes, damsons and rowanberries. You can also experiment with mixtures of fruits. Cook them separately if one needs more cooking than the other.

Proceed as for blackberry and apple cheese to the point where the fruit is cooked and soft. Then strain the juice through a cloth. Don't succumb to the temptation of squeezing it to speed it up or the finished jelly will be cloudy. Measure the juice and add 1 lb (0.9 kg) sugar to each 1 pint (0.5 liters) of juice. Cook until setting point is reached and can and label in the usual way. If you are very economically minded you can stew up the residue of fruit in the jelly bag with more water, then either extract more juice or make a fruit cheese by sieving it. Follow the instructions given above if you want to do this.

Fruit syrups

Fruit syrups are made in the same way as fruit jellies, though you don't need to add so much sugar to syrups. To prevent spoiling by fermentation (when you would be on the way to making wine) you have to sterilize syrups and keep them well sealed. They make very refreshing drinks and milkshakes in summer, or you can use them as sauces for desserts and cereals.

Extract the juice from any unsweetened cooked fruit you like, as for jelly, or, if you wish, extract it by pressing then straining. Measure the amount and then add 1 lb (0.9 kg) sugar per 1 pint (0.5 liter) of juice. Heat it until the sugar is just dissolved – no more or it will start to set like jelly. Let it cool. Sterilize the bottles and their lids, preferably the screw-cap sort, by immersing in boiling water for 15 minutes. Drain, then fill with syrup. Screw up tightly then unscrew by half a turn, so that the heating syrup will be able to expand (leave about a 1-inch/2.5-cm gap at the top of each bottle). Stand the bottles in a pan deep enough for the water to come up to their tops. If possible use a pan like a pressure cooker that has a false bottom. Bring slowly to the boil and keep boiling for 20–30 minutes. Take out the bottles and screw the lids on tightly as soon as they are cool enough. If you are doubtful about the tightness of the seal, coat with melted candle wax.

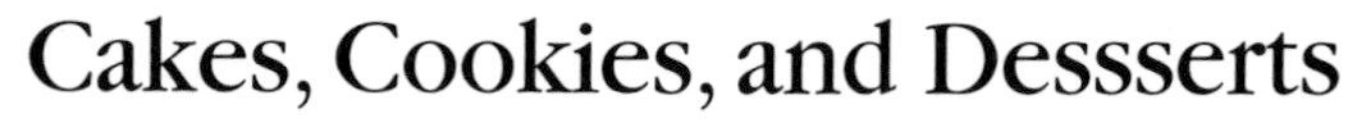

Cakes, Cookies, and Dessserts

Cakes, cookies, and desserts – now this is where the real magic of cooking lies for me. Somehow, over thousands of years, dedicated humans have experimented with all sorts of mixtures and ovens, and today we can enjoy the results. I've no doubt the chemistry of flour, eggs, yeast, and baking powder is complex indeed – and I certainly never studied it in school – but the end products are straightforward enough. With modern mixing machines there is no excuse for missing out on the excitement of a weekly session of making your own desserts and treats. So what is the key to all this magic? All equipment must be clean and cool.

Try to keep one specific board, preferably made of marble or slate, for rolling pastry. The rolling pin should not be too heavy – in fact, a round glass bottle filled with cold water is ideal. You have to make pastry in as cool a place as possible so that the cooking process creates lightness by expanding the cool air trapped in the dough. People with hot hands simply cannot make good pastry! Keep plenty of flour on hand for dusting over the pastry to prevent it from sticking. Roll it lightly and try to press evenly with both hands; always roll away from you, taking short, quick strokes and lifting the rolling pin between each stroke.

Here are just a few of the endless recipes for cakes, pastry, and desserts to enjoy with family and friends.

Farmhouse carrot cake

This is a great way to use up the eggs and carrots from your garden as it makes a marvelously moist and flavorsome cake. You will need:

450 g (1 lb) confectioner's sugar
4 eggs
1 cup olive oil
8 oz (225 g) carrots, finely grated
8 oz (225 g) plain flour
1 heaping teaspoon of baking powder
1 teaspoon of ground allspice and 1 of ground cinnamon
For the icing you need:
8 oz (225 g) icing sugar
1 cup of softened cream cheese
2 oz (56 g) of butter
1 teaspoon of vanilla extract
6 oz (170 g) of chopped nuts (try walnuts)
A little milk, if required

Mix together the sugar, eggs, oil, and grated carrots in a large mixing bowl. Sift all the dry ingredients together in a separate bowl. Add a small amount of the dry ingredients to the mixture a bit at a time and mix together until you have blended all the ingredients.

Grease and flour two 9–in (22–cm) cake tins. Divide the mixture between the two tins. Cook for about 40 minutes in a preheated oven at about 375°F (190°C). Check if it is cooked by inserting a skewer into the center of the cake. If it comes out clean, it is ready; if the mixture is attached to the skewer you need to let the cake cook for a little longer.

Once cooked, let the cakes cool in their tins for a few minutes and then tip them out onto wire racks to let them cool thoroughly.

To make the icing, combine all the ingredients, except the walnuts, together until you have a smooth, spreadable consistency. You may need to add milk if the mix is too dry. Add the walnuts and blend together. Spread over the top of one cake layer, top with the other cake, and then spread the remaining icing over the surface.

Doughnuts

You won't eat a store-bought doughnut again after you've made your own. These doughnuts are made from bread dough but you also add these ingredients during mixing:

2 oz (56 g) melted butter
2 oz (56 g) sugar
1 egg; and milk (substitute this for the water used in making a normal bread dough)
pinch of salt
1 lb (0.5 kg) flour
1 oz (28 g) yeast or ½ oz (14 g) dried yeast

Mix the dough until smooth and soft. Cover with a cloth and leave it to rise in a warm place for about one hour. After it has risen, knead it vigorously for about 4–5 minutes. Roll out the dough on a floured board. Use a large glass or cutter to press out a circular shape. To make the rings, use a bottle top and press down in the center of the circle. Don't worry if the holes look small as they will more than double in size during cooking. Cover them with a cloth and leave in a warm place to prove for 20 minutes.

Once proved, fry them on both sides, a few at a time, in deep, boiling fat. The spherical ones will turn themselves over at half time, leaving a pale ring round the equator. Drain the doughnuts on kitchen paper and then roll in powdered or confectioner's sugar. Eat at once.

Flap Jacks

These make a wonderfully healthy and quick snack.

4 oz (112 g) butter
2 ½ oz (70 g) sugar
1 tablespoon syrup
6 oz (170 g) of porridge oats

Melt the butter, sugar, and syrup into a pan. Stir in the porridge oats and mix well. Spread onto a greased baking tin, press down firmly, and, with a sharp knife, divide into squares. Bake in a moderate oven at 375°F (190°C) for 15–20 minutes. Allow to cool and remove by breaking each square off the block.

Cheese Scones

Quick to cook and delicious to eat warm and crumbly from the oven, these savory scones make an appetizing addition to any feast. You will need:

1 oz (28 g) butter
6 oz (170 g) self-raising flour
3 oz (85 g) strong cheddar cheese, grated finely
¼ teaspoon of mustard and ½ teaspoon of salt
1 egg; and 2 good tablespoons of water

Rub the butter into the flour and then add the grated cheese and seasonings. Add the egg and the water and mix together. Once you have a firm dough, roll it out so it is about ½ in (1 cm) thick. Sprinkle a little more grated cheese over the top and cut out circular shapes with a cutter or a glass. Place onto a greased tray and bake in the oven at 425°F (220°C) for 15 minutes.

Meats

To the self-supporter, meat is not merely "flesh." Each animal has its own life saga with escapes, injuries, and always a shared sympathy between living beings. Seeing an animal happily content with its accommodation, its food, and its "carer" is a pleasure indeed. But there will have been frustrations and furies, too – the day the beast escaped into the strawberry bed or the time it broke its water trough and water flooded the food store. Finally comes the day when animal becomes meat to be eaten or preserved.

Smoking

One very useful way of helping to preserve the meat is to smoke it. This also helps it dry out, and probably helps it mature quicker. It is also much easier than people seem to think. If you have a big open chimney, simply hang the meat high up in it, well out of reach of the fire, and leave it there for about a week, keeping a wood fire going the while. There is a lot of mysticism about which wood to use for smoking: Americans swear by hickory, the British will hear of nothing but oak. In my experience it matters very little provided you use hard woods and not pine.

Whatever you use don't let the temperature go above 120°F (50°C): 100–110°F (39–43°C) is fine. Building a smokehouse is a matter of common sense and a little ingenuity. For years we used a brick outdoor lavatory (we didn't use it for its original purpose, of course). We had a slow-combustion, wood-burning stove outside, with the chimney pipe poking through the wall of the outhouse, and we hung up the meat from lengths of angle-iron under the roof. It does seem a pity though not to make use of the heat generated by the smoking fuel, so surely it is better to have your burning unit inside a building, even if the smoke chamber itself is outside. Often a slow-combustion wood burning stove can heat a house efficiently and, with no increase in fuel consumption, it will automatically smoke whatever you like.

> For smoking, Americans swear by hickory.

There are two kinds of smoking: cold-smoking and cooked-smoking. The latter is common in America and Germany but almost unknown in Britain. It consists of smoking at a higher temperature, from 150–200°F (65–93°C), so that the meat is cooked as well as smoked. Meat thus smoked must be eaten within a few days because it will not keep as cold-smoked meat will.

Thawing meat

Always take your meat from the freezer to the fridge 24 hours before you intend to cook it. Meat should be thawed slowly, overnight at room temperature. Once thawed the meat should be cooked immediately, as it will not keep.

Bones

Many butchers like to "bone" joints of meat. This is not something I recommend. I know people hate the idea of paying for bone but if they would just pause for a moment, they would realize that boned meat actually costs more and they are really paying for the butcher's time in doing the boning. The fact is that meat on the bone cooks better and the marrow and presence of the bone add an extra flavor.

Larding and barding

I don't hear these terms used much today because real bacon is such a rarity. But if you make your own bacon from your own pigs then you are likely to have a fair bit of "fatty" bacon which can be used in roasting other meats. Larding is simply threading pieces of bacon through a \ roast using a "larding needle." "Barding" means covering lean or exposed parts of a roast with a few slices of fatty bacon. This provides fat to prevent burning and imparts an extra boost to the flavor.

Roasting

I try to have an open-air roast over a fire once or twice a year, and very delicious and exciting it is, too. If you want to roast a pig or lamb like this you need at least 12 hours burning time: the longer the better. So start your fire early in the morning; you will need two strong metal supports to hold your rotating spit rod and you must fasten the carcass to this, using wire. Keep the meat high up to start with and progressively lower it during the day. Always have a good supply of well-dried timber for the fire and appoint a responsible person to be "in charge" at all times. With an oven, start at a moderately hot temperature, say 375°F (190°C), to "seal" the roast. Keep an eye on the meat to ensure it does not dry out and baste with fat as often as necessary. If you want to make fat or skin crisp then rub in some salt before cooking. If you suspect your oven temperature may be uneven then use cooking foil to cover parts of the joint exposed to "hot spots." Do not think that there are fixed times for making a perfect roast: each piece of meat will have its own characteristics and a long, thin roast will cook much quicker than a fat, round one. Something like 20 minutes to the pound will not be far wrong, plus 20 minutes extra. Pork, lamb, and veal should cook longer than beef.

Braising

This is a superb way of cooking the tougher less attractive joints of meat by effectively combining roasting and boiling. If possible use a heavy cast-iron cooking pot with a close-fitting lid. Tie the meat up with string if necessary. Partially fill the pot with water suitably spiced up with whatever takes your fancy: dried tomatoes and black peppercorns are brilliant. Then cook for however long it takes for the meat to become tender. The oven temperature will be lower than for a roast, perhaps 300°F (150°C). Make sure the liquid does not boil away. If the meat is fatty, allow the whole lot to cool overnight before reheating the next day. All the fat will solidify on the surface and can be removed.

Stewing

For me this is ideal slow cooking to tenderize the less attractive, tougher parts of the animal. The first job is to cut up the meat into lumps about 1 sq in (6 sq cm), removing all unnecessary fat and gristle. These must now be "sealed" with a quick burst of strong heat using good fat or olive oil and perhaps a few chopped onions. Now make up your chosen mixture of vegetables and seasoning before allowing everything to simmer gently in a slow oven for three or four hours. You can keep a good stew going for several days simply by adding fresh vegetables and stock – but it must be boiled up strongly once each day, or it will go bad.

Fish

I vividly remember catching mackerel from a yacht as I entered a small anchorage on the Scottish island of Gomera near Mull. Within a couple of minutes I had the fish filleted; the sails came down and I made anchor. So quick was the journey from ocean to the grill that the fillets actually jumped off the grill. Freshly grilled with lemon juice, mackerel is delicious. What did this tell me? That well-cooked fresh fish is one of the great delicacies of the world. But how often have we been disappointed in restaurants to find the meal either soggy and overcooked or almost raw? So, aside from finding a fish shop or local fisherman and timing your cooking to perfection, bear in mind these tips:

Gutting fish

You must clean and gut fish properly – usually by slitting the fish on the underside from the head halfway to the tail and carefully removing the insides. Always handle fish gently to avoid bruising. If there is a roe in the fish you can either replace it if it is small or cook it separately.

Make sure you take out all of the guts, including any black skin lining the body cavity. Rub this out with salt because if you leave it, there will be a bitter taste. Wash the fish out well with cold water; use a running tap rather than soaking the fish or you will find they become watery. If there are scales on the fish, then these must be removed by scraping from tail to head with a sharp knife. Angle the knife against the fish and scrape slowly so the scales do not fly everywhere. Sometimes the scales are tough to remove: if so, dip the fish quickly into boiling water. If you are going to serve the fish whole then cut off the fins and the head (or take out the eyes with a sharp pair of scissors!).

> Well-cooked fresh fish is one of the great delicacies of the world.

Skinning and filleting

Round fish are skinned from head to tail. You make a cut along the sides of the fish close to the fins and then make a cut in the skin just below the head. Now start pulling the skin away downward, using a knife to hold down the flesh. Put your hands in salt if the fish is too slippery – or use a cloth to hold it. Flat fish are skinned in similar fashion but starting at the tail. The skin of flat fish can be pulled off quickly once the sides have been cut and loosened – just hold down the tail to keep it steady.

You will need a very sharp knife and a fair bit of practice to make a good job of separating the flesh from the bones. The way to fillet is to make a cut down the whole of the back of the fish down to the backbone. Then carefully scrape away the fillets of flesh from either side; you make two fillets from each side. It is usually easiest to work the first fillet from the left-hand side of the fish working from head to tail. Then turn the fish around and work the second fillet from tail to head. Now turn the fish over and repeat for the other side.

Fish stock

Making a good fish stock is the essence of cooking a fine fish sauce. The best stock is made from fresh fish trimmings after filleting. Discard any black-looking skin and break the bones up into small pieces. Put the trimmings into a saucepan with water and/or milk, a small piece of onion, white peppercorns, and some parsley. Simmer the mixture on a low heat for about half an hour and then strain off your stock. Add white wine instead of milk if you prefer.

Boiling fish

This is a good way to cook large fish. They should be left unskinned with the heads on and eyes removed. Fish should be put into the water when it is piping hot but not boiling, and the water should be salted, with a little vinegar or lemon juice added. If you do not make the water slightly acid, the fish will not be white and firm when cooked.

A fish kettle is the best way to boil fish. This will have a drainer to take off the water and avoid breaking the fish. If you do not have a fish kettle, then you can use an ordinary large saucepan. Put a plate in the bottom and rest the fish on this tied up in muslin. By hanging the ends of the muslin over the sides of the cooking vessel you can remove the fish whole without breaking it.

Weigh the fish before you boil it: 8–10 minutes per pound and ten minutes over, is a good guide. Do not put too much liquid over the fish or the boiling will shake it about and damage the skin. About 2 in (5 cm) above the fish should be sufficient.

Grilling fish

This is a good way to cook smaller fish like herring, mackerel, and trout. Prepare the fish carefully and score the skin on both sides to prevent it from cracking when cooking. Season the fish with pepper and salt and brush it all over with oil or melted butter. Alternatively you may want to split the fish open, removing the bone and coating it lightly in flour or fine oatmeal. Make sure the broiler is hot before you start cooking. Allow 7–10 minutes for cooking and turn the fish at least once. It should look nicely browned when ready and should be served immediately.

Frying

Probably the most popular way to cook fish, as well as one of the trickiest to do well. There are two important things to remember: first, make sure your fish is as dry as possible before you cook it, and second, coat the fish in some mixture which will prevent it absorbing the cooking fat. There are several different ways of coating fish for frying. The easiest way is simply to dip the fish into sieved flour. Alternatively, you can use the familiar batter coating: this is a weak batter of flour, milk, and egg. I prefer to use egg and breadcrumbs and this certainly looks the best when the fish is cooked. Make sure the fat is always kept very hot: do not put too many pieces of fish in the pan at any one time, and let the fat heat up again before putting in a fresh piece of fish. Drain the fish on paper towels before serving so as to remove excess grease.

Baking, poaching or steaming

Fish can be baked very simply in an open dish in a moderate oven. Add the seasoning of your choice. Baking is a dry way to cook fish, so you may need to add some butter, fat, or milk to provide moisture. With the correct equipment poaching and steaming are two other excellent ways to cook fish.

Vegetables

Almost certainly the major sin when cooking vegetables is to overcook and boil into oblivion. Better a little crunchy than soggy bland mush!

Artichokes

Brilliantly simple to cook and prepare, artichokes make a most tasty and sociable appetizer. Choose the larger flower heads but make sure they are still tender and there is no sign of the actual flower appearing. Soak in water (probably one or two per person) with a little vinegar added to bring out any bugs. After half an hour take out, wash, and drop into a large pan of rapidly boiling water. After five or six minutes lower the heat and simmer for another 40 minutes to one hour, depending on the size of the artichokes. You can tell when they are cooked when the leaves peel off easily. Remove from the water, drain, and serve with butter or your own dressing, or my favorite, which is a mixture of soy sauce, lemon juice, and olive oil in equal parts.

Broad beans

Do not pod these until just before you are going to cook them. In all cases other than when beans are very fresh and young, you will have to remove the skins of each bean. Do this by dropping the podded beans into boiling water for a few minutes, then remove and the skins will be removed easily. Now you can boil in salted water. Remove any scum as it appears and test regularly to see when they become tender. Drain and serve with melted butter and salt and pepper as you like.

Green beans

Pick these before they are fully grown so you avoid the risk of the dreaded "string" bean. Small and tender is better than big and stringy! If the beans are very small and young you can simply cut off the heads and tails and serve them whole. Older beans must be thinly sliced diagonally into lozenge-shaped pieces. Drop the sliced beans into a pan of salted boiling water. When the beans are ready they will sink to the bottom of the pan. Serve with hot butter and plenty of salt and pepper.

Beets

Small, well-shaped beets make an excellent hot meal. Choose your beets carefully, scrub clean, and then boil in salted water for at least one hour, possibly more. Test if they are cooked and tender by using a finger – if you spear them with a fork all the color will tend to leak out into your cooking water. Once cooked, remove from water and take off the skins.

Carrot croquettes

Do not cook your carrots too soft. Grate about 1 cupful per person. Now melt together butter and flour in a saucepan (equal parts, 1 oz/28 g per person) together with about one cupful of milk per person. Cook steadily until the mixture begins to draw away from the sides of the pan, stirring constantly. Now add your grated carrot plus the yolk of one egg for each person to be served. Add seasoning to taste (salt and pepper plus some sugar) and turn out onto a plate to cool. Then you can form into shapes as you choose – use a little flour to stop them from sticking together.

Baked eggplant

This is a very quick and delicious way to cook eggplants, especially if you have a large stove that is always hot. Wipe or wash the eggplants and cut off the stalk ends. Cut the eggplants down the centers to split into two halves. Put the halves into a baking tray, cut side uppermost, and drizzle on a little olive oil to stop them from sticking. Now grate some cheese onto the upturned flat sides of eggplant. Put into a moderately hot oven at about 325°F (170°C) for around 40 minutes.

Creamed leeks

Wash five or six leeks and clean them carefully. Cut off the roots and most of the green leaves. Split them open lengthwise and cut into pieces about 2 in (5 cm) long. Throw these pieces into boiling water, slightly salted, and cook for ten minutes, then drain. Now put them into a pan with half a pint of milk seasoned with pepper and salt. Simmer them slowly until they are tender. Now strain off the milk and arrange the leeks carefully in a warmed vegetable dish. Melt about 1 oz (28 g) of butter in a pan and mix with one tablespoon of flour. Then pour in the milk you have strained off the leeks. Stir the mixture until it boils and cook for a couple of minutes. Now add the cream at the end and pour the entire sauce over the leeks. Sprinkle with parsley and serve hot.

Baked mushrooms

Wash and peel your mushrooms, then remove the stems. Now put them hollow side uppermost in a baking tray greased with a little olive oil. Sprinkle them with salt and pepper and a few drops lemon juice, then add a small piece of butter to each one. Give them about 15 minutes in a moderate oven. Of course, you can add crushed garlic to the butter for extra flavor.

Potatoes *au gratin*

Make mashed potatoes in the normal way but add plenty of milk and butter together with grated cheese – add as much cheese as you like depending on the strength of the cheese. Season with salt and pepper and add a little mustard. Now pour the mixture into an ovenproof dish. Grate cheese to cover the top and add a few handfuls of breadcrumbs. Spread a little melted butter over the surface and then brown in a hot oven at 425°F (220°C).

Baked tomatoes

Choose moderately sized tomatoes and cut out the stalk and the hard part at the root of the stalk. Place the tomatoes on a buttered baking tray and put a small piece of butter into the hole left after removing the stalks. Sprinkle with pepper and salt and bake in a moderate oven for about 15 minutes. Serve in a hot dish.

Baked cauliflower/eggplant

This is a quick and tasty way to cook large vegetables. Get your oven reasonably hot, say 375°F (190°C). Grease a baking tray (I like to use olive oil). Place your prepared vegetable in the center (large lumps for cauliflower, cut in half for eggplant) and sprinkle grated cheese (cheddar is fine) over the top with a little pepper and salt. Bake it for about half an hour.

Brewing Basics

Brewing, wine-making, and distilling have been major influences on the development of entire civilizations. Today they remain the cornerstone of success for several of the largest companies on Planet Earth, not to mention vital sources of revenue for the national governments. How fortunate, then, that alcohol is so conveniently produced in the natural world by yeasts that are ever present on the food we eat and the air we breathe.

Yeast works in mysterious ways

Different strains of yeast behave differently and we need to choose one that suits our purposes best (see also p.156). Some yeasts will float on the top of the brew, others sink to form a mud on the bottom. Still others remain suspended as a colloidal mess – definitely not the brewer's favorite. Some yeasts work quickly but cannot stand high temperatures or too much alcohol. Other yeasts work slowly but go on to produce much more alcohol over many months. The first types of yeast are excellent, aggressive plants ideal for beer, while the second are what we want for wine but are very easily displaced and upset by interlopers. This is why we can ferment beer quickly in relatively unsealed containers while we have to treat wine much more carefully.

Racking off

When we make beer (or wine for that matter) we must carefully separate the delicious-tasting part from the build-up of sludge and yeast. A fine, clear end result can only be achieved by managing a process called "racking off."

To do this well, firstly don't rack off beer or cider until the major fermentation process has stopped. While fermentation continues, the minute bubbles of carbon dioxide gas carry sediment with them into the body of the brew. When fermentation calms down, there are less bubbles and less sediment. With wines we may want to rack off several times during the much slower fermentation – and we do this once a solid body of sludge has built up.

Secondly, cool liquid holds less sediment than a warm one. So put your brew in a cool place at least 24 hours before you finally rack off the finished product. And if possible put the demijohn or fermenting bin on a high table in this position so it's ready for racking off without having to move it again. The more height you have, the more quickly you can siphon off the brew! Also do make sure you have some device for preventing the end of your siphon from going too far down into the sludge (or near it) for suction will pull it up. There are all sorts of special devices sold for this purpose in brewing shops, but I prefer to use a good solid copper nail fastened onto the pipe with elastic band. A copper or galvanized nail will not taint the brew and its weight helps keep the siphon pipe down.

Finally (and I say this from bitter experience) don't put newly corked bottles straight into storage. You will be storing them horizontally with labels uppermost so that the cork breathes properly and the sediment settles on the opposite side from the label. In this position you will lose everything in a big, smelly mess if the corks blow out. So leave freshly corked bottles upright for at least 48 hours, and examine them carefully to make sure the corks are secure before laying them down.

Distilling

If you get a big copper boiler with a fire under it, half fill it with beer, float a basin on the beer, and place a shallow dish wider than the boiler on the top of the boiler, you will get whiskey. Alcohol will evaporate from the beer, condense on the undersurface of the big dish, run down to the lowest point of it, and drip down into the basin. It is an advantage if you can run cold water into, and out of, the top dish to cool it. This speeds up condensation. And if distilling is illegal in your part of the world and some inquisitive fellow comes down the drive, it doesn't take a second to be washing clothes in the boiler, making porridge in the floating basin, and bathing the baby in the big flat dish. And what could be more innocent than that?

Marvelous malt

Something that has contributed over the millennia to keeping humans human, even if it sometimes gives them headaches, is the invention of malt. One imagines that very soon after men discovered grain, they also discovered that if you left it lying around in water, the water would ferment, and if you drank enough of it, it would make you drunk. Later on in history some genius discovered that if you sprouted the grain first, it made better beer and made you even more drunk. He didn't know the reason for this, of course, but we do. It is because alcohol is made from sugar. Yeast, which is a microscopic mold or fungus, eats sugar and turns it into alcohol. It can also do the same, in a much more limited way, with starch. Now grain is mostly starch, or carbohydrate, and you can make an inferior sort of beer out of it before it sprouts by fermenting it with yeast. But if you cause the grain to sprout, that is start to grow, the starch gets turned, by certain enzymes, into sugar, and you can make much better, stronger beer. So to make beer, we civilized people sprout our barley before we ferment it. This process is known as malting, and the sprouted grain is called malt. You can malt any grain, but barley, being highest in starch, makes the best malt.

Malting barley

Put your barley, inside a porous sack if you like, into some slightly warm water and leave it for four days. Pull it out and heap it on a floor and take its temperature every day. If the latter goes below 63°F (17°C) pile it up in a much thicker heap. In the trade this is called "couching" it. If the temperature goes above 68°F (20°C) spread it out more thinly and turn it often. Turning cools it. Keep it moist but not sodden: sprinkle warmish water on it occasionally. Remember you want to make it grow. After about ten days of this, the acrospire, or shoot of the grain (not the root, which will also be growing), should have grown about two-thirds the length of the grain. The acrospire is to be seen growing below the skin of the grain. Couch it for 12 hours when you think it has grown enough.

Kilning the malt

After this you must kiln the grain. This means bringing it to a temperature of 120°F (50°C) over a fire or stove, or in an oven with the door open to keep the hot air moving through the grain. Keep it moving in the kiln, which is simply a perforated steel plate over a fire, until it is dry.

Turn the page for more on brewing.

Making Beer

Before Tudor times there were no hops in Britain and the stuff people drank – fermented malt – was called ale. At about that time hops were introduced from Continental Europe and used for flavoring and preserving ale, and the resultant drink was called beer. Beer is bitterer than ale was and, when you get used to it, much nicer. Nowadays the nomenclature has got confused and the words beer and ale are used indiscriminately. However, if you can it is well worth growing your own hops.

Home for hops

Hops like a deep, heavy, well-drained loam and liberal manuring, preferably with farmyard manure. But they will produce some sort of a crop on most land, provided they are well fertilized and the land is not waterlogged, and if you grow your own hops for your own beer, some sort of a crop is all you need: you need a few pounds, not tons.

Clean your piece of land thoroughly first. Make sure you get out all perennial weed roots and grass. Beg, borrow, or steal a dozen bits of hop root. Bits of root about a foot in length are fine. Hops produce an enormous mass of roots every year and an established hop plant just won't miss 1–2 ft (30–60 cm) of root. Plant these bits of root at intervals of about 2–3 ft (60–90 cm), with plenty of farmyard manure or compost. Arrange horizontal wires, some high and others down near the ground. Put vertical strings between the wires for

“I normally make one brew each week and somehow it all seems to disappear.

the hops to climb up, three or four strings for each bit of root. When the hops begin to grow they will race each other up the strings – they grow so fast you can almost see them move. Watch for aphids. If you get them, spray with nicotine, pyrethrum, or other nonpersistent insecticide. Pick the flowers when they are in full bloom, and full of the bitterly fragrant yellow powder that is the virtue of the hop. Dry the flowers gently. If you put them on a wire, burlap, or some other perforated surface over a stove, that will do. When they are thoroughly dry, store them, preferably in woven sacks.

Malt, malt extract and brewing beer

You can brew beer from malt extract, which you can buy from the store, or in "brewing kits" from various enterprises. The beer you brew will be strong (or can be), will taste quite good (or can do), but it will not be the same as real beer brewed from real malt. The best beer will be the stuff you brew from the malt you have made yourself (see p.185). But you can also buy malt in sacks, and this is preferable to malt extract. The difference between beer brewed from malt and beer brewed from malt extract is great and unmistakable. If you once get used to beer brewed from malt you will not be content to go back to extract beer – nor to the liquid you sip from a six-pack.

In the evening, before you go to bed, boil some 10 gallons (45 liters) of water. While it is boiling, make a strainer for your mash-tub or kive (otherwise known as a brewing vat). This is a tub holding 20 gallons (90 liters), but with the top cut off. You can make the strainer by tying a bundle of straw, or hay, or gorse leaves with a piece of string, poking the string through the taphole of the kive, pulling it tight so as to haul the bundle hard up against the hole inside, and banging the tap in. The tap then holds the piece of string. Or, if you like, you can have a hole in the bottom of your kive with an ash stick pushed down into it to close it. When you pull the ash stick out, of course, it opens the hole. If you lay a layer of gorse in the bottom of your kive, some straw on top of this, then a flat stone with a hole in the middle of it, and then poke your ash stick through this hole, you have a magnificent strainer.

"Mashing" the malt

When the water has boiled let it cool to 150°F (66°C). Then dump one bushel (about 55 lb or 25 kg) of cracked malt into it and stir until the malt is wet through. This is called "mashing," and once this stage is completed the malt is now the "mash." It is most important that the water should not be hotter than 150°F (66°C) because if it is, it will kill the enzymes. Cover up the kive with a blanket and go to bed.

Early in the morning get up and open the cock, or draw the ash stick, to allow the wort, as the liquid is now called, to run out into buckets. Pour it from the buckets into the boiler, together with 1 lb (0.5 kg) of dried hops tied in a pillowcase, and boil it. While the wort is dribbling out, "sparge" (brewer's word for sprinkle) the mash with boiling water. (You don't care about the enzymes now – they have done their work and converted the rest of the starch into sugar.) Go on sparging until 10 gallons (45 liters) of wort have drained out. Much of the original quantity has been absorbed by the mash. Now boil off the 10 gallons (45 liters) of wort, and the hops in the pillowcase, for an hour.

BEER-MAKING

To make consistently good home-brew you must start off with scrupulously scrubbed, scalded, and disinfected kives and barrels.

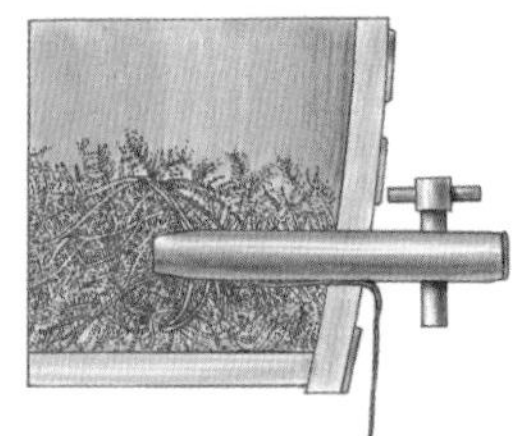

1 Boil up 10 gallons (45 liters) of water. Make a strainer for the kive (brewing vat). Tie a small bundle of gorse, hay, or straw with a piece of string and drop it in the kive, poke the loose end through the bung-hole and pull hard. Then bang in the tap (wooden cock).

2 When the water boils let it cool to 150°F (66°C) and pour half into the kive.

3 Dump in a bushel (55 lb/25 kg) of malt, the rest of the hot water, and stir thoroughly. Then tuck the kive up for the night. Cover with a clean sheet and a blanket. The enzymes in the malt plus the water will then go to work extracting the malt sugar.

4 Next morning, open the cock and drain the "wort" (liquid) into a bucket.

5 "Sparge" (sprinkle) the spent malt with kettle after kettle of boiling water to remove all sugar, until 10 gallons (45 liters) of wort have drained out.

6 Pack 1 lb (0.5 kg) of hops into a pillowcase and plunge it into the wort. If you want to cheat by stirring in sugar, honey, or malt extract – 6 lb (2.7 kg) to 10 gallons (45 liters) of wort – now is the time to do it. Boil for at least an hour. Meanwhile, get on with cleaning out the kive. The mash makes splendid food for pigs or cows.

7 Draw a jugful of boiling wort and cool quickly by immersing in icy water. When it has cooled to 60°F (16°C), plop in your yeast – either packet beer yeast, about 1 oz (28 g) will do – or a couple of tablespoons of "barm" which you have strained off the top of your last brew and kept covered in a cool place. Then transfer the rest of the boiling wort back into the kive.

8 Cool most of the wort quickly by lowering buckets of cold water into it without spilling.

9 As soon as the bulk of the wort has cooled to hand-hot, i.e. 60°F (16°C), pour in the "starter," a jugful of foaming, yeasty wort, and stir. Cover with blankets to keep out vinegar flies. Leave for three days. Then skin off the "barm." After fermenting stops at five to eight days, "rack" (pour off without stirring up the sediment).

If you want the beer to be very strong, add 6 lb (2.7 kg) of sugar now, or honey if you can spare it. Or, another way of cheating is to add 6 lb (2.7 kg) of malt extract. But you needn't add anything at all. You will still get very strong beer. Clean the mash out of the kive and set it aside.

Transfer the boiling wort back into the clean kive. Take a jugful of wort out and cool it by standing it in cold water. When it is hand-hot, or about 60°F (16°C), dump some yeast into it. This can be yeast kept from a previous fermentation, or yeast you have bought especially for beer. Bread yeast will do, but beer yeast is better. Bread yeast is a "bottom-fermenting" yeast; it sinks to the bottom in beer. Beer yeast is "top-fermenting" and is marginally better. The faster your bulk of wort cools now, the better. An "in-churn" milk cooler put into the wort with cold water running through it is very helpful. If you haven't got this you can lower in buckets of cold water, but be sure no water spills out and that the outside of the bucket is clean. Quick cooling allows less time for disease organisms to get into the wort before it is cool enough to take the yeast.

When the main body of the wort has cooled to 60°F (16°C), dump your jugful of yeasty wort into it and stir. This is the time when you should pray. Cover up very carefully to keep out all vinegar flies and dust. Try to keep away from the stuff for at least three days. Then skim the floating yeast off. Otherwise it will sink, which is bad. When it has stopped fermenting, after five to eight days, "rack" it. That means pour it gently, without stirring up the sediment in the bottom, into the vessels in which you intend to keep it and cover these securely. From now on no air must get in. You have made beer.

You can use plastic trash containers instead of wooden or earthenware vessels; I don't like them, but they have their advantages for hygiene and accessibility. If you use wooden vessels, though, you must keep them scrupulously clean.

Beer from kits

Specialized stores or health-food shops often sell beer kits and usually all the equipment to go with them. Experiment with different recipes – and don't think the most expensive is always the most delicious. For years I bought the cheapest cans of malt/beer extract made by Irish monks – they were delicious, but now alas, the monks have died out. Keep a note of what you have brewed and how you brewed it.

Your key items of equipment are a large fermenting vessel, normally 40 pints (23 liters), with a well-fitting airtight top, a decanting siphon tube with rigid pipes at each end and a tap at the end you will put into bottles, and a heating mat for keeping the fermentation at the right temperature. Your kit will come with yeast and instructions.

Remember at the beginning to swish out your fermenting vessel (which should be kept nice and clean – replace it if it gets old and worn) with a kettle full of boiling water to kill any beasts and bugs. Pour in your malt extract (after pre-warming it on the stove to make it pour easily), add 2 lb (1 kg) of sugar (you'll need plenty of sugar in reserve) and then two kettles full of boiling water. Stir it all together and when well mixed, fill up the vessel with cold water before adding the yeast. Keep the lid firmly sealed and place on your heating mat in a calm place for about one week. Siphon with care!

Making Wine

Strict cleanliness is essential in wine-making, for wine is made by a living organism (yeast) and if other living organisms (wild yeasts or other molds or bacteria) get into the act, either the tame yeasts that you want to use for your wine cannot do their job, or you get putrefaction, bad tastes, and odors. So keep all wine-making equipment scrupulously clean. Use boiling water whenever possible. Aside from that important point, you can ignore the plethora of books about home wine-making, each one blinding us with science more effectively than the last. There are a few other basics to bear in mind: chiefly that you are unlikely to get more than 3 lb (1.4 kg) of sugar to ferment in 1 gallon (4.5 liters) of water, so keep to approximately this ratio if you want strong wine. You must ferment at the temperature most favorable to vital yeasts. You must give your special cultivated yeast every help and an unfair advantage over the wild yeasts and other organisms that might ruin your brew. You must keep all contaminants out of your wine, especially vinegar flies, those little midges that hang around rotting fruit, carrying the bugs that turn wine to vinegar. You must "rack" or pour off the wine from the lees and sediments before the latter spoil its flavor. You must allow the wine to settle and clear in the cool after the yeast has done its work.

Finally, having safely bottled your wine, you must try to keep your mitts off it for at least a year with red wine, if you can, and at least three months with white wine.

> Keep all equipment scrupulously clean.

Equipment

You need jars, barrels, or bottles for fermentation. You also need fermentation locks (if you can get them). The purpose of these is to allow the gases produced by fermentation to escape while keeping out air, which is always germ-laden, and vinegar flies. Many a vat of fine wine has been made without a fermentation lock and with just a plug of cotton balls stuffed in the neck of the vessel. Many a gallon of wine has been ruined this way, too. A fermentation lock is a very useful thing. A thermometer is not to be despised, either. You also need a flexible tube – rubber or plastic – for "racking" or syphoning, a funnel or two, and containers for the final bottling of the wine. A corking gun is very good for driving in corks, which have to be driven in dead tight or air gets in and the wine goes bad. Polythene sealers are quite a good substitute for corks if you do not want to invest in a corking gun.

Materials

You will need yeast. Old-fashioned country wine makers, including myself, have used all kinds of yeasts but undoubtedly it is best to buy wine yeasts from a store. For very good and strong results some people use yeast nutrients, also bought from a store. Acid is another thing you may have to add. Lemons will provide this, as will citric acid, which you can buy. Tannin, too, can be bought, but tea or apples – particularly crabapples – will provide it. The reader may say that it is not being self-sufficient to buy all this stuff from a store. True, but I would say that a trivial expenditure on this sort of thing is necessary if you are going to make a great deal of fine, drinkable wine.

GRAPE WINE

There is no wine like grape wine. Red grape wine is made by fermenting the grape skins in with the wine. White wine is made by taking the skins out. White wine is often made with red or black grapes, for all grapes are white inside. It is easier to make red or rosé wine than white because the tannin in the skins helps the "must" (the wine-to-be) to ferment better, and the quicker it ferments, the less chance there is of bad organisms getting in to do their deeds. As for crushing your grapes, personally, I could not drink wine if I had seen somebody treading it with his bare feet, so I would use some sort of pestle and mortar. If you want to make white wine, press the broken grapes in a press (a car jack will do), having first wrapped them in strong calico "cheeses." In the case of red or rosé, press in the same way, but then add a proportion of the skins to the wine.

WINE-MAKING EQUIPMENT

Don't attempt to make your own wine without arming yourself beforehand with plenty of containers, to hold the must (wine-to-be) at each of its many stages.

Bottles and bottling are only the end stages of a long fermentation process, during which you will need at least several containers, such as jugs and jars – and possibly vats and barrels, too.

Key
1 Fermentation barrel
2 Corking gun
3 Jug
4 Bottle
5 Sieve
6 Bottle brush
7 Funnel
8 Hydrometer
9 Measuring cylinder
10 Screw-top bottle
11 Plastic or rubber siphon
12 Earthenware vessel
13 Barrel and tapped vat
14 Fermentation jar and lock
15 Cork and plastic sealer

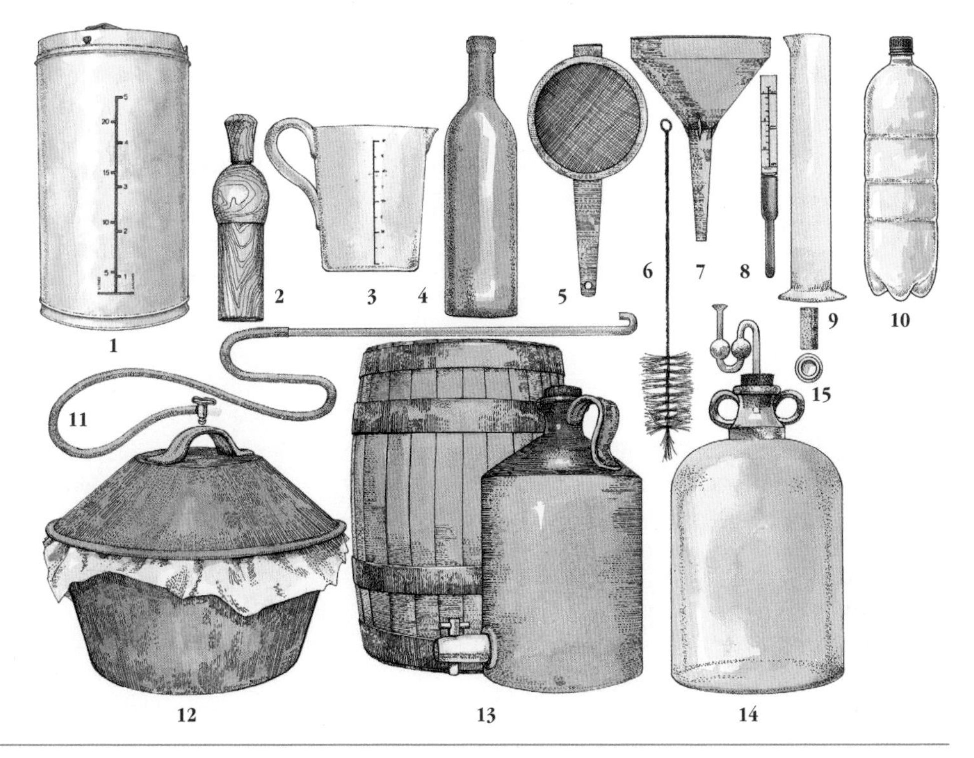

The more you add, the deeper the red color of the wine, but, in cold climates at any rate, the deeper red ones may contain too much tannin and will be a little bitter as a result. Now in real wine-growing climates (where you will not be reading instructions like this anyway, since your neighbors will initiate you), you don't need to add any sugar. In less sunny climates add between 4–6 lb (1.8–2.7 kg) of sugar to every 10 gallons (45 liters) of wine-to-be. If there has been a hot season and the grapes are sweet, you need less; if a bad season, more.

Fermenting

Let the juices and skins ferment in a vat. Grapes have their own yeasts in the "bloom" on their skins, but you had better add a wine yeast culture bought from a store, if you can get one. Warm a bottle of the must (juice) to 75°F (24°C), dump the yeast culture into it, and stand it in a warm place with some cotton balls in the neck. Meanwhile, try to get your main body of must to 75°F (24°C). When the "starter" or culture in the bottle has started to fizz, pour it into the main body.

If you keep the temperature at about 75°F (24°C) fermentation will be so active that there is no danger of air getting to the must, for the carbon dioxide given off will prevent this. Don't let the temperature rise above 80°F (27°C) or some of your yeast will be killed. By the same token, don't let the temperature fall below 70°F (21°C), or your yeast will get sleepy and foreign yeasts will gain advantage. Always keep the skins stirred into the must. They will float on top, so don't let them form a dry, floating crust.

Racking

When the first violent fermentation has ceased, rack off the must, squeeze the juice out of the skins so as not to waste it, and pour the juice into a barrel or carboy, so that the must fills it completely. Be careful not to leave an air space above it.

Let the temperature fall now to a temperature of about 60°F (16°C). Check, and when you think most of the sediment has sunk to the bottom, rack the wine into another container. At this stage people in continental climates often put wine out of doors in winter so that it almost freezes, because this hastens the settling-down of sediment. Now rack it again. After another month or two of it sitting quietly, you can then bottle it in the way I am now going to describe.

Bottling

Bottles must be completely cleaned and then sterilized. It is no good "sterilizing" anything with dirt in it; the dirt must first be removed. Sterilize by heating slowly so you do not crack the bottles. You can do this in an oven if you like. Then pour in boiling water, or put in cold water and slowly bring to the boil and boil for 5 minutes. Hang the bottles upside down immediately to let them drain and stop dust from floating down into them. Either use as soon as they are cool or cork until you want them. Boil the corks before you use them and whack them in with a special corker. Store bottled wine on its side to keep the corks wet. If they dry out they will shrink, and air and vinegar bacillus will get in. Store wine in the dark, at a cool, even temperature. A cellar or basement is ideal.

MAKING ROSE HIP WINE

The addition of a wine yeast to your brew starts off the fermentation process, which can take as long as three months.

1 Take 3 quarts (3.4 liters) of rose hips, clean them, and chop them up finely. Crush with a wooden spoon or mallet.

2 Put the crushed hips into a deep bowl and pour 1½ gallons (6.8 liters) of boiling water over them. You can add the rind and juice of an orange.

3 Add 2 lb (0.9 kg) of sugar, and heat it to 75°F (24°C). Stir in a teaspoon of fresh yeast. You can put this first into a bottle of "starter," which you add to the brew when it starts fermenting. Add a teaspoon of citric acid and then ½ teaspoon of tannin.

4 Cover the must overnight to keep out vinegar flies and all other contaminants.

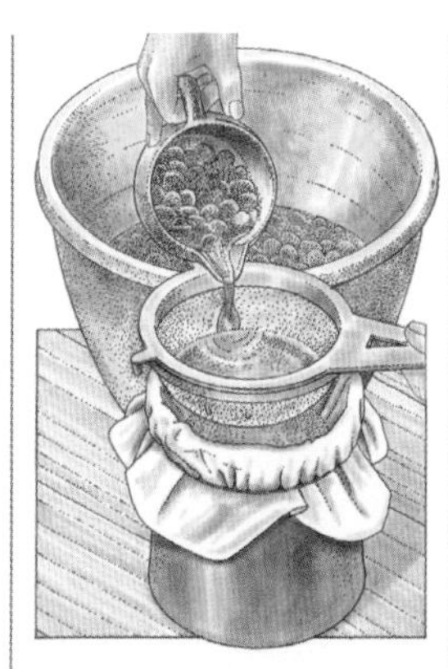

5 Strain the must from the hips through a sieve or muslin cloth. For even clearer must, use both these methods.

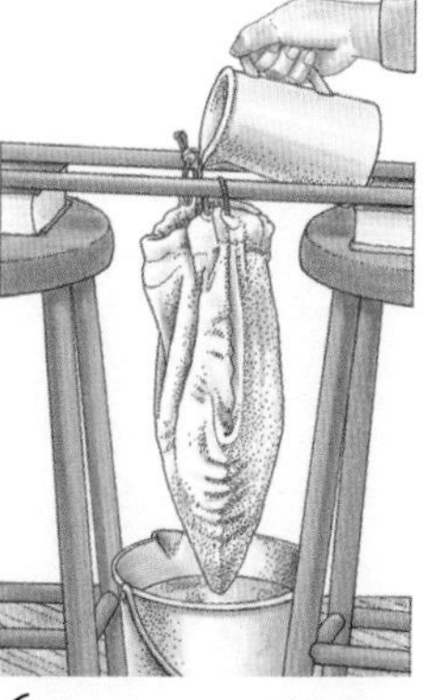

6 Or you can strain through a jelly bag, suspended from two stools. Don't press it, or it will get cloudy.

7 Strain the must into fermentation jars. Use a funnel. Keep at 75°F (24°C).

8 A fermentation lock keeps air out but allows gases to escape. When fermentation stops, rack the wine off the lees into bottles. Use a rubber or a plastic tube.

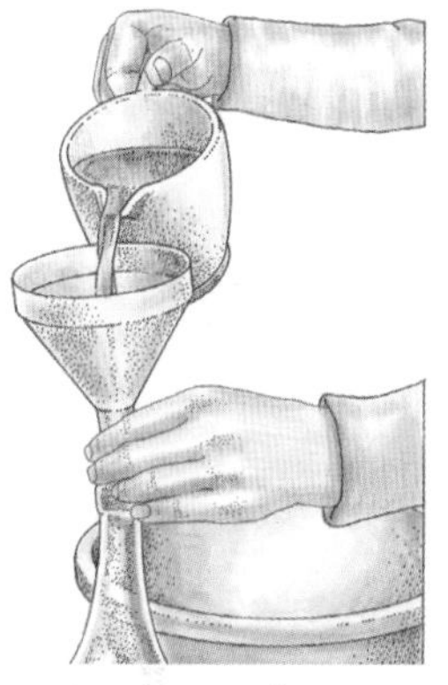

9 If you have no tube, use a hand jug and a funnel. Leave 1 in (2.5 cm) at the top for corks when filling the bottles.

10 A corking gun is excellent for driving corks in tight, but a wooden mallet will do. Date, label, and leave for a year.

COUNTRY WINES

I am going to give you some recipes for "country wines" that work, as I know from long experience. I would not put anybody off "scientific wine-making," which is reliable and produces good wines, but country people all over Europe and North America have used the sort of recipes I give for centuries, and very seldom have failures; indeed, their wines are very good. One point worth noting is that the larger the bulk of wine you make, the less likely you are to have a failure. My old friends in an English village, who all brew rhubarb wine in the summer and parsnip in the winter, in batches of 60 gallons (273 liters) stored in huge cider barrels, have never known what a failure is. Their spouses cry in vain for them to grow something else in their gardens, but their wine is superb.

Flower wines

Pour 1 gallon (4 liters) of boiling water over an equivalent quantity of whatever flowers you wish to use; allow to cool, and press the water from the flowers. Add 4 lb (1.8 kg) of sugar, ½ lb (228 g) of raisins (optional), and the juice of three lemons. As the flowers don't give much nutriment for the yeast, and sugar alone is not enough for it, add some yeast nutriment if you have some. A tablespoon of nutriment to 1 gallon (4 liters) of wine is about right. Then, when the temperature has fallen to 75°F (24°C), add yeast. A bought wine yeast is best. Put the wine in a vessel with a fermentation lock, and leave it to ferment. Rack off and bottle when ready. I have made wines from broom flowers, gorse flowers, elderflower (superb, see right, above), cowslip, and dandelion, and I have drunk good rose wine.

To make elderberry wine you'll need:

- 6 lb (2.7 kg) elderberries
- 3 lb (1.4 kg) sugar
- 1 gallon (4 liters) water
- 2 oz (56 g) citric acid or lemon juice; and add yeast

You're meant to get all the berries off the stalks, but I've shoved in stalks and all and it's made no difference. After all, if you can save a lot of work by departing from slavish convention, why not? Pour the boiling water on, mash hard with a potato masher, cover and leave to soak for 24 hours. Put the sugar and yeast in and leave it alone – the longer, the better. When it has finished fermenting, rack it into bottles or other containers, so as to leave the sediment behind. You do this with all wines. The above recipe can be applied to any wine that is made from berries or currants.

MEAD

To supply what you might guess is about 3 lb (1.4 kg) of honey to 1 gallon (4.5 liters) of water, you want comb cappings, odd bits of "wild comb" that you can't put through the extractor, and perhaps some pure honey (from the main storage pot when your spouse isn't looking!). Melt the honey in the water and ferment. Honey is deficient in acid, so put the juice of a few lemons or citric acid in a gallon. Mead likes some tannin to feed the yeast, so add some crushed crabapples. I have heard of people putting tea in mead. I once dumped some rose hip syrup into my mead, which wasn't fermenting very well, and it started to ferment like blazes. Mead goes on fermenting for a long time. Don't hurry it; if you can leave it in a bottle for a few years, do.

Making Cider and Vinegar

Cider should be made from a mixture of apples. The ideal mixture is a selection of apples rich in acid, tannin, and sugar, so a good combination mixes very sweet apples with very sour ones, perhaps with some crabapples thrown in to provide the tannin.

Cider can be made with unripe apples but it is never very successful. Ideally, the apples should be picked ripe and then allowed to lie in heaps for 2 or 3 days until they begin to soften a little. A few bad or bruised apples in the press don't seem to affect the quality of the cider at all. Apples vary greatly in juice content, so it is not possible to tell exactly how much cider you will get from a given number of apples. As a rough estimate, 10–14 lb (4½–6 kg) of apples make 1 gallon (4.5 liters).

Over the centuries cider-making was one of the best ways of preserving the "food" value of apples over the winter. Alcohol and the fermentation process are like a magic preserving process. By the miracle of nature, cloudy and dirty apple juice become a delicious (if slightly intoxicating) golden liquor. Apples are produced in great quantities during the autumn. Some varieties store fairly well, Coxes for example, but most will only last a couple of months, and then only if they are picked in perfect condition (windfalls will be bruised and useless for storage). In the modern world very few people know how to deal with their apple crops and we find we have lots of friends who are only too happy for us to appear with a party of kids to gather up all their windfalls. Cider-making parties with kids are a pleasant way of enjoying a fall day.

Crushing

When you have collected a pile of apples – a wheelbarrow-full at least – you're ready to start cider-making. A few strong helpers will be useful if you can find them. You will need chopping equipment, a crusher, a fruit press, and a 5-gallon (4-liter) fermentation bin. You then crush the apples. Crushing is an arduous task. Traditionally, this was done by a horse or an ox pulling a huge, round stone round a circular stone trough. I did have one friend who used to put his apples through a horizontal mangle, which reduced them to pulp very effectively.

Firstly, get all the equipment cleaned from storage and set up. Make sure your fruit press is fastened to a solid, heavy object. I have made a small, heavy table for the purpose and screw the press down so strength can be exerted without knocking things around. The apples go from the wheelbarrow into a chopping box, where they can be chopped with a clean spade. Once chopped, the apples can be put through the crusher – watch out for catching fingers here. When your press is full, start the squeezing. The first juice is always exciting – and delicious to drink straight from the press.

Direct the juice from the press straight into your large fermenting bin and do not worry too much at this stage about bits of apple or grass floating about in the vat. When all the juice has been squeezed from the first batch of apples, you must undo the press to take out the "cheese" of crushed pulp. I keep a separate wheelbarrow to hand for this. You can feed some pulp to pigs and cattle, but most must go on the compost heap. Refill the press and continue the process until your fermenting vessel is nearly full.

Covering and fermenting the apple juice

Your vat of apple juice is full of natural yeasts from the skins and the orchard. It will probably have a fair bit of other bits and pieces in it, too. The next step is to cover with a muslin cloth to keep out the vinegar flies, then leave the vat overnight in a sink. In the first day or so there is likely to be a rapid fermentation and you want this to bubble over the sides. This trick means that the bubbles carry with them large quantities of dirt and muck over the edge and down the drain. As soon as any violent fermentation has finished you can decant the whole bin into another clean fermentation bin through a sieve. This removes any remaining bits and pieces of apple, and you can leave behind any heavy sediment that may have formed in the first vessel. You should now have 5 gallons (23 liters) of reasonably clean apple juice ready to complete its fermentation. At this stage I normally add a few teaspoonfuls of commercial brewing yeast and 1–2 lb (0.5–1 kg) of granulated sugar. The yeast makes sure that you get completion of a good fermentation as you cannot altogether rely on natural yeasts. The amount of added sugar is up to you – more sugar makes a stronger cider that will keep much better than a watery version. Add the sugar by making up a syrup with a couple of pints of boiling water: pour this into your vat. Put a tight-fitting lid on your fermenting vessel and keep it warm; you can use a warming pad, a heated belt or mat (electronically-

THREE SIMPLE STEPS

1 The chopping box Use a strong wooden box for chopping your apples with a clean, sharp spade. Fill it full enough so the apples cannot move around, but not so full that the pieces spill out.

2 The crusher Put your chopped apples into the crusher when they are no more than 1 in (3 cm) square. Crush the pulp straight into the fruit press – and be careful you don't catch your fingers.

3 Pressing the juice Fix your press to a stout table or work surface and squeeze the juice straight into the fermenting vessel. Remove the "cheeses" of squeezed pulp, feed a bit to the pigs, with the rest for your compost heap.

heated wraps to keep fermentation at a constant temperature), or an airing cupboard. The brew needs to ferment completely so that all the sugars are transformed into alcohol. This may take anything from 10 days to 3 weeks. You can check on progress by looking at the brew to see if there are still bubbles coming up or by tasting it (if it is still sweet, then there is a long way to go). When fermentation is complete, the liquid will begin to clear and a brown scum of yeast will be left around the edges. You are now ready to rack off into bottles for storage. Take the fermenting vessel into a cool place, preferably where you are going to rack it off. Leave it for at least 24 hours so it can settle; then rack it off into bottles just as you would beer. Add a little more sugar to each if you wish to ensure a secondary fermentation, but this often happens on its own. I have stored flatish cider through the winter months (outside), then, when the warmer months come, a secondary fermentation starts and gives an excellent fizzy lift. Cider improves greatly with age and will certainly keep for up to a year.

Vinegar

Vinegar is wine, beer, or cider in which the alcohol has been turned into acetic acid by a species of bacteria. This bacillus can only operate in the presence of oxygen, so you can prevent your wines, beers, and ciders from turning to vinegar by keeping them protected from the air.

Yeast produces carbon dioxide in large quantities, and this expels the air from the vessel that the beverage has been stored in. But yeast cannot operate in more than a certain strength of alcohol, so fermentation ceases when so much sugar has been converted into alcohol that the yeast is killed or inhibited by its own action. This is the moment when the vinegar-forming bacillus, *Acetobacter,* gets active, and the moment when your beverages need protecting most rigorously from fresh air and bacterial infection.

However, if you want to make vinegar you must take your wine, beer, or cider and expose it to the air as much as possible. If you just leave it in an open barrel it will turn into vinegar in a few weeks. But it is better to speed up the process, to ensure that smells from the surrounding atmosphere do not taint the vinegar and hostile bacteria have little time to attack.

To hasten the process, take a barrelful of beech shavings. Beech is a traditional component for this stage of the proceedings but, really, any shavings will do as long as they do not come from a very resinous tree. First, soak the shavings well in a good vinegar of the type you are trying to make (see illustration below). Then, put a perforated wooden plate in the barrel over the shavings and pour your wine, beer, or vinegar on to this plate.

MAKING VINEGAR
Soak a barrelful of beech shavings in vinegar of the sort you are making. Put a wooden plate, perforated with pin-sized holes, on top of the shavings in the barrel. Pour your alcohol on to the plate. The liquid will drip slowly through the shavings through the holes in the barrel (which must be tiny, about the size of pin-holes) and be well exposed to air and the vinegar-forming bacillus. After a week in an open cask, it will turn into vinegar. At the barrel's bottom the vinegar-to-be is drawn off through a cock.

CHAPTER FIVE

ENERGY AND WASTE

"Every householder should have several small bins: one for organic waste, one for aluminum, one for non-returnable glass, one for tin cans, and one for plastic. Plastic, by the way, is hugely overused. It hadn't been invented fifty years ago, or most of it hadn't, and the world got on surprisingly well without it. We should refuse to buy goods which are overwrapped in plastic. As far as recycling goes, by far the best solution is one that has been developed in Germany: melting it down and turning it into building panels which are strong and good insulators. Our poor suffering old planet just cannot stand the wastage and pollution of garbage dumping any more. We owe it to our children and our children's children to put an end to this scandal: we are rifling their inheritance."

John Seymour *Changing Lifestyles* 1991

Food for the Garden

If you pile up vegetable matter upon vegetable matter in a heap, it will rot and turn into compost. But to make good compost, and to make it quickly, you have to do more than this. Of course the self-supporter with livestock can make the best compost in the world in just 12 hours by putting vegetable matter through the guts of an animal. Otherwise using just the natural waste of the garden will take you months, whatever you do. Either way, the principle of compost-making is this.

Making compost

The vegetation should be broken down by aerobic organisms. These are bacteria and fungi, which require oxygen in order to live. The bacteria that break down cellulose in plant matter need available nitrogen to do it. If they get plenty of available nitrogen they break down the vegetable matter very quickly, and in doing so they generate a lot of heat. The heat kills the weed seeds and disease organisms in the compost. If there is a shortage of available nitrogen, it takes the organisms a very long time to break the vegetable matter down. So in order to speed the process up as much as you can, you try to provide the things that the compost-making organisms need: air, moisture, and nitrogen. You can provide the air by having rows of bricks with gaps between them underneath the compost and, if you like, by . leaving a few posts in the heap as you build it, so you can pull them out to leave "chimneys."

> Compost-making organisms need air, moisture, and nitrogen.

You can provide the moisture either by letting rain fall on the heap, or by throwing enough water on it to moisten it well. And you can provide the nitrogen by adding animal manure (chicken dung and horse dung are especially good), urine, fish meal, inorganic nitrogen, or anything you can get that has a fairly high nitrogen content.

Dung and fertilizers

The natural, and traditional, way to make compost is to throw your vegetable matter (generally straw) at the feet of yarded cattle, pigs, or other animals. The available nitrogen in the form of the animal's dung and urine "activates" the compost. The urine also provides moisture and enough air gets between the straw. After a month or two, you dig the heap out and stack it carefully out of doors. More air gets into it and makes it rot down further. Then, after a few months, you cart it out and spread it on your vegetable plot and elsewhere as fertilizer.

But if you don't have any animals your best bet is to build compost piles by putting down a layer of bricks or concrete blocks with gaps in them, and laying coarse, woody material on these to let the air through. Then you need to put down several layers of vegetable matter, sprinkling a dusting of some substance with a high nitrogen content between them. About 10 in (25 cm) of vegetable matter and 2–3 in (5 cm) of chicken dung, or a thick sprinkling of a high-nitrogen inorganic fertilizer, would be ideal. Some people alternate lime with the nitrogen.

Keep the sides vertical using walls of either wood, brick, or concrete, and keep it decently moist but not sopping wet. Don't forget that anyone can pile up stuff to make a heap but only a pro can make a good stack with vertical sides. You will be surprised how much material from the garden you can deal with in this way. Just make sure you spread out each addition into a thin layer rather than a heap. And mix plenty of rich green stuff (weeds, grass cuttings, and so on) with the more woody wastes so you keep a good mix. Keep piling vegetable wastes in for a whole season. Make sure you allow enough space to do this – 8 x 4 ft (2.5 x 1.2 m) does it for our half an acre of garden. The compost pile will grow with new material one week and shrink back down the next as the material decomposes; in fact you will be surprised just how much shrinkage takes place.

At the end of the season (October or November) you will stop adding any further material to your season's compost. From now on you will use the second composting area, leaving the first to ferment undisturbed. When it comes to early spring (February or March) you will be able to take off the top and unrotted material from the outside of last season's heap and put this into the bottom of the second heap. You can then spread your rotted compost on the garden as you like: some for the pole bean bed, some for the soft fruits, some for new deep beds. If you can, try to also obtain farmyard manure from a local farmer. You often see farm signs for compost or manure along the roads, but you'll need a trailer of some sort.

IDEAL TWO-BIN COMPOSTER
Here is the ideal two-bin composter for garden and kitchen wastes. Make each bin large enough to contain one season's waste – at least 4 sq ft (0.5 sq m).

Use one bin only during the season – and keep piling stuff in as it shrinks with the composting process.

Walls of the bins can be old pallets or treated timber.

The front planks are optional (loading is quicker without them) but movable to allow for emptying.

Pound in treated posts, square or round to make the corners.

Flagstones in the loading area keep down mud and help keep the area tidy (but are not essential).

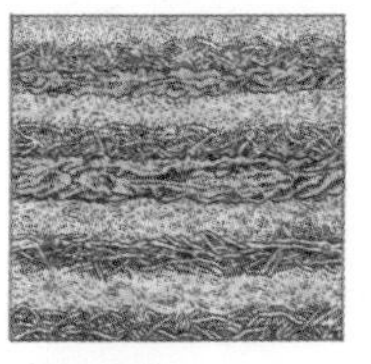

COMPOST
Every possible object of vegetable or animal origin should go in the compost heap. The base should be bare soil covered by branches or straw for aeration.

The closed urban composter

I like to keep a closed plastic composting bin for the richer kitchen wastes that attract the flies and rats. Again if you can buy these with a closing top and a rat-proof base from garden centers, do so; and check whether your local government is supplying these or similar bins (many now do at a low cost). Of course, if you have a composting toilet, then most of this stuff can go down that route.

Essentially the same principles apply as to the open garden compost heap: a good mixture and plenty of it. I put an aluminum sheet with holes punched through it as a base for my plastic composter and this keeps out rats but lets in worms. Once you have sufficient mixture to generate a good fermentation you will see the material rapidly shrinking. Add urine if you feel it needs extra nitrogen. The composting bin has a hatch in the bottom which can be opened to shovel out the rotted material after several months of fermentation. You may want to add this to your existing garden compost heap if it is not quite ready.

Worm composting

In warm climates worm composters are very popular and easy to use. These depend on small red manure worms which either appear naturally from nowhere or that can be bought from bait stores. Worms need moisture and warmth to thrive. And one neat way of providing this is to use a column of used car tires as a container for organic wastes. Add manure worms at the bottom and they will steadily multiply and eat their way upward. You can then remove the lower tire (and its compost) as the column fills up. The worms will have moved upward by then, so you keep the process on-going.

PLASTIC URBAN COMPOSTER

Typical store-bought composter suitable for urban use. Made of heavy-grade plastic and should be both fly- and rat-resistant.

Body made of strong plastic with closing top and removable base.

Base must be rat-resistant yet allow worms to enter and moisture to leave; perforated aluminum sheeting is ideal. Sliding door allows rotted material to be removed.

WORM COMPOSTING

A pile of old car tires can make a good container for worm composting with manure worms. The worms like warmth and heat. You remove the bottom tire regularly as the worms move up the stack.

Managing Waste

Over the last 50 years, garbage collection and the processing of human waste has become a major challenge for urban civilization. We take from nature, we use (briefly) and we throw away – tons and tons of supposedly useless "waste." Most of this is put into landfills which will, of course, become the mines of tomorrow if not the methane power stations of the 22nd century. Much more than half of this "waste" is paper and kitchen waste and lots more is glass, metal, or clothing that can be recycled. Every self-sufficient holding should take pride in producing as little waste as possible – indeed, zero waste should be the goal. The first and most elementary step is to avoid buying in waste in the first place (i.e. the bulky Sunday papers). The second step is to separate your waste for the following:

Compost heap Your main compost heap (see also p.200) takes bulk vegetable waste like potato peelings, weeds, leaves, fruit skins, apple pulp, and so on. Your closed composter takes stuff that would attract rats – for example composting disposable diapers, old tea bags, and rotten meat or fish unsuitable for poultry.

Poultry bucket This takes waste food and scraps and must be emptied and washed out daily to keep it fresh. Stale cakes and buns, pasta, fish skins – these are pure heaven for your chickens.

Paper Recycling is the first option, followed by burning, or composting (after shredding which is tiresome).

Plastic Almost impossible to avoid in the modern world beholden to the oil industry. Recycle those plastic 2-liter bottles and keep clean for bottling your beer and cider.

Cans Most local governments now recycle both aluminum and steel cans so you need to separate these out. Aluminum cans are crushed easily while steel cans will flatten if you take off both ends.

Glass The crashing of green, brown, and clear glass bottles is now a regular sound at recycling centers as people get rid of waste glass. Quite why we have to smash up perfectly good bottles when millions of kilowatts of energy could be saved by having a few standardized shapes beats me. The fuel companies would hate us but for goodness sake we could even take wine bottles to be refilled as they still do in parts of France; and I do remember a time when milk came in bottles that were reused without difficulty.

With all the above check with your local government first to find out their latest recycling offers (you might be surprised); but the best recycling is that of composting your garbage to use later as a fantastic fertilizer for your crops.

The black art of moving muck

We are told that the Zen master of housework spends a lifetime perfecting the job of doing the dishes so that the activity ultimately becomes an art form of sublime pleasure and satisfaction. What greater success could there be in life? What magic is it that can transform drudgery into pleasure?

On the previous pages I've discussed how to make the best compost for your garden, but here I'd also like to cover an even better source of food for next year's vegetables (and even if you don't own a cow, sheep, or pig I do hope you find this illuminating). It may seem like a foul task as I'm speaking of emptying out a winter's build-up of cow manure and straw.

Let's face it, digging out and wheelbarrowing ten tons of smelly manure does not sound immediately appealing. But in the art of self-sufficiency the good student will enjoy great satisfaction from the sight of a beautiful heap of rotting manure. Just think of the hot, sweaty, smelly shoveling as being like riding a bike up a beautiful mountain; the pain of the climb is more than balanced by the prospect of whizzing downhill for many miles on the other side. In this case the pain of the shoveling is more than compensated for by the prospect of fabulous "food" for next year's vegetables.

The fork and wheelbarrow

The first requirement, as all students of Zen will know, is to get to know and love your tools, in this case, the manure fork and the wheelbarrow. The right equipment is vital. Your manure fork will have four prongs or tines made of spring steel and with curved shoulders, like a pitchfork. The tines should have a nice curve on them which not only allows you to carry more manure but also serves as a vital lever to prize up layers of heavy, downtrodden, wet straw. The curved shoulders mean that straw is less likely to stick to the fork when you toss it into the barrow. A heavy, square garden fork is absolutely the wrong tool for this job: it is straight, its tines are too thick, and its shoulders catch constantly on the straw.

Your wheelbarrow has to be strong enough to carry up to 220 lb (100 kg) of muck at a time. The wheel should be of the inflatable type, as this runs more smoothly. And don't forget you can use different grades of tire. The more expensive are much less likely to give problems with punctures. A galvanized steel barrow is probably the best of all. You will also want your wheelbarrow to fit close to the cowshed gate so you do not have to take more than a couple of steps each time you put a forkful into the barrow.

Now get yourself organized so you have a clear run between the cowshed and the compost-manure heap: you would not want this to be more than 25 yd (23 m). Make sure your manure heap has good strong sides than can take the pressure of a few tons of manure – drive in extra treated posts with your post rammer if necessary. We are talking here about a manure pile which might typically be 10 ft (3 m) across by 6 ft (1.8 m) deep. It will be open at one side and bounded on the other three by timber slats held in place by treated fence posts. If you have steps or similar to push up, then you will make sure any ramp is well secured and supported before you start. The straw bedding will be heavily compacted by the weight and hooves of the animals. As each barrowload may weigh over 220 lb (100 kg), you'll need a good run to get up any slopes.

The art of digging

You cannot dig out manure like sand. Instead you must push in your fork tines at a low angle and use the curve of the tines to act as a fulcrum as you lever gently down on the handle of the fork. This will slowly lift up a layer of manure perhaps 3 in (7.5 cm) thick with a sucking sound as the compaction is released. You can then lift this, with a bit of jiggling, and toss the forkful into your barrow. You can pile up the barrow pretty high, as the manure holds itself together well. Take care not to put your hand over the end of the fork handle because if you bump a wall, it will hurt!

An almost inevitable spin-off from the manure moving will be, alas, a broken fork handle. Manure is heavy stuff and it is very easy to press a bit hard and break your fork handle. Many modern tools are sold with poor quality handles. You want one made of ash where you can see a good straight grain running down the handle. It should be thicker in the middle, tapering to the top. If you break your fork handle, you can look forward to a nice rainy day job.

Making a straight-edged stack

Now you have the task of making a good stack of manure to compost. This is an art form in itself for, as every country person knows, anyone can make a pile, but only a country person can make a good stack. And a stack is going to be there for all to see as a work of art, or otherwise, for perhaps a year or more! The key to making a good stack is to have the material (straw in this case) sloping down into the stack from the edges. If it is sloping down from the center to the outside then it's going to slip and you will not get a straight vertical side to your stack. In the old days of farming the stacking of the crop was a vital skilled task, for a stack that slipped or let in the weather was a major disaster. Stacking your manure heap is not quite that important but a neat stack will keep its shape and give you a better compost than a loose heap. To make a straight-edged stack you must start by putting material along the outside edge. You want a wide mat of material with plenty of long strands, ideally running at right angles to the edge of the stack. If you have a forkload of loose material which is in small pieces then discard it for the moment: toss it to the back of the space. By building up a straight edge right across the front of the heap about 9 in (23 cm) high and then working back from it, you will make sure your material is sloping down away from the edge. Every time you have a good forkload with long strands, use this to strengthen the edge. The long strands will be trapped by the other material above them and hold the edge firm.

You have a major strategic choice to make when digging out your compost. Do you make a solid heap of manure which will compost itself? Or do you keep your good manure in reserve so you can take out a 6–in (15–cm) layer every couple of weeks to add to your general compost heap? By mixing manure with other material for composting you will achieve an excellent result. There is a lot to be said for taking a little time over moving tons of muck. Like many tasks in the world of self-sufficiency, a great deal can be achieved by regular application on a small scale.

More on manuring

If your land has had proper additions of farmyard manure or the dung of animals added direct, or seaweed (which has in it every element), or compost, it is most unlikely to be deficient in anything. By getting your soil analyzed when you take it over, and adding once and for all whatever element the analysis shows the soil to be deficient in (nitrogen, phosphorus, potassium, or calcium), and thereafter husbanding in a sound organic way, the "heart" (fertility) of your land should increase continually until it is at a very high level. There should be no need to spend any further money at all on "fertilizers." And, very often, if land is virgin, or if it has been properly farmed in the past, you may not even need to get it analyzed.

Saving Energy

THE ALTERNATIVES

I have advocated throughout an integrated approach to the land: the encouragement of organic beneficial interaction of soil, crops, and animals. When considering energy we must adopt this same approach. We should look upon our holding of land as having a certain energy potential that we can use for our own good purposes, and we should aim to make our holding autonomous in this respect, as we have aimed to make it for food.

There is something wrong about burning coal to heat water on a hot, sunny day, or burning oil to warm a house when there is a fast-flowing stream next to it. Or, for that matter, using electricity to drive a mill or a power loom, when there is potential wind or water power nearby.

Water power can be harnessed in hilly, rainy countries and wind power in flat lands; but wind power should never be used where water power is available. The simple reason is that the wind is fickle, while water is relatively reliable and consistent. Where there is hot sun it is ridiculous not to use it. It is obviously unproductive to feed cold water into your water boiler when the corrugated iron roof over your shed is so hot you can't hold your hand on it.

A characteristic of natural sources of energy is that they lend themselves much more to small-scale use than to large-scale exploitation. For example, more energy can be got out of a given river more cheaply by tapping it with a hundred small dams and waterwheels right down its length, than by building one enormous dam and driving one set of huge turbines. The wind's energy can be tapped better, and now increasingly is (thankfully for our environment) by a myriad of small windmills, rather than some gigantic wind-equivalent of a power station.

> Where there's hot sun it's ridiculous not to use it.

It doesn't need an "Earth Summit" to tell you that every house in a city could have a solar roof, and derive a great part of its energy requirement from it, whereas a solar collector big enough to supply a community is still in the realms of fantasy. Scattered farms can easily make their own methane gas, but to cart muck from a hundred farms to some central station, make gas from it, and then redistribute it would be madly uneconomical. So these "alternative energy devices" commend themselves especially to the self-supporter.

Combining natural energy sources

Now it may well be that it is better for the self-supporter to combine several sources of energy instead of concentrating on just one. For example, you could have a big wood-burning furnace that does the cooking for a large number of people, and heats water for dairy, kitchen, butchery, bathroom, and laundry. If you preheated the water that went into it with solar panels on the roof, you would need less wood to heat more water. Then you might have a methane plant to utilize animal and human waste and use the methane to bring the hot water from the furnace to steam-heat for sterilizing dairy equipment. Then you could use a pumping windmill to pump up water from the clear, pure well below your holding, instead of having to use the very slightly polluted water from the hill above.

HEAT LOSS

A house built in the traditional way loses vast amounts of heat through the roof, doors, windows, floor, and outside walls. Use a combination of the methods illustrated and you can save as much as two-thirds of your annual domestic energy requirement.

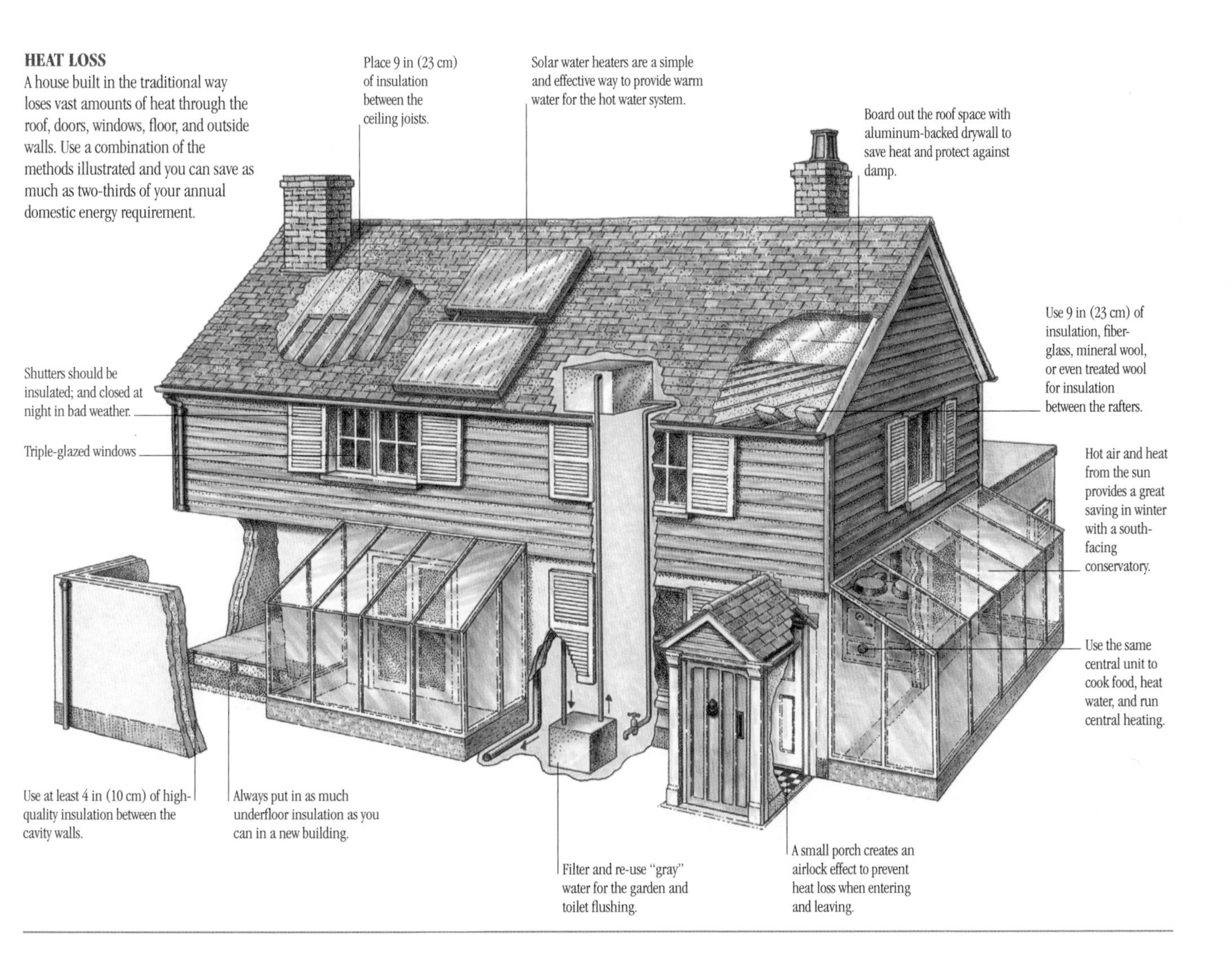

And what about lighting your buildings using the stream that runs nearby to drive a small turbine? All these things are possible, would be fairly cheap, and would pay for themselves by saving on energy brought in from outside.

Keeping heat in

There is little point in creating elaborate systems for getting heat from natural sources until you have plugged the leaks in the systems you have already got.

For keeping heat in a house there is nothing to beat very thick walls of stone, pise (rammed earth), or brickwork with small windows and a thatched roof. The thin cavity walls of modern brick or concrete block housing only insulate well if plastic foam or some other insulating material is put between the walls and laid on the joists in the roof. The big "picture windows" beloved of modern architects are terrible heat-losers. Dual glazing may help, but it is very expensive. Country folk, working out of doors for most of the day as people were designed to do, want to feel, when they do go indoors, that they are indoors; they get plenty of "views" when they are out in it and are part of the view themselves. Therefore, for country housing, big windows are a mistake.

Huge chimneys, very romantic and fine when there are simply tons of good dry firewood, send most of their heat up to heat the sky. In a world short of fuel they are inexcusable. Long, straggly houses are also great heat-wasters. A compact shape is more desirable. A round building will lose less heat than a square one, because it has a smaller surface area in comparison with its volume (the Mongolian herdsmen know a thing or two about this). And a square building is obviously better than an oblong one. It is always best to have your primary heat source in the middle of the building rather than against an outside wall. Most insulation nowadays is achieved with high technology products, and these are very expensive. What we can do is search for cheaper and more natural materials. Wherever the cork oak will grow it should be grown, for it provides excellent insulation, and in large quantities.

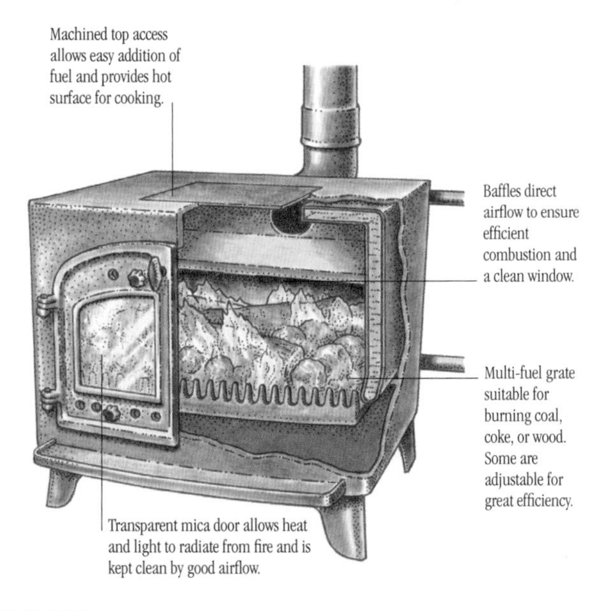

CLOSED BOILER

Most wood stoves and ranges will burn almost anything combustible. Wood and all other inflammable trash provide additional free fuel which can be saved and stored during summer and fall for use in winter. A large old-fashioned cast-iron range can supply the major source of domestic heat as well as being used for cooking meals.

Heat from the Sun

The most practical solar collector is a wood, for woodland can collect the sun's rays from vast areas, and, properly managed, can continually convert them into energy, while to cover a few square yards with a man-made solar collector costs a lot of effort and money. But if collecting and storing the sun's heat can be done relatively easily and cheaply, as it usually can on the roof of an existing house or wall, then, if nothing more, solar energy can be used to reinforce other sources of energy. The drawback is that in cold climates we want heat in the winter and we get it in the summer, but if the winter gap is filled in with wind or water power a consistent system can be evolved.

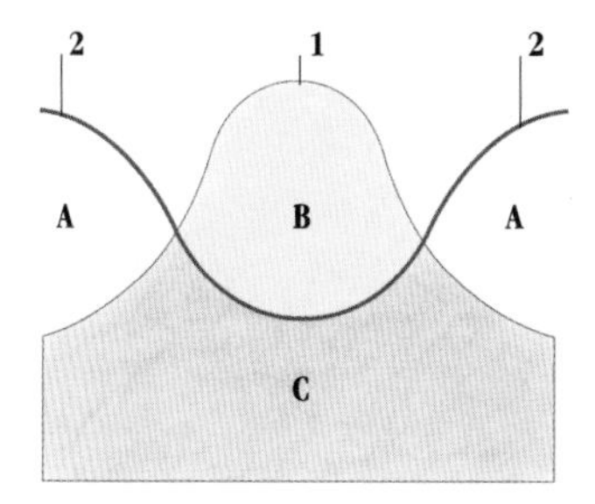

SOLAR ENERGY
Solar energy (**1**) is most abundant in mid-summer while our heating requirements (**2**) are greatest in mid-winter. Most solar collectors provide more heat than we need in summer (**B**) and less than we need in winter (**A**). The productive use of solar energy (**C**) reaches peaks in spring and fall. Received energy per day per sq m might be 4 or 5 kW-hr in summer, and ½ to 1 kW-hr in winter in a temperate climate.

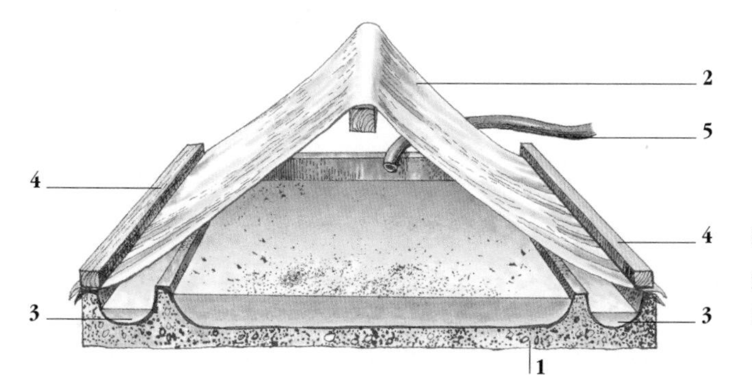

SOLAR STILL
This shallow concrete basin (**1**), painted black or tarred contains a few inches of polluted water. A heavy-gauge polythene tent encloses this (**2**), and condensation runs down the inside surface of the tent into a pair of collecting gutters (**3**). The condensation is pure distilled water which you can syphon off. Hold down the plastic sheeting with heavy wooden battens (**4**) and close the cover ends rather like a ridge tent. You can replenish the polluted water through a hose (**5**).

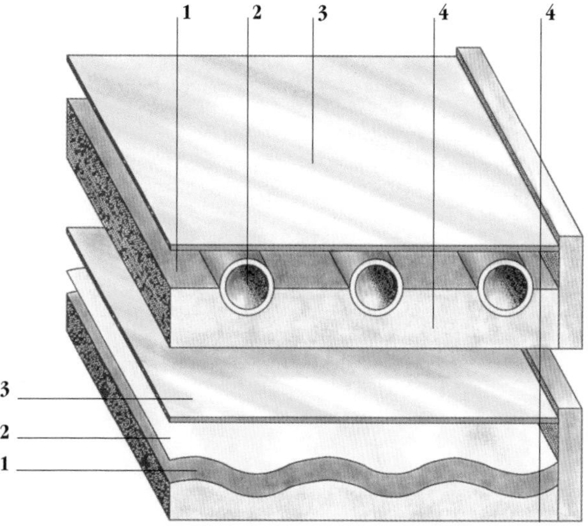

FLAT-PLATE SOLAR COLLECTORS
Most solar energy collectors use a black surface (**1**) to absorb the sun's radiation and produce heat. You transfer the heat into a hot water tank, or to heat space, by passing water, or air in some cases, through pipes or channels (**2**) behind the absorbing surface. A glass or plastic covering (**3**) prevents heat loss from the front of the collector, while insulation (**4**) prevents it from escaping from the rear and sides.

The practical choices open to a self-supporter in temperate climates are:

1 Heating water by letting it trickle over a black-painted corrugated roof under a transparent covering that turns the roof into a heat collector. You will have to buy your transparent covering and a pump to circulate the water. All the same, this will allow you to collect the sun over a large area.

2 A second option is heating water with black-painted pipes behind transparent material. This has the advantage that there is no obscuration by misting-up and you don't need a circulatory pump because hot water rises. But it is expensive to cover large areas.

3 Solar stills: these are arrangements for using the heat of the sun directly for distilling water or other liquids.

4 Solar dryers: these can be used for drying fruit, grain vegetables, malt, and many other things (see below).

5 Solar hot air heaters: provide extra heat for a greenhouse.

6 Solar-heated walls such as the Trombe wall (see right): store heat during the day and release it during the night.

HEATING AIR: THE TROMBE WALL

Named after Professor Trombe, this is a clever method for making use of solar energy in winter. The Professor perfected the wall high up in the Pyrénées, where the sun shines quite often in winter, albeit weakly. You use a vertical dual-glazed plate glass window (**1**) which faces south, and allow a black-painted wall (**2**) behind it to catch and trap the sun's heat. When you require heat inside the house you open ventilators (**3**), and these allow warm air to circulate between the glass and the wall (**4**). An over-hanging roof (**5**) prevents the high summer sun from striking the glass and also protects the building from getting overheated. An alternative to the Trombe wall is a glass-covered extension to your house – in other words, a conservatory. This will warm the house if properly ventilated.

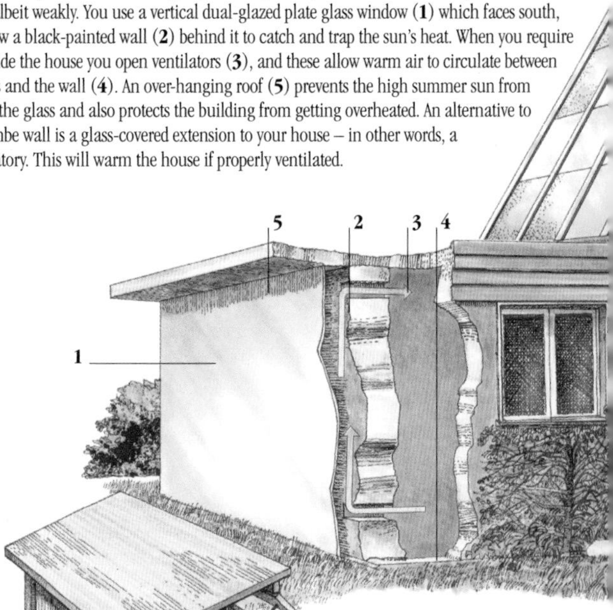

SOLAR DRIER

An inclined, glazed, flat-plate solar air heater admits air through an adjustable flap (**A**). The air heats up as it crosses over a blackened absorber surface (**B**), because the heat is trapped by glass panels (**C**). The heated air rises through a bed of rocks (**D**) and then through a series of gratings which hold the produce to be dried. A flap (**E**) under the overhanging roof allows air supply to be adjusted or closed off. The rock bed heats up in the course of the day and continues releasing a measure of warmth to the crop after sunset, thereby preventing condensation from occurring. There is a door in the unit's back to allow crops to be added or removed.

TRICKLE ROOF HEATER

Providing an entire south-facing roof for a solar water heater won't be cheap but can be a very worthwhile investment in the long run, by having water trickle down a blackened, corrugated, aluminum roof behind an area of glazing. Insulation behind the aluminum prevents overheating of the roof space and keeps most of the heat in the water. A small pump drives water round the system whenever a sensor on the roof tells a control-box that the roof temperature is higher than that of the water in the copper immersion heater.

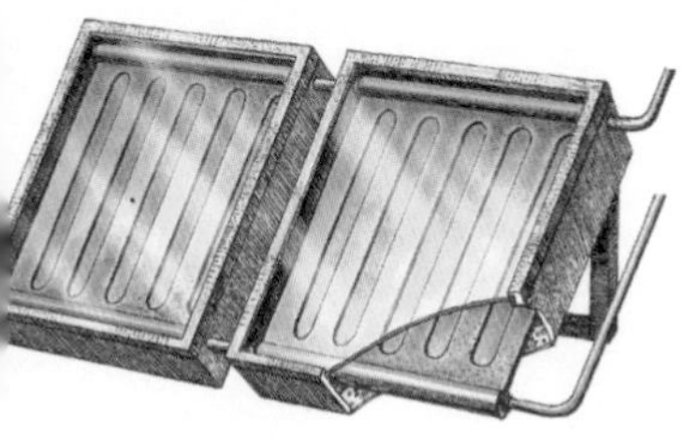

SOLAR WATER HEATERS

Mount a domestic radiator, painted black, in a mattress of fiberglass, and put it inside a box with a glazed lid. Place it at an angle of 45° to 60° to catch the sun. Join this to your water system and collect the heated water. A simpler method is to remove the bases of old bottles (see right), thread the bottles onto a garden hose, and spread them out to catch the sun. Run water through the hose slowly.

Power from the Wind

The common, factory-built steel pumping windmill, seen in all lands where water has to be pumped up from deep boreholes, is one of the most effective devices ever conceived by humans. Many an old steel "wind pump" has been turning away, for 30 or 40 years, never failing in its job. Such machines will pump water comfortably from 1,000 ft (300 meters) and work in very little wind at all. The tail-vane is arranged on a pivot so that the windmill can turn itself sideways to the wind in a storm.

Wind power for households, however, is still in its infancy (any modern wind turbine attached to a home generally requires planning permission), but without doubt low-powered but high-speed devices are now wanted for driving dynamos to produce electricity.

Unpredictable power

The wind, of course, is completely unpredictable, and so you must either accept that you cannot use a machine in calm weather, or in severe gales, or you must be able to store electricity, and that is very expensive. However, if you can use the power when it is available – even to power low-energy light bulbs – the total wind energy available over a period of time tends to be fairly constant and over the years will repay the investment.

TYPES OF WINDMILLS

Sail windmill
This is a variation on a Mediterranean sail windmill. Used for irrigation water pumping by market gardeners on Crete, it is readily improvised.

All-metal
This typical, all-metal windmill is used for pumping water. A swinging tail-vane turns it out of the wind in a storm. You might be able to renovate an old one.

Tubular steel
A water-pumping windmill in which the rotor runs in the lee of the tubular steel tower; weights at the blade roots swing them into a feathered position in gales.

Triple-blade
This windmill needs only three aerodynamically profiled blades. The machine trickle-charges a bank of batteries to supply low-powered appliances.

Sailwing
This is the simple and cheap sailwing, developed at Princeton University. A fabric sleeve is stretched between the two edges of the "wings."

Vertical axis
Reading University, England, developed this vertical axis windmill. Aerofoil blades are spring-loaded and fold outward to prevent over-speeding.

Wind power is hard to win and store, so you should always use wind-generated electricity sparingly. To exploit wind power you must have an average wind speed of at least 9 mph (14 km/h), with no lengthy periods of low winds; even so you will need battery storage to cover up to 20 consecutive days of calm. Apart from an electricity-generating windmill, you need a voltage regulator and a cut-out to prevent the battery from over-charging. Total battery storage capacity needs to be 20 x average current needed in amps (watts ÷ volts) x average usage time in hours per day, measured in amp hours. Major domestic electric appliances requiring 220 volts AC. can be driven from a bank of 12 volt (DC) batteries by an electronic inverter. Alternatively, some low-voltage appliances may be used directly. A typical 2–kW, commercially manufactured windmill will often generate at 110 volts DC to charge a bank of low-voltage batteries, wired in series. You might get 5,000 kW-hr annually from a 2–kW windmill. One kW is equal to one unit of electricity.

Traditional electricity-generating windmills are available in kit form or as a DIY design, while modern wind turbines are also now becoming popular. In theory you could generate enough electricity to sell it back to the grid, and wouldn't that be nice?

CHAPTER SIX

CRAFTS AND SKILLS

"No machine-made artifact can be beautiful. Beauty in artifacts can only be put there by the hands of the craftsman, and no machine will ever be built that can replace these. Machines might one day be made which will appreciate the beauty of articles made by other machines. People can only be truly pleased by articles made by other people. As far as possible we buy only things that have been made by people, not machines. I do not mean necessarily by the bare hands of people – hands can be magnified by tools and machines – but the hands must be there. Cloth woven on a loom by a person is fine. Cloth woven on a loom by an automatic device is dull. It is grudging... it only serves the one purpose."

John Seymour *The Fat of the Land* 1976

The Workshop

In real life things are always breaking and wearing out – usually just when you don't want them to. If you have all your tools to hand, in good shape, and a suitable place to use them, your blood pressure will benefit greatly.

The bare necessities

First things first: a workshop needs to have a good solid worktop. You need ½ in (1 cm) of good quality plywood; this will just about do, but 2–in (5–cm) planking would be better. Make a few large holes in the worktop with an augur so you can put in wooden pins to keep work still. You will also need a good vise. You must have good light to work effectively – but you do not want hot sun coming through your window so a big northern skylight would be ideal (you will see these in many old factories). The workshop does not need to be huge – 8 sq ft (6 or 7 sq m) would do. It should have electric power outlets in convenient places – at working height. The workshop should have a floor that is easy to brush clean, but it must not be slippery: plain concrete or unvarnished boarding is ideal.

It is true that one of the new portable workbenches can be a great help for the self-supporter. I have two and both have now reached a battered old age; believe me, these things suffer serious punishment. So don't buy one unless it's robust: the deck should be marine-quality plywood and not any form of chipboard. The fittings should be rust-resistant. Anything else will disintegrate pretty rapidly.

Tools are worse than useless unless they are sharp. And being sharp in my book means blades with straight edges and no chips. The blades on chisels and planes have been heat tempered on the edges and are very easily chipped if they are dropped, put down carelessly, or used as scrapers or levers. All too often they are borrowed by would-be helpers who use them to scrape off paint or lever up nails – this spells disaster and many hours of hard work to get back a decent edge. My tip to avoid this is to keep good chisels tucked away safely out of sight and leave an old one out on a rack or workbench, where it will be an effective decoy for visitors or helpers who are searching for a tool!

Sharpening stone and guides

If you want to have planes and chisels with straight edges, then you need to buy a first-rate carborundum or diamond stone: this will not come cheap but your tools are no good without it. And the way you use the stone will affect the flatness of the surface and hence the straightness of the blade. To keep the surface flat you must use the full width of the stone and turn it around from time to time so both ends get worn equally. You simply cannot do decent work without properly sharpened tools. I always have two sharpening stones. When a stone is worn and old I leave it out on the bench as a decoy (much like my chisel duplication). That is how seriously you need to take this crusade for properly sharpened tools. When you sharpen chisels or planes, always use a rolling guide to keep the blade at exactly the correct angle. You can see whether you are on the right track by looking at the bright, shining area produced by the stone. If your angle is correct this should cover the entire area of the blade. There is no way you can sharpen tools effectively without the guide.

IDEAL WORKSHOP LAYOUT

Large north-facing skylight illuminates without overheating. Even 8 sq ft (6 or 7 sq m) will make a good workspace and turn irritating chores into satisfying challenges. All tools have a habit of "walking," so keep them in their place and make sure putting tools back is rule number one in your workshop.

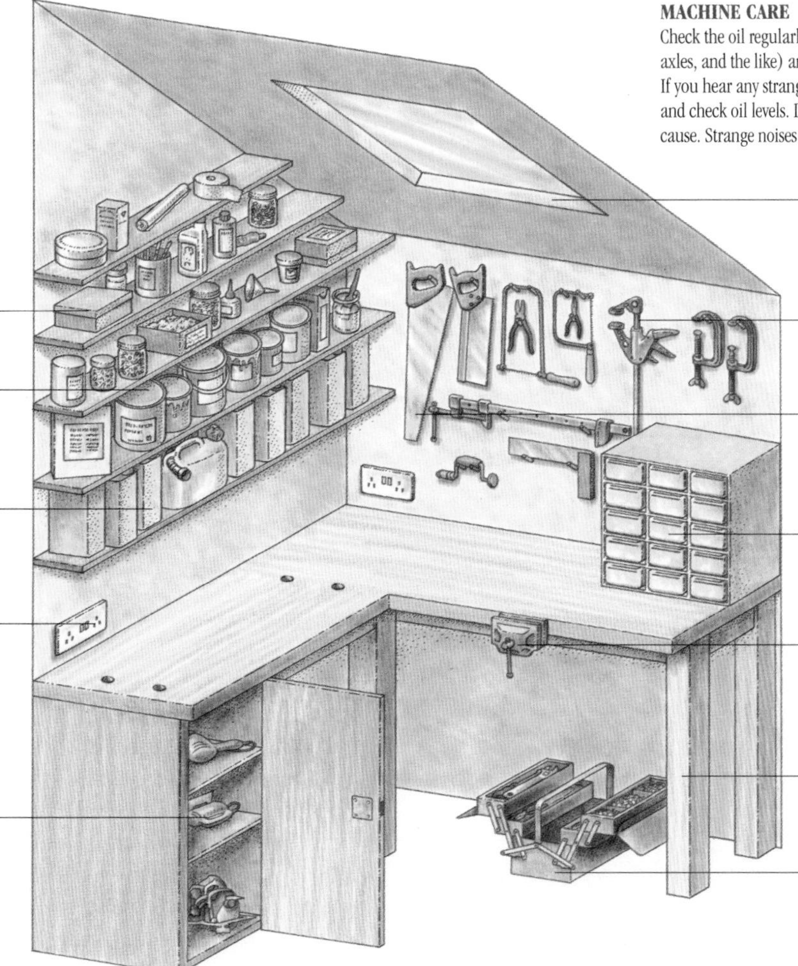

Top shelves
This is for nasties like rat poison, wood preservers, and glues.

Recycle plastic
Use old plastic containers or margarine tubs for storing small fixings. Transparent containers are best, but avoid glass, which breaks.

Fuel store
Keep spare gas cans and mark them separately for 2-stroke, regular, and diesel.

Power source
Several double wall sockets will be needed at least.

Power tools
Keep power tools out of sight in cupboards when not in use.

MACHINE CARE

Check the oil regularly on all engines (and gearboxes, back axles, and the like) and change it as to maker's instructions. If you hear any strange noises – stop! Check for loose nuts and check oil levels. Do not continue until you find the cause. Strange noises can be very expensive.

Light and air access
Overhead window gives light and ventilation.

Clamps
Modern, quick-action clamps are well worth buying.

Hang it all up
Buy a wall rack or make your own using nails to keep clamps, saws, large pliers, and other tools in view.

Screws and fixings
Keep your small fixings, screws, nails, and so on in a set of purpose-built, small drawers.

Vise
Fix a strong vise permanently to your workbench.

Workbench
Hammering and planing need a firm base with strong and sturdy legs.

Metal toolbox
Use a strong, portable toolbox for all small tools so you can carry it with you.

Building

For some reason the self-supporter often seems to spend considerable time building. Sometimes this amounts to repair work to keep existing buildings going against the ravages of damp and weather. More often the self-supporter simply wants to extend his or her accommodation and storage space, whether for humans, animals, or equipment.

The cheapest and ideal way to construct a solid building as far as I'm concerned is to use mud and thatch, and don't be put off by the way it sounds. Mud is rot-proof and fire-proof, and it keeps sounds out and heat in pretty efficiently. Mud for buildings should be fairly free of organic matter, so dig it from well below the surface: say 2–3 ft (60–90 cm). Save your humus-laden topsoil for growing things! I admit it may not be so practical these days, but even if you go for the easier breeze block, your building should be simple, with large areas of unbroken wall, few and small windows, all loads well spread, and no outward thrusting roofs.

It's all in the planning

If you are building anything substantial you ought to contact your local building inspector. You may well need planning permission – which means paperwork. Do not be deterred. In most cases the building inspector can offer you very constructive advice about the pitfalls and peculiarities of local conditions. Far better to get advice early than have to knock down your prized blockwork and start again. Building is labor-intensive but much of the work is far less skilled than you might imagine. It is a great help if you have a good eye for straight lines and right angles, and you do need to be fairly systematic. The vital first step is to make sensible plans. Sensible in terms of where you are siting your building, how big you are going to make it, what materials you are going to use, and how much of a financial budget you expect to have available. Last but not least, do not take on more than you can manage: start with a small, simple project and move on from there. A great deal of the work in building consists of lugging heavy, uncomfortable material from one place to another, often lifting up a considerable height.

> The vital first step is to make sensible plans.

There is a wide choice of materials available for building. Bricks, concrete blocks, breeze blocks, wood, and metal are the most common. Local stone may be an option if you are lucky and there is an abundance of suitable building stone. Of course you can also use more outlandish materials such as straw bales or rammed earth, but for most practical self-supporters it is easier to make a trip to the home-improvement store. For a cheap, strong, and long-lasting building my preferred material is concrete block: you can face this with cement, or plaster or wood

Before you buy materials, ask around to find out which suppliers have the best quality and most reasonable prices. You will find enormous variations in both. Many suppliers will deliver much more cheaply if you buy direct from the factory. This means buying a truckload (and making sure your access is suitable for such) which probably amounts to over 1,000 blocks. One thing about blocks and building materials is that this kind of thing does not deteriorate and believe me, you will always find uses for blocks.

Make sure you think things through carefully before you tell the truck driver where to stack the blocks. The modern trucks have very long reach with their hydraulic cranes. Get the blocks as close as you can to where they will be used. Damp is the great enemy of the self-sufficient builder. If you have damp in your floors or walls you can expect all sorts of trouble from rot. So a good roof, good damp-proof course, proper membrane under any concrete slab, and well-made cavities between walls are essential. Concrete and plaster act like blotting paper and seem to have an uncanny knack for absorbing any moisture.

Roofing

Materials for roofing also come in all shapes and sizes – from thatch to artificial tiles at one extreme to corrugated iron at the other. In between you have tiles and natural slates. Each type of roofing material requires a different approach. Your choice will obviously depend on your design, your budget, and what is easily available locally.

If you are using heavy roofing materials you will need to construct a strong wooden framework. Slates and tiles are extremely heavy – this is one reason they make a good roof that will resist the ravages of the wildest winter storms. Make sure the roof is well ventilated to prevent damp rotting the timber. Use stainless steel, aluminum, or copper nails for fastening roof coverings.

Basic block laying

First load out your blocks in piles close to where they will be needed. Make sure you have a couple of spot boards for dumping mortar ready for use. Mix your cement (usually a 4-to-1 mixture of sand and cement respectively) and add some mortar plasticizer to make the cement flow better. With practice you will get the sloppiness just right: not too wet and not too dry (wetter is probably better than drier to start with). With your large trowel lay a bed of wet mortar in the place where your first block is to go. Place the block carefully in position exactly to the markers you have set up in advance (corner and line). Slide it backward and forward to ease it into the mortar. Check with your pocket level that it is level in all directions. Tap it with the lump hammer end if it refuses to settle correctly. Block after block, keep each one positioned accurately to your builder's line.

Building foundations and a wall

Here are the basic steps:

1 Mark out the foundations with posts and lines. Corners and diagonals must have exact measurements. Dig by hand or mark out with white lime for a small digger to work to. As a rule, dig to at least 2 ft (60 cm).

2 Tap your metal bars into the bottom of your trenches until their upper ends are in exactly the right place to give you the correct thickness of concrete.

3 Check your levels carefully across the tops of the metal bars. Use a long, straight piece of wood in conjunction with your long level – and be fussy: re-check several times.

4 Pour your concrete to the tops of the metal bars and spread it out carefully. Tamp it down with a long, straight piece of wood, making sure the levels are correct.

5 When the foundations have set solid, you're ready to begin your "footings." Get the corners precise before you set up lines from them for the rest of the blocks.

BUILDING FOUNDATIONS AND A WALL

1 Mark out the foundations with posts and lines. Corners and diagonals must be exact. Dig by hand or mark out with white lime for a small digger to work to. As a rule dig to at least 2 feet (60 cm).

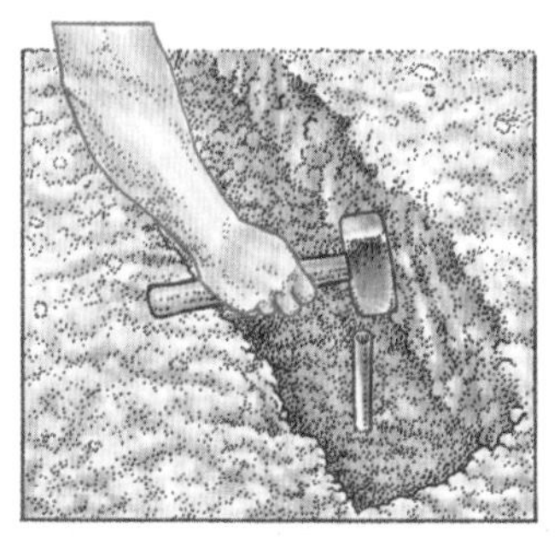

2 Tap your metal bars into the bottom of your trenches until their upper ends are in exactly the right place to give you the correct thickness of concrete.

3 Check your levels carefully across the tops of the metal bars. Use a long, straight piece of wood in conjunction with your long level – and be fussy. Mistakes at this stage will cost you time and frayed nerves later.

4 Pour your concrete to the tops of the metal bars and spread it out carefully. Tamp the concrete down with a long, straight piece of wood, making sure the levels are correct.

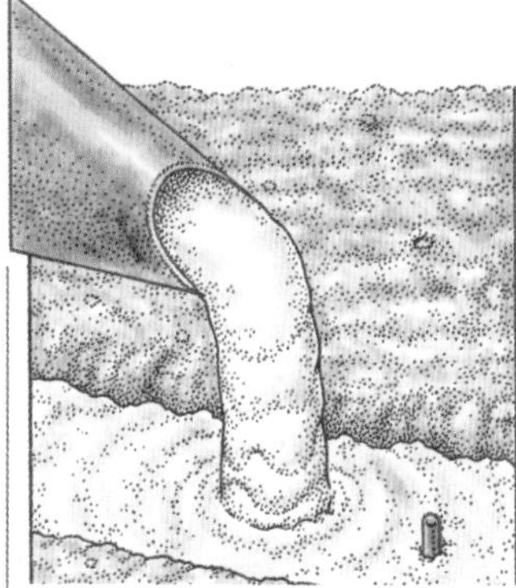

5 When the foundations have set solid, you are ready to begin your "footings." Again, make sure you have your corners marked accurately and take great care to get the corners precise before you set up lines from them for the rest of the blocks.

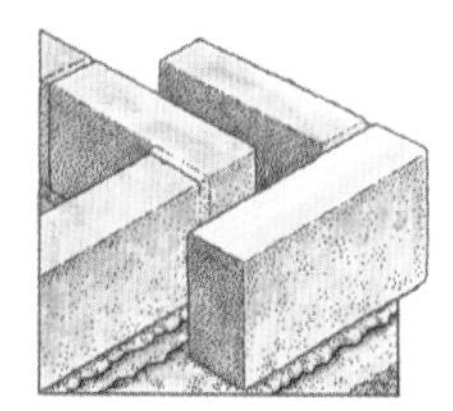

6 Place the inner course of blocks in exactly the right position inside the original blocks. Spacing must be exactly right for a substantial layer of insulation material (usually at least 4 in/10 cm). Do not forget to put in wall ties to connect the two walls every few feet. And never let mortar drop down between the walls, since this can cause damp if it bridges the gap.

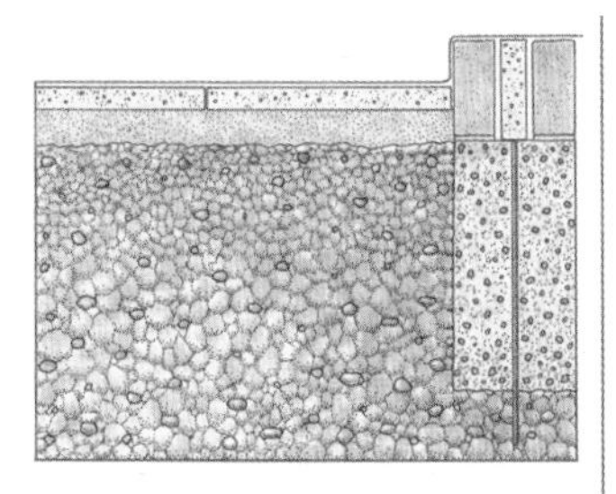

Cross section
This shows the foundations, footings, and layers of insulation. There is insulation under the concrete slab and between the two courses of blocks that form the walls. You also have a strong damp-proof membrane between the slab and the earth underneath.

7 Use reinforcing mesh to strengthen your concrete slab if the area to be covered is large. Support this several inches up with a few pieces of stone or brick.

8 Find or make a long, stiff wooden batten to extend right across the slab so you can "tamp" down the concrete to a perfect flat, level surface. Always pour a little more concrete than you need so you can pull off the excess with the batten.

9 Lay your damp course carefully over the top of the footings on a bed of wet mortar. The damp course must be well above ground level if it is to work effectively to keep out damp.

10 Split blocks to size using a lump hammer and bolster. Cut a shallow groove in each side of the block using a few blows at a time.

11 Use your long level with great care to make sure corners are exactly vertical on both sides. Don't cut corners or the project will go awry.

12 Once the corners are set, use a builder's line pulled tight between the pins at each corner. Check levels regularly using a hanging level at the middle of the line.

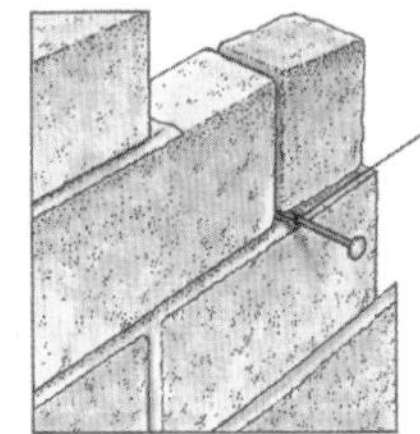

Knots and Ropework

The use of rope and string is probably older than the wheel. Their use is certainly one of the greatest of all human inventions. If string and rope came first, then knots, nets, and weaving came pretty soon afterward. Ropes and cordage are made in all sorts of clever ways by spinning and twisting strong fibers together. Hemp, linen, cotton, and wool are obvious examples of fibers used in making rope and cord. But today we are more likely to come across the modern plastic equivalents in terylene, nylon, and other so-called synthetics.

The right knot for the right job

The right knot is one that does the job it is intended for with minimum effort. One of the most satisfying moments a teacher can have on any self-sufficiency topic is the look of amazement on a student's face on seeing how years of struggling with rope can be swiftly brought to an end with the right knot. My father always used to tell the tale of how the "thief" knot was used instead of reef knots to tie up important packages. The reef knot is the simplest of knots: right over left and left over right and the sails are tied up tightly in place as the wind strengthens. It is so simple that the knot is invariably used to tie up packages. On first glance the thief knot looks just like a reef knot: left over right and right over left – certainly sufficient to deceive a would-be snooper. But there is one crucial difference: the loose ends of string in a reef knot come out both on the same side of the tight string, while the ends on a thief knot come out on opposite sides. The simple logic of the story was that you could always tell if someone had meddled with your mail if it was tied with thief knot. (Just for the record, the reef knot is often used for tying together two pieces of rope, yet it is quite unsuitable for this as it will come undone if the tension of the rope is varied or jerked. The correct knot for tying together two pieces of rope is the sheet bend, or double sheet bend if the ropes are of different thicknesses.)

Managing rope and cord

All ropes should be properly coiled when not in use. They should be kept free of knots and kinks which will, in time, weaken them. And their ends should not be allowed to fray. Ends can be kept tidy in three ways:

1 Using heat from a match or hot piece of steel if the rope is of synthetic material. Watch out if you are doing this and the rope catches fire: the molten material that drips off can cause very nasty burns.

2 Applying strong twine in the form of a whipping which binds the loose ends together over at least 1 in (2.5 cm).

3 Undertaking a back splice on three or four stranded ropes, which makes the job much more permanent.

Ropes have a nasty habit of getting twisted and knotted. There is one very simple reason for this. When a rope is made into a single coil, it has to be twisted to make it coil neatly. So if both ends are tied and the rope unravels, it can only do so with all the twists intact. As soon as tension comes off the rope and it gets loose, then it seems to tie itself up in knots. (You often have this problem with telephone cords.) Opposite are some very useful basic knots for the self-supporter.

ESSENTIAL KNOTS

Bowline
The bowline is the essential method of making a loop in rope that will not slip and will not jam – an important factor when stringing a bow (for which this knot was originally intended). If you only ever learn one knot, this should be it.

Sheetbend
The sheetbend rivals the bowline in importance. It is the definitive knot for tying together two pieces of rope under tension. The thin rope can be passed around twice for extra security to make a double sheet bend. For extra security whip the loose end of the thicker rope tight against the part under tension (the "standing" part).

Falconer's hitch
Learn to tie this knot with one hand as you have to hold the animal with the other. One pull on the loose end undoes the knot, letting a struggling animal free.

Rolling hitch
A rolling hitch is used to fasten a rope to a pole or beam. The tension on the rope should be pulling against the double turn side of the knot which jams the turns tight and thus prevents slippage.

Clove hitch
This is a quick way to take tension on a pole or post. But it does slip so cannot be used for a permanent fastening without adding a couple of half hitches.

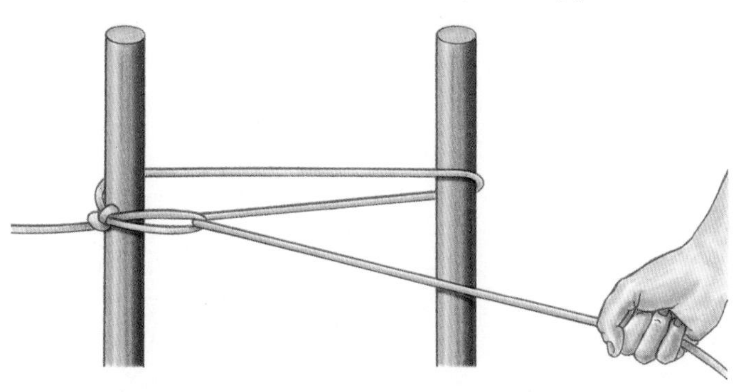

Lorryman's hitch
Use this knot to tighten up a rope already under tension. The loop acts like a block and tackle to double your force. You can then secure with a quick half hitch against the loop, or a slip half hitch if you want to undo it more easily. This knot is now largely replaced by the use of woven straps with hooks at each end and a ratchet tightener. These are powerful tools; I always keep a couple in the workshop.

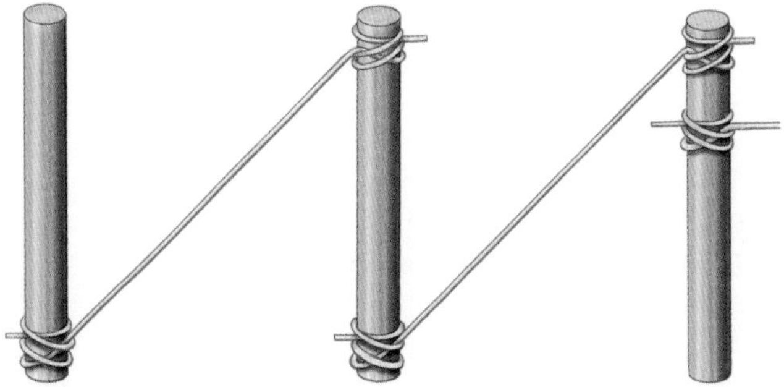

Holdfast
Driving three posts into the softest mud or soil can achieve amazing staying power with this layout of holdfast. This is the way to pull a machine or animal out of the mud if you have a block and tackle but no convenient tree to pull on. Each post should be 3 ft (1 m) long and driven well into the ground. Use rolling hitches to fasten the ropes. You can use a similar setup to anchor the ends of stock fencing before applying tension: drill holes in the center of the posts to fasten your wires.

Woodworking

Woodworking is a vital skill for the self-supporter. It may be making a small box to store apples, repairing stalls for animals, building a henhouse, or making a roof. Hardly a day will pass without some activity connected to woodworking. The modern, cordless, powered screwdrivers and drills are absolutely indispensable. Combined with crosshead posi-drive screws, these tools have revolutionized woodworking.

No longer is it necessary to drill pilot holes for wood screws. The new design of screws mean that they simply make their own holes. But remember, a screw which has no smooth length to the shank will not pull two pieces of wood tight together. Always keep a decent supply of screws and fastenings, glues, mastics, paints, and thinners. Generally, it is much easier to buy screws by the box, and you will be surprised how quickly they get used up. There is a vast range of screws and nails available from your local home-improvement store: nails are usually sold by weight.

Choosing your wood

For most of your tasks you will be selecting your wood from the home-improvement store or lumber yard. And I mean selecting: do not trust the yard man to choose timber for you or you will certainly end up with all the lengths left by others. Remember, too, that each lumber yard will have its own standards. Some managers will be very fussy about the timber they will accept from suppliers; others simply do not give quality of timber any priority and get whatever is cheapest. Try to use a local store or lumber yard that sets reasonably high standards if you can find one: it will save you a lot of trouble, even if it costs a bit more. As a quick checklist, here is what to look for in your timber.

1 You need wood that is straight. Use your good, old "mark one" eyeball, that is, inspect thoroughly for warps; you may be horrified by what you might have been fobbed off with.

2 You need wood that has no splits.

3 You need wood without many knots in the wrong places.

4 You need wood that has, if possible, the grain running in a way that will prevent future warping. This is particularly important for critical items like door posts.

5 You need wood that comes in quarter-sawn planks for any kind of quality carpentry. When you look at the grain end-on, it should run at right angles to the side of the board all the way across. Remember that the businessmen are trying to get as many planks as they can from each tree, and this is a much more important consideration for them than cutting for stability.

QUICKFIT CLAMPS

A quick and easy (and lighter) alternative to the traditional vise, quickfit clamps allow you to clamp pieces of wood firmly and quickly to your bench (or simply a large plank if you are working on a building site), and you can clamp pieces together easily to assist with fixing. The one-hand quick-release mechanism is very handy when you have several tasks on the go at the same time. I also keep a much larger pair of what are called "sash cramps," which I tend to use to hold together large pieces of work during fixing and gluing. Like all tools, these do not deteriorate over time, so having a couple to hand is usually a good investment.

ESSENTIAL FIXINGS

Here are the essential screws and nails needed for any woodworking projects. Keep a selection of these handy in your tool box.

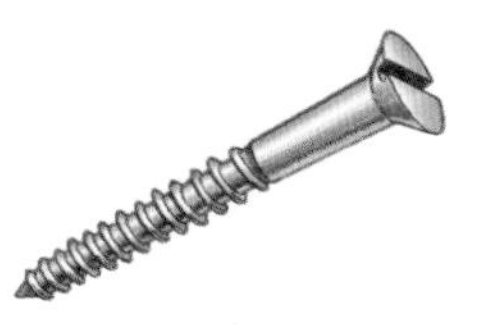

Countersunk wood screw

Traditional fixing screw for woodwork. It needs a hole drilled first to avoid splitting the wood plus countersink to recess head. Use with a screw-cup for added strength.

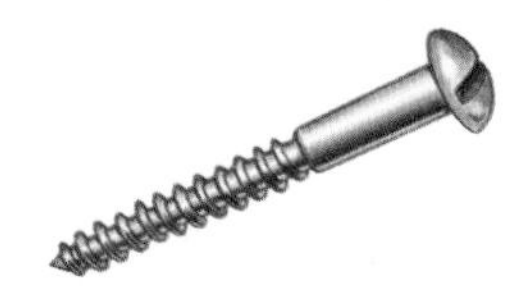

Roundhead screw

Another traditional fixing which requires a hole drilled first and leaves the head proud.

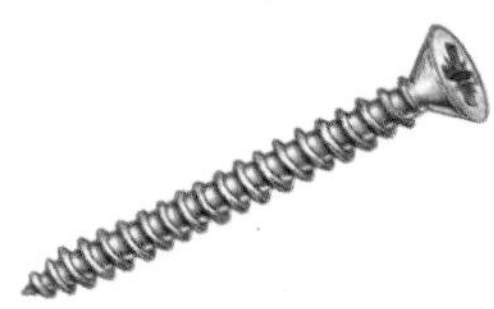

Posi-drive screw

Now almost universally used with cordless, powered screwdrivers. The beauty of these screws is that no pilot hole is required. The fixing will also grip tight even if screwed into endgrain wood.

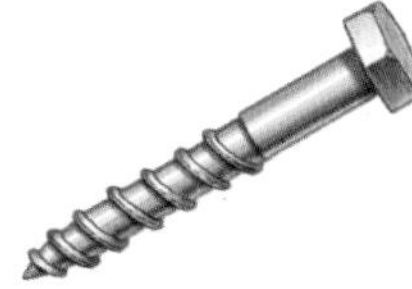

Coach screw

The coach screw is a very strong fixing for outdoor work. It requires a pilot hole and must be tightened with a wrench. Use the galvanized versions for long life.

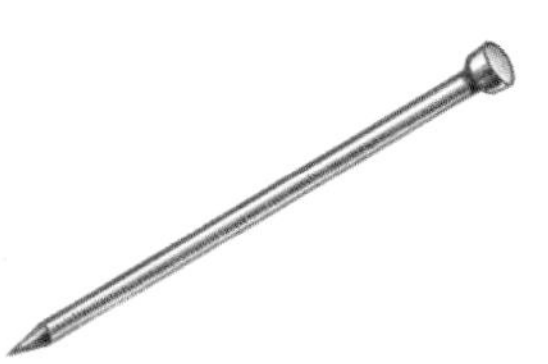

Lost head nail

The "lost" element refers to the small round head that is easily knocked into the work, especially useful for floorboards. You might well need to use a nail punch to push it below the surface and make it invisible.

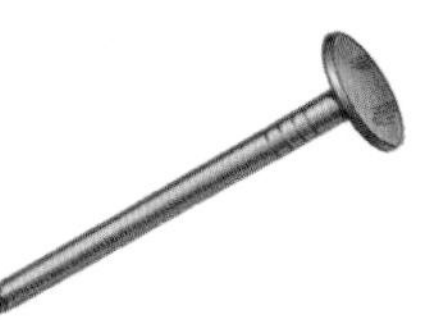

Clout-galvanized nail

A nail for external work such as for fixing roofing battens. These nails also provide a cheap way to fasten slates. Clouts come in all shapes and sizes – both length and thickness. Make sure you know exactly which size you need, especially if fixing roofing where you do not want sharp ends going through your felting.

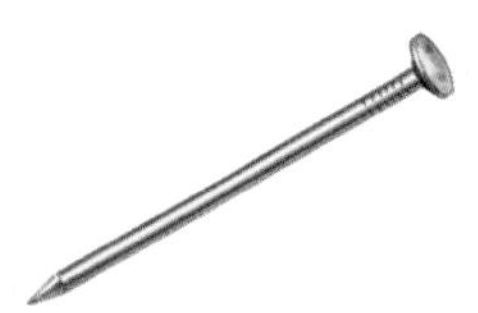

Flathead wire nail

The standard nail for fixing. It also comes in galvanized form for outdoor use. You can't have too many of these handy fixers.

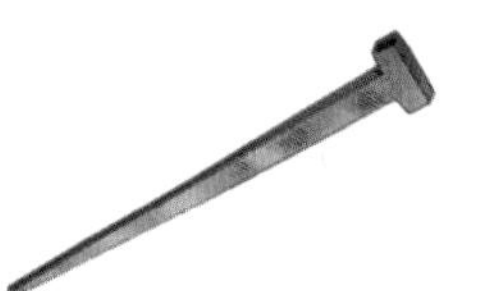

Cut clasp nail

Often used for fastening floorboards, this square section nail is excellent for avoiding splits in the wood.

Roofing nail

A heavy, twisted and galvanized nail which will not pull out of roofing in wind or gales. Use for roof sheeting.

Masonry nail

Toughened steel nail made for fastening directly into masonry. Can be difficult to use: watch out for sparks and splinters.

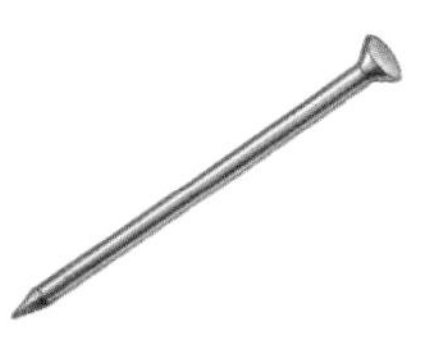

Ribbed flooring nail

A nail used to fix hardboard and chipboard flooring down so it will not loosen and squeak under use.

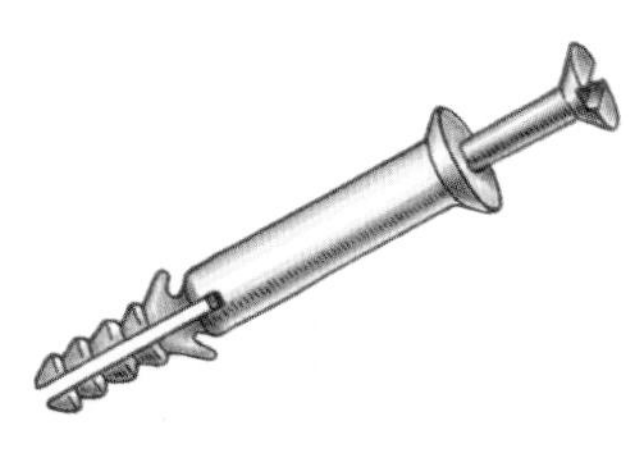

Anchor fixing

A wallplug-type fixing in many sizes which is simply hammered home into the correct sized hole made by a masonry drill.

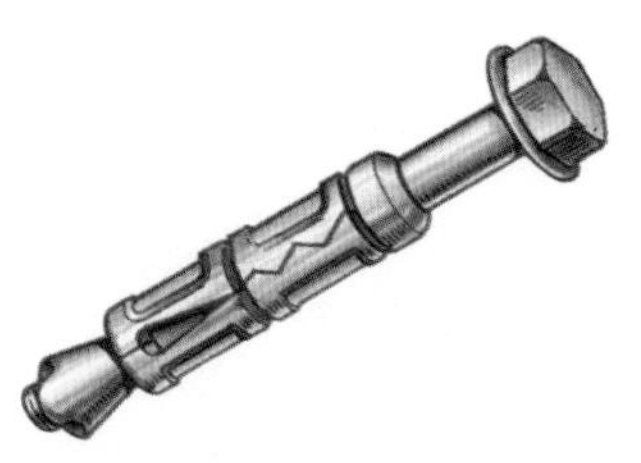

Expanding masonry bolt

The ultimate fixing for fastening into stone or masonry. Tremendous load-bearing capabilities. An expanding masonry bolt requires the correct size of masonry bit to make a good joint.

DOWEL JOINTS

For a neat, strong, and relatively easy joint between two pieces of wood, you can now buy dowel kits from most good hardware stores. The kit has short lengths of different diameter hardwood doweling rod, a set of wood drills exactly the right size to take each size of doweling rod, plus a small plug cutter so you can seal and disguise doweling holes if you need to. To achieve workable dowels, holes of exactly the right size must be drilled in each piece to be joined.

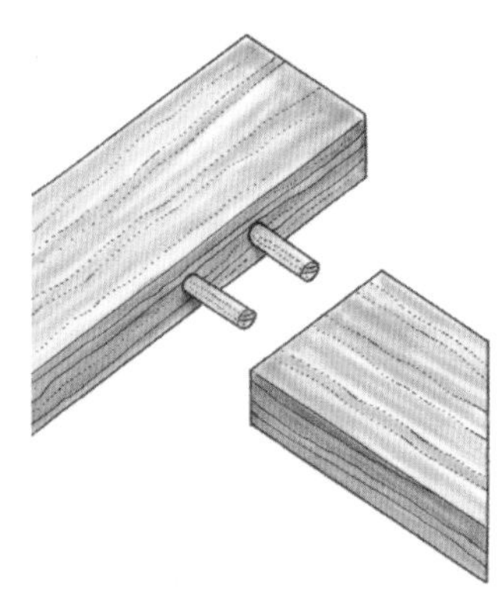

Positioning must be exact so the dowels (round pins) match up in correct alignment within the glued joint.

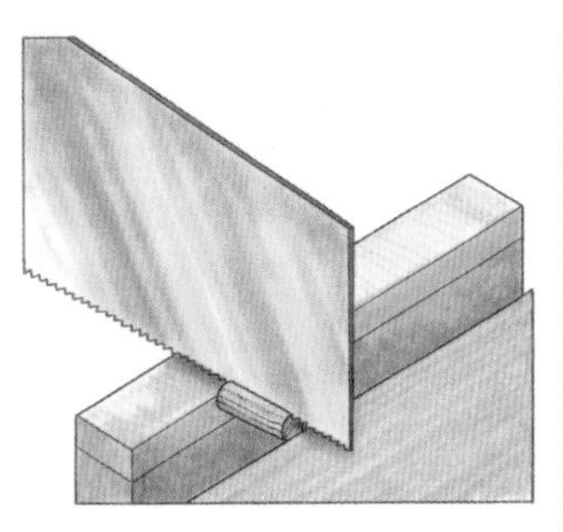

1 Cut wood to the exact size for a flush fit against the piece to be joined. Use a set square and make sure you cut the correct side of the drawn line.

2 Mark the center of the end grain with a sharp scribe.

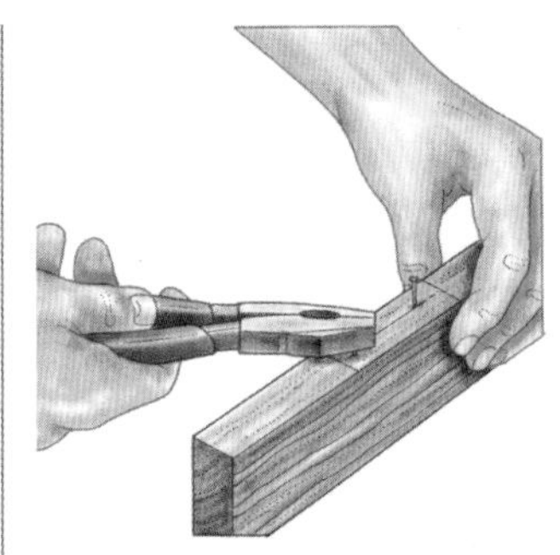

3 Drill holes in the piece to be joined and insert dowels with glue to half their length.

4 Now marry up the fixed dowels to the end grain of the marked piece. Mark centers exactly and use a set square to drop down to center line.

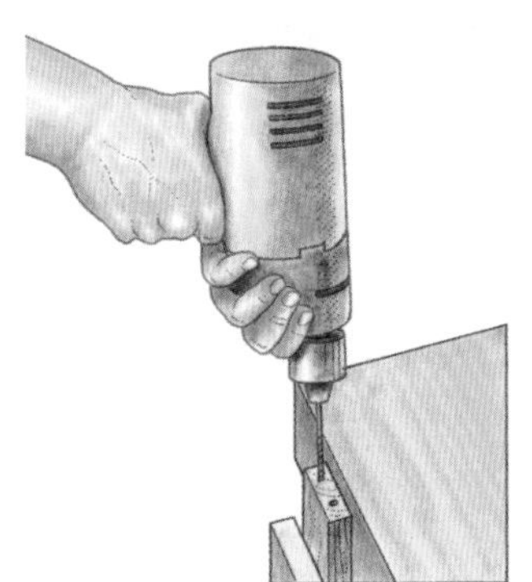

5 Now drill out the two final dowel holes, taking care to keep the drill perfectly perpendicular to the end grain.

6 Hand-join the two bits of wood and tap the dowels home with a little glue, and your joint is complete. Clamp if necessary until the glue is set.

MORTISE-AND-TENON JOINTS

The basic joint for the "joiner" who graduates from using dowels is the mortise-and-tenon joint. The joint, or variants of it, would be useful for tables or gates. With a little practice and care you will soon get the hang of it and produce strong and neat results. Accurate marking out is vitally important, and you must learn to decide whether to cut lines off or cut inside them. Think about this carefully or your tolerances will be too great. Always use a good glue to finish the job.

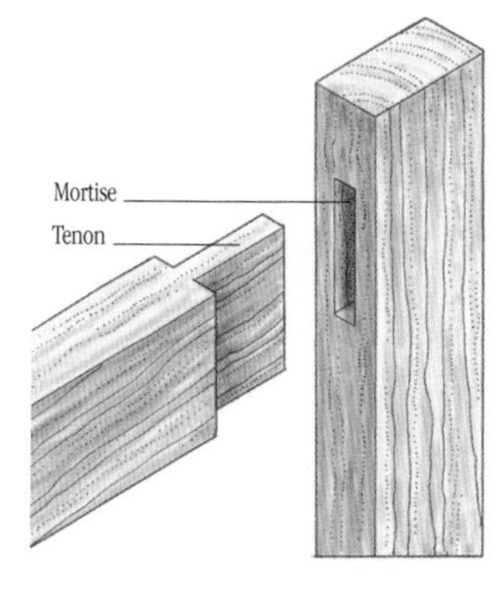

A slot (mortise) is cut into the siderail exactly the correct length and width to fit a "tenon" cut out of the endgrain of the crossrail.

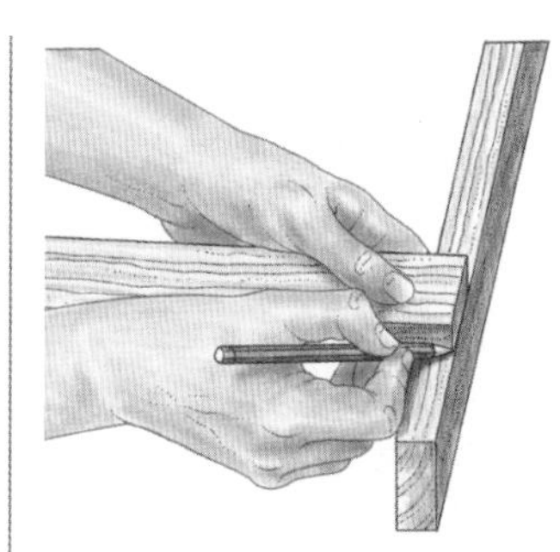

1 Mark out the length of the mortise carefully using the crossrail. Use a set square throughout the task to extend lines across the rail.

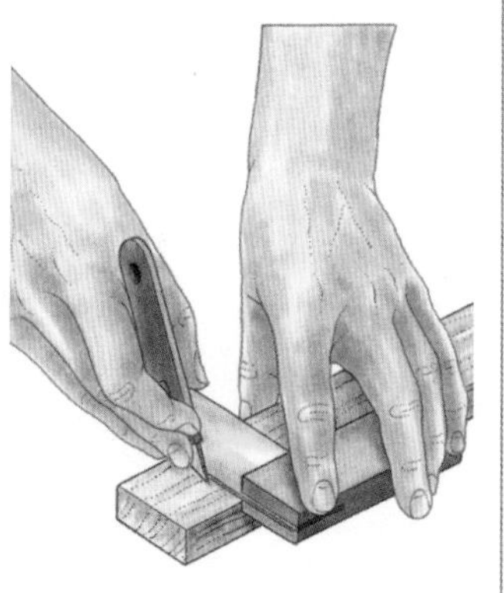

2 Mark off the length of the tenon (again, with a set square). Don't make it too long or you may go through the back of the mortise on the siderail.

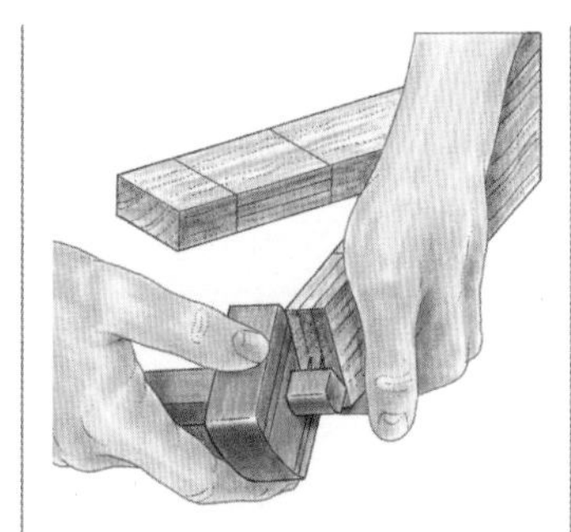

3 Carefully scribe the marks for the edges of the tenons at each end of the crossrails. Cut these out accurately with a sharp saw and a firm vise. Pare down with a sharp chisel if the saw goes awry.

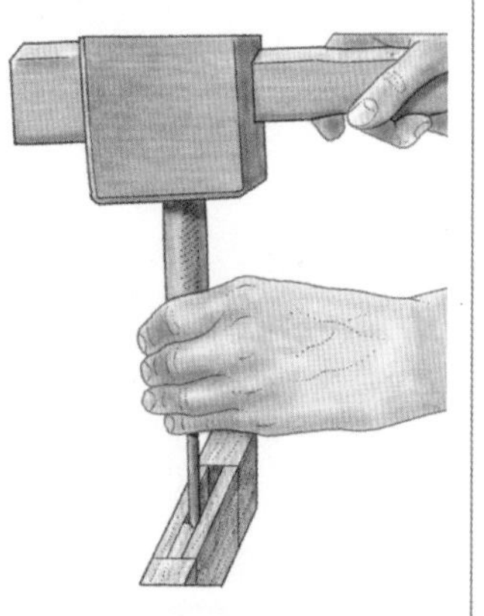

4 Mark out the correct width for the mortise. With a sharp chisel and wooden mallet, cut it out bit by bit. The mortise is better too small, than too large.

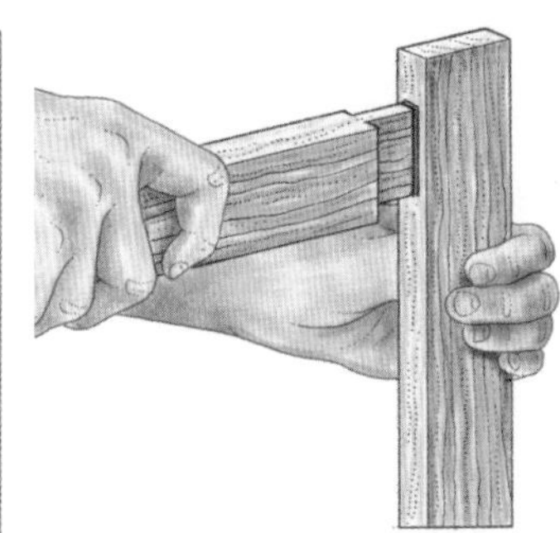

5 Offer up the tenon into the mortise to check for a tight fit. Use your chisel again if you need to perfect the fit. You will see why a smaller mortise is better.

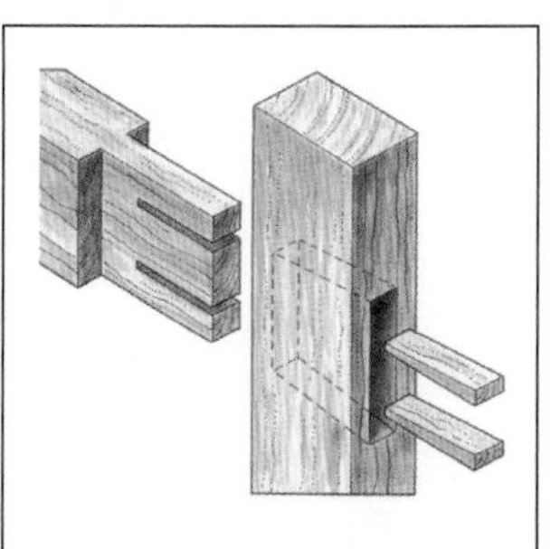

THROUGH MORTISE-AND-TENON JOINT

Mortise right through the siderail for a really strong joint. Cut slots into the tenon; make correct-size long wedges to hammer in from the outside when the joint is positioned.

MAKING A BOX

This is a simple but effective method of constructing a strong wooden box which will come in handy for all sorts of useful jobs on your self-sufficient holding. Use good quality plywood and well chosen 6–in x 1–in (15–cm x 2.5–cm) pine planking. For best results add round beading to the inside and up the insides of the corners.

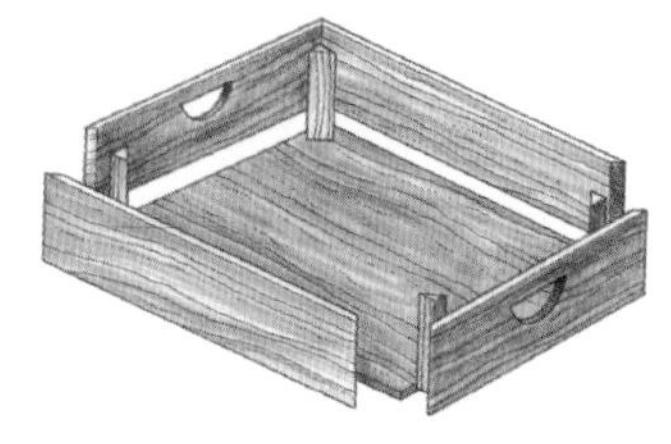

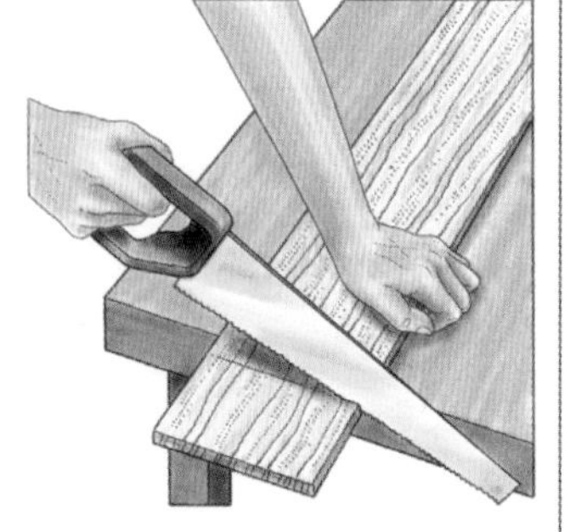

1 Cut your 6-inch (15-cm) planking to accurate lengths, using a set square to make sure the ends are exactly at 90 degrees to the sides. Next, cut the plywood base to the correct size.

2 When you cut the plywood base, make sure again that you have corners which are accurate right angles. Cut the base too big rather than too small so you can plane down later.

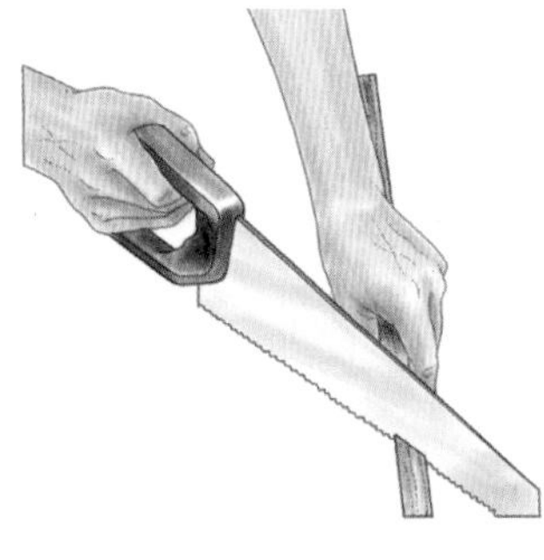

3 Take off any rough edges with sandpaper or a sharp plane. This applies to saw edges as well as the sides of the planking. You'll need to apply some pressure as you sandpaper.

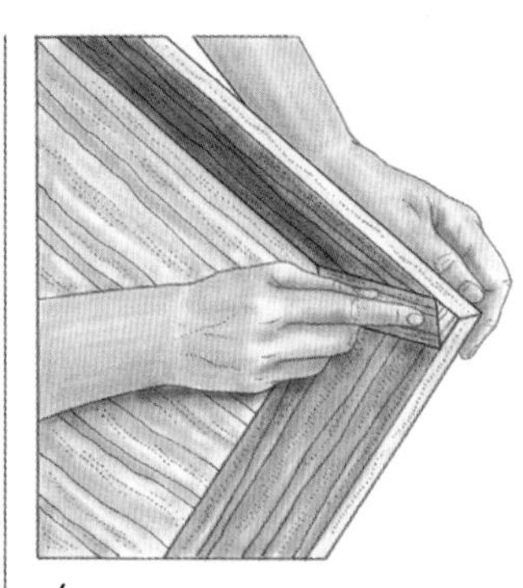

4 Now screw the ends of the box on to the plywood base. Use countersunk screws either galvanized or brass for outdoor use. These are purpose-made for weathering.

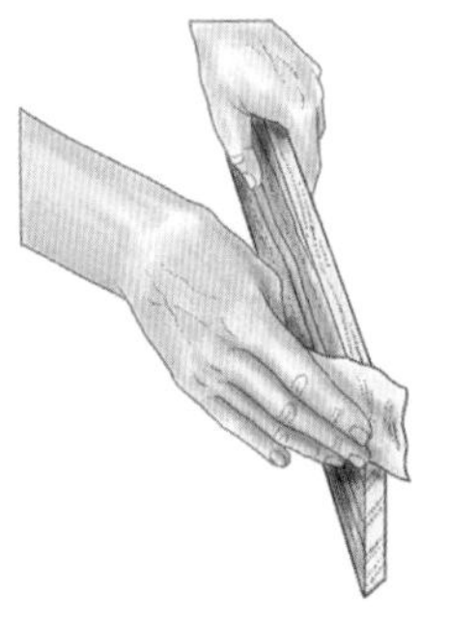

5 The sides can now be screwed into the end grain of the ends which have already been fixed. Posi-drive screws work well for this and will pull themselves into the wood.

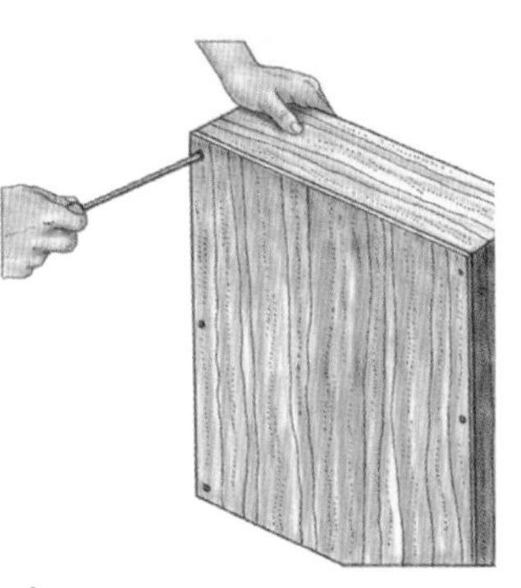

6 Make sure corners fit exactly and sand off any rough or overlapping edges. You have to work quite hard at this as the corners are quite tricky to make contact with. Complete screwing on the base and use plenty of screws to make the job effective. Battery-powered screwdrivers are best for this. Cut handle holes if necessary using a drill and a power jigsaw.

7 Cut hand holes as needed. First use a drill to make a hole large enough to accept the blade of the jigsaw. Then carefully cut out the hand holes, smoothing down with sandpaper afterward to finish off.

TURNING A BOWL ON A LATHE

These pictures show a bowl being turned on a simple lathe powered by electricity, but you can turn a bowl in the same way on a treadle lathe, or, rather laboriously, on a chair bodger's pole lathe.

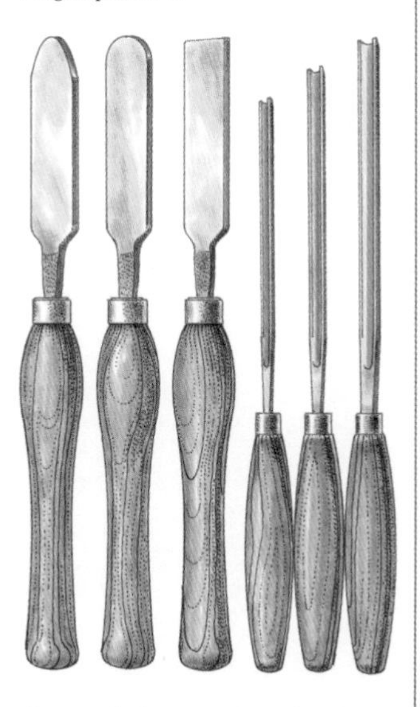

If you use the latter, you must replace the stock with a rod fixed to a chuck to which the bowl can be attached. For the heavy work of removing unwanted wood you need three gouges of differing thicknesses (*above right*), and for the more delicate shaping and smoothing you need scrapers (*above left*). Never press hard with any tool, particularly a gouge. If they stick, you are in trouble. Keep your tools sharp.

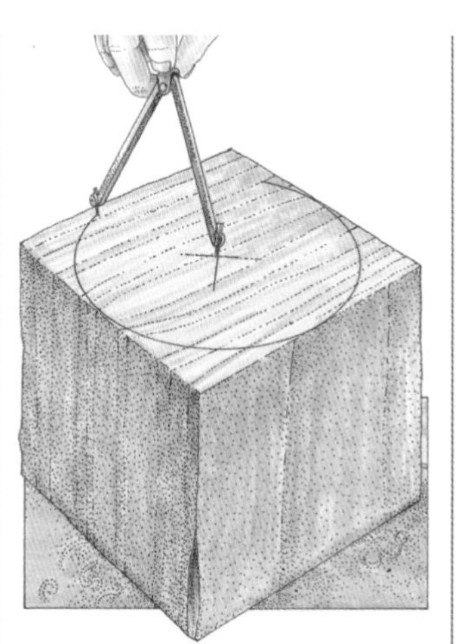

1 Take a block of wood, mark the center with a cross, and draw a circle with a compass slightly larger – say ¼ in (6 mm) – than the intended diameter of your bowl.

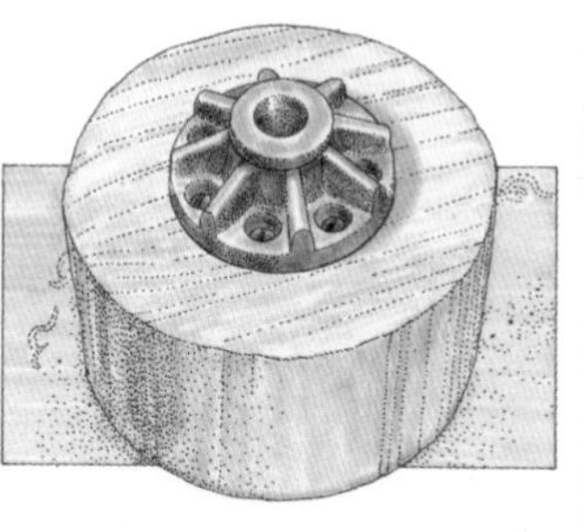

2 Saw roughly around your circle. Find the midpoint for your chuck and screw it on evenly. The base of your bowl must be thicker than the screws are long.

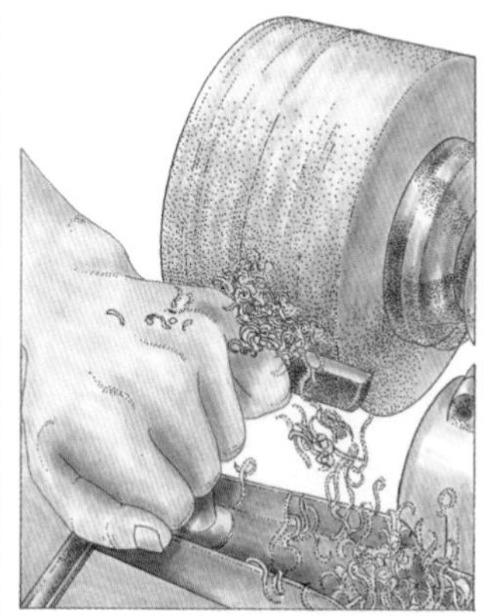

3 Round off edges with a large gouge.

4 Shape the outside with a smaller gouge. Use the handrest and keep the gouge moving slowly along it.

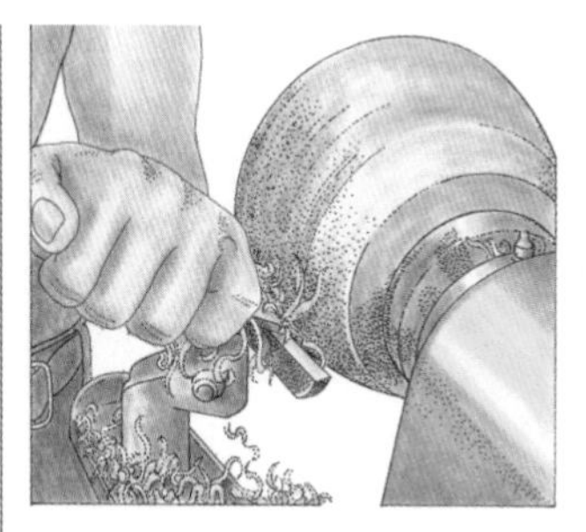

5 Smooth off the outside with your scrapers. Then, keeping the bowl on the lathe, rub with sandpaper, which will give the wood a gloriously smooth finish.

6 Move the handrest to work on the inside. The unbreakable rule for hollowing wood on a lathe is: begin at the outside and work towards the center. Start with a gouge, then scrape with rounded scrapers only, and finally sandpaper it smooth. Remove the chuck from the lathe, unscrew it, and fill the holes with plastic wood. Polish it all with beeswax and glue felt on the bottom.

Basketry

You can go for a walk in the country with no tools other than a sharp knife and come back with a basket. Traditionally, one-year shoots from willow (called osiers) are used for the strongest baskets, but you can use other materials, such as straw or rushes too. Osiers are grown by a very simple process of pushing stout lengths of willow into the ground. These should be about 1 ft (30 cm) long and at least ½ in (1.5 cm) thick, planted about 18 in (45 cm) apart with rows 2 ft (60 cm) apart. These will sprout roots at one end and rods at the other. The rods are cut in winter when the sap is down. Sort the rods into lengths after harvesting. You can let them dry naturally, you can strip the bark, or you can boil to obtain different finishes. Rods are tied into "bolts" (bundles) for sale.

Basic basketry

Good willow should be smooth and straight, with nice thin tips. It can only be worked when it has been soaked. Choosing rods the correct size for what you need is more critical than you might think. Even small variations in thickness can allow the stronger rods to dominate the work.

The base of your basket, the "slath," can be round, oval, or square. The base is the foundation for your work and must be firm and well-shaped. Choose strong, smooth rods and use "pairing" to form them into the shape required. The uprights are then pushed firmly into the base to begin weaving the sides. To make uprights for a square basket you must cut away the willow at the butt of the stake to make what is called a "slype."

Otherwise simply use the traditional bodkin (*see opposite*) to insert a stake into the weave on each side of each stick of the base. Push the stake right to the center of the base if you can. If the stakes are too stiff then you will have to prick them—that is to say, make a small crease with your thumb or the back of a knife at the point about ¼ in (½ cm) from the base edge where they are to turn up. Now tie the ends of the stakes together as you prepare to weave. The first few rows of your weave (the "upsett") are critical to the shape of the finished basket. The weave used for this is called the "waling." It is vital to get the stakes into the correct positions with this weave and you will probably use a rapping iron to firm them down. You always finish a round with the tip ends.

Borders A good border is critical. We show one border here (another common border is the 3-rod-behind-1). Once you have three pairs of rods facing towards you from three consecutive spaces you simply take the right-hand rod of the left-hand set in front of the next upright and behind the next. You can then bend the first upright down beside it and continue the sequence.

Handles A bow handle is made by forcing a stout rod of the correct length down into the weave on each side of a basket. Use a bodkin and grease to ease the sharpened rod into position as far down the weave as you can. Now cover the handle bow with thin rods, taking four at a time, pushing them in besides the handle. Wind them around the bow three times as you go to the other side where they can be woven in. Repeat this process with another four rods from the opposite side. Add more rods until the handle is evenly covered.

BASKET-MAKING EQUIPMENT
The bodkin is a heavy iron rod, tapered down to a pointed end to part the weave in order to insert a new rod. The grease horn stores the bodkin when not in use. Use cheesecloth soaked in tallow for the grease. A curved knife with a sharp point is really useful for cutting scalloms. Weights are heavy chunks of metal to keep work in place. The rapping iron is a heavy flat strip of metal used to tap down each row of the weave. The screwblock is a clamp used to hold weaves flat, particularly for making bases. For a measure use a rigid steel or retractable wooden rule. The pruning shears are for cutting rods.

As for the rods, depending on the type of basket you want, as a rule of thumb work with the following lengths: 3.3 ft (1 m) for small baskets, 4–5 ft (1.2–1.6 m) for shopping baskets, and 8 ft (4 m) for large items. Sort into four groups of matching thickness.

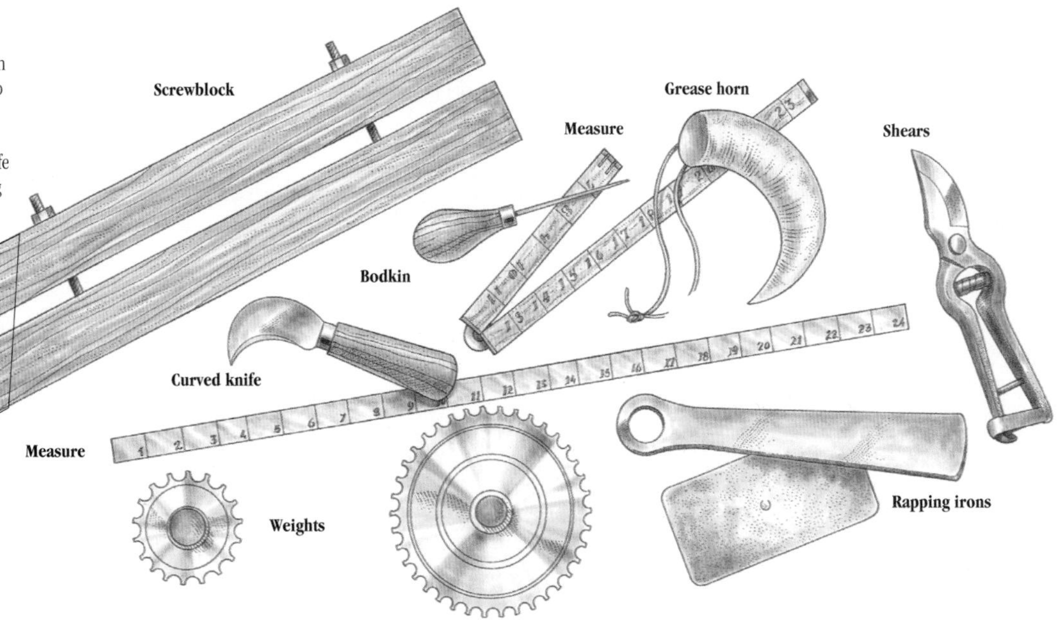

To make a twisted rope handle, take four rods long enough to reach across the handle twice with some to spare. Slype the first one and insert it beside one end of the handle. Twist and wind the rod five times around the handle to the other side. Pass the rod through or under the border and bring it back keeping the twist beside the first. Tuck the loose end through the weave to keep it in place and repeat the process with each successive rod. Twist the loose ends of the weavers together and weave them under the border to complete the handle.

STRUCTURE OF A WILLOW ROD

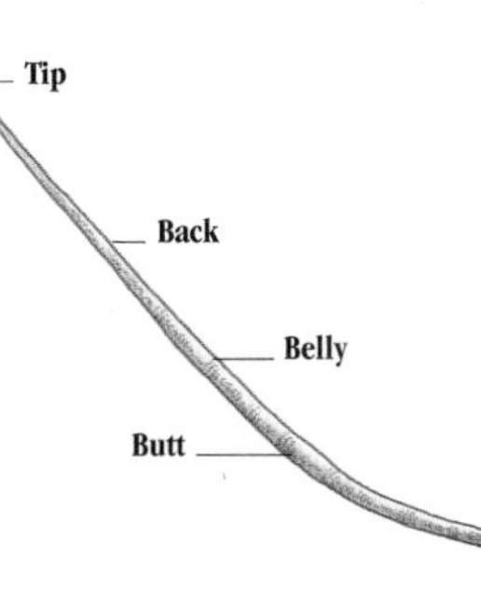

MAKING A HARD BASKET
You need three different types of rod: eight short, stout rods for the "slath," or base; a number of strong but bendy rods for your side stakes; and some weavers—the long, thin whippy rods that hold the basket together. Side stakes should be about 8 in (20 cm) longer than the intended height of the basket. Weavers can be any length (and varying thickness), but long enough to go around the basket once. Soak all your rods for an hour before using them, in a container big enough to hold them all. They might need to be weighed down to keep them under water.

CHAPTER SEVEN

THINGS YOU NEED TO KNOW

"Well, what have we learned? What has altered since I wrote The Fat of the Land? The first big change is that now we are not alone. When we found ourselves becoming self-sufficient in food we were probably the only family in England living in this way. Now there are hundreds doing it – and tens of thousands who would like to. Other changes are the soaring price of land, the drying-up of the empty cottages [to rent], of cheap horse-drawn and other old implements and the even greater intrusion of the State into every corner of private life.

But the thing that I have learned is that it was a mistake to try to live like this alone. We have tried to do too much, have worked too hard, have forgotten what it is to sit and listen to music in the evening, or read something for pleasure, or to engage for hours in amusing and interesting conversation."

John Seymour *The Fat of the Land* 1976

Becoming a Self-Supporter

I hope that by the time you have reached this final chapter you will have found at least one or two activities which inspire you to make a change in the way you live. Our chief experience in our courses with those who have a determination to change their lives has been one of great success. But often this success does not come in the package you are dreaming of or expecting. It is the very fact that one door has been closed and another opened that changes everything. Growing your own food and managing the essentials of life (bread, beer, wine, jam, pickles, etc.) is a very satisfying way to get more enjoyment from life.

This book is primarily aimed at those who will continue to live in a village, town, or city but I would not be honest if I did not admit to a belief that getting a little more space in the country is really the ultimate goal. A rural way of life is particularly satisfying for those with young children because there is so much useful work they can do and enjoy as part of the family team. It is a way of life which means you no longer have to wait in traffic jams or rush off to the gym in your leisure time. It is way of life where the pressures of debt repayment and career demands simply disappear. So here are a few pointers you may find useful if you are considering making a major change.

Choosing a smallholding

The first challenge for those searching after the "good life" is to decide just exactly what you want to do. Do you like animals and all the excitements and worries they bring? How much physical work do you want to do? Will you have the scope to have extra accommodation so that you can take on volunteers to help with manual work? There are excellent world wide volunteer schemes where bed, board, and practical experience are given in return for work which can be a great help. (Organizations such as the Working Weekends on Organic Farms, now called WWOOF, are one of many such schemes—check out the websites.) And how much land do you really want? Do you like building work and doing odd jobs around the house that might be perfect for renovating an older property?

On the financial side of things you must never expect to make your fortune by growing food. Governments in many countries Europe have done everything they can to make this virtually impossible. If you are going to move to part-time work, then you will want to avoid taking on debt like the proverbial plague itself. So cash in your town home together with your big mortgage and buy a smallholding well within your means.

Get hands-on experience

All those above questions are important—and even if you think you know what you want, most people have dreams that are rather too large for their experience, skills, and endurance. So it is a really good idea to get some hands-on experience before you take the plunge. You can do this either by taking one of the various courses on offer or by becoming a volunteer yourself and visiting and helping out on other people's smallholdings (as described above). This is really an invaluable experience—there is much to be gained by learning from others, be it the tips and tricks, or the mistakes, and virtually nothing to be lost.

Putting the strategic questions to one side, we can say that you probably need around one acre (over half a hectare) of decent land to make any effective attempt at producing a good quantity of your own food. And if you buy more than 4 acres (1.5 hectares), then you will have to accept the responsibilities of fencing and managing a large area. You can, of course, put a good part of your land into woodlands but even this needs to be fenced and managed.

And when you do buy your dream farm don't forget that you can (and must) keep the land under control. The simplest way to do this if you do not have grazing animals is to cut all the grass (weeds, brambles etc.) just once or twice a year. Do this preferably in June and September with a good sharp scythe. You can make a bit of hay or compost the cuttings. Over time you will find all the nasty weeds are eliminated and the whole affair of creating a garden with more time and experience on your hands becomes that much easier. City people often forget that in the countryside nature is vibrant and often in turmoil. Good food attracts many and varied beasts and bugs whose antennae and senses are finely tuned to such things. Walls, fences, and nets may be needed to keep such pests away—and pests might include the neighbor's herd of cattle and the "delightful" kiddies who come to visit. There is constant interaction, nay warfare, going on out there in the garden and you will want to make sure your troops keep on top.

Choosing the right place

Once you have given some careful thought to the things you want to do then you have to find the right place. There are two different ways to approach this: either buying a bare site on the one hand or buying an older property to improve on the other. In either case the position, aspect, type of land, history of cultivation, shelter, and mature trees will be very important factors to consider. We should consider these general factors in turn.

Position

You will probably want to be fairly close to a reasonable shopping center without being so close as the encourage thieving and vandalism from the town hooligans. Some five miles (eight kilometers) is probably about right—and if you are further than eight miles (12 km) or thereabouts then you will end up doing a lot of driving to fetch supplies, ferry kids to friends, and follow your own social life.

Climes and aspect

Rainfall and weather conditions will also vary considerably from one area to another. Generally west means wet, east means dry. High up means windy, cold, and wet—and take care, even a mere 200 ft (60 m) or so can make a big difference. Low down may be shaded and badly drained. Your ideal site will be gently sloping towards the south, preferably with some shelter to the north and east. You are unlikely to be interested in a north facing site unless there are other very important benefits. This is because sunshine is so important to successful growing in a northern climate.

Type of land

If you have ever tried using a spade to dig wet clay then you will not need to be told twice about the importance of soil type. Clay is hard work but productive if well drained.

Sandy, light soil is a joy for carrots but can be difficult in hot, dry weather and may need a lot of compost added. Good quality loam that has been fallow (uncultivated) for a number of years may be best *(see pp.22-23 for soil types)*.

Take a spade with you when you visit your potential site and dig down in a few likely spots to see what's actually down there. Also look out for rushes anywhere on the site as they will surely indicate wet areas or poor drainage. If possible, visit the site in winter especially after wet weather and see if water is lying on the land.

Find out what has been growing on the land in recent years and how it has been cultivated. If land has been intensively used for cereals or sugar beet production, this is likely to have destroyed much of the inherent fertility and

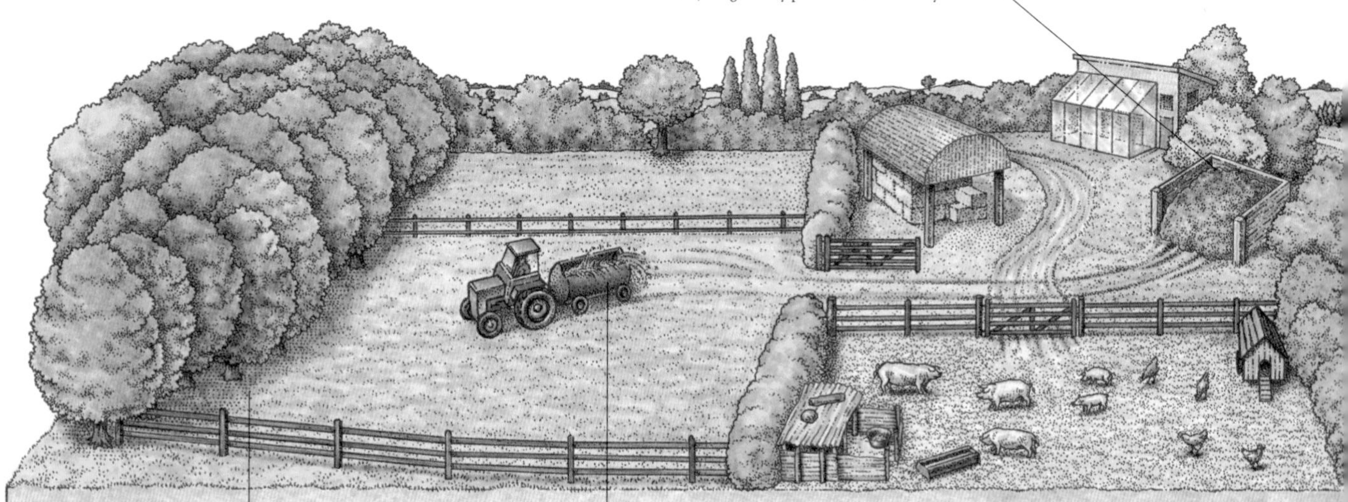

soil structure. Old, well managed grassland would be best—with as few deep-rooted weeds as possible (i.e. thistles docks, ragwort, nettles, and the like).

The existence and location of hedges and mature trees will have a large effect on the comfort and micro-climate of your site. Mature trees are a very rare luxury these days and you want them on the north or east side of your site.

SUSTAINABLE LIVING ON LAND

By understanding the nitrogen cycle and nature's law of return we can steadily build up the fertility and production from our land. A healthy soil is the prime agent which we depend upon to convert natural wastes into fertility and food. But a healthy soil needs careful management and a constant supply of nutrients from human and animal wastes. A healthy soil must not be poisoned by strong chemicals or fed artificially with factory-made nutrients. If the soil is to increase in depth and fertility, then it must contain good quantities of vegetable material (humus). Without humus from decaying plant material, the soil will either blow away or wash away in winter rains.

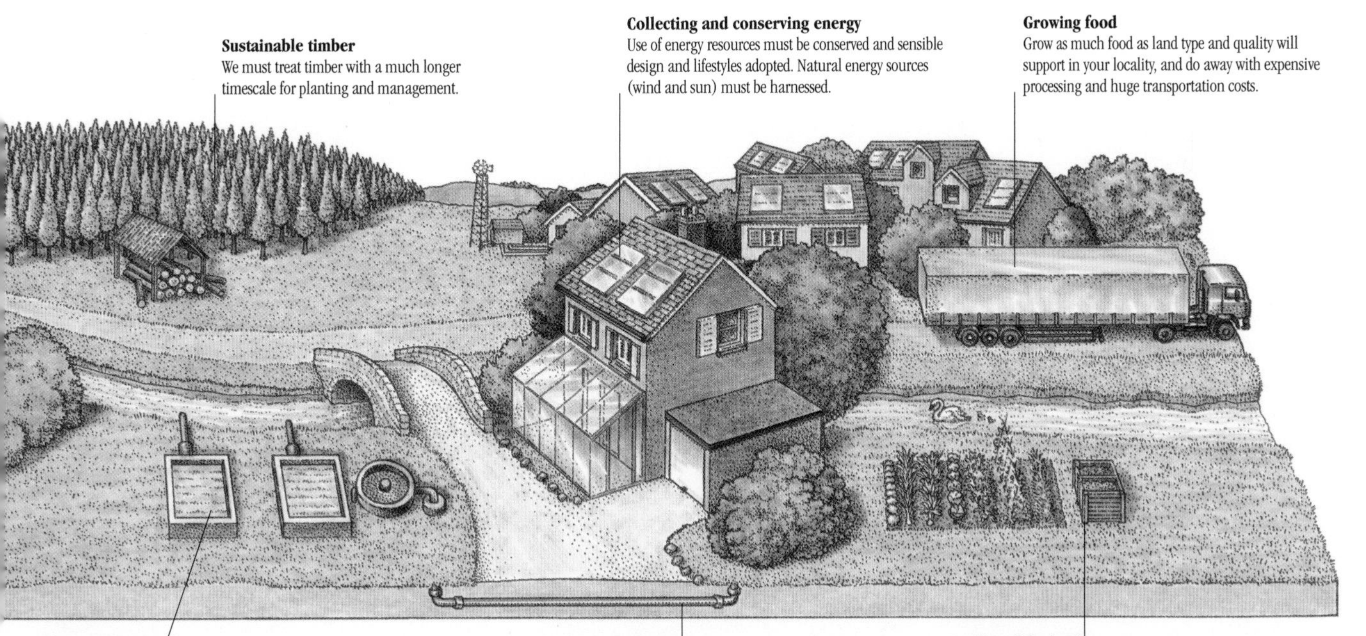

Sustainable timber
We must treat timber with a much longer timescale for planting and management.

Collecting and conserving energy
Use of energy resources must be conserved and sensible design and lifestyles adopted. Natural energy sources (wind and sun) must be harnessed.

Growing food
Grow as much food as land type and quality will support in your locality, and do away with expensive processing and huge transportation costs.

Nitrate-free water
By careful use of organic methods we prevent serious contamination of drinking water caused by farming's massive dependence on highly soluble cheap chemical nitrates.

Dual water systems
Current use of expensively treated drinking water for flushing wastes, washing cars, or watering must be stopped by creating dual water systems to collect "gray" water for re-use.

Fertility of the land
The challenge of constantly increasing fertility must be one of organic farming's highest objectives. Using chemicals for short-term profit can only damage long-term fertility.

Generally you want a site which sees plenty of sun in the south and west—and it is a bonus if you can see the setting sun from your dining room window. We have looked at general factors for choosing the best site for you in the likelihood that it will be either a bare site or an established older property such as a farmhouse with outbuildings. Let's now look at those specific two options in more detail, and the number of other factors you might need to take into consideration.

Option 1: The bare site

A bare site is unlikely to have the charm of an older property. But equally it won't have too many hidden snags. You can more or less see—and visualize—what you are in for. Don't forget that the location of the main dwelling needs to fit into a plan for the garden and field structure. For example, if you are going to have a pigsty, then you want this to be downwind of the dwelling house—while at the same time you should also be looking to locate your composting area away from the house. On the other hand you will probably want a space to the south of the house for a grassed area for recreation, whilst you will want good growing areas reasonably close on the east side for salad crops and possibly herbs that you want near to the kitchen. The orchard and the chickens can be further away from the house, and so on… the list and options gets longer.

There is much more that can be said about the planning of your farm, but we do not have space to do it justice here. It is wise to take advice from someone with experience just as soon as you have a really good idea what it is you want to do.

Option 2: Established, older property

It is still possible, but not easy, to find an old farmhouse with outbuildings in a more or less abandoned condition. This generally happens after an old "local" has died or maybe a farmer has moved out into a modern home. Many such properties will not be on any realtor's books and you will have to do your own research.

If an old building has sound roofing then you may have a bargain. But more than likely the venture will only be possible for those who have very deep pockets or plenty of their own time to devote to sorting things out. Old buildings are the very devil to sort out—and often full of very nasty surprises.

Don't be put off however by the doomsters. If you do have the enthusiasm and the place feels right, then you may find yourself with new skills as a builder that you never expected. We know a couple of families who left the city to grow and farm but actually found the rebuilding work much more interesting at the end of the day!

Working with others

Whatever the physical size and shape of your smallholding you will also need to think about working with others. Your neighbors will be a first port of call and their attitude will have a big impact on your activities. You will also want to discover whether other like-minded souls are living in the area. This is important particularly if you are thinking of having livestock. Almost certainly you will be looking for somebody to help look after these if you want to go on holiday or be away from your smallholding for any time. In a town job you meet your workmates easily through socializing at the workplace but it is not quite so easy in the countryside, and you will have to make a conscious effort to build a network of useful contacts. Never lose the opportunity of doing a favor for your neighbors; in the countryside this will always be paid back many times over.

The last word

We may hoe our potatoes, pickle our beets, drink our wonderful homemade beer, and many other splendid things beside, but be in no doubt that Mother Nature, and our mysterious universe, will always have the last laugh. Many and various are the great civilizations that have come and gone before us. Many and various are the bright souls who have tried to put their worlds to rights over a fine glass of wine around the supper tables of history. But the great cultural juggernauts of civilizations cannot be so easily diverted from their journeys toward oblivion. Are we now in another such juggernaut without even a brake let alone a steering wheel?

Can we make of sense of the views of the so-called experts, the great and the good, the pundits, prophets, and politicians? The planet is getting warmer, our wilderness is disappearing, more and more species are becoming extinct, and the violence of war is a regular feature of our daily news. Politicians will try to persuade us to burn less carbon and have fewer children. Pressure groups will clamor for more donations to protect threatened species. Religious leaders will pray for us to be more spiritual. Corporations will greenwash their race to exploit the planet's resources as quickly as possible. Banks will smile sweetly while continuing to direct the world's resources so they make the biggest money profits. Many of us will do our bit to save energy and recycle our piles of waste and packaging as we try to salve our consciences about the growing gap between the rich and the poor. But still the juggernaut of our consumer civilization will roll remorselessly onward.

The broader perspective

It's not exactly a pleasant prospect! But just for a moment take let's take a broader perspective. Every night if we look up to the stars we see billions of tons of hydrogen furiously burning and, in the process, producing more heavy elements that will eventually form planets so new life can begin again and again. For it was in the stars a billion years ago that the atoms of our world were created. A lifetime for us is merely a microsecond for the universe, so does it really matter?

Quite apart from the fact that becoming extinct is likely to be an extremely uncomfortable reality for future generations, there is also the quite extraordinary fact that the human being is almost certainly the most complex ordered structure that the process we call life has yet produced. So it would be a pity somehow if we were to mess things up having got so far.

Powered from the bottom up

Of course many thousands of words have been written already on the why's, wherefores and "what next" of this ultimate challenge. Brilliant minds have delved into every facet of the problem and there is a huge body of wise and constructive advice which is available to us. Has any of it really done any good? I somehow doubt it.

It seems to me that we can simply ignore any prospect of real change arising from new leaders or gurus of whatever persuasion.

Natural processes only really work successfully when they are powered from the bottom up rather than the top down. The magnificent creature at the top of the food chain is ultimately controlled by, and dependent upon, the activities of microscopic bacteria and fungi that process nutrients in the soil. This essential and crucial fact is the cornerstone of everything even though it is ignored and completely written out of the script of our modern lives.

We are the Problem and We are the Solution

The critical insight which we now need to grasp is that it is we who are the problem and only we who can provide the solution. If we fail to understand this crucial fact then we become like the energetic but desperate crabs who could never get out of their basket. Each was so determined to get out before his neighbor that they continually pulled each other down and ultimately they all perished together. Could the human species really be as stupid as this? Do we really have to let our systems of money, greed, and democracy drag us over the abyss?

The first thing I would say about this is that there is much more to life than money and consumer goods. True it is hard to shake off the conditioning of childhood, school, and advertising where competition and "success" are drummed into us from an early age. I am reminded of a story told to me by one of our students. He was a very bright and caring fellow with several university degrees who applied for a well-paid job with one of our major corporations. "Tell me" asked his interviewer, "what are the three most important ingredients for success in modern business?" Doing his best to think this through, our student replied "hard work, honesty, and intelligence." "No" snapped his interviewer—"attack, attack, attack!" The interview did not progress much further.

It's true of course that the advertising industry spends billions of dollars persuading us that we need the latest gizmos—indeed in many cases the advertising message has actually become part of the product. You only need to think of those expensive labels which make the same piece of clothing cost three times as much!

Changing our Conditioning

In a modern world which is run by corporations who act like "merchants of greed" our conditioning makes it hard to refocus on what we need rather than what we want. And, of course, it is hard to be different from our friends and neighbors. It is hard but it can be done and it can be fun too—especially if you have a few simple basic skills to help you on your way.

Not only can you grow your own food; you can build your own house, brew your own wine and beer, make your own entertainment and even educate your own children. If you have a little courage and moderate determination all these things can be done and the vicious circle can be broken. Surely this must be an optimistic and constructive way to press forward the frontiers of living. Surely this is one certain way of moving from the Age of Plunder towards the Age of Healing (to which I alluded at the start of this book), and now you can make a start!

"Getting it Together"

If you really want to make a change in your lifestyle then you are going to need help from others. And, what's more, the bigger the spread of talents you can find, the better your self-sufficient lifestyle will become. It makes no sense, for example, to imagine you can milk a cow just for a single family. You will have far too much milk and far too much of a tie that means you can never take a day off. You are unlikely to have all the skills—make clothes, shoes, furniture, buildings, pottery, and the like. But find others who can do these things and your life will become more interesting and much more satisfying.

A network of self-supporters

This logic does not simply apply to those who are seeking the rural idyll, it applies probably even more strongly to those who live in towns and want to make some important changes in how they live. Of course some will be able to take on community gardens or make vegetable gardens; others will keep bees, chickens, or rabbits; some will be experts at bicycle repair; others will know of local farmers who produce organic food; then there will be those who enjoy making bread, or beer, or wine. And so it goes on. Your challenge is to find such people and, having found them, to energize them and yourself to do things differently. By developing and using these different skills you can make a richer, happier, and healthier lifestyle for you and your family. Yes, and even create more of your own entertainment, too—meeting socially for parties, music, walks, poetry readings, meals, and visits.

All this human interaction and mutual support is what we mean by "getting it together." Strangely, these skills in human relations have been all but destroyed by our modern urban lifestyle. This puts all the emphasis on tight, little nuclear families and a separate social life at the workplace. Each family has to paddle its own canoe, so to speak, earning its own money, paying its own bills, and surviving its own crises. Work, school, and survival take up so much time it seems there is no spare time left to develop alternative human contacts. Now is the time you can begin to change all of that.

Finding or starting a self-supporting group

The first thing you will want to do is to find out whether a self-supporting group is already meeting anywhere on a regular basis. Try local papers, store bulletin boards, and the local library for starters. If nothing has been done to bring people together, then it is up to you to make the first move. To some, this will be second nature, but to others it may take quite a bit of courage.

There are really a couple of sensible options to try, such as organizing an "at home" evening or perhaps a session at the local restaurant or other meeting place. The important thing is to try. It is a great chance to exchange ideas, to laugh about your mistakes, and to find out what else is going on in your area. As you get to know each other better you can plan more joint activities and develop a barter of goods and skills. Once you have got the ball rolling, make sure you meet regularly—try for at least once each month to make a good start. Now, here are a few tips and hints about how to have successful meetings.

Selecting an appropriate venue

The first thing you may want to do is to search out a local restaurant or coffee shop that seems suitable for meetings. A public place is good because it is neutral ground and does not involve anyone in having to "show off" or tidy up, or prepare food at home. And you can go there without involving all the other members of your family in the meeting. A local health food restaurant may be another option, or even a local hotel.

One way or another my preference would be a place with real beer, real wood, and an owner who is happy to have you. Very often bars and restaurants have separate function rooms that you can reserve free of charge—but don't use these unless they have a good atmosphere. Somewhere that is cold and dusty without any "buzz" is not going to be a pleasant meeting.

Calling your first meeting

If you find a positive response from your first contact list then take a stab at finding a convenient date for a first meeting. This will be quite exciting if you haven't met face to face before although it can be daunting to those trying it out for the first time. To those who are confident and outgoing it is a relatively simple matter to meet up with and get to know new faces. But to many it will seem hard and you may have some tense silences while people try to figure out what they are supposed to be doing and what you all have in common.

Size of groups

With small groups (six or less) it is pretty simple to have a joint conversation where everyone has a chance to take part. If groups get bigger then the conversations will split up or, alternatively, you will need more rules about how each person can make their contribution. Some groups will be very able to "police" themselves so as to make sure everyone feels included.

Others will have to work harder and may need a bit of leadership, or what is called "facilitation," if they are to work successfully. It is really helpful if you have someone in the group who is used to working with people, and has a sensitivity to the mood and the needs of the meeting.

Chairing a meeting

If you have "called the meeting" and set things moving, then people will expect you to take a lead in getting things started. Usually people like to introduce themselves and say a little bit about what they do, their family perhaps, and what they are doing at the moment to be self-sufficient.

If things are tense you can invite people to speak either by starting yourself and taking each person in turn around the table, going alphabetically, or writing down names on slips of paper and pulling them out of a hat. This is not as far-fetched as it sounds, and is actually more fun and gets better results because people speak more spontaneously when they do not know when their turn will come.

Remember, the only important objectives of the first meeting are really to get to know each other and to fix a date for the next meeting. Do not be put off if you find some of the people irritating or bizarre in some way. You have to remember that several of these people are likely to become very good friends as time goes by.

Contacts and References

On the following pages you will find organizations, societies, associations, cooperatives, and the like who, in my opinion, have something to say to the self-supporter. I have also listed several reference books that I have found genuinely helpful, and hopefully you may find them of use too. Websites, which are so useful if you're a self-suporter out in the sticks, are given (when I started out on the road to self-sufficiency the world wide web didn't exist). Bear in mind that web addresses, like telephone numbers, change with alarming rapidity, but they were accurate at the time of going to press. Certainly, the home computer can really help the self-supporter, especially for getting in contact with like-minded souls. Good luck and good searching!

Every effort has been made to check the accuracy of telephone numbers, and email and website addresses, at the time of going to press. However, the content, as well as the addresses, are subject to frequent changes, and the publisher can accept no responsibility for any inconvenience or distress arising from such changes.

The John Seymour School for Self-Sufficiency
Killowen,
New Ross,
County Wexford, Ireland
Tel/Fax 00353 51388945
Web: www.self-sufficiency.net

Each year the "School" takes up to eight students at a time on week-long courses which provide hands-on experience of life on a mixed smallholding. There is accommodation on site and the courses include occasional visits to neighbours, local pubs, and the local town. The Killowen smallholding is only 3.5 acres with about an acre taken up by the house and garden. Courses cover a wide range of practical skills which vary depending on the seasons and include: Organic Vegetable Growing; Planning a Smallholding; Top Fruit and Soft Fruit Growing; Pig and Cow Husbandry; Poultry Management; Dairy Work; Bee keeping; Basket making; Wine, Beer and Juice making; Jam and Bread making; Scything and Grass Management; Composting; Blockwork and Basic Building.

COMMUNITIES & ASSOCIATIONS

Eco Village Network
The Create Centre, Smeaton Road
Bristol, BS1 6XN
Web: www.gaia.org.uk
An organisation and magazine promoting the eco-village concept

Earth Village Network
Postbus 1179
1000BD Amsterdam
Netherlands
also at Edinburgh Crescent, Leamington Spa, CV31 3LL
Gives help and advice on forming sustainable permaculture communities.

Eco-Design Association
The British School
Siad Road, Stroud, Gloucestershire GL5 1QW
Source of information on ecological architecture.

Permaculture Academy
8 Helen Road, Oxford OX2 0DE
Promotes the philosophy of working with nature through permaculture.

Sustainable Land Trust
7 Chamberlain Street
London NW1 8XB
Organization dedicated to sound management of the land.

Smallholder's Society (N. Yorkshire)
Web: www.smallholder.org.uk
For information email
roger-walker@tesco.net
Set up in 1999 and now expanding rapidly, this site provides a comprehensive listing of smallholder activity and information, including meetings and local associations.

SEED International
(Sustainability Education and Ecological Design)
Crystal Waters Permaculture Village
MS 16, Maleny, QLD 4552 Australia
Tel: +61 7 5494 4833
Web: www.seedinternational.au.com

ENERGY

Centre for Renewable Energy and Sustainable Technology
Centre for Alternative Technology
Machynlleth
Powys, SY20 9AZ
Tel: 01654 705959
Web: www.cat.org.uk
Extremely active and wide-ranging centre for all aspects of alternative technology; produces many fact sheets, runs courses.

INTERMEDIATE TECHNOLOGY

The Schumacher Centre for Technology and Development
Bourton Hall, Bourton-Dunsmore
Rugby, Worcestershire CV23 9QZ
Tel. 01926 634400
Web: www.itdg.org.uk
This organization exists to promote all types of intermediate and alternative technology in line with the philosophy of E. F. Schumacher.

WIND AND SOLAR ENERGY

Alternative Energy Systems Co.
1469 Rolling Hills Rd., Conroe, Texas, US 77303
Tel: +41 936 264 4873
Web: www.poweriseverything.com
Has a very large selection of subjects and related information.

Alternative Technology Association, CERES
8 Lee St, Brunswick East ,VIC 3057 Australia
Tel: +61 3 9388 9311
Web: www.ata.org.au

Energy Development Co-operative Ltd
The Old Brewery, Oulton Broad
Industrial Estate,
Harbour Road, Oulton Broad
Suffolk NR32 3LZ
Tel: 0870 745 1119
Web: www.unlimited-power.co.uk
Comprehensive supplier of alternative energy equipment:

British Wind Energy Association
Renewable Energy House, 1 Aztec Row,
Berners Road, London N1 0PW
Tel: 020 7689 1960
Web: www.bwea.com
Trade association promoting wind energy.

MAGAZINES

Smallholder Magazine
3 Falmouth Business Park,
Bicklandwater Road,
Falmouth, Cornwall TR11 4SZ
Tel: 01326 213303
Web: www.smallholder.co.uk
Monthly magazine for smallholders, with news and sources.

Country Smallholder Magazine
Fair Oak Close, Exeter Airport Business Park,
Clyst Honiton, Exeter EX5 2UL
Tel: 01392 447711
Another monthly magazine for smallholders, with news and information.

Earthgarden Magazine
PO Box 2, Trentham VIC 3458 Australia
Web: www.earthgarden.com.au

Green Futures
Circa, 13–17 Sturton Street,
Cambridge CB1 2SN
Tel: 01223 564334
Web: www.greenfutures.org.uk
A forum on all issues re progress towards sustainable development.

Smallholder Bookshop
High Street, Stoke Ferry, Nr Kings Lynn,
Norfolk PE33 9SF
Tel: 01366 500466
Web: www.smallholderbooks.co.uk
Useful smallholder mail order bookshop.

FURTHER HELP

Department for the Environment, Food and Rural Affairs
Development and Advisory Service
Ergon House, 17 Smith Square,
London SW1P 3JR
helpline@defra.gsi.gov.uk
Tel: 0845 9335577
Web: www.defra.gov.uk
Useful first stop for the would-be self-supporter. Regional offices in UK provide advice and pamphlets (many free) on most agricultural subjects

Agricultural Development and Advisory Service
Whitehall Place, London SW1A 2HH
Tel: 0845 7660085
Web: www.adas.co.uk
For advice and information on general aspects of farming (not free).

The Forestry Commission (GB)
Silvan House, 231 Corstorphine Road,
Edinburgh EH12 7AT
Tel: 0870 1214180
Web: www.forestry.gov.uk
For advice and pamphlets on woodland.

ASI, Importers and Wholesale Distributors
Alliance House, Snape Maltings,
Saxmundham,
Suffolk IP17 1SW
For a wide range of guns (to purchase you must have a licence and go through a dealer).

Organic Federation of Australia
PO Box Q455
QVB Post Office,
Sydney NSW 1230 Australia
Tel: +61 2 9299 8016
Web: www.ofa.org.au

Wright Rain Irrigation
No4 Millstream Industrial Estate,
Christchurch Road, Ringwood, Hampshire,
BH24 3SB
Tel: 01425 472251
For irrigation equipment.

Garden Organic (formerly HDRA)
Ryton Organic Gardens
Wodston Lane, Ryton-on-Dunsmore,
Coventry, CV8 3LG
Tel: 024 7630 3517
Web: www.gardenorganic.org.uk
Email: enquiry@hdra.org.uk
For general information on soil and organic gardening.

Global Action Plan
Web: www.globalactionplan.org.uk
The section on this small environmental charity's Eco Teams explains all about household eco-audits for energy saving.

Donnachadh McCarthy
Web: www.3acorns.co.uk
Website belonging to Donnachadh McCarthy's eco-audit work which includes home visit and follow-up reports for a fee, plus green lifestyle coaching.

Beyond Green
Web: www.beyondgreen.co.uk
With sections on sustainable lifestyles and ways to change the world.

Gadsby and Son Ltd
Huntworth Business Park, Bridgewater,
Somerset TA6 6TS
Tel: 01278 437123
For basketware.

Essex Kilns Ltd
Furnace Manufacturers,
Woodrolfe Road,
Tollesbury, Maldon,
Essex CM9 8SE
Tel: 01672 869342.

Harris Looms
Wotton Road, Ashford, Kent TN23 6JY
Tel: 01233 622686

Jacobs, Young and Westbury
Bridge Road, Haywards Heath,
Sussex RH16 1UA
Tel: 01444 412411
For rushes and loom cord.

FURTHER HELP

Frank Herring and Sons
27 High West Street, Dorchester, Dorset DT1 1UP
Tel: 01305 264449
For spinning wheels.

Alec Tiranti Ltd
27 Warren Street, London W1T 5NB
Tel: 020 7636 8565
Web: www.tiranti.co.uk
For all stone masonry tools, also clay.

Basket Makers Association UK
Membership Secretary: Sally Goymer, 37 Mendip Road, Cheltenham, Gloucestershire GL52 5EB
Web: www.basketassoc.org;
Also for willow basketmakers see www.basketmakers.org

British Goat Society
34–36 Fore Street,
Bovey Tracey,
Newton Abbot,
Cornwall TQ13 9AD
Tel: 01626 833168
Web: www.allgoats.com
A large website with comprehensive coverage of different breeds and suppliers.

Pig Breeders
SM PO Box 233,
Sheffield S35 0BP
Tel: 0114 286 4638
Web: www.thepigsite.com
Comprehensive information about different pig breeds and where to obtain them – mostly slanted towards the commercial operator.

Linda & Derek Walker/Oxmoor Smallholders Supplies
Harlthorpe,
East Yorkshire YO8 6DW
Tel: 01757 288186

Bridport Gundy Marine
The Court,
Bridport,
Dorset DT6 3QU
Tel: 01308 422222
Lines and nets supplier

Art of Brewing
Tel: 020 8549 5266
Web: www.art-of-brewing.co.uk
Comprehensive source of all brewing supplies – can be viewed online.

Buck and Ryan Ltd
101 Tottenham Court Road,
London W1T 4DY
Tel: 020 7636 8565
For metal-working tools.

General Woodworking Supplies
76/80 Stoke Newington High Street,
London N16 7PA
Tel: 020 7254 6052
For wide range of British and imported woods.

SPR Centre
Greenfield Farm, Fontwell Avenue,
Eastergate, Chichester,
Sussex PO20 6RU
Tel: 01243 542815
Web: www.sprcentre.co.uk
A supplier of a large range of animal foodstuffs for smallholders.

Ascott Smallholding Supplies
Anvil House,
Dudleston Heath, Ellesmere,
Shropshire, SY12 9LJ
Tel: 0870 7740750
Web: www.ascott-shop.co.uk
Mail-order supplier of a large range of animal foodstuffs, precision seeders, and the like for smallholders.

Moorlands Cheesemakers
Brewhamfield Farm, North Brewham,
Bruton,
Somerset BA10 0QQ
Tel: 01749 850108
Cheese-making supplies and equipment.

Solartwin
Freepost, NWW7 888A, Chester CH1 2ZU
Tel: 0845 1300137
Solar power suppliers.

Solar Sales
97 Kew St, Welshpool WA 6986 Australia
Tel: +61 8 9362 2111
Web: www.solarsales.com.au

Cheeselinks
15 Minns Rd
Little River, VIC 3211 Australia
Tel: +61 3 5283 1396
Web: www.cheeselinks.com.au

Chr. Hansen UK Ltd
Rennet Manufacturers, 2 Tealgate,
Hungerford,
Berkshire RG17 0YT
Tel: 01488 689800
For starters and pure cultures for cheese-making.

E. H. Thorne Beehives Ltd
Beehive Works, Wragby, Market Raisen,
Lincolnshire LN8 5LA
Tel: 01673 858555
Web: www.thorne.co.uk
For bee equipment.

Burntstone Ceramics Ltd
19 Redgate, Walkington, Beverley, HUM 8TS
Tel: 01482 868 706
Web: www.burntstone.co.uk
A supplier of furnaces and kilns.

Kings Seeds
Monks Farm, Kelvedon
Colchester, Essex CO5 9PG
Tel: 01376 570000
Web: www.kingseeds.com
Big supplier and of organic seed.

Countrywide
Email: enquiries@countrywidefarmers.co.uk
Livestock care and feed, plant production, and energy needs for smallholders.

BOOKS

The Living Soil
Lady Eve Balfour; Faber and Faber, 1933
One of the definitive books on the health-giving powers of the organic management of soil and garden. Lady Balfour was effectively one of the founders of the reborn "organic" movement.

The Growth Illusion
Richard Douthwaite; Green Books, 1999
A painstakingly researched exploration showing how propaganda about the importance of "economic growth" is largely fallacious.

Short Circuit
Richard Douthwaite; Green Books 1996
A useful and comprehensive collection of alternative economic systems which bring back control to a more local level. There is also a powerful statement explaining the importance of adopting more of such systems.

Soil and Civilisation
Edward S. Hyams; HarperCollins, 1976
An accurate and perceptive description of the vital link between soil and the development of modern civilisation. Sooner or later the fate of every urban culture is decided by the wisdom with which they manage their soil.

Eco Villages and Sustainable Communities
Gaia Trust research publication commissioned from Context Institute, 1991. Gaia Trust, Skyumvej 101, 7752 Snedsted, Denmark Context Institute, PO Box 946, Langley, WA 98260 USA www.context.org
Extremely important and comprehensive review of the theory and practice of eco-villages worldwide. The report reaches a sobering conclusion that the huge majority of eco-villages fail not because of physical or technical deficiencies but because of financial and social problems.

The Guide to Co-operative Living
(annual)
Diggers and Dreamers c/o Edge of Time Ltd, BCM Edge, London WC1N 3XX
Useful practical handbook (and other catalogues and information about communities) for people seriously intent on exploring community living. There is a large index of communities from England, Scotland, and Wales.

Ecotopia
Ernest Callenbach; Pluto Press, 1978
A thought provoking novel which really explores what living in a self-sufficient eco-culture would be like. Full of practical examples of how to do things differently.

Blueprint for A Small Planet
John Seymour and Herbert Girardet, Dorling Kindersley, 1987
Comprehensive and common sense review of actions that could be taken in all the routing activities of daily life to save the future of the planet. Full of neat diagrams and plenty of frightening facts about the consequences of our present Western approach to ordinary living.

The Forgotten Arts & Crafts
John Seymour; Dorling Kindersley, 1984, 1987, 2001
This very beautiful and thorough book gives detailed and well-illustrated insights into the skills of traditional life. It is an invaluable and extremely interesting reference book – the result of many months of painstaking research and visits to some of the last of the true traditional craftsmen.

The New Complete Book of Self-Sufficiency
John Seymour; Dorling Kindersley, 2002
The original 1970s classic guide for dreamers and realists, digitally re-coloured, enhanced and expanded.

Home Farm
Paul Heiney; Dorling Kindersley, 1998
As the title suggests, lots of practical help on pig-, sheep-, horse-, and chicken-keeping and other self-sufficient skills (with photographic step-by-steps).

Textbook of Fish Culture – Breeding and Cultivation of Fish
Marcel Huet; Fishing News Books Ltd, 1971
A definitive book on fish culture by the Director of the Belgian Research Station for Water and Forests .

The Fat of the Land
John Seymour; Carningli, 1991
This is the original personal story of how John and Sally Seymour developed their desire for self-sufficiency in rural Suffolk. Packed with anecdotes and real-life dramas, the book makes entertaining reading as well as giving a warning about some of the less expected consequences of searching for self-sufficiency.

Organic Gardening
Maria Rodale; Rodale Press, Emmaus, PA 18098 USA, 1999
An inspirational book celebrating the beauty of organic growing and discussing many of its leading ideas

HDRA Encyclopedia of Organic Gardening
Pauline Pears; Dorling Kindersley, 2001
About as complete as you can get and with the Henry Doubleday Research Association seal of approval (Europe's largest and most respected organic gardening association, now called Garden Organic).

The Organic Garden Book
Geoff Hamilton; Dorling Kindersley, 1987
For growing better tasting fruit and vegetables untainted by chemicals from a much missed man.

Flora Britannica
Richard Mabey; Sinclair-Stevenson, 1987
A vivid testimony as to how nature and self-sufficiency have collaborated over the centuries.

The Complete Encyclopedia of Home Freezing
Jeni Wright (editor); Octopus
Out of print but useful A-Z guide (if you can get it) to freezing techniques and recipes for the freezer.

The Complete Book of Preserving
Mary Cameron-Smith; Marshall Cavendish Books, 1986
Gives all the technical know-how on a huge range of fruit and vegetable.

The Gaia Atlas of Planetary Management
Norman Myers; Pan Books, 1985
This is an ideal book to give younger people a good idea about what is happening on planet Earth. Lots of exemplary pictures, flow charts, and information.

An Inconvenient Truth
Al Gore; Bloomsbury, 2006
Sub-titled "The Planetary Emergency of Global Warning and What we Can Do About It". Trying the most rudimentary self-sufficiency would be a start.

Index

G

H,I

R

S

Y

Acknowledgements

Acknowledgments to 1st Edition
I would like to thank the many people who have helped me with information and advice, particularly Sally Seymour without whom this book would never have been written. The students on my farm, Fachongle Isaf, also assisted in many ways, especially Oliver Harding and David Lee who helped with the drawings and diagrams.
John Seymour

Dorling Kindersley would also like to express their gratitude to Sally Seymour and the many people associated with Fachongle Isaf. In addition they would like to thank the following for their special contribution to the book:
Susan Campbell, Peter Fraenkel, Mr. Woodsford of W. Fenn Ltd., Cleals of Fishguard, Peter Minter of Bulmer Brick & Tile Co., Mr. Fred Patton of Cummins Farm, Aldham, Rachel Scott, Fred'k Ford Ramona Ann Gale, John Norris Wood, Richard Kindersley, Barbara Fraser, Michael Thompson and the staff of Photoprint Plates, Barry Steggle, John Rule, Murray Wallis, Mel Hobbs, Peter Rayment and the staff at Diagraphic.

Artists
Dorling Kindersley would also like to thank Eric Thomas, Jim Robins, Robert Micklewright, and David Ashby for their major contributions to the illustrations in this book. Also Norman Barber, Helen Cowcher, Michael Craig, Brian Craker, Roy Grubb, Richard Jacobs, Ivan Lapper, Richard Lewis, Dave Nash, Richard Orr, Edward Kinsey and Alastair Campbell at QED, Christine Roberts, Rodney Shackell, Kathleen Smith, Harry Titcombe, Justin Todd, Roger Twinn, Ann Winterbottom, Elsie Wrigley.

Acknowledgments to the 2nd edition
Kinsey & Harrison (design and editorial) would like to thank Patricia Hymans; Mel Hobbs and Peter Rayment at Brightside; David and Ann Sears.

Digital Color Enhancement
All existing and new line illustrations were digitally colored by Simon Roulstone.

Linocut Illustrations
Jeremy Sancha produced the linocuts.

New Line Illustrations
Sally Launder, Kathleen McDougall, John Woodcock, David Ashby, Simon Roulstone and Peter Bull Associates,

Measurements and oven temperatures

Weights and measures in this book, (including temperatures) have approximate metric and Imperial conversions (rounded up or down); this applies to the recipes, too. When referring to these measurements, including recipe temperatures (see below), do not mix metric with Imperial.

Gas Mark			
	1	275°F	140°C
	2	300°F	150°C
	3	325°F	170°C
	4	350°F	180°C
	5	375°F	190°C
	6	400°F	200°C
	7	425°F	220°C
	8	450°F	230°C
	9	475°F	240°C